Holt Spanish 1B

Lesson Planner
with Differentiated Instruction

HOLT, RINEHART AND WINSTON

A Harcourt Education Company

Orlando • **Austin** • New York • San Diego • Toronto • London

Contributing Writers:
Jodee Costello

Copyright © by Holt, Rinehart and Winston

All rights reserved. No part of this publication may be reproduced or transmitted in any form or by any means, electronic or mechanical, including photocopy, recording, or any information storage and retrieval system, without permission in writing from the publisher.

Teachers using ¡EXPRÉSATE! may photocopy complete pages in sufficient quantities for classroom use only and not for resale.

HOLT and ¡EXPRÉSATE! are trademarks licensed to Holt, Rinehart and Winston, registered in the United States of America and/or other jurisdictions.

Printed in the United States of America

ISBN 0-03-074389-3

1 2 3 4 5 6 7   170   06 05 04

Table of Contents

To the Teacher iv
Differentiated Instruction Strategies and Tips v
Homework Calendar xii
Progress Report xiii
Standards for Foreign Language Learning xiv
Geoculture Lesson Plan Suggestions xv

50-Minute Lesson Plans

Bridge Chapter 1
Chapter 6 11
Chapter 7 41
Chapter 8 71
Chapter 9 101
Chapter 10 131

90-Minute Lesson Plans

Bridge Chapter 162
Chapter 6 172
Chapter 7 200
Chapter 8 228
Chapter 9 256
Chapter 10 284

Substitute Teacher Lesson Plans

Bridge Chapter 315
Chapter 6 316
Chapter 7 317
Chapter 8 318
Chapter 9 319
Chapter 10 320

To the Teacher

You will find that the *¡Exprésate! Lesson Planner* facilitates the planning, execution, and documentation of your classroom work.

For more help in organizing your lessons, use the *One-Stop Planner* CD-ROM. For each chapter, this computer-ready version of the *Lesson Planner* includes: editable lesson plans with direct links to teaching resources, printable worksheets from resource books, direct launches to the HRW Internet activities, video and audio segments, the *Test Generator,* and clip art for vocabulary items.

Standards for Foreign Language Learning

At the top of each page of the lesson plan is a box showing the correlations of the *Pupil's Edition* and the *Annotated Teacher's Edition* to the Standards for Foreign Language Learning. In addition, the chart on page xiv provides a summary of the five major goals and the standards within each goal, so that you can more easily understand the correlation within each section of the *Lesson Planner.*

Calendario de tareas cotidianas

On page xii you will find a homework calendar (**Calendario de tareas cotidianas**) that you can copy and distribute to your class so that you and your students can keep track of their assignments each week.

Chapter-Specific Lesson Plans

Each daily or block lesson plan consists of timed suggestions for core instruction (regular lesson plans total 50 minutes, block lesson plans total 90 minutes each), Optional Resources (also timed) that can be integrated into the lesson plan, and correlations to the Standards for Foreign Language learning. There are 30 50-minute lesson plans and 14 90-minute lesson plans per chapter.

Differentiated Instruction

Within each chapter's lesson plans are suggestions for differentiating instruction.
- ▲ Advanced Learners
- ◆ Slower Pace Learners
- ● Students with Special Learning Needs
- ■ Heritage Speakers

Geocultura

Suggestions for presenting and teaching **Geocultura** are on page XV.

Substitute Teacher Lesson Plans

These lesson plans have been designed with the goal of making class time productive on the days when a substitute teacher conducts class. They provide instructive activities that can be administered by a substitute who does not speak Spanish. Each chapter has several days' worth of suggestions for activities.

Holt Spanish 1B

Lesson Planner

Copyright © by Holt, Rinehart and Winston. All rights reserved.

Differentiated Instruction Strategies and Tips

Mayanne Wright

In today's classroom no two students are exactly alike. Students vary in their readiness to learn, the ways in which they learn, and their interests. In order to meet each student's learning needs, many teachers are turning to differentiated instruction in order to teach all students in an effective and equitable manner. Advanced, on-level, and struggling students, as well as students with special academic, behavioral, or language needs can all be taught in the same classroom when instruction is differentiated.

Instruction may be differentiated by varying one of three components in a lesson: content, process, or product. Teachers differentiate by varying either what students learn, or the activities they use to comprehend and practice what they learn, or how they express what they've learned. They decide how to differentiate instruction based on students' readiness, on their interests, and on their learning profiles or preferred styles and modes of learning.

There are four steps to follow when planning a differentiated lesson using *¡Exprésate!* First, determine what the essential knowledge is that all students must learn. Review the learning objectives listed in the *Teacher's Edition* and at the top of each page of this *Lesson Planner* to help you make this determination. Second, decide if and when grouping might be appropriate during different phases of the learning process based on students' readiness, interests, and learning profiles. Consider how to group students and what each group will do differently. The *Student Edition* has many activities that are already marked for pairs and groups. You may decide to have students do these as marked, and you may also choose for students to do individual activities in pairs or groups. The *Teacher's Edition* also offers suggestions for adapting activities. Third, choose what part of the lesson to vary: content, process, or product. Do not vary everything in one lesson; instead, focus on one area, based on students' needs. For suggestions regarding ways to differentiate your lessons, begin with the wrap in the *Teacher's Edition*. There you will find suggestions for varying presentations, activities, products, and assessments according to students' different learning styles, preferred modes of learning, and interests. Also, see the coded lesson plans in this *Lesson Planner* and the teaching strategies outlined in this essay. Finally, determine how you will evaluate students' needs and progress, and what the final assessment will be. To evaluate student progress, there are culminating activities featured in each chapter of the *Student Edition* and *Teacher Edition*, as well as in the *Interactive Tutor* and various ancillaries. See the coded lesson plans in this *Lesson Planner* for ideas. To assess what students have learned when instruction has been completed, *¡Exprésate!* offers several options. You may choose to use the tests featured in the *Testing Program*, use one of the alternative assessments in the *Assessment Program*, or create your own test using the *Test Generator*.

As you work through the four steps above, you may wish to consider using one of the instructional strategies that follow. Each strategy is designed to address the special needs of advanced, on-level, and struggling learners as well as native speakers. They will provide you with concrete tools for varying the content, process, or product in each of the following areas of foreign language learning: vocabulary, grammar, listening, speaking, reading, writing, culture, and assessment.

Vocabulary

Using Multiple Resources

One of the most effective ways to vary the content of a lesson is to use **multiple resources.** Using a variety of resources to teach essential vocabulary allows teachers to meet the needs of students with different learning profiles and varied readiness to learn. Teachers may use the

Student Edition, which presents vocabulary visually and verbally; the *Teacher's Edition*, which provides suggestions for presenting vocabulary using a variety of instructional techniques; the *Teaching Transparencies* and accompanying teaching suggestions; the *Interactive Tutor*; and the **Novela en video** in the *Video/DVD Program*, which presents vocabulary in context. Each resource lends itself to different intelligences, learning styles, and paces. Each also provides for different grouping possibilities, from whole class to individual instruction, and multiple entry points to learning, from the very concrete to the more complex. For example, the **Novela en video** might be more appropriate for native speakers and advanced learners, since the vocabulary is presented in a more complex manner, while the teaching suggestions in the *Teacher's Edition* and for the *Teaching Transparencies* might better address the needs of struggling and on-level learners.

Jigsaw

Jigsaw is a cooperative learning strategy. The teacher divides students into heterogeneous base groups and gives them a vocabulary assignment consisting of several components. For example, in order to review a particular chapter's vocabulary, the teacher might have students complete selected activities from the *Student Edition*, *Teacher's Edition*, *Teaching Transparencies Binder*, *Vocabulary and Grammar Workbook*, *Activity Workbook*, or the *Interactive Tutor*. Members of the base groups divide the assignment among themselves. Each member takes responsibility for teaching or leading students through one or more of the activities from the list. Members then work individually to decide how they will teach their activities to fellow group members. Finally, students return to their base groups to teach their material. Jigsaw activities differentiate by allowing students to use their preferred learning styles, set their own pace, and choose the level of difficulty for a particular task. Thus, this type of activity is ideal for students at all levels of learning. See the Cooperative Learning activities in the wrap of the *Teacher's Edition* for jigsaw ideas or create your own using the resources listed above.

Grammar

Stations

To practice a grammar concept, the teacher might create **stations** at different locations in the classroom, where students work on various tasks simultaneously. Each station has materials that practice the chosen grammar concept at a different level of difficulty. For example, the first station might provide reteaching and guided practice. At this station the teacher provides instruction, then guides student practice using resources such as the *Interactive Tutor*. The second station might provide simple independent practice using selected core activities from the *Student Edition*, **Juegos interactivos**, *Activity Workbook*, or *Vocabulary and Grammar Workbook*. The third station might provide more complex independent practice, using the same resources as the second station. The fourth and fifth stations might have students using the grammar concept in communicative contexts such as those featured in the culminating activities of the *Student Edition*, *Activity Workbook*, **Cuaderno para hispanohablantes**, or *Activities for Communication*. Some students will need to go to several stations, while others will not. For example, struggling students might go to the first three stations, on-level students might go to the second, third, and fourth stations; advanced students might go to the third, fourth, and fifth stations; and native speakers might go only to the fourth and fifth stations. Students will also spend different amounts of time at each station, according to their needs.

Tiered Activities

Tiered activities allow all students to focus on the same essential knowledge and skills, but at different levels of complexity, abstractness, and open-endedness. By assigning tiered grammar activities, teachers ensure challenge and success for all learners. To create a tiered activity to practice a grammatical concept, follow these steps:

- Select the concept to be practiced.
- Assess students' readiness, interests, and learning profiles.
- Choose an activity from the *Student Edition*.
- Assess the complexity and level of the activity.
- Adapt the activity to different student levels by choosing an alternative activity from the *Teacher's Edition*, or from one of the following: *Interactive Tutor*, **Juegos interactivos**, *Activities for Communication*, *Vocabulary and Grammar Workbook*, or *Activity Workbook*.
- Match the original and adapted activities to the appropriate students. Assign the most concrete and close-ended version of the activity to struggling learners and the most complex and open-ended version to advanced learners. On-level learners do the activity that falls somewhere in-between.

Listening

Using Multiple Resources

Students vary greatly in their ability to listen, due to different learning styles and the degree to which they are comfortable with the language and learning contexts. An excellent way to address students' differing needs is to vary the lesson content by using **multiple resources.** For struggling and on-level students, teachers may choose from listening activities in the *Student Edition*; **Expresavisión** and **Gramavisión**; the suggestions in the *Teacher's Edition*; or the suggested activities accompanying the *Teaching Transparencies*. All levels of students may practice their listening skills through the pair and group work activities in the *Student Edition*, *Teacher's Edition*, or *Activities for Communication*. The *Interactive Tutor* is also appropriate for all levels of students, particularly struggling learners, since it provides a great deal of repetition. By choosing a variety of resources, teachers provide listening practice at an appropriate level for each student while addressing students' different learning styles and preferences.

Vary The Task

Teachers can also **vary the listening task** to meet students' level of readiness. There are two ways to vary a listening task. One way is to vary the complexity of what students listen for. For example, struggling students may listen for the main idea in a story, on-level students listen for the main idea and a few significant details, and advanced students listen for more specific detailed information. The second way to adapt a listening task is to vary how students demonstrate what they comprehend. Struggling students may demonstrate comprehension by listing items, on-level students by summarizing the text, and advanced students by interpreting what they heard. See the *Teacher's Edition* for more ideas about varying listening tasks.

Speaking

Tiered Assignments

Tiered assignments allow students to express essential knowledge and skills at different levels of complexity, abstractness, and open-endedness. To create a tiered speaking assignment, take the following steps:

- Choose a function or set of functions to be demonstrated.
- Assess students' readiness, interests, and learning profiles.
- Choose a speaking activity from the *Student Edition*, *Teacher's Edition*, *Activities for Communication*, or Picture sequences, Portfolio, or Performance Assessment in the *Assessment Program*.
- Determine where on a continuum of difficulty the activity falls. Is it closed or open-ended? Is there just one task to complete or several? Is the assignment highly or loosely structured?

- Adapt the assignment or choose alternate assignments from one of the resources previously mentioned. Give advanced students multi-faceted, open-ended, more complex assignments; assign simpler and more closed-ended assignments to struggling students; and have on-level students complete assignments that fall somewhere in between.

Learning Scenarios

Learning scenarios give teachers a framework for organizing instruction, and provide students with the opportunity to carry out communicative functions in culturally authentic situations. Students can adapt the scenarios to reflect their personal interests, preferred learning styles, and level of learning. To develop a scenario, decide what type of situation students should be able to handle when they complete a chapter. For ideas, see the culminating activities in the *Student Edition*; projects or role-plays from the *Teacher's Edition*; activities in *Activities for Communication*; and, suggestions in the *Assessment Program*. Next, teach the functions, grammar, vocabulary, culture, and life skills students need in order to carry out the scenario. Use the *Student Edition* as a guide, but add to or subtract content based on your students' needs. For example, you may need to focus on some components of the chapter more than on others, or review skills and information from previous chapters. Finally, create a checklist of activities that students need to complete to prepare them for the scenario. After students complete the checklist, divide them into heterogeneous groups to carry out the scenario.

Reading

Varied Graphic Organizers

A **graphic organizer** is a visual framework that helps students make connections between concepts. They may be used before, during, and after reading to aid students in comprehension. Some common graphic organizers are Venn diagrams, which help to compare and contrast information; time lines or flow charts, which help with sequencing events; and multiple causes-or-effects maps, which help to identify cause-and-effect relationships. By using different graphic organizers for a particular reading, teachers can adjust the reading objectives or tasks to match students' readiness, as well as address a variety of learning styles. For example, a time line to sequence events in a story may be appropriate for struggling learners, while a multiple causes-and-effects map may be more appropriate for on-level students. See the *Reading Strategies and Skills Handbook* for a variety of graphic organizers to use with *Student Edition* readings and the *¡Lee conmigo!* readers.

Choice Boards

A **choice board** is a menu of activities set up like a Bingo card. Each column on the board reflects a different level of learning, and each activity in a given column calls for the use of a different learning style. The teacher directs students to a particular column on the board from which they choose an activity. By asking students to select an activity from a particular row, the teacher addresses students' learning needs while at the same time allowing students to make choices based on their preferred learning styles and interests. For activities to include on a choice board, see the *Student Edition, Teacher's Edition, Activity Workbook,* **Cuaderno para hispanohablantes,** *¡Lee conmigo!,* and *Reading Strategies and Skills Handbook*. You may also wish to use the following sample choice board as a model. The first column's activities are directed toward struggling learners, the second column toward on-level learners, and the third column toward advanced learners.

Sample Choice Board For A Story

Column 1	Column 2	Column 3
Act out the story and perform it for a small group or the class.	Create a Venn diagram comparing and contrasting two characters in the story.	Create a treasure chest of symbols that represent each of the characters, the main events of the story, and the theme(s) of the story. Present your treasure chest to the class.
Create a timeline of key events in the story.	Retell the story from the perspective of another character.	Write an essay that compares and contrasts your qualities and faults, or those of one character, with those of another character.
Make four illustrations to accompany the story.	Create a collage that expresses the personality of one of the characters.	Interview students about their reactions to the story, graph their answers, and write a summary of the results.

Writing

R.A.F.T.

R.A.F.T. is an instructional strategy that allows students to pick the **Role** of the writer, the **Audience**, the **Format**, and/or the **Topic** of a writing assignment. By allowing students to choose one or more of these components, teachers can address students' different interests and learning styles. Such choices make this strategy appropriate for students at all levels of learning and for native speakers. To create a R.A.F.T. assignment, teachers may choose from among the writing activities in the *Student Edition*, *Teacher's Edition*, and the *Activity Workbook*, as well as the portfolio suggestions in the *Assessment Program*. Although many of these activities provide general guidelines for the role of the writer, audience, format, and topic, teachers may invite students to narrow their focus within each of these components, or they may adapt the activities by allowing students to change one of the R.A.F.T. components. For example, a writing activity might ask students to write a letter to an exchange student describing their family members and typical family activities. In a R.A.F.T. assignment, students may be asked to narrow their focus by deciding exactly who the exchange student is (audience), who their family members are, and what activities they will talk about (topic). Or, teachers may suggest that students change the format of the assignment, creating a family album, scrapbook, journal entry, song, or poem instead of writing a letter.

Cubing

Cubing is a strategy that allows students to think about a topic, idea, or task from different angles. Each facet of a cube features a writing prompt that describes the task to be completed. Cubes can differentiate instruction by having prompts that practice the same skills, but call for different learning styles. For example, one cube will have six different prompts, each one calling for a different learning style. Three possible prompts on one cube might be:

- Create a timeline of the activities you did last week (for mathematical/logical learners).
- Write a paragraph describing what you did last week (for verbal learners).
- Create a cartoon strip about what you did last week (for visual learners).

Students then choose the prompt they prefer. Another way cubes can differentiate instruction is by having prompts at different levels of difficulty. For example, the teacher might create four different cubes for an assignment, one for struggling learners, one for on-level learners, one for advanced learners, and one for native speakers. Students would then choose an activity from the cube that best matches their level of learning. Teachers may choose from among the writing activities in the *Student Edition*, *Teacher's Edition*, *Interactive Tutor*, and ***Cuaderno para hispanohablantes*** or from among the portfolio and performance assessment suggestions in the *Assessment Program* to feature on a cube. These activities can be used as written, or the teacher can adapt one or more of them to meet their students' needs.

Culture

Learning Centers

A **learning center** is a location in a classroom where students use activities and materials to learn about, reinforce, or expand on a particular topic. Students explore a different topic at each center. Because centers feature a variety of materials and activities, they can easily be designed to meet the needs of students' multiple intelligences, different learning styles, and varying degrees of readiness. To use centers for teaching culture, first decide on the topic to be taught at each center. For example, centers for the following topics might be created to study Puerto Rican culture: music, festivals, sports, food, and traditions. Next, select materials and activities that explore each topic. Each center should have activities that reflect the different levels of learning in the classroom. For example, at the center on music, struggling learners might write their impressions of a music selection that they listen to while on-level learners might compare the selection to other types of music they've heard. Some resources to use in centers are the presentations and activities in the *Student Edition*; the notes, suggestions, and projects in the wrap of the *Teacher's Edition* as well as the projects and activities featured in the interleaf pages; the *Video/DVD Program* and accompanying activity masters in the *Video Guide*; the *Interactive Tutor*; and, the activities in the ***Cuaderno para hispanohablantes*** and *Activity Workbook*. You may also choose to use resources from your community or that you've collected. Once you've selected appropriate materials and activities, create a checklist of activities for each learning level for each center. Finally, assign or let students choose a center. Give each student the checklist that is appropriate for him/her. You may wish to have students complete the tasks at every center or at only one or two of the centers according to their individual interests.

Interest-Based Mini-Lessons

After having taught the essential culture for a particular chapter, you may wish to provide an opportunity for students to further explore a topic or learn about something totally different. One way to provide such an opportunity is to create **interest-based mini lessons** for your students to complete. By allowing students to choose what they would like to study and how to demonstrate what they have learned, you can address the needs of different learning profiles. For expanding on a cultural topic already covered in the *Student Edition*, you may suggest that students choose from among the activities in ***Cuaderno para hispanohablantes***, *Activity Workbook*, *Video Guide*, *Interactive Tutor*, or in the wrap of the *Teacher's Edition*. For ideas regarding other topics for students to explore, see the wrap and the Projects and Traditions interleaf pages of the *Teacher's Edition*.

Assessment

Alternative Assessments

One of the best ways to assess whether every student has mastered essential knowledge and skills is to offer **alternative assessments**. By choosing the appropriate assessment tool based on students' learning profile and readiness, you can better determine what students have actually learned. First, determine the essential knowledge and skills all students should have learned. Next, decide whether the assessment should be objective or performance-based, or a combination of the two. Then decide on the assessment mode based on students' learning profiles. Which would be more appropriate: a pencil-and-paper test, a test taken on a computer, a product, or a performance? Finally, adapt the assessment instrument to match the level of students' learning by altering testing items, simplifying directions, reducing the number of tasks, or varying the rubric for evaluating a product or performance. The following assessment options will allow you to address a variety of learning profiles and may be adapted to students' level of learning: Grammar and Vocabulary quizzes, *Aplicación, Lectura, Escritura,* and *Geocultura* quizzes, *Assessment Program,* and *Test Generator.*

Choice Board

An assessment **choice board** is a menu of tests, performances, and products from which students choose to demonstrate that they have learned a particular set of concepts or skills. Assessment choice boards allow you to better address the needs of your students when evaluating what they have learned. They are set up like Bingo cards with three columns and three rows. Each column on the board reflects a different type of assessment while each activity in a column calls for the use of a different learning style. To address different levels of learning, there may be different choice boards for different students. Students choose one activity from each column of the choice board given to them to demonstrate mastery of essential knowledge and skills. For options to include in the test column, see *Assessment Program* or *Test Generator.* For product options, see the project suggestions in the wrap and interleaf pages of the *Teacher's Edition* and the portfolio suggestions in the *Assessment Program.* For performance options, see the portfolio and performance suggestions in the *Assessment Program.*

Sample Assessment Choice Board
(based on Chapter 5, Level 1 *¡Exprésate!*)

Test Options Column	Product Options Column	Performance Options Column
Chapter 5 Test, *Assessment Program, Test Generator*	Written Portfolio Suggestion for Chapter 5, *Assessment Program*	Oral Portfolio Suggestion for Chapter 5, *Assessment Program*
Chapter 5, *Grammar and Vocabulary Quizzes*	Project: **Árbol genealógico,** *Annotated Teacher's Edition*	Performance Assessment for Chapter 5, *Assessment Program*

Differentiated Instruction Bibliography

The following references are a starting point for the teacher interested in learning more about the topic of differentiated instruction.

Gardner, H. *Multiple Intelligences: The Theory in Practice.* New York: Basic Books, 1993.
Tomlinson, C., and Eidson, C. *Design for Differentiation: Curriculum for the Differentiated Classroom, Grades 5–9.* Alexandria, VA: Association for Supervision and Curriculum Development (in press).
Tomlinson, C. *The Differentiated Classroom: Responding to the Needs of All Learners.* Alexandria, VA: Association for Supervision and Curriculum Development, 1999.
Tomlinson, C. *How to Differentiate Instruction in Mixed-Ability Classrooms,* 2/e. Alexandria, VA: Association for Supervision and Curriculum Development, 2001.
Tomlinson, C., and Allan, S. *Leadership for Differentiating Schools and Classrooms.* Alexandria, VA: Association for Supervision and Curriculum Development, 2000.
Udall, A., and Daniels, J. *Creating the Thoughtful Classroom: Strategies to Promote Student Thinking.* Tucson, AZ: Zephyr Press, 1991.
Winebrenner, S. *Teaching Gifted Kids in the Regular Classroom.* Minneapolis, MN: Free Spirit, 1992.
Winebrenner, S. *Teaching Kids with Learning Difficulties in the Regular Classroom.* Minneapolis, MN: Free Spirit, 1996.

Calendario de tareas cotidianas

Fechas: del **lunes** _____ al **viernes** _____

Día	Tareas
lunes, el _____ _____ _____ _____	*Textbook:* _____ ***Cuaderno de actividades:*** _____ ***Cuaderno de vocabulario y gramática:*** _____ *CD-ROM:* _____ *Other:* _____
martes, el _____ _____ _____ _____	*Textbook:* _____ ***Cuaderno de actividades:*** _____ ***Cuaderno de vocabulario y gramática:*** _____ *CD-ROM:* _____ *Other:* _____
miércoles, el _____ _____ _____ _____	*Textbook:* _____ ***Cuaderno de actividades:*** _____ ***Cuaderno de vocabulario y gramática:*** _____ *CD-ROM:* _____ *Other:* _____
jueves, el _____ _____ _____ _____	*Textbook:* _____ ***Cuaderno de actividades:*** _____ ***Cuaderno de vocabulario y gramática:*** _____ *CD-ROM:* _____ *Other:* _____
viernes, el _____ _____ _____ _____	*Textbook:* _____ ***Cuaderno de actividades:*** _____ ***Cuaderno de vocabulario y gramática:*** _____ *CD-ROM:* _____ *Other:* _____

Holt Spanish 1B   Lesson Planner

STUDENT PROGRESS REPORT

Name _____ Class _____ Date _____

From _____ To _____

	1 Very poor	2 Poor	3 Average	4 Good	5 Excellent	Comments
Reading						
Speaking						
Writing						
Quizzes/Tests						
Completion of assignments						
Class participation						

Overall effort and involvement in language learning

_____

_____

_____

Teacher signature   Parent or guardian signature

Holt Spanish 1B   Lesson Planner

Copyright © by Holt, Rinehart and Winston. All rights reserved.

STANDARDS FOR FOREIGN LANGUAGE LEARNING

Communication Communicate in Languages Other Than English	**Standard 1.1**	Students engage in conversations, provide and obtain information, express feelings and emotions, and exchange opinions.
	Standard 1.2	Students understand and interpret written and spoken language on a variety of topics.
	Standard 1.3	Students present information, concepts, and ideas to an audience of listeners or readers on a variety of topics.
Cultures Gain Knowledge and Understanding of Other Cultures	**Standard 2.1**	Students demonstrate an understand-ing of the relationship between the practices and perspectives of the culture studied.
	Standard 2.2	Students demonstrate an understand-ing of the relationship between the products and perspectives of the culture studied.
Connections Connect with Other Disciplines and Acquire Information	**Standard 3.1**	Students reinforce and further their knowledge of other disciplines through the foreign language.
	Standard 3.2	Students acquire information and recognize the distinctive viewpoints that are only available through the foreign language and its cultures.
Comparisons Develop Insight into the Nature of Language and Culture	**Standard 4.1**	Students demonstrate understanding of the nature of language through comparisons of the language studied and their own.
	Standard 4.2	Students demonstrate understanding of the concept of culture through comparisons of the cultures studied and their own.
Communities Participate in Multilingual Communities at Home and Around the World	**Standard 5.1**	Students use the language both within and beyond the school setting.
	Standard 5.2	Students show evidence of becoming life-long learners by using the language for personal enjoyment and enrichment.

"National Standards Report" from *Standards for Foreign Language Learning: Preparing for the 21st Century.* Copyright © 1996 by **National Standards in Foreign Language Education Project**. Reprinted by permission of the publisher.

Geocultura

The Geocultura pages precede the chapter core and highlight different locations throughout the Spanish-speaking world. Levels 1A, 1B, and 1 present eight countries and two U.S. States. Level 2 presents ten cities, and Level 3 presents the Spanish-speaking world divided into five major regions.

The first two pages of each **Geocultura** section explore the geography of the country, city, or region presented. The following pages take a closer look at other characterizing features, such as local cuisine, architecture, festivals and celebrations, art, history, customs, and others.

Geografía

- To familiarize students with the geographic location of the **Geocultura** present the locator map under the title first. From there, lead students to the location map and have them point out any distinguishing geographical features such as oceans, rivers, lakes, mountain ranges and so on. This provides the opportunity to compare and contrast the geographical features of the studied country, city, or region with the students' own.
- Next, you might have students scan the surrounding photos and captions and have them find the location of each photo on the map. Then, have students read the captions and comment on them. Point out that the photo will help them understand the caption. Audio for all captions is available in the *¡Exprésate! Online Edition*.
- After students have achieved some familiarity with the geography, you might present the **Almanaque** and the **¿Sabías que...?** fact. Another **¿Sabías que...?** fact provides additional information for the students.
- For comprehension assessment, have students answer the question or questions under **¿Qué tanto sabes?**

A conocer...

- Have students first scan the photos and then have them focus on one section at a time. For orientation, have students find the location of each photo on the map. All sections on these pages lend themselves to comparing and contrasting between the location studied and the place where the students live, or places that they have visited.
- At the end of the **Geocultura** you will find a **Conexión** linking the content to another subject area. The **Conexión** always includes a student activity that can be done in class or assigned as homework. .
- Throughout the chapter—in the **Nota cultural,** the **Cultura,** the **Novela,** and the **Integración**—you will find references to the location that expand on the information presented in the **Geocultura**. At these points in the chapter you might want to revisit the **Geocultura** to reinforce and refresh what students have learned, or simply use the map for reference.
- At any point in the chapter, you may want to follow the Traditions, Projects, and Recipes suggestions in each chapter of the *Teacher Edition* interleaf pages. Each of these is specific to the location covered in the corresponding chapter **Geocultura** and provides opportunities to present additional cultural information.
- The **Geocultura** activities you assign can be easily adapted for Differentiated Instruction. You may want to assign further research or cultural projects to advanced learners or have slower pace learners spend additional time studying the information. Interdisciplinary Links and the topics of the **Geocultura** can be targeted for each of the Multiple Intelligences; for example, you might assign projects focusing on architecture for Logical-Mathematical Intelligences, research on traditional music in each location for Musical Intelligences, Internet research projects based on location-specific flora and fauna for Naturalist Intelligences, and so on.

- **GeoVisión,** a video counterpart to **Geocultura,** features a local teen presenter who introduces students to highlights of his or her country or city. Each **GeoVisión,** shot on location, allows student to see and hear the sights and sounds of the area and also to hear someone their own age who speaks with the location's regional accent. See *Video Guide* for specific suggestions on how to present **GeoVisión.**

For your reference, here is a chart of the **Geocultura** locations for all levels of *¡Exprésate!*

Chapter	Levels 1A, 1B, 1	Level 2	Level 3
1	Spain	Mexico City	Castilla-La Mancha
2	Puerto Rico	Cuzco	
3	Texas (El Paso)	Santo Domingo	Caribbean
4	Costa Rica	Miami	
5	Chile	San José	Southwestern US/Mexico
6	Mexico	Segovia	
7	Argentina	San Juan	Andean Highlands
8	Florida (Miami)	Santiago	
9	Dominican Republic	El Paso	Southern Cone
10	Peru	Buenos Aires	

50-Minute Daily Lesson Plans

Teacher's Name _____ Class _____ Date _____

Capítulo puente

CAPÍTULO
P

DAY 1 50-MINUTE LESSON PLAN

STANDARDS FOR FOREIGN LANGUAGE LEARNING: DAY 1

Chapter Opener
Communication 1.2: Students understand and interpret written and spoken language on a variety of topics.

Vocabulario en acción 1
Communication 1.1: Students engage in conversations, provide and obtain information, express feelings and emotions, and exchange opinions.

Communication 1.2: Students understand and interpret written and spoken language on a variety of topics.
Cultures 2.1: Students demonstrate an understanding of the relationship between the practices and perspectives of the culture studied.
Comparisons 4.1: Students demonstrate understanding of the nature of language through comparisons of the language studied and their own.

CORE INSTRUCTION

Warm-Up
(5 min.) Present Objetivos, p. T74.

Chapter Opener
- (5 min.) See Using the Photo, p. T74.

Vocabulario en acción 1
- (15 min.) Present **Vocabulario 1**, pp. 2–3 using Teaching **Vocabulario**, p. 2.
- (10 min.) Play Audio CD 6, Tr. 1 for Activity 1, p. 4.
- (15 min.) Have students do Activities 2–5, pp. 4–5.

Wrap-Up
- (5 min.) Have students answer questions about the pictures in Activity 5 (¿Quién es...? ¿Cómo es...?)

OPTIONAL RESOURCES
- (5 min.) TPR, p. 3
- (10 min.) Slower Pace Learners, p. 3 ◆
- (5 min.) Special Learning Needs, pp. 3, 5 ●
- (5 min.) Advanced Learners, p. 5 ▲
- (5 min.) **Comunicación**, p. 5
- (5 min.) See Common Error Alert, p. 5. Remind students to prepare for **Prueba: Vocabulario 1**.

Practice Options
- *Lab Book*, pp. 9–10 ▲ ◆
- *Cuaderno de vocabulario y gramática*, pp. 1–5 ▲ ◆ ●
- *Teaching Transparencies: Vocabulario y gramática* Answers, pp. 1–5 ▲ ◆ ●
- *Interactive Tutor* (Disc 1) or *DVD Tutor* (Disc 1) ▲ ● ■
- Online Practice, **Capítulo puente** (go.hrw.com, Keyword: EXP1B CHP)

▲ = Advanced Learners   ◆ = Slower Pace Learners   ● = Special Learning Needs   ■ = Heritage Speakers

Holt Spanish 1B   Lesson Planner

Teacher's Name _____ Class _____ Date _____

Capítulo puente

CAPÍTULO
P

DAY 2 50-MINUTE LESSON PLAN

STANDARDS FOR FOREIGN LANGUAGE LEARNING: DAY 2

Vocabulario en acción 1

Communication 1.1: Students engage in conversations, provide and obtain information, express feelings and emotions, and exchange opinions.
Communication 1.2: Students understand and interpret written and spoken language on a variety of topics.
Cultures 2.1: Students demonstrate an understanding of the relationship between the practices and perspectives of the culture studied.
Comparisons 4.1: Students demonstrate understanding of the nature of language through comparisons of the language studied and their own.

Gramática en acción 1

Communication 1.1: Students engage in conversations, provide and obtain information, express feelings and emotions, and exchange opinions.
Communication 1.2: Students understand and interpret written and spoken language on a variety of topics.
Communication 1.3: Students present information, concepts, and ideas to an audience of listeners or readers on a variety of topics.

CORE INSTRUCTION

Warm-Up
- (5 min.) See Bell Work CP.1, p. 2.

Vocabulario en acción 1
Assess
- (10 min.) Give **Prueba: Vocabulario 1.**

Gramática en acción 1
- (5 min.) Have students do Bell Work CP.2, p. 6.
- (10 min.) Present **Gramática:** *The verbs* ser *and* estar, p. 6 using Teaching **Gramática**, p. 6.
- (15 min.) Have students do Activities 6–9, p. 7.

Wrap-Up
- (5 min.) Have pairs of students read their emails from Activity 9 to each other.

OPTIONAL RESOURCES
- (10 min.) Special Learning Needs, p. 7 ●
- (10 min.) **Comunicación**, p. 7
- (5 min.) See Slower Pace Learners, p. 7. ◆

Practice Options
- **GramaVisión**, Level 1A, Ch. 2, 5
- *Lab Book*, pp. 9–10 ▲ ◆
- *Cuaderno de vocabulario y gramática*, pp. 1–5 ▲ ◆ ●
- *Teaching Transparencies:* Bell Work CP.1, CP.2; **Vocabulario y gramática** Answers, pp. 1–5 ▲ ◆ ●
- *Interactive Tutor* (Disc 1) or *DVD Tutor* (Disc 1) ▲ ● ■
- Online Practice, **Capítulo puente** (go.hrw.com, Keyword: EXP1B CHP)
- **Assessment Options**
- *Assessment Program*: **Prueba: Vocabulario 1**, pp. 1–2
- Test Generator

▲ = Advanced Learners   ◆ = Slower Pace Learners   ● = Special Learning Needs   ■ = Heritage Speakers

Holt Spanish 1B   Lesson Planner

Teacher's Name _____ Class _____ Date _____

CAPÍTULO
P

Capítulo puente

DAY 3 50-MINUTE LESSON PLAN

STANDARDS FOR FOREIGN LANGUAGE LEARNING: DAY 3

Gramática en acción 1
Communication 1.1: Students engage in conversations, provide and obtain information, express feelings and emotions, and exchange opinions.

Communication 1.2: Students understand and interpret written and spoken language on a variety of topics.

CORE INSTRUCTION

Warm-Up
- (5 min.) Have students do Bell Work CP.3, p. 8.

Gramática en acción 1
- (10 min.) Present **Gramática**: *The verbs* **gustar** *and* **tener**, p. 8 using Teaching **Gramática**, p. 8.
- (5 min.) Have students do Activity 10, p. 8.
- (10 min.) Play Audio CD 6, Tr. 2 for Activity 11, p. 9.
- (10 min.) Have students do Activities 12 and 13, p. 9.

Wrap-Up
- (10 min.) Play Audio CD 6, Tr. 3 for Activity 14, p. 14. Remind students to prepare for **Prueba: Gramática 1**.

OPTIONAL RESOURCES
- (5 min.) Advanced Learners, p. 9 ▲
- (5 min.) **Comunicación** (TE), p. 9
- (5 min.) See Multiple Intelligences, p. 9.

Practice Options
- *Lab Book,* pp. 9–10 ▲ ◆
- *Cuaderno de vocabulario y gramática,* pp. 1–5 ▲ ◆ ●
- *Cuaderno de actividades,* pp. 1–4 ▲ ● ■
- *Teaching Transparencies:* Bell Work CP.3; *Vocabulario y gramática* Answers, pp. 1–5 ▲ ◆ ●
- *Interactive Tutor* (Disc 1) or *DVD Tutor* (Disc 1) ▲ ● ■
- Online Practice, **Capítulo puente** (go.hrw.com, Keyword: EXP1B CHP)

▲ = Advanced Learners   ◆ = Slower Pace Learners   ● = Special Learning Needs   ■ = Heritage Speakers

Holt Spanish 1B   Lesson Planner

Teacher's Name _____ Class _____ Date _____

Capítulo puente

CAPÍTULO
P

DAY 4 50-MINUTE LESSON PLAN

STANDARDS FOR FOREIGN LANGUAGE LEARNING: DAY 4

Gramática en acción 1
Communication 1.1: Students engage in conversations, provide and obtain information, express feelings and emotions, and exchange opinions.
Communication 1.2: Students understand and interpret written and spoken language on a variety of topics.

Vocabulario en acción 2
Communication 1.1: Students engage in conversations, provide and obtain information, express feelings and emotions, and exchange opinions.

Communication 1.2: Students understand and interpret written and spoken language on a variety of topics.
Communication 1.3: Students present information, concepts, and ideas to an audience of listeners or readers on a variety of topics.
Comparisons 4.1: Students demonstrate understanding of the nature of language through comparisons of the language studied and their own.

CORE INSTRUCTION

Warm-Up
- (5 min.) See Bell Work CP.4, p. 12.

Gramática en acción 1
Assess
- (20 min.) Give **Prueba: Gramática 1**

Vocabulario en acción 2
- (10 min.) Present **Vocabulario 2**, pp. 12–14 using Teaching **Vocabulario**, p. 12.
- (10 min.) Have students do Activities 16 and 18, p. 15.

Wrap-Up
(5 min.) Have pairs of students pretend to have a phone conversation using the dialog they created in Activity 16, p. 15

OPTIONAL RESOURCES
- (5 min.) TPR, p. 13
- (5 min.) Slower Pace Learners, p. 13 ◆
- (5 min.) Special Learning Needs, p. 13 ●

Practice Options
- *Lab Book,* pp. 11–12 ▲ ◆
- *Cuaderno de vocabulario y gramática,* pp. 6–10 ▲ ◆ ●
- *Teaching Transparencies:* Bell Work CP.4; *Vocabulario y gramática* Answers, pp. 6–10 ▲ ◆ ●
- *Interactive Tutor* (Disc 1) or *DVD Tutor* (Disc 1) ▲ ● ■
- Online Practice, **Capítulo puente** (go.hrw.com, Keyword: EXP1B CHP)

Assessment Options
- *Assessment Program*: **Prueba: Gramática 1**, pp. 3–4
- Test Generator

▲ = Advanced Learners   ◆ = Slower Pace Learners   ● = Special Learning Needs   ■ = Heritage Speakers

Holt Spanish 1B

Lesson Planner

Teacher's Name _____ Class _____ Date _____

CAPÍTULO P

Capítulo puente

DAY 5 50-MINUTE LESSON PLAN

STANDARDS FOR FOREIGN LANGUAGE LEARNING: DAY 5

Gramática en acción 2

Communication 1.1: Students engage in conversations, provide and obtain information, express feelings and emotions, and exchange opinions.

Communication 1.2: Students understand and interpret written and spoken language on a variety of topics.

Communication 1.3: Students present information, concepts, and ideas to an audience of listeners or readers on a variety of topics.

CORE INSTRUCTION

Warm-Up
- (5 min.) Have students do Bell Work CP.5, p. 16.

Gramática en acción 2
- (20 min.) Present **Gramática: querer, ir a + infinitive, and pronouns,** p. 16 using Teaching **Gramática,** #1–2, p. 16.
- (10 min.) Play Audio CD 6, Tr. 4 for Activity 19, p. 16.
- (10 min.) Have students do Activities 20 and 22, p. 17.

Wrap-Up
- (5 min.) Have pairs of students ask and answer the questions they wrote in Activity 21. Remind students to study for **Prueba: Vocabulario 2.** ◆

OPTIONAL RESOURCES
- (10 min.) **Comunicación** (TE), p.17
- (5 min.) See Slower Pace Learners, p. 17.
- (5 min.) See Special Learning Needs, p. 17. ●

Practice Options
- *Lab Book,* pp. 11–12 ▲ ◆
- *Cuaderno de vocabulario y gramática,* pp. 6–10 ▲ ◆ ●
- *Cuaderno de actividades,* pp. 5–8 ▲ ● ■
- *Teaching Transparencies:* Bell Work CP.5; *Vocabulario y gramática* Answers, pp. 6–10 ▲ ◆ ●
- *Interactive Tutor* (Disc 1) or *DVD Tutor* (Disc 1) ▲ ● ■
- Online Practice, **Capítulo puente** (go.hrw.com, Keyword: EXP1B CHP)

▲ = Advanced Learners   ◆ = Slower Pace Learners   ● = Special Learning Needs   ■ = Heritage Speakers

Holt Spanish 1B   Lesson Planner

Teacher's Name _____ Class _____ Date _____

Capítulo puente

CAPÍTULO **P**

DAY 6 50-MINUTE LESSON PLAN

STANDARDS FOR FOREIGN LANGUAGE LEARNING: DAY 6

Vocabulario en acción 2

Communication 1.1: Students engage in conversations, provide and obtain information, express feelings and emotions, and exchange opinions.
Communication 1.2: Students understand and interpret written and spoken language on a variety of topics.
Communication 1.3: Students present information, concepts, and ideas to an audience of listeners or readers on a variety of topics.
Comparisons 4.1: Students demonstrate understanding of the nature of language through comparisons of the language studied and their own.

Gramática en acción 2

Communication 1.1: Students engage in conversations, provide and obtain information, express feelings and emotions, and exchange opinions.
Communication 1.2: Students understand and interpret written and spoken language on a variety of topics.
Communication 1.3: Students present information, concepts, and ideas to an audience of listeners or readers on a variety of topics.

CORE INSTRUCTION

Warm-Up
- (5 min.) Have students do Bell Work CP. 6, p. 18.

Vocabulario en acción 2

Assess
- (20 min.) Give **Prueba: Vocabulario 2.**

Gramática en acción 2
- (5 min.) See Teaching **Gramática,** #3, p. 16.
- (10 min.) Have students do Activities 23 and 24, pp. 18–19.
- (5 min.) Have students do Activity 26, p. 19.

Wrap-Up
- (5 min.) Read Activity 25 aloud as a class. Remind students to prepare for **Prueba: Gramática 2.**

OPTIONAL RESOURCES
- (10 min.) See **Comunicación,** p. 19.

Practice Options
- *Lab Book,* pp. 11–12 ▲ ◆
- *Cuaderno de vocabulario y gramática,* pp. 6–10 ▲ ◆ ●
- *Teaching Transparencies:* Bell Work CP.6; **Vocabulario y gramática** Answers, pp. 6–10 ▲ ◆ ●
- *Interactive Tutor* (Disc 1) or *DVD Tutor* (Disc 1) ▲ ● ■
- Online Practice, **Capítulo puente** (go.hrw.com, Keyword: EXP1B CHP)

Assessment Options
- *Assessment Program:* **Prueba: Vocabulario 2,** pp. 5–6
- *Test Generator*

▲ = Advanced Learners   ◆ = Slower Pace Learners   ● = Special Learning Needs   ■ = Heritage Speakers

Holt Spanish 1B   Lesson Planner

Teacher's Name _____ Class _____ Date _____

Capítulo puente

DAY 7 50-MINUTE LESSON PLAN

STANDARDS FOR FOREIGN LANGUAGE LEARNING: DAY 7

Gramática en acción 2
Communication 1.1: Students engage in conversations, provide and obtain information, express feelings and emotions, and exchange opinions.
Communication 1.2: Students understand and interpret written and spoken language on a variety of topics.
Communication 1.3: Students present information, concepts, and ideas to an audience of listeners or readers on a variety of topics.

Vocabulario en acción 3
Communication 1.2: Students understand and interpret written and spoken language on a variety of topics.
Cultures 2.1: Students demonstrate an understanding of the relationship between the practices and perspectives of the culture studied.

CORE INSTRUCTION

Warm-Up
- (5 min.) Have students do Bell Work CP.7, p. 22.

Gramática en acción 2

Assess
- (15 min.) Give **Prueba: Gramática 2**.

Vocabulario en acción 3
- (10 min.) Present **Vocabulario 3**, pp. 22–23. See Teaching **Vocabulario**, p. 22.
- (5 min.) Have students do Activities 27 and 28, p. 24.
- (10 min.) Play Audio CD 6, Tr. 5 for Activity 29, p. 25.

Wrap-Up
- (5 min.) Have students do Activity 30, p. 25.
- Remind students to prepare for **Prueba: Vocabulario**.

OPTIONAL RESOURCES
- (10 min.) TPR, p. 23
- (5 min.) See Slower Pace Learners, p. 23. ◆

Practice Options
- *Lab Book,* pp. 13–14 ▲ ◆
- *Cuaderno de vocabulario y gramática,* pp. 11–15 ▲ ◆ ●
- *Teaching Transparencies:* Bell Work CP.7; *Vocabulario y gramática* Answers, pp. 11–15 ▲ ◆ ●
- *Interactive Tutor* (Disc 1) or *DVD Tutor* (Disc 1) ▲ ● ■
- Online Practice, **Capítulo puente** (go.hrw.com, Keyword: EXP1B CHP)

Assessment Options
- *Assessment Program*: **Prueba: Gramática 2**, pp. 7–8
- Test Generator

▲ = Advanced Learners   ◆ = Slower Pace Learners   ● = Special Learning Needs   ■ = Heritage Speakers

Teacher's Name _____ Class _____ Date _____

Capítulo puente

CAPÍTULO
P

DAY 8 50-MINUTE LESSON PLAN

STANDARDS FOR FOREIGN LANGUAGE LEARNING: DAY 8

Vocabulario en acción 3
Communication 1.2: Students understand and interpret written and spoken language on a variety of topics.
Cultures 2.1: Students demonstrate an understanding of the relationship between the practices and perspectives of the culture studied.

Gramática en acción 3
Communication 1.1: Students engage in conversations, provide and obtain information, express feelings and emotions, and exchange opinions.
Communication 1.2: Students understand and interpret written and spoken language on a variety of topics.
Communication 1.3: Students present information, concepts, and ideas to an audience of listeners or readers on a variety of topics.

CORE INSTRUCTION

Warm-Up
- (5 min.) Have students do Bell Work CP. 8, p. 26.

Vocabulario en acción 3
- (5 min.) Have students do Activity 31, p. 25 as a class activity.

Assess
- (10 min.) Give **Prueba: Vocabulario 3**.

Gramática en acción 3
- (10 min.) Present **Gramática:** *The present tense of -er and -ir verbs,* p. 26 using Teaching **Gramática**, #1–2, p. 26.
- (10 min.) Have students do Activities 32 and 33, pp. 26–27.
- (5 min.) Have students do Activity 34, p. 27.

Wrap-Up
- (5 min.) Have students check answers to Activity 32 with a partner.

OPTIONAL RESOURCES
- (10 min.) **Comunicación** (TE) pp. 25, 27
- (10 min.) See Slower Pace Learners, p. 27. ◆
- (5 min.) Activity 35, p. 27

Practice Options
- *Lab Book*, pp. 13–14 ▲ ◆
- *Cuaderno de vocabulario y gramática,* pp. 11–15 ▲ ◆ ●
- *Cuaderno de actividades*, pp. 9–12 ▲ ● ■
- *Teaching Transparencies:* Bell Work CP.8; **Vocabulario y gramática** Answers, pp. 11–15 ▲ ◆ ●
- *Interactive Tutor* (Disc 1) or *DVD Tutor* (Disc 1) ▲ ● ■
- Online Practice, **Capítulo puente** (go.hrw.com, Keyword: EXP1B CHP)

Assessment Options
- *Assessment Program*: **Prueba: Vocabulario 3**, pp. 9–10
- *Test Generator*

▲ = Advanced Learners   ◆ = Slower Pace Learners   ● = Special Learning Needs   ■ = Heritage Speakers

Teacher's Name _____ Class _____ Date _____

Capítulo puente

CAPÍTULO
P

DAY 9 50-MINUTE LESSON PLAN

STANDARDS FOR FOREIGN LANGUAGE LEARNING: DAY 9

Gramática en acción 3
Communication 1.1: Students engage in conversations, provide and obtain information, express feelings and emotions, and exchange opinions.
Communication 1.2: Students understand and interpret written and spoken language on a variety of topics.
Communication 1.3: Students present information, concepts, and ideas to an audience of listeners or readers on a variety of topics.
Communities 5.2: Students show evidence of becoming life–long learners by using the language for personal enjoyment and enrichment.

CORE INSTRUCTION

Warm-Up
- (5 min.) Have students do Bell Work CP. 9, p. 28.

Gramática en acción 3
- (10 min.) Present **Gramática:** *Stem-changing verbs*, p. 28 using Teaching **Gramática**, p. 28.
- (10 min.) Play Audio CD 6, Tr. 6 for Activity 36, p. 28.
- (10 min.) Have students do Activities 37–39, p. 29.
- (5 min.) Have students go over **Repaso: El mundo hispanohablante,** pp. 30–31.
- (5 min.) Have students complete **¿Quién eres?**, pp. 32–33.

Wrap-Up
- (5 min.) See Fold-n-Learn, p. 32. Remind students to prepare for Chapter Test.

OPTIONAL RESOURCES
- (10 min.) **Comunicación**, p. 29
- (10 min.) Advanced Learners, p. 29 ▲
- (5 min.) See Special Learning Needs, p. 29. ●

Practice Options
- *Lab Book,* pp. 13–14 ▲ ◆
- *Cuaderno de vocabulario y gramática,* pp. 11–15 ▲ ◆ ●
- *Cuaderno de actividades,* p. 13 ▲ CIRCE, ■
- *Teaching Transparencies:* Bell Work CP.9; *Vocabulario y gramática* Answers, pp. 11–15 ▲ ◆ ●
- *Interactive Tutor* (Disc 1) or *DVD Tutor* (Disc 1) ▲ ● ■
- Online Practice, **Capítulo puente** (go.hrw.com, Keyword: EXP1B CHP)

▲ = Advanced Learners   ◆ = Slower Pace Learners   ● = Special Learning Needs   ■ = Heritage Speakers

Holt Spanish 1B   Lesson Planner

Teacher's Name _____ Class _____ Date _____

Capítulo puente

CAPÍTULO **P**

DAY 10 50-MINUTE LESSON PLAN

CORE INSTRUCTION

Warm-Up
- (5 min.) Let students practice with their Fold-n-Learns (see Day 9) for five minutes.

Chapter Assessment

Assess
- (40 min.) Give the Chapter Test.

Wrap-Up
- (5 min.) Preview **Geocultura: México**, pp. 34–37.

OPTIONAL RESOURCES
- Have students do the project on page T73C.

Practice Options
- Online Practice, **Capítulo puente** (go.hrw.com, Keyword: EXP1B CHP)

Assessment Options
- *Assessment Program*: **Examen: Capítulo puente**, pp. 121–131
- *Assessment Program*: **Examen oral: Capítulo puente**, p. 132
- Test Generator

▲ = Advanced Learners ◆ = Slower Pace Learners ● = Special Learning Needs ■ = Heritage Speakers

Holt Spanish 1B — Lesson Planner

Teacher's Name _____ Class _____ Date _____

¡A comer!

CAPÍTULO 6

DAY 1 50-MINUTE LESSON PLAN

STANDARDS FOR FOREIGN LANGUAGE LEARNING: DAY 1

Chapter Opener
Communication 1.2: Students understand and interpret written and spoken language on a variety of topics.

Vocabulario en acción 1
Communication 1.2: Students understand and interpret written and spoken language on a variety of topics.

Before starting **Capítulo 6,** you may wish to Teach **Geocultura: México,** pp. 34–37. For Teaching suggestions, see pp. xv–xvi of this Lesson Planner.

CORE INSTRUCTION

Warm-Up
- (5 min.) See Learning Tips, p. 39.

Chapter Opener
- (10 min.) See Using the Photo and **Más vocabulario,** p. 38.
- (5 min.) See **Objetivos,** p. 38.

Vocabulario en acción 1
- (15 min.) See Teaching **Vocabulario,** p. 40.
- (10 min.) Present other expressions from **¡Exprésate!,** p. 41.

Wrap-Up
- (5 min.) See **También se puede decir,** p. 41.

OPTIONAL RESOURCES
- (5 min.) Common Error Alert, pp. 40, 41
- (10 min.) Advanced Learners, p. 41 ▲
- (5 min.) Multiple Intelligences, p. 41

Practice Options
- *Lab Book,* pp. 37, 38 ▲ ♦
- *Cuaderno de vocabulario y gramática,* pp. 17–19 ▲ ♦ ●
- *Activities for Communication,* pp. 21–22 ▲ ■
- *Cuaderno para hispanohablantes,* Chapter 6 ■
- *Teaching Transparencies:* **Vocabulario** 6.1, 6.2; *Vocabulario y gramática* Answers, pp. 17–19 ▲ ♦ ●
- *Video Guide,* pp. 51, 52, 54–55, 56 ▲ ● ■
- *TPR Storytelling Book,* pp. 30–31 ▲ ●
- *Interactive Tutor* (Disc 2) or *DVD Tutor* (Disc 2) ▲ ● ■
- Online Practice, Chapter 6 (go.hrw.com, Keyword: EXP1B CH6)

▲ = Advanced Learners   ♦ = Slower Pace Learners   ● = Special Learning Needs   ■ = Heritage Speakers

Holt Spanish 1B   Lesson Planner

Teacher's Name _____ Class _____ Date _____

¡A comer!

CAPÍTULO 6

DAY 2 50-MINUTE LESSON PLAN

STANDARDS FOR FOREIGN LANGUAGE LEARNING: DAY 2

Vocabulario en acción 1

Communication 1.2: Students understand and interpret written and spoken language on a variety of topics.

Cultures 2.1: Students demonstrate an understanding of the relationship between the practices and perspectives of the culture studied.

Connections 3.1: Students reinforce and further their knowledge of other disciplines through the foreign language.

Comparisons 4.2: Students demonstrate understanding of the concept of culture through comparisons of the cultures studied and their own.

CORE INSTRUCTION

Warm-Up
- (5 min.) Have students do Bell Work 6.1, p. 40.

Vocabulario en acción 1
- (10 min.) Show **ExpresaVisión,** Ch. 6.
- (10 min.) Review **Vocabulario 1** and **¡Exprésate!,** pp. 40–41.
- (5 min.) Present **Nota cultural,** p. 42.
- (5 min.) Have students do Activity 1, p. 42.
- (10 min.) Play Audio CD 6, Tr. 1 for Activity 2, p. 42.

Wrap-Up
- (5 min.) See Game, p. 42.

OPTIONAL RESOURCES
- (5 min.) TPR, p. 41
- (5 min.) **Más práctica,** p. 42
- (10 min.) Fold-n-Learn, p. 42

Practice Options
- *Lab Book,* pp. 16; 38 ▲ ◆
- *Cuaderno de vocabulario y gramática,* pp. 17–19 ▲ ◆ ●
- *Activities for Communication,* pp. 21–22 ▲ ■
- *Cuaderno para hispanohablantes,* Chapter 6 ■
- *Teaching Transparencies:* Bell Work 6.1; **Vocabulario** 6.1, 6.2; *Vocabulario y gramática* Answers, pp. 17–19 ▲ ◆ ●
- *Video Guide,* pp. 54–55, 56 ▲ ● ■
- *TPR Storytelling Book,* pp. 30–31 ▲ ●
- *Interactive Tutor* (Disc 2) or *DVD Tutor* (Disc 2) ▲ ● ■
- Online Practice, Chapter 6 (go.hrw.com, Keyword: EXP1B CH6)

▲ = Advanced Learners   ◆ = Slower Pace Learners   ● = Special Learning Needs   ■ = Heritage Speakers

Holt Spanish 1B   Lesson Planner

Teacher's Name _____ Class _____ Date _____

¡A comer!

CAPÍTULO 6

DAY 3 50-MINUTE LESSON PLAN

STANDARDS FOR FOREIGN LANGUAGE LEARNING: DAY 3

Vocabulario en acción 1

Communication 1.1: Students engage in conversations, provide and obtain information, express feelings and emotions, and exchange opinions.

Communication 1.2: Students understand and interpret written and spoken language on a variety of topics.

Communication 1.3: Students present information, concepts, and ideas to an audience of listeners or readers on a variety of topics.

Cultures 2.1: Students demonstrate an understanding of the relationship between the practices and perspectives of the culture studied.

Connections 3.1: Students reinforce and further their knowledge of other disciplines through the foreign language.

Comparisons 4.2: Students demonstrate understanding of the concept of culture through comparisons of the cultures studied and their own.

CORE INSTRUCTION

Warm-Up
- (5 min.) Have students tell a partner how they feel about the foods listed in Activity 2, p. 42.

Vocabulario en acción 1
- (25 min.) Have students do Activities 3–6, pp. 42–43.
- (15 min.) See Teaching ¡Exprésate!, p. 44.

Wrap-Up
- (5 min.) Have some students read aloud their answers for Activity 4.

OPTIONAL RESOURCES
- (5 min.) Slower Pace Learners, p. 43 ◆
- (5 min.) Special Learning Needs, p. 43 ●
- (10 min.) **Comunicación** (TE), p. 43
- (5 min.) Language Note, p. 45

Practice Options
- *Lab Book,* p. 38 ▲ ● ■
- *Cuaderno de vocabulario y gramática,* pp. 17–19 ▲ ◆ ●
- *Activities for Communication,* pp. 21–22 ▲ ■
- *Cuaderno para hispanohablantes,* Chapter 6 ■
- *Teaching Transparencies:* **Vocabulario** 6.1, 6.2; *Vocabulario y gramática* Answers, pp. 17–19 ▲ ◆ ●
- *Video Guide,* pp. 54–55, 56 ▲ ● ■
- *TPR Storytelling Book,* pp. 30–31 ▲ ●
- *Interactive Tutor* (Disc 2) or *DVD Tutor* (Disc 2) ▲ ● ■
- Online Practice, Chapter 6 (go.hrw.com, Keyword: EXP1B CH6)

▲ = Advanced Learners ◆ = Slower Pace Learners ● = Special Learning Needs ■ = Heritage Speakers

Holt Spanish 1B — Lesson Planner

Teacher's Name _____ Class _____ Date _____

¡A comer!

CAPÍTULO 6

DAY 4 50-MINUTE LESSON PLAN

STANDARDS FOR FOREIGN LANGUAGE LEARNING: DAY 4

Vocabulario en acción 1

Communication 1.1: Students engage in conversations, provide and obtain information, express feelings and emotions, and exchange opinions.

Communication 1.2: Students understand and interpret written and spoken language on a variety of topics.

Communication 1.3: Students present information, concepts, and ideas to an audience of listeners or readers on a variety of topics.

Comparisons 4.2: Students demonstrate understanding of the concept of culture through comparisons of the cultures studied and their own.

CORE INSTRUCTION

Warm-Up
- (5 min.) Have students do Bell Work 6.2, p. 46.

Vocabulario en acción 1
- (10 min.) Review **¡Exprésate!**, p. 44.
- (25 min.) Have students do Activities 7–10, pp. 44–45.

Wrap-Up
- (10 min.) Have pairs of students present their dialogs to the class. Remind students to study for **Prueba: Vocabulario 1.**

OPTIONAL RESOURCES
- (5 min.) Extension, p. 44
- (5 min.) Multiple Intelligences, p. 45
- (10 min.) **Comunicación TE,** p. 45
- (10 min.) See Advanced Learners, p. 45.

Practice Options
- *Lab Book,* p. 38 ▲ ● ■
- ***Cuaderno de vocabulario y gramática,*** pp. 17–19 ▲ ●
- *Activities for Communication,* pp. 21–22 ▲ ■
- ***Cuaderno para hispanohablantes,*** Chapter 6 ■
- *Teaching Transparencies:* Bell Work 6.2; **Vocabulario** 6.1, 6.2; ***Vocabulario y gramática*** Answers, pp. 17–19 ▲ ●
- *Video Guide,* pp. 54–55, ▲ ● ■
- *TPR Storytelling Book,* pp. 30–31 ▲ ●
- *Interactive Tutor* (Disc 2) or *DVD Tutor* (Disc 2) ▲ ● ■
- Online Practice, Chapter 6 (go.hrw.com, Keyword: EXP1B CH6)

▲ = Advanced Learners   ◆ = Slower Pace Learners   ● = Special Learning Needs   ■ = Heritage Speakers

Holt Spanish 1B   Lesson Planner

Teacher's Name _____ Class _____ Date _____

¡A comer!

CAPÍTULO 6

DAY 5 50-MINUTE LESSON PLAN

STANDARDS FOR FOREIGN LANGUAGE LEARNING: DAY 5

Vocabulario en acción 1

Communication 1.1: Students engage in conversations, provide and obtain information, express feelings and emotions, and exchange opinions.
Communication 1.2: Students understand and interpret written and spoken language on a variety of topics.
Communication 1.3: Students present information, concepts, and ideas to an audience of listeners or readers on a variety of topics.

Cultures 2.1: Students demonstrate an understanding of the relationship between the practices and perspectives of the culture studied.
Connections 3.1: Students reinforce and further their knowledge of other disciplines through the foreign language.
Comparisons 4.2: Students demonstrate understanding of the concept of culture through comparisons of the cultures studied and their own.

CORE INSTRUCTION

Warm-Up
- (5 min.) Review responses for Activity 8, p. 45.

Vocabulario en acción 1

Assess
- (20 min.) Review **Vocabulario en acción 1**, pp. 40–45.
- (20 min.) Give **Prueba: Vocabulario 1**.

Wrap-Up
- (5 min.) Preview **Gramática en acción 1**, pp. 46–51.

OPTIONAL RESOURCES
- (5 min.) See Advanced Learners, p.45.
- (5 min.) See Multiple Intelligences, p. 45.

Practice Options
- *Lab Book*, p. 38 ▲●■
- *Cuaderno de vocabulario y gramática,* pp. 17–19 ▲●
- *Activities for Communication,* pp. 21–22 ▲■
- *Cuaderno para hispanohablantes,* Chapter 6 ■
- *Teaching Transparencies:* **Vocabulario** 6.1, 6.2; *Vocabulario y gramática* Answers, pp. 17–19 ▲●
- *Video Guide,* pp. 54–55, 56 ▲●■
- *TPR Storytelling Book,* pp. 30–31 ▲●
- *Grammar Tutor for Students of Spanish,* Chapter 6 ●■
- *Interactive Tutor* (Disc 2) or *DVD Tutor* (Disc 2) ▲●■
- Online Practice, Chapter 6 (go.hrw.com, Keyword: EXP1B CH6)

Assessment Options
- *Assessment Program*: **Prueba: Vocabulario 1**, pp. 17–18
- *Assessment Program*: Alternative Assessment Guide, pp. 241, 249, 257 ▲●■
- Test Generator

▲ = Advanced Learners ◆ = Slower Pace Learners ● = Special Learning Needs ■ = Heritage Speakers

Holt Spanish 1B Lesson Planner

Teacher's Name _____ Class _____ Date _____

¡A comer!

CAPÍTULO 6

DAY 6 50-MINUTE LESSON PLAN

STANDARDS FOR FOREIGN LANGUAGE LEARNING: DAY 6

Gramática en acción 1
Communication 1.1: Students engage in conversations, provide and obtain information, express feelings and emotions, and exchange opinions.

Communication 1.2: Students understand and interpret written and spoken language on a variety of topics.

CORE INSTRUCTION

Warm-Up
- (10 min.) Ask students to give examples of how they have used **estar** and **ser** in previous lessons.

Gramática en acción 1
- (20 min.) Present **Gramática: ser** and **estar**, p. 46. See Teaching **Gramática,** p. 46.
- (10 min.) Have students do Activity 11, p. 46.
- (5 min.) Present **Nota cultural,** p. 46. See Special Learning Needs, p. 47. ●

Wrap-Up
- (5 min.) See Career Path, p. 47.

OPTIONAL RESOURCES
- (5 min.) See Slower Pace Learners, p. 47.
- (5 min.) See Special Learning Needs, p. 47.

Practice Options
- *Lab Book,* p. 38 ▲ ● ■
- *Cuaderno de vocabulario y gramática,* pp. 20–22 ▲ ●
- *Cuaderno de actividades,* pp. 15–18 ▲ ● ■
- *Activities for Communication,* pp. 21–22 ▲ ■
- *Cuaderno para hispanohablantes,* Chapter 6 ■
- *Teaching Transparencies; Vocabulario y gramática* Answers, pp. 20–22 ▲ ●
- *Video Guide,* pp. 54–55, 56–57 ▲ ● ■
- *Grammar Tutor for Students of Spanish,* Chapter 6 ● ■
- *Interactive Tutor* (Disc 2) or *DVD Tutor* (Disc 2) ▲ ● ■
- Online Practice, Chapter 6 (go.hrw.com, Keyword: EXP1B CH6)

▲ = Advanced Learners   ◆ = Slower Pace Learners   ● = Special Learning Needs   ■ = Heritage Speakers

Holt Spanish 1B
Lesson Planner

Teacher's Name _____ Class _____ Date _____

¡A comer!

CAPÍTULO 6

DAY 7 50-MINUTE LESSON PLAN

STANDARDS FOR FOREIGN LANGUAGE LEARNING: DAY 7

Gramática en acción 1

Communication 1.1: Students engage in conversations, provide and obtain information, express feelings and emotions, and exchange opinions.

Communication 1.2: Students understand and interpret written and spoken language on a variety of topics.

Communication 1.3: Students present information, concepts, and ideas to an audience of listeners or readers on a variety of topics.

Cultures 2.2: Students demonstrate an understanding of the relationship between the products and perspectives of the culture studied.

Communities 5.2: Students show evidence of becoming life–long learners by using the language for personal enjoyment and enrichment.

CORE INSTRUCTION

Warm-Up
- (5 min.) Have students do Bell Work 6.3, p. 48.

Gramática en acción 1
- (10 min.) Show **GramaVisión 6**, Segment 1
- (30 min.) Have students do Activities 12–15, p. 47.

Wrap-Up
- (5 min.) Have students review their letters from Activity 13 with a partner.

OPTIONAL RESOURCES
- (10 min.) **Comunicación** (TE), p. 47
- (10 min.) *Lab Book,* pp. 38–39
- (5 min.) See Slower Pace Learners, p. 47. ◆

Practice Options
- *Lab Book,* p. 38 ▲ ● ■
- ***Cuaderno de vocabulario y gramática,*** pp. 20–22 ▲ ◆ ●
- ***Cuaderno de actividades,*** pp. 15–18 ▲ ● ■
- *Activities for Communication,* pp. 21–22 ▲ ■
- ***Cuaderno para hispanohablantes,*** Chapter 6 ■
- *Teaching Transparencies:* Bell Work 6.3; *Vocabulario y gramática* Answers, pp. 20–22 ▲ ◆ ●
- *Video Guide,* pp. 54–55, 56 ▲ ● ■
- *Grammar Tutor for Students of Spanish,* Chapter 6 ● ■
- *Interactive Tutor* (Disc 2) or *DVD Tutor* (Disc 2) ▲ ● ■
- Online Practice, Chapter 6 (go.hrw.com, Keyword: EXP1B CH6)

▲ = Advanced Learners   ◆ = Slower Pace Learners   ● = Special Learning Needs   ■ = Heritage Speakers

Holt Spanish 1B — Lesson Planner

Teacher's Name _____ Class _____ Date _____

CAPÍTULO
6

¡A comer!

DAY 8 50-MINUTE LESSON PLAN

STANDARDS FOR FOREIGN LANGUAGE LEARNING: DAY 8

Gramática en acción 1

Communication 1.2: Students understand and interpret written and spoken language on a variety of topics.

CORE INSTRUCTION

Warm-Up
- (5 min.) See Practices and Perspectives, p. 49.

Gramática en acción 1
- (5 min.) Show **GramaVisión 6**, Segment 2
- (15 min.) Present **Gramática: pedir** and **servir**, p. 48 using Teaching **Gramática,** p. 48.
- (10 min.) Play Audio CD 6, Tr. 2 for Activity 16, p. 48.
- (5 min.) Have students do Activity 17, p. 48.

Wrap-Up
- (10 min.) See **Comunicación** (TE)**,** p. 49. You might want to assign it as homework.

OPTIONAL RESOURCES
- (5 min.) See Advanced Learners, p. 49.
- (10 min.) See Multiple Intelligences, p. 49.

Practice Options
- *Lab Book,* pp. 16, 38 ▲●■
- *Cuaderno de vocabulario y gramática,* pp. 20–22 ▲♦●
- *Cuaderno de actividades*, pp. 15–18 ▲●■
- *Activities for Communication,* pp. 21–22 ▲■
- *Cuaderno para hispanohablantes,* Chapter 6 ■
- *Teaching Transparencies: Vocabulario y gramática* Answers, pp. 20–22 ▲♦●
- *Video Guide,* pp. 56 ▲●■
- *Grammar Tutor for Students of Spanish,* Chapter 6 ●■
- *Interactive Tutor* (Disc 2) or *DVD Tutor* (Disc 2) ▲●■
- Online Practice, Chapter 6 (go.hrw.com, Keyword: EXP1B CH6)

▲ = Advanced Learners   ♦ = Slower Pace Learners   ● = Special Learning Needs   ■ = Heritage Speakers

Holt Spanish 1B   Lesson Planner

Teacher's Name _____ Class _____ Date _____

¡A comer!

CAPÍTULO 6

DAY 9 50-MINUTE LESSON PLAN

STANDARDS FOR FOREIGN LANGUAGE LEARNING: DAY 9

Gramática en acción 1

Communication 1.1: Students engage in conversations, provide and obtain information, express feelings and emotions, and exchange opinions.

Communication 1.2: Students understand and interpret written and spoken language on a variety of topics.

Communication 1.3: Students present information, concepts, and ideas to an audience of listeners or readers on a variety of topics.

Cultures 2.1: Students demonstrate an understanding of the relationship between the practices and perspectives of the culture studied.

CORE INSTRUCTION

Warm-Up
- (5 min.) Review **ser** and **estar**, p. 46.

Gramática en acción 1
- (15 min.) Have students do Activities 18–20, p. 49.
- (15 min.) Present **Gramática: preferir, poder** and **probar**, p. 50 using Teaching **Gramática**, p. 50.
- (10 min.) Show **GramaVisión 6**, Segment 3.

Wrap-Up
- (5 min.) See Advanced Learners, p. 49.

OPTIONAL RESOURCES
- (5 min.) See Multiple Intelligences, p. 49.

Practice Options
- *Lab Book*, p. 38
- ***Cuaderno de vocabulario y gramática,*** pp. 20–22 ▲ ◆ ●
- ***Cuaderno de actividades***, pp. 15–18 ▲ ● ■
- *Activities for Communication*, pp. 21–22 ▲ ■
- ***Cuaderno para hispanohablantes,*** Chapter 6 ■
- *Teaching Transparencies:* ***Vocabulario y gramática*** Answers, pp. 20–22 ▲ ◆ ●
- *Video Guide*, pp. 54–55, 56 ▲ ● ■
- *Grammar Tutor for Students of Spanish*, Chapter 6 ● ■
- *Interactive Tutor* (Disc 2) or *DVD Tutor* (Disc 2) ▲ ● ■
- Online Practice, Chapter 6 (go.hrw.com, Keyword: EXP1B CH6)

▲ = Advanced Learners   ◆ = Slower Pace Learners   ● = Special Learning Needs   ■ = Heritage Speakers

Holt Spanish 1B — Lesson Planner

Teacher's Name _____ Class _____ Date _____

¡A comer!

CAPÍTULO 6

DAY 10 50-MINUTE LESSON PLAN

> **STANDARDS FOR FOREIGN LANGUAGE LEARNING: DAY 10**
>
> **Gramática en acción 1**
> **Communication 1.1:** Students engage in conversations, provide and obtain information, express feelings and emotions, and exchange opinions.
> **Communication 1.2:** Students understand and interpret written and spoken language on a variety of topics.
> **Communication 1.3:** Students present information, concepts, and ideas to an audience of listeners or readers on a variety of topics.

CORE INSTRUCTION

Warm-Up
- (5 min.) Have students do Bell Work 6.4, p. 50.

Gramática en acción 1
- (15 min.) Review **preferir, poder,** and **probar,** p. 50.
- (20 min.) Have students do Activities 21–24, p. 50–51.

Wrap-Up
- (10 min.) Have students volunteer to read their sentences from Activity 23. Remind students to study for **Prueba: Gramática 1**.

OPTIONAL RESOURCES
- (10 min.) **Comunicación** (TE), p. 51
- (5 min.) See Slower Pace Learners, p. 51.
- (5 min.) Special Learning Needs, p. 51. ◆ ●

Practice Options
- *Lab Book,* pp. 38–39 ▲ ● ■
- *Cuaderno de vocabulario y gramática,* pp. 20–22 ▲ ◆ ●
- *Cuaderno de actividades,* pp. 15–18 ▲ ● ■
- *Activities for Communication,* pp. 21–22 ▲ ■
- *Cuaderno para hispanohablantes,* Chapter 6 ■
- *Teaching Transparencies:* Bell Work 6.5; **Vocabulario y gramática** Answers, pp. 20–22 ▲ ◆ ●
- *Video Guide,* p. 56 ▲ ● ■
- *Grammar Tutor for Students of Spanish,* Chapter 6 ● ■
- *Interactive Tutor* (Disc 2) or *DVD Tutor* (Disc 2) ▲ ● ■
- Online Practice, Chapter 6 (go.hrw.com, Keyword: EXP1B CH6)

▲ = Advanced Learners   ◆ = Slower Pace Learners   ● = Special Learning Needs   ■ = Heritage Speakers

Holt Spanish 1B   Lesson Planner

Teacher's Name _____ Class _____ Date _____

CAPÍTULO 6

¡A comer!

DAY 11 50-MINUTE LESSON PLAN

STANDARDS FOR FOREIGN LANGUAGE LEARNING: DAY 11

Gramática en acción 1

Communication 1.1: Students engage in conversations, provide and obtain information, express feelings and emotions, and exchange opinions.

Communication 1.2: Students understand and interpret written and spoken language on a variety of topics.

Communication 1.3: Students present information, concepts, and ideas to an audience of listeners or readers on a variety of topics.

Cultura

Communication 1.2: Students understand and interpret written and spoken language on a variety of topics.

Cultures 2.2: Students demonstrate an understanding of the relationship between the products and perspectives of the culture studied.

Comparisons 4.2: Students demonstrate understanding of the concept of culture through comparisons of the cultures studied and their own.

Communities 5.1: Students use the language both within and beyond the school setting.

Communities 5.2: Students show evidence of becoming life–long learners by using the language for personal enjoyment and enrichment.

CORE INSTRUCTION

Warm-Up
- (10 min.) Have students repeat Bell Work 6.3, p. 48.

Gramática en acción 1
- (10 min.) Review **Gramática en acción 1**, pp. 46–51.

Assess
- (20 min.) Give **Prueba: Gramática 1.**

Cultura
- (5 min.) See Teaching **Cultura,** #1–2, p. 52.

Wrap-Up
- (5 min.) See Map Activities, p. 52.

OPTIONAL RESOURCES
- (5 min.) Heritage Speakers, p. 52 ■
- (10 min.) Special Learning Needs, p. 53
- (10 min.) Advanced Learners, p. 53

Practice Options
- *Lab Book,* pp. 38–39 ▲ ● ■
- *Cuaderno de actividades,* p. 19 ▲ ● ■
- *Activities for Communication,* pp. 21–22 ▲ ■
- *Cuaderno para hispanohablantes,* pp. 45–52 ■
- *Video Guide,* pp. 54–55, 56, 57 ▲ ● ■
- *Interactive Tutor* (Disc 2) or *DVD Tutor* (Disc 2) ▲ ● ■
- Online Practice, Chapter 6 (go.hrw.com, Keyword: EXP1B CH6)

Assessment Options
- *Assessment Program*: **Prueba: Gramática 1**, pp. 19–20
- *Assessment Program*: **Prueba: Aplicación 1**, pp. 21–22
- *Assessment Program*: Alternative Assessment Guide, pp. 241, 249, 257 ▲ ● ■
- *Audio CD 6,* Tr. 15
- Test Generator

▲ = Advanced Learners ◆ = Slower Pace Learners ● = Special Learning Needs ■ = Heritage Speakers

Holt Spanish 1B — Lesson Planner

Teacher's Name _____ Class _____ Date _____

¡A comer!

CAPÍTULO 6

DAY 12 50-MINUTE LESSON PLAN

STANDARDS FOR FOREIGN LANGUAGE LEARNING: DAY 12

Cultura
Communication 1.2: Students understand and interpret written and spoken language on a variety of topics.
Cultures 2.2: Students demonstrate an understanding of the relationship between the products and perspectives of the culture studied.
Comparisons 4.2: Students demonstrate understanding of the concept of culture through comparisons of the cultures studied and their own.
Communities 5.1: Students use the language both within and beyond the school setting.

Communities 5.2: Students show evidence of becoming life–long learners by using the language for personal enjoyment and enrichment.

Vocabulario en acción 2
Communication 1.2: Students understand and interpret written and spoken language on a variety of topics.
Comparisons 4.1: Students demonstrate understanding of the nature of language through comparisons of the language studied and their own.

CORE INSTRUCTION

Warm-Up
- (5 min.) See Products and Perspectives, p. 53.

Cultura
- (10 min.) Have students read the interviews, pp. 52–53.
- (5 min.) See Teaching **Cultura,** #3, p. 52.
- (5 min.) Present and assign **Comunidad,** p. 53.

Vocabulario en acción 2
- (15 min.) Present **Vocabulario 2,** pp. 54–55 using Teaching **Vocabulario,** p. 54.

Wrap-Up
- (10 min.) Present Language Note and **También se puede decir,** p. 55.

OPTIONAL RESOURCES
- (5 min.) **Comunidad,** p. 53
- (5 min.) Products and Perspectives, p. 53
- (5 min.) Community Link, p. 53
- (10 min.) Special Learning Needs, p. 55 ●

Practice Options
- *Lab Book,* pp. 39, 40 ▲ ● ■
- *Cuaderno de vocabulario y gramática,* pp. 23–25 ▲ ◆ ●
- *Activities for Communication,* pp. 23–24 ▲ ■
- *Cuaderno para hispanohablantes,* Chapter 6 ■
- *Teaching Transparencies:* **Vocabulario** 6.3, 6.4; *Vocabulario y gramática* Answers, pp. 23–25 ▲ ◆ ●
- *Video Guide,* pp. 54–55, 57, 58 ▲ ● ■
- *TPR Storytelling Book,* pp. 32–33 ▲ ●
- *Interactive Tutor* (Disc 2) or *DVD Tutor* (Disc 2) ▲ ● ■
- Online Practice, Chapter 6 (go.hrw.com, Keyword: EXP1B CH6)

▲ = Advanced Learners ◆ = Slower Pace Learners ● = Special Learning Needs ■ = Heritage Speakers

Holt Spanish 1B — Lesson Planner

Teacher's Name _____ Class _____ Date _____

¡A comer!

CAPÍTULO 6

DAY 13 50-MINUTE LESSON PLAN

STANDARDS FOR FOREIGN LANGUAGE LEARNING: DAY 13

Vocabulario en acción 2

Communication 1.1: Students engage in conversations, provide and obtain information, express feelings and emotions, and exchange opinions.
Communication 1.2: Students understand and interpret written and spoken language on a variety of topics.
Communication 1.3: Students present information, concepts, and ideas to an audience of listeners or readers on a variety of topics.

Cultures 2.1: Students demonstrate an understanding of the relationship between the practices and perspectives of the culture studied.
Comparisons 4.1: Students demonstrate understanding of the nature of language through comparisons of the language studied and their own.

CORE INSTRUCTION

Warm-Up
- (5 min.) Have students ask a partner the questions from ¡Exprésate!, p. 55.

Vocabulario en acción 2
- (10 min.) Show **ExpresaVisión**, Ch. 6.
- (15 min.) Review **Vocabulario 2,** pp. 54–59.
- (5 min.) Present **Nota cultural,** p. 56.
- (10 min.) Have students do Activities 25–26, p. 56.

Wrap-Up
- (5 min.) Do TPR Activity, p. 55.

OPTIONAL RESOURCES
- (10 min.) Advanced Learners, p. 55 ▲
- (5 min.) Practices and Perspectives, p. 56
- (10 min.) Game, p. 56

Practice Options
- *Lab Book,* p. 40 ▲●■
- *Cuaderno de vocabulario y gramática,* pp. 23–25 ▲◆●
- *Activities for Communication,* pp. 23–24 ▲■
- *Cuaderno para hispanohablantes,* Chapter 6 ■
- *Teaching Transparencies:* **Vocabulario** 6.3, 6.4; *Vocabulario y gramática* Answers, pp. 23–25 ▲◆●
- *Video Guide,* pp. 54–55, 58 ▲●■
- *TPR Storytelling Book,* pp. 32–33 ▲●
- *Interactive Tutor* (Disc 2) or *DVD Tutor* (Disc 2) ▲●■
- Online Practice, Chapter 6 (go.hrw.com, Keyword: EXP1B CH6)

▲ = Advanced Learners   ◆ = Slower Pace Learners   ● = Special Learning Needs   ■ = Heritage Speakers

Holt Spanish 1B

Lesson Planner

Teacher's Name _____ Class _____ Date _____

¡A comer!

CAPÍTULO 6

DAY 14 50-MINUTE LESSON PLAN

> **STANDARDS FOR FOREIGN LANGUAGE LEARNING: DAY 14**
>
> **Vocabulario en acción 2**
> **Communication 1.1:** Students engage in conversations, provide and obtain information, express feelings and emotions, and exchange opinions.
> **Communication 1.2:** Students understand and interpret written and spoken language on a variety of topics.
> **Communication 1.3:** Students present information, concepts, and ideas to an audience of listeners or readers on a variety of topics.
>
> **Cultures 2.1:** Students demonstrate an understanding of the relationship between the practices and perspectives of the culture studied.
> **Comparisons 4.1:** Students demonstrate understanding of the nature of language through comparisons of the language studied and their own.

CORE INSTRUCTION

Warm-Up
- (5 min.) Have students do Bell Work 6.5, p. 54.

Vocabulario en acción 2
- (5 min.) Present **Nota Cultural**, p. 56
- (35 min.) Have students do Activities 27–31, pp. 56–57.
- (10 min.) **Comunicación** (TE), p. 57

Wrap-Up
- (5 min.) Present Language Note, p. 57.

OPTIONAL RESOURCES
- (5 min.) Slower Pace Learners, p. 57 ◆
- (5 min.) Multiple Intelligences, p. 57

Practice Options
- *Lab Book*, p. 40 ▲ ● ■
- *Cuaderno de vocabulario y gramática,* pp. 23–25 ▲ ◆ ●
- *Activities for Communication,* pp. 23–24 ▲ ■
- *Cuaderno para hispanohablantes,* Chapter 6 ■
- *Teaching Transparencies:* Bell Work 6.6; **Vocabulario** 6.3, 6.4; *Vocabulario y gramática* Answers, pp. 23–25 ▲ ◆ ●
- *Video Guide,* pp. 54–55, 58 ▲ ● ■
- *TPR Storytelling Book,* pp. 32–33 ▲ ■
- *Interactive Tutor* (Disc 2) or *DVD Tutor* (Disc 2) ▲ ● ■
- Online Practice, Chapter 6 (go.hrw.com, Keyword: EXP1B CH6)

▲ = Advanced Learners ◆ = Slower Pace Learners ● = Special Learning Needs ■ = Heritage Speakers

Holt Spanish 1B — Lesson Planner

Teacher's Name _____ Class _____ Date _____

CAPÍTULO 6

¡A comer!

DAY 15 50-MINUTE LESSON PLAN

STANDARDS FOR FOREIGN LANGUAGE LEARNING: DAY 15

Vocabulario en acción 2

Communication 1.1: Students engage in conversations, provide and obtain information, express feelings and emotions, and exchange opinions.

Communication 1.2: Students understand and interpret written and spoken language on a variety of topics.

Communication 1.3: Students present information, concepts, and ideas to an audience of listeners or readers on a variety of topics.

CORE INSTRUCTION

Warm-Up
- (5 min.) Have several students read their sentences describing the pictures in Activity 28, p. 57.

Vocabulario en acción 2
- (15 min.) See Teaching ¡Exprésate!, p. 58.
- (10 min.) Play Audio CD 6, Tr. 6 for Activity 32, p. 58.
- (15 min.) Have students do Activities 33–35, pp. 58–59.

Wrap-Up
- (5 min.) Have students check answers to Activity 35 with a partner.

OPTIONAL RESOURCES
- (5 min.) Language to Language, p. 58
- (10 min.) Extension, p. 59
- (10 min.) Slower Pace Learners, p. 59 ◆
- (10 min.) Special Learning Needs, p. 59 ●

Practice Options
- *Lab Book,* p.17, 40 ▲ ● ■
- ***Cuaderno de vocabulario y gramática,*** pp. 23–25 ▲ ◆ ●
- *Activities for Communication,* pp. 23–24 ▲ ■
- ***Cuaderno para hispanohablantes,*** Chapter 6 ■
- *Teaching Transparencies:* **Vocabulario** 6.3, 6.4; ***Vocabulario y gramática*** Answers, pp. 23–25 ▲ ◆ ●
- *Video Guide,* pp. 54–55, 58 ▲ ● ■
- *TPR Storytelling Book,* pp. 32–33 ▲ ●
- *Interactive Tutor* (Disc 2) or *DVD Tutor* (Disc 2) ▲ ● ■
- Online Practice, Chapter 6 (go.hrw.com, Keyword: EXP1B CH6)

▲ = Advanced Learners ◆ = Slower Pace Learners ● = Special Learning Needs ■ = Heritage Speakers

Holt Spanish 1B — Lesson Planner

Teacher's Name _____ Class _____ Date _____

¡A comer!

CAPÍTULO 6

DAY 16 50-MINUTE LESSON PLAN

> **STANDARDS FOR FOREIGN LANGUAGE LEARNING: DAY 16**
>
> **Vocabulario en acción 2**
> **Communication 1.1:** Students engage in conversations, provide and obtain information, express feelings and emotions, and exchange opinions.
> **Communication 1.2:** Students understand and interpret written and spoken language on a variety of topics.
> **Communication 1.3:** Students present information, concepts, and ideas to an audience of listeners or readers on a variety of topics.
>
> **Cultures 2.1:** Students demonstrate an understanding of the relationship between the practices and perspectives of the culture studied.
> **Comparisons 4.1:** Students demonstrate understanding of the nature of language through comparisons of the language studied and their own.

CORE INSTRUCTION

Warm-Up
- (10 min.) Review the phrases in **¡Exprésate!**, p. 58.

Vocabulario en acción 2
- (10 min.) Have students do Activity 36, p. 59.
- (20 min.) Review **Vocabulario en acción 2**, pp. 54–59.

Wrap-Up
- (10 min.) Answers questions students might have about **Prueba: Vocabulario 2**.

OPTIONAL RESOURCES
- (10 min.) Game, p. 56
- (10 min.) **Comunicación** (TE), p. 59

Practice Options
- *Lab Book*, p. 40 ▲ ● ■
- ***Cuaderno de vocabulario y gramática,*** pp. 23–25
- *Activities for Communication*, pp. 23–24 ▲ ■
- ***Cuaderno para hispanohablantes,*** Chapter 6 ■
- *Teaching Transparencies:* **Vocabulario** 6.3, 6.4; *Vocabulario y gramática* Answers, pp. 23–25 ▲ ● ■
- *Video Guide*, pp. 54–55, 58 ▲ ● ■
- *TPR Storytelling Book*, pp. 32–33 ▲ ●
- *Interactive Tutor* (Disc 2) or *DVD Tutor* (Disc 2) ▲ ● ■
- Online Practice, Chapter 6 (go.hrw.com, Keyword: EXP1B CH6)

▲ = Advanced Learners   ◆ = Slower Pace Learners   ● = Special Learning Needs   ■ = Heritage Speakers

Holt Spanish 1B

Lesson Planner

Teacher's Name _____ Class _____ Date _____

¡A comer!

CAPÍTULO 6

DAY 17 50-MINUTE LESSON PLAN

STANDARDS FOR FOREIGN LANGUAGE LEARNING: DAY 17

Vocabulario en acción 2

Communication 1.1: Students engage in conversations, provide and obtain information, express feelings and emotions, and exchange opinions.
Communication 1.2: Students understand and interpret written and spoken language on a variety of topics.
Communication 1.3: Students present information, concepts, and ideas to an audience of listeners or readers on a variety of topics.

Cultures 2.1: Students demonstrate an understanding of the relationship between the practices and perspectives of the culture studied.
Comparisons 4.1: Students demonstrate understanding of the nature of language through comparisons of the language studied and their own.

Gramática en acción

Communication 1.2: Students understand and interpret written and spoken language on a variety of topics.

CORE INSTRUCTION

Warm-Up
- (5 min.) Have students do Bell Work 6.6, p. 60.

Vocabulario en acción 2

Assess
- (20 min.) Give **Prueba: Vocabulario 2**.

Gramática en acción 2
- (20 min.) Present **Gramática**: *Direct objects and direct object pronouns*, p. 60 using Teaching **Gramática**, p. 60.

Wrap-Up
- (5 min.) See Common Error Alert, p. 60.

OPTIONAL RESOURCES
- (10 min.) See Multiple Intelligences, p. 61.

Practice Options
- *Lab Book,* p. 40 ▲ ● ■
- ***Cuaderno de vocabulario y gramática,*** pp. 26–28 ▲ ♦ ●
- *Activities for Communication,* pp. 23–24 ▲ ■
- ***Cuaderno de actividades***, pp. 20–23 ▲ ● ■
- ***Cuaderno para hispanohablantes,*** Chapter 6 ■
- *Teaching Transparencies:* **Vocabulario y gramática** Answers, pp. 26–28 ▲ ♦ ●
- *Grammar Tutor for Students of Spanish,* Chapter 6 ● ■
- *Video Guide,* pp. 54–55, 58 ▲ ● ■
- *Interactive Tutor* (Disc 2) or *DVD Tutor* (Disc 2) ▲ ● ■
- Online Practice, Chapter 6 (go.hrw.com, Keyword: EXP1B CH6)

Assessment Options
- *Assessment Program*: **Prueba: Vocabulario 2**, pp. 23–24
- *Assessment Program*: Alternative Assessment Guide, pp. 241, 249, 257 ▲ ● ■
- Test Generator

▲ = Advanced Learners   ♦ = Slower Pace Learners   ● = Special Learning Needs   ■ = Heritage Speakers

Holt Spanish 1B   Lesson Planner

Teacher's Name _____ Class _____ Date _____

¡A comer!

CAPÍTULO 6

DAY 18 50-MINUTE LESSON PLAN

STANDARDS FOR FOREIGN LANGUAGE LEARNING: DAY 18

Gramática en acción 2

Communication 1.1: Students engage in conversations, provide and obtain information, express feelings and emotions, and exchange opinions.

Communication 1.2: Students understand and interpret written and spoken language on a variety of topics.

Communication 1.3: Students present information, concepts, and ideas to an audience of listeners or readers on a variety of topics.

CORE INSTRUCTION

Warm-Up
- (5 min.) See Teacher to Teacher activity, p. 61.

Gramática en acción 2
- (10 min.) Show **GramaVisión 6**, Segment 1.
- (10 min.) Review direct objects and direct object pronouns, p. 60.
- (15 min.) Have students do Activities 37–39, pp. 60–61.

Wrap-Up
- (10 min.) Review answers to Activities 38 and 39 as a class.

OPTIONAL RESOURCES
- (10 min.) Present **Nota Cultural**, p. 62.
- (10 min.) See Slower Pace Learners, p. 61. ◆

Practice Options
- *Lab Book,* p. 40 ▲ ● ■
- ***Cuaderno de vocabulario y gramática,*** pp. 26–28 ▲ ◆ ●
- *Activities for Communication,* pp. 23–24 ▲ ■
- ***Cuaderno de actividades,*** pp. 20–23 ▲ ● ■
- ***Cuaderno para hispanohablantes,*** Chapter 6 ■
- *Teaching Transparencies:* **Vocabulario y gramática** Answers, pp. 26–28 ▲ ◆ ●
- *Grammar Tutor for Students of Spanish,* Chapter 6 ● ■
- *Video Guide,* pp. 54–55, 58 ▲ ● ■
- *Interactive Tutor* (Disc 2) or *DVD Tutor* (Disc 2) ▲ ● ■
- Online Practice, Chapter 6 (go.hrw.com, Keyword: EXP1B CH6)

▲ = Advanced Learners   ◆ = Slower Pace Learners   ● = Special Learning Needs   ■ = Heritage Speakers

Holt Spanish 1B   Lesson Planner

Teacher's Name _____ Class _____ Date _____

¡A comer!

CAPÍTULO 6

DAY 19 50-MINUTE LESSON PLAN

STANDARDS FOR FOREIGN LANGUAGE LEARNING: DAY 19

Gramática en acción 2

Communication 1.1: Students engage in conversations, provide and obtain information, express feelings and emotions, and exchange opinions.

Communication 1.2: Students understand and interpret written and spoken language on a variety of topics.

Communication 1.3: Students present information, concepts, and ideas to an audience of listeners or readers on a variety of topics.

Cultures 2.1: Students demonstrate an understanding of the relationship between the practices and perspectives of the culture studied.

Comparisons 4.2: Students demonstrate understanding of the concept of culture through comparisons of the cultures studied and their own.

CORE INSTRUCTION

Warm-Up
- (5 min.) Have students do Bell Work 6.7, p. 62.

Gramática en acción 2
- (10 min.) Have students do Activity 40, p. 61. See Multiple Intelligences, p. 61.
- (25 min.) Present **Gramática**: *Affirmative informal commands*, p. 62 using Teaching **Gramática**, p. 62.

Wrap-Up
- (10 min.) Have students practice using the verbs from Point 3, p. 62 by giving commands to a partner.

OPTIONAL RESOURCES
- (10 min.) **Comunicación** (TE), p. 61

Practice Options
- *Lab Book*, p. 40 ▲●■
- ***Cuaderno de vocabulario y gramática***, pp. 26–28
- *Activities for Communication*, pp. 23–24 ▲■
- ***Cuaderno de actividades***, pp. 20–23 ▲●■
- ***Cuaderno para hispanohablantes***, Chapter 6 ■
- *Teaching Transparencies:* Bell Work 6.7; ***Vocabulario y gramática*** Answers, pp. 26–28 ▲♦●
- *Grammar Tutor for Students of Spanish*, Chapter 6 ●■
- *Video Guide*, pp. 54–55, 58 ▲●■
- *Interactive Tutor* (Disc 2) or *DVD Tutor* (Disc 2) ▲●■
- Online Practice, Chapter 6 (go.hrw.com, Keyword: EXP1B CH6)

▲ = Advanced Learners   ♦ = Slower Pace Learners   ● = Special Learning Needs   ■ = Heritage Speakers

Holt Spanish 1B   Lesson Planner

Teacher's Name _____ Class _____ Date _____

¡A comer!

CAPÍTULO 6

DAY 20 50-MINUTE LESSON PLAN

STANDARDS FOR FOREIGN LANGUAGE LEARNING: DAY 20

Gramática en acción 2
Communication 1.1: Students engage in conversations, provide and obtain information, express feelings and emotions, and exchange opinions.
Communication 1.2: Students understand and interpret written and spoken language on a variety of topics.
Communication 1.3: Students present information, concepts, and ideas to an audience of listeners or readers on a variety of topics.

Cultures 2.1: Students demonstrate an understanding of the relationship between the practices and perspectives of the culture studied.
Comparisons 4.2: Students demonstrate understanding of the concept of culture through comparisons of the cultures studied and their own.

CORE INSTRUCTION

Warm-Up
- (5 min.) Give students a few informal commands that they can act out.

Gramática en acción 2
- (10 min.) Show **GramaVisión 6,** Segment 2.
- (10 min.) Review affirmative informal commands, p. 62.
- (15 min.) Have students do Activities 41–43, pp. 62–63.

Wrap-Up
- (10 min.) Review commands from Activity 42.

OPTIONAL RESOURCES
- (10 min.) Teacher to Teacher, p. 63
- (10 min.) Advanced Learners, p. 63 ▲
- (10 min.) See Special Learning Needs, p. 63. ●

Practice Options
- *Lab Book,* p. 40 ▲ ● ■
- ***Cuaderno de vocabulario y gramática,*** pp. 26–28 ▲ ◆ ●
- *Activities for Communication,* pp. 23–24 ▲ ■
- ***Cuaderno de actividades***, pp. 20–23 ▲ ● ■
- ***Cuaderno para hispanohablantes,*** Chapter 6 ■
- *Teaching Transparencies:* ***Vocabulario y gramática*** Answers, pp. 26–28 ▲ ◆ ●
- *Grammar Tutor for Students of Spanish,* Chapter 6 ● ■
- *Video Guide,* pp. 54–55, 58 ▲ ● ■
- *Interactive Tutor* (Disc 2) or *DVD Tutor* (Disc 2) ▲ ● ■
- Online Practice, Chapter 6 (go.hrw.com, Keyword: EXP1B CH6)

▲ = Advanced Learners   ◆ = Slower Pace Learners   ● = Special Learning Needs   ■ = Heritage Speakers

Holt Spanish 1B

Lesson Planner

Teacher's Name _____ Class _____ Date _____

¡A comer!

CAPÍTULO 6

DAY 21 50-MINUTE LESSON PLAN

STANDARDS FOR FOREIGN LANGUAGE LEARNING: DAY 21

Gramática en acción 2

Communication 1.1: Students engage in conversations, provide and obtain information, express feelings and emotions, and exchange opinions.
Communication 1.2: Students understand and interpret written and spoken language on a variety of topics.
Communication 1.3: Students present information, concepts, and ideas to an audience of listeners or readers on a variety of topics.

Cultures 2.1: Students demonstrate an understanding of the relationship between the practices and perspectives of the culture studied.
Comparisons 4.2: Students demonstrate understanding of the concept of culture through comparisons of the cultures studied and their own.

CORE INSTRUCTION

Warm-Up
- (5 min.) Have students give these informal commands to partner: take out a pencil, write your name, open your book, speak Spanish.

Gramática en acción 2
- (5 min.) Have students do Activity 44, p. 63.
- (20 min.) Present **Gramática:** *Affirmative informal commands with pronouns*, p. 64 using Teaching **Gramática**, p. 64.
- (15 min.) Have students do Activities 45–46, p. 64.

Wrap-Up
- (5 min.) Have students do Bell Work 6.8, p. 64.

OPTIONAL RESOURCES
- (10 min.) **Comunicación** (TE), p. 63

Practice Options
- *Lab Book,* p. 40 ▲ ♦ ●
- *Cuaderno de vocabulario y gramática,* pp. 26–28 ▲ ♦ ●
- *Activities for Communication,* pp. 23–24 ▲ ■
- *Cuaderno de actividades,* pp. 20–23 ▲ ● ■
- *Cuaderno para hispanohablantes,* Chapter 6 ■
- *Teaching Transparencies:* Bell Work 6.8; *Vocabulario y gramática* Answers, pp. 26–28 ▲ ♦ ●
- *Grammar Tutor for Students of Spanish,* Chapter 6 ● ■
- *Video Guide,* pp. 54–55, 58 ▲ ● ■
- *Interactive Tutor* (Disc 2) or *DVD Tutor* (Disc 2) ▲ ● ■
- Online Practice, Chapter 6 (go.hrw.com, Keyword: EXP1B CH6)

▲ = Advanced Learners   ♦ = Slower Pace Learners   ● = Special Learning Needs   ■ = Heritage Speakers

Holt Spanish 1B   Lesson Planner

Teacher's Name _____ Class _____ Date _____

¡A comer!

CAPÍTULO 6

DAY 22 50-MINUTE LESSON PLAN

STANDARDS FOR FOREIGN LANGUAGE LEARNING: DAY 22

Gramática en acción 2

Communication 1.1: Students engage in conversations, provide and obtain information, express feelings and emotions, and exchange opinions.

Communication 1.2: Students understand and interpret written and spoken language on a variety of topics.

Communication 1.3: Students present information, concepts, and ideas to an audience of listeners or readers on a variety of topics.

Cultures 2.1: Students demonstrate an understanding of the relationship between the practices and perspectives of the culture studied.

Comparisons 4.2: Students demonstrate understanding of the concept of culture through comparisons of the cultures studied and their own.

CORE INSTRUCTION

Warm-Up
- (5 min.) Review class answers to Activities 45–46, p. 64.

Gramática en acción 2
- (5 min.) Show **GramaVisión 6**, Segment 6.
- (10 min.) Play Audio CD 6, Tr. 7 for Activity 47, p. 65.
- (15 min.) Have students do Activities 48–49, p. 65. See Slower Pace Learners, p. 65. ◆
- (10 min.) Review **Gramática en acción 2**, pp. 60–65.

Wrap-Up
- (5 min.) Have students give their answers from Activity 48. Remind students to study for **Prueba: Gramática 2**.

OPTIONAL RESOURCES
- (20 min.) Multiple Intelligences, p. 65

Practice Options
- *Lab Book*, p. 40 ▲ ● ■
- ***Cuaderno de vocabulario y gramática,*** pp. 26–28 ▲ ◆ ●
- *Activities for Communication*, pp. 23–24 ▲ ■
- ***Cuaderno de actividades***, pp. 20–23 ▲ ● ■
- ***Cuaderno para hispanohablantes,*** Chapter 6 ■
- *Teaching Transparencies:* **Vocabulario y gramática** Answers, pp. 26–28 ▲ ● ■
- *Grammar Tutor for Students of Spanish*, Chapter 6 ● ■
- *Video Guide*, pp. 54–55, 58 ▲ ● ■
- *Interactive Tutor* (Disc 2) or *DVD Tutor* (Disc 2) ▲ ● ■
- Online Practice, Chapter 6 (go.hrw.com, Keyword: EXP1B CH6)

▲ = Advanced Learners ◆ = Slower Pace Learners ● = Special Learning Needs ■ = Heritage Speakers

Teacher's Name _____ Class _____ Date _____

¡A comer!

CAPÍTULO 6

DAY 23 50-MINUTE LESSON PLAN

STANDARDS FOR FOREIGN LANGUAGE LEARNING: DAY 23

Gramática en acción 2
Communication 1.1: Students engage in conversations, provide and obtain information, express feelings and emotions, and exchange opinions.
Communication 1.2: Students understand and interpret written and spoken language on a variety of topics.
Communication 1.3: Students present information, concepts, and ideas to an audience of listeners or readers on a variety of topics.
Cultures 2.1: Students demonstrate an understanding of the relationship between the practices and perspectives of the culture studied.
Comparisons 4.2: Students demonstrate understanding of the concept of culture through comparisons of the cultures studied and their own.

Conexiones culturales
Communication 1.1: Students engage in conversations, provide and obtain information, express feelings and emotions, and exchange opinions.
Cultures 2.1: Students demonstrate an understanding of the relationship between the practices and perspectives of the culture studied.
Cultures 2.2: Students demonstrate an understanding of the relationship between the products and perspectives of the culture studied.
Connections 3.1: Students reinforce and further their knowledge of other disciplines through the foreign language.
Comparisons 4.2: Students demonstrate understanding of the concept of culture through comparisons of the cultures studied and their own.

CORE INSTRUCTION

Warm-Up
- (5 min.) Do Activity 48 as a class activity.

Gramática en acción 2
- (10 min.) Review **Gramática en acción 2,** pp. 60–65.

Assess
- (20 min.) Give **Prueba: Gramática 2.**

Conexiones culturales
- (10 min.) See Teaching **Conexiones culturales,** #1–2, p. 66.

Wrap-Up
- (5 min.) See Advanced Learners, p. 67. Assign some words as homework. ▲

OPTIONAL RESOURCES
- (10 min.) Multiple Intelligences, p. 67

Practice Options
- *Lab Book,* p. 40–41 ▲●■
- *Cuaderno de vocabulario y gramática,* pp. 26–28 ▲◆●
- *Activities for Communication,* pp. 23–24 ▲■
- *Cuaderno de actividades,* pp. 20–23 ▲●■
- *Cuaderno para hispanohablantes,* Chapter 6 ■
- *Teaching Transparencies: Vocabulario y gramática* Answers, pp. 26–28 ▲●■
- *Grammar Tutor for Students of Spanish,* Chapter 6 ●■
- *Video Guide,* pp. 54–55, 58 ▲●■
- *Interactive Tutor* (Disc 2) or *DVD Tutor* (Disc 2) ▲●■
- Online Practice, Chapter 6 (go.hrw.com, Keyword: EXP1B CH6)

Assessment Options
- *Assessment Program*: **Prueba: Gramática 2,** pp. 25–26
- *Assessment Program*: **Prueba: Aplicación 2,** pp. 27–28
- Audio CD 6, Tr. 16
- *Assessment Program*: Alternative Assessment Guide, pp. 241, 249, 257 ▲●■
- Test Generator

▲ = Advanced Learners   ◆ = Slower Pace Learners   ● = Special Learning Needs   ■ = Heritage Speakers

Holt Spanish 1B — Lesson Planner

Teacher's Name _____ Class _____ Date _____

¡A comer!

CAPÍTULO 6

DAY 24 50-MINUTE LESSON PLAN

STANDARDS FOR FOREIGN LANGUAGE LEARNING: DAY 24

Conexiones culturales
Communication 1.1: Students engage in conversations, provide and obtain information, express feelings and emotions, and exchange opinions.
Cultures 2.1: Students demonstrate an understanding of the relationship between the practices and perspectives of the culture studied.
Cultures 2.2: Students demonstrate an understanding of the relationship between the products and perspectives of the culture studied.
Connections 3.1: Students reinforce and further their knowledge of other disciplines through the foreign language.
Comparisons 4.2: Students demonstrate understanding of the concept of culture through comparisons of the cultures studied and their own.

Novela en video
Communication 1.1: Students engage in conversations, provide and obtain information, express feelings and emotions, and exchange opinions.
Communication 1.2: Students understand and interpret written and spoken language on a variety of topics.
Cultures 2.1: Students demonstrate an understanding of the relationship between the practices and perspectives of the culture studied.
Connections 3.2: Students acquire information and recognize the distinctive viewpoints that are only available through the foreign language and its cultures.
Comparisons 4.2: Students demonstrate understanding of the concept of culture through comparisons of the cultures studied and their own.

CORE INSTRUCTION

Warm-Up
- (5 min.) Have students share some of the food vocabulary they found in the activity from Advanced Learners, p. 67.

Conexiones culturales
- (20 min.) See Teaching **Conexiones culturales**, #3–6, p. 66.
- (10 min.) Have students do Activity 3, p. 67.

Novela en video
- (10 min.) See Teaching **Novela en video,** #1–2, p. 68.

Wrap-Up
- (5 min.) See Gestures, p. 68.

OPTIONAL RESOURCES
- (5 min.) Practices and Perspectives, p. 67
- (5 min.) Suggestion, p. 67
- (5 min.) Comparing and Contrasting, p. 69
- (5 min.) Culminating Project, p. 70

Practice Options
- *Lab Book,* p. 42 ▲●■
- *Video Guide,* pp. 54–55, 59 ▲●■
- *Interactive Tutor* (Disc 2) or *DVD Tutor* (Disc 2) ▲●■
- Online Practice, Chapter 6 (go.hrw.com, Keyword: EXP1B CH6)

▲ = Advanced Learners ◆ = Slower Pace Learners ● = Special Learning Needs ■ = Heritage Speakers

Holt Spanish 1B — Lesson Planner

Teacher's Name _____ Class _____ Date _____

CAPÍTULO
6

¡A comer!

DAY 25 50-MINUTE LESSON PLAN

STANDARDS FOR FOREIGN LANGUAGE LEARNING: DAY 25

Novela en video
Communication 1.1: Students engage in conversations, provide and obtain information, express feelings and emotions, and exchange opinions.
Communication 1.2: Students understand and interpret written and spoken language on a variety of topics.
Cultures 2.1: Students demonstrate an understanding of the relationship between the practices and perspectives of the culture studied.
Connections 3.2: Students acquire information and recognize the distinctive viewpoints that are only available through the foreign language and its cultures.
Comparisons 4.2: Students demonstrate understanding of the concept of culture through comparisons of the cultures studied and their own.

Leamos y escribamos
Communication 1.3: Students present information, concepts, and ideas to an audience of listeners or readers on a variety of topics.
Connections 3.1: Students reinforce and further their knowledge of other disciplines through the foreign language.
Connections 3.2: Students acquire information and recognize the distinctive viewpoints that are only available through the foreign language and its cultures.
Comparisons 4.2: Students demonstrate understanding of the concept of culture through comparisons of the cultures studied and their own.
Communities 5.1: Students use the language both within and beyond the school setting.

CORE INSTRUCTION

Warm-Up
- (5 min.) See Visual Learners, p. 68.

Novela en video
- (25 min.) See Teaching **Novela en video,** #3–5, p. 68.

Leamos y escribamos
- (15 min.) See Teaching **Leamos,** #1–2, p. 72.

Wrap-Up
- (5 min.) Present Practices and Perspectives, p. 73.

OPTIONAL RESOURCES
- (5 min.) Language Note, p. 70
- (5 min.) **Más práctica,** p. 71
- (5 min.) Applying the Strategies, p. 72

Practice Options
- *Lab Book*, p. 42 ▲ ● ■
- *Cuaderno de actividades*, p. 24 ▲ ● ■
- *Cuaderno para hispanohablantes,* pp. 45–52 ■
- *Reading Strategies and Skills Handbook*, Chapter 6 ▲ ● ■
- *¡Lee conmigo!* Level 1 Reader ▲ ■
- *Video Guide*, pp. 54–55, 59 ▲ ● ■
- *Interactive Tutor* (Disc 2) or *DVD Tutor* (Disc 2) ▲ ● ■
- Online Practice, Chapter 6 (go.hrw.com, Keyword: EXP1B CH6)

▲ = Advanced Learners   ◆ = Slower Pace Learners   ● = Special Learning Needs   ■ = Heritage Speakers

Holt Spanish 1B   Lesson Planner

Teacher's Name _____ Class _____ Date _____

¡A comer!

CAPÍTULO 6

DAY 26 50-MINUTE LESSON PLAN

STANDARDS FOR FOREIGN LANGUAGE LEARNING: DAY 26

Leamos y escribamos

Communication 1.3: Students present information, concepts, and ideas to an audience of listeners or readers on a variety of topics.

Connections 3.1: Students reinforce and further their knowledge of other disciplines through the foreign language.

Connections 3.2: Students acquire information and recognize the distinctive viewpoints that are only available through the foreign language and its cultures.

Comparisons 4.2: Students demonstrate understanding of the concept of culture through comparisons of the cultures studied and their own.

Communities 5.1: Students use the language both within and beyond the school setting.

CORE INSTRUCTION

Warm-Up
- (5 min.) Have a few students volunteer to summarize the story, **La montaña del alimento**, in English.

Leamos y escribamos
- (10 min.) Have students read **Leamos** silently, p. 72.
- (10 min.) See Teaching **Leamos**, #3, p. 72.
- (10 min.) Present **Taller del escritor**, p. 73 using Teaching **Escribamos**, #1–2, p. 72.
- (10 min.) Have students complete the first part of step 2 in **Taller del escritor,** p. 73. Assign the rest as homework. See Special Learning Needs, p. 73. ●

Wrap-Up
- (5 min.) Read the recipe for **Salsa**, p. 73, and make sure all students understand the ingredients and instructions.

OPTIONAL RESOURCES
- (10 min.) Advanced Learners, p. 73 ▲
- (5 min.) Additional Reading, pp. 266–267

Practice Options
- *Cuaderno de actividades*, p. 24 ▲ ● ■
- *Cuaderno para hispanohablantes,* pp. 45–52 ■
- *Reading Strategies and Skills Handbook*, Chapter 6 ▲ ● ■
- *¡Lee conmigo!* Level 1 Reader ▲ ■
- *Interactive Tutor* (Disc 2) or *DVD Tutor* (Disc 2) ▲ ● ■
- Online Practice, Chapter 6 (go.hrw.com, Keyword: EXP1B CH6)

▲ = Advanced Learners   ◆ = Slower Pace Learners   ● = Special Learning Needs   ■ = Heritage Speakers

Holt Spanish 1B   Lesson Planner

Teacher's Name _____ Class _____ Date _____

¡A comer!

CAPÍTULO 6

DAY 27 50-MINUTE LESSON PLAN

STANDARDS FOR FOREIGN LANGUAGE LEARNING: DAY 27

Leamos y escribamos

Communication 1.3: Students present information, concepts, and ideas to an audience of listeners or readers on a variety of topics.

Connections 3.1: Students reinforce and further their knowledge of other disciplines through the foreign language.

Connections 3.2: Students acquire information and recognize the distinctive viewpoints that are only available through the foreign language and its cultures.

Comparisons 4.2: Students demonstrate understanding of the concept of culture through comparisons of the cultures studied and their own.

Communities 5.1: Students use the language both within and beyond the school setting.

Repaso

Communication 1.2: Students understand and interpret written and spoken language on a variety of topics.

Communication 1.3: Students present information, concepts, and ideas to an audience of listeners or readers on a variety of topics.

Cultures 2.1: Students demonstrate an understanding of the relationship between the practices and perspectives of the culture studied.

Cultures 2.2: Students demonstrate an understanding of the relationship between the products and perspectives of the culture studied.

CORE INSTRUCTION

Warm-Up
- (5 min.) Review the writing rubric you will use to assess this assignment.

Leamos y escribamos
- (15 min.) Have students complete the second half of step 2 and step 3, **Taller del escritor,** p. 73.

Repaso
- (25 min.) Have students do Activities 1–4, pp. 74–75.

Wrap-Up
- (5 min.) Have students ask and answer the questions in Activity 3 with a partner.

OPTIONAL RESOURCES
- (10 min.) Fold-n-Learn, p. 74
- (5 min.) Reteaching, p. 74

Practice Options
- *Activities for Communication,* pp. 48, 65–66 ▲ ■
- *Cuaderno para hispanohablantes,* Chapter 6 ■
- *Teaching Transparencies:* **Situación, Capítulo 6**; Picture Stories, Chapter 6 ▲ ● ■
- *TPR Storytelling Book,* pp. 34–35 ▲ ●
- *Grammar Tutor for Students of Spanish,* Chapter 6 ● ■
- *Interactive Tutor* (Disc 2) or *DVD Tutor* (Disc 2) ▲ ● ■
- Online Practice, Chapter 6 (go.hrw.com, Keyword: EXP1B CH6)

▲ = Advanced Learners   ◆ = Slower Pace Learners   ● = Special Learning Needs   ■ = Heritage Speakers

Holt Spanish 1B — Lesson Planner

Teacher's Name _____ Class _____ Date _____

¡A comer!

CAPÍTULO 6

DAY 28 50-MINUTE LESSON PLAN

STANDARDS FOR FOREIGN LANGUAGE LEARNING: DAY 28

Repaso

Communication 1.2: Students understand and interpret written and spoken language on a variety of topics.

Communication 1.3: Students present information, concepts, and ideas to an audience of listeners or readers on a variety of topics.

Cultures 2.1: Students demonstrate an understanding of the relationship between the practices and perspectives of the culture studied.

Cultures 2.2: Students demonstrate an understanding of the relationship between the products and perspectives of the culture studied.

CORE INSTRUCTION

Warm-Up
- (5 min.) Do Activity 3, p. 74 as a class activity.

Repaso
- (10 min.) Have students do Activity 5, p. 75.
- (10 min.) Play Audio CD 6, Tr. 10 for Activity 6, p. 75.
- (10 min.) Have students do Activity 7, p. 75.
- (10 min.) Play Audio CD 6, Tr. 11–13 for **Letra y sonido,** p. 76.

Wrap-Up
- (5 min.) See Game, p. 77. Remind students to study for Chapter Test.

OPTIONAL RESOURCES
- (5 min.) **Letra y sonido,** p. 76

Practice Options
- *Lab Book,* pp. 18, 41 ▲●■
- *Activities for Communication,* pp. 48, 65–66 ▲■
- *Cuaderno para hispanohablantes,* Chapter 6 ■
- *Teaching Transparencies:* **Situación, Capítulo 6**; Picture Stories, Chapter 6 ▲●■
- *Video Guide,* pp. 54–55, 60 ▲●■
- *TPR Storytelling Book,* pp. 34–35 ▲●
- *Grammar Tutor for Students of Spanish,* Chapter 6 ●■
- *Interactive Tutor* (Disc 2) or *DVD Tutor* (Disc 2) ▲●■
- Online Practice, Chapter 6 (go.hrw.com, Keyword: EXP1B CH6)

▲ = Advanced Learners   ◆ = Slower Pace Learners   ● = Special Learning Needs   ■ = Heritage Speakers

Holt Spanish 1B

Teacher's Name _____ Class _____ Date _____

¡A comer!

CAPÍTULO 6

DAY 29 50-MINUTE LESSON PLAN

STANDARDS FOR FOREIGN LANGUAGE LEARNING: DAY 29

Integración

Communication 1.1: Students engage in conversations, provide and obtain information, express feelings and emotions, and exchange opinions.

Communication 1.2: Students understand and interpret written and spoken language on a variety of topics.

Communication 1.3: Students present information, concepts, and ideas to an audience of listeners or readers on a variety of topics.

Communities 5.1: Students use the language both within and beyond the school setting.

CORE INSTRUCTION

Warm-Up
- (5 min.) See Fine Art Connection, Introduction, p. 79.

Integración
- (10 min.) Play Audio CD 6, Tr. 14 for Activity 1, p. 78.
- (25 min.) Have students do Activities 2–4, pp. 78–79.

Wrap-Up
- (10 min.) Review for Chapter Test.

OPTIONAL RESOURCES
- (5 min.) **Más práctica,** p. 78
- (10 min.) Culture Project, p. 78

Practice Options
- *Lab Book,* pp. 18, 40 ▲●■
- *Cuaderno de actividades,* pp. 25–26 ▲●■
- *Teaching Transparencies:* Fine Art, Chapter 6 ▲●■
- *Interactive Tutor* (Disc 2) or *DVD Tutor* (Disc 2) ▲●■
- Online Practice, Chapter 6 (go.hrw.com, Keyword: EXP1B CH6)

▲ = Advanced Learners ◆ = Slower Pace Learners ● = Special Learning Needs ■ = Heritage Speakers

Holt Spanish 1B — Lesson Planner

Teacher's Name _____ Class _____ Date _____

¡A comer!

CAPÍTULO 6

DAY 30 50-MINUTE LESSON PLAN

CORE INSTRUCTION

Chapter Assessment
- (50 min.) Give Chapter Test.

OPTIONAL RESOURCES
- (5 min.) Preview **GeoCultura: Argentina,** pp. 80–83.

Assessment Options
- *Assessment Program*: **Examen, Capítulo 6,** pp. 133–143
- *Assessment Program*: **Examen oral: Capítulo 6,** p. 144
- *Audio CD 6*, Tr. 17–18
- *Assessment Program*: Alternative Assessment Guide, pp. 241, 249, 257 ▲ ● ■
- *Standardized Assessment Tutor,* Chapter 6
- Test Generator ▲ ◆ ●
- Online Practice, Chapter 6 (go.hrw.com, Keyword: EXP1B CH6)

▲ = Advanced Learners   ◆ = Slower Pace Learners   ● = Special Learning Needs   ■ = Heritage Speakers

Holt Spanish 1B   Lesson Planner

Teacher's Name _____ Class _____ Date _____

CAPÍTULO 7

Cuerpo sano, mente sana

DAY 1 50-MINUTE LESSON PLAN

STANDARDS FOR FOREIGN LANGUAGE LEARNING: DAY 1

Chapter Opener
Communication 1.2: Students understand and interpret written and spoken language on a variety of topics.

Vocabulario en acción 1
Communication 1.2: Students understand and interpret written and spoken language on a variety of topics.

Before starting **Capítulo 7,** you may wish to teach **Geocultura: Argentina,** pp. 80–83. For teaching suggestions, see pp. xv–xvi of this *Lesson Planner.*

CORE INSTRUCTION

Warm-Up
- (5 min.) See Learning Tips, p. 85.

Chapter Opener
- (5 min.) See Using the Photo and **Más vocabulario,** p. 84.
- (5 min.) See **Objetivos,** p. 84.

Vocabulario en acción 1, pp. 86–91
- (30 min.) Introduce **Vocabulario en acción 1,** pp. 86–87 using Teaching **Vocabulario,** p. 86.

Wrap-Up
- (5 min.) Have students practice pronunciation of all new vocabulary words.

OPTIONAL RESOURCES
- (5 min.) Common Error Alert, p. 87
- (5 min.) **También se puede decir,** p. 87
- (10 min.) Advanced Learners, p. 87 ▲
- (10 min.) Multiple Intelligences, p. 87
- (5 min.) Bell Work 7.1, p. 86

Practice Options
- *Lab Book,* pp. 43, 44 ▲●■
- *Cuaderno de vocabulario y gramática,* pp. 29–31
- *Activities for Communication,* pp. 25–26 ▲■
- *Cuaderno para hispanohablantes,* Chapter 7 ■
- *Teaching Transparencies:* Bell Work 7.1; **Vocabulario** 7.1, 7.2; *Vocabulario y gramática* Answers pp. 29–31 ▲♦●
- *Video Guide,* pp. 61–62, 64–65, 66 ▲●■
- *TPR Storytelling Book,* pp. 36–37 ▲●
- *Interactive Tutor* (Disc 2) or *DVD Tutor* (Disc 2) ▲●■
- Online Practice, Chapter 7 (go.hrw.com, Keyword: EXP1B CH7)

▲ = Advanced Learners   ♦ = Slower Pace Learners   ● = Special Learning Needs   ■ = Heritage Speakers

Holt Spanish 1B   Lesson Planner

Teacher's Name _____ Class _____ Date _____

Cuerpo sano, mente sana

CAPÍTULO 7

DAY 2 50-MINUTE LESSON PLAN

STANDARDS FOR FOREIGN LANGUAGE LEARNING: DAY 2

Vocabulario en acción 1
Communication 1.1: Students engage in conversations, provide and obtain information, express feelings and emotions, and exchange opinions.

Communication 1.2: Students understand and interpret written and spoken language on a variety of topics.

CORE INSTRUCTION

Warm-Up
- (5 min.) Have students do Bell Work 7.1, p. 86.

Vocabulario en acción 1
- (10 min.) Show **ExpresaVisión,** Ch. 7.
- (10 min.) Review **Vocabulario 1** and **¡Exprésate!,** pp. 86–87.
- (20 min.) Have students do Activities 1–3, p. 88.

Wrap-Up
- (5 min.) See **Más práctica,** p. 88.

OPTIONAL RESOURCES
- (10 min.) TPR, p. 87
- (10 min.) Fold-n-Learn, p. 88

Practice Options
- *Lab Book,* p. 44 ▲●■
- *Cuaderno de vocabulario y gramática,* pp. 29–31 ▲◆●
- *Activities for Communication,* pp. 25–26 ▲■
- *Cuaderno para hispanohablantes,* Chapter 7 ■
- *Teaching Transparencies:* Bell Work 7.1; **Vocabulario** 7.1, 7.2; *Vocabulario y gramática* Answers pp. 29–31 ▲◆●
- *Video Guide,* pp. 64–65, 66 ▲●■
- *TPR Storytelling Book,* pp. 36–37 ▲●
- *Grammar Tutor for Students of Spanish,* Chapter 7 ●■
- *Interactive Tutor* (Disc 2) or *DVD Tutor* (Disc 2) ▲●■
- Online Practice, Chapter 7 (go.hrw.com, Keyword: EXP1B CH7)

▲ = Advanced Learners ◆ = Slower Pace Learners ● = Special Learning Needs ■ = Heritage Speakers

Holt Spanish 1B Lesson Planner

Teacher's Name _____ Class _____ Date _____

CAPÍTULO
7

Cuerpo sano, mente sana

DAY 3 50-MINUTE LESSON PLAN

STANDARDS FOR FOREIGN LANGUAGE LEARNING: DAY 3

Vocabulario en acción 1

Communication 1.1: Students engage in conversations, provide and obtain information, express feelings and emotions, and exchange opinions.

Communication 1.2: Students understand and interpret written and spoken language on a variety of topics.

Cultures 2.1: Students demonstrate an understanding of the relationship between the practices and perspectives of the culture studied.

CORE INSTRUCTION

Warm-Up
- (5 min.) Have students review answers to Activity 3, p. 88.

Vocabulario en acción 1
- (25 min.) Have students do Activities 4–5, p. 89. See Slower Pace Learners, p. 89. ◆
- (15 min.) Present ¡Exprésate!, p. 90 using Teaching ¡Exprésate!, p. 90.

Wrap-Up
- (5 min.) Have students work with a partner to practice the phrases in ¡Exprésate!

OPTIONAL RESOURCES
- (10 min.) **Comunicación** (TE), p. 89
- (5 min.) Multiple Intelligences, p. 89

Practice Options
- *Lab Book*, p. 44 ▲●■
- *Cuaderno de vocabulario y gramática*, pp. 29–31 ▲◆●
- *Activities for Communication*, pp. 25–26 ▲■
- *Cuaderno para hispanohablantes*, Chapter 7 ■
- *Teaching Transparencies:* **Vocabulario** 7.1, 7.2; *Vocabulario y gramática* Answers pp. 29–31 ▲◆●
- *Video Guide*, pp. 64–65, 66 ▲●■
- *TPR Storytelling Book*, pp. 36–37 ▲●
- *Interactive Tutor* (Disc 2) or *DVD Tutor* (Disc 2) ▲●■
- Online Practice, Chapter 7 (go.hrw.com, Keyword: EXP1B CH7)

▲ = Advanced Learners ◆ = Slower Pace Learners ● = Special Learning Needs ■ = Heritage Speakers

Holt Spanish 1B   Lesson Planner

Teacher's Name _____ Class _____ Date _____

CAPÍTULO 7

Cuerpo sano, mente sana

DAY 4 50-MINUTE LESSON PLAN

STANDARDS FOR FOREIGN LANGUAGE LEARNING: DAY 4

Vocabulario en acción 1

Communication 1.1: Students engage in conversations, provide and obtain information, express feelings and emotions, and exchange opinions.

Communication 1.2: Students understand and interpret written and spoken language on a variety of topics.

Cultures 2.1: Students demonstrate an understanding of the relationship between the practices and perspectives of the culture studied.

CORE INSTRUCTION

Warm-Up
- (5 min.) Review **¡Exprésate!**, p. 90.

Vocabulario en acción 1
- (10 min.) Play Audio CD 7, Tr. 1 for Activity 6, p. 90.
- (10 min.) Present **Nota cultural,** p. 90.
- (20 min.) Have students do Activities 7–9, pp. 90–91. See Special Learning Needs, p. 91. ●

Wrap-Up
- (5 min.) Have students work with a partner to check answers to Activity 7. Remind students to study for **Prueba: Vocabulario 1**.

OPTIONAL RESOURCES
- (5 min.) Science Link, p. 90
- (5 min.) Geography Link, p. 90
- (10 min.) **Comunicación** (TE), p. 91

Practice Options
- *Lab Book*, pp. 19, 44 ▲●■
- *Cuaderno de vocabulario y gramática,* pp. 29–31 ▲◆●
- *Activities for Communication,* pp. 25–26 ▲■
- *Cuaderno para hispanohablantes,* Chapter 7 ■
- *Teaching Transparencies:* **Vocabulario** 7.1, 7.2; *Vocabulario y gramática* Answers pp. 29–31 ▲◆●
- *Video Guide,* pp. 64–65, 66 ▲●■
- *TPR Storytelling Book,* pp. 36–37 ▲●
- *Interactive Tutor* (Disc 2) or *DVD Tutor* (Disc 2) ▲●■
- Online Practice, Chapter 7 (go.hrw.com, Keyword: EXP1B CH7)

▲ = Advanced Learners   ◆ = Slower Pace Learners   ● = Special Learning Needs   ■ = Heritage Speakers

Holt Spanish 1B

Lesson Planner

Teacher's Name _____ Class _____ Date _____

CAPÍTULO 7

Cuerpo sano, mente sana

DAY 5 50-MINUTE LESSON PLAN

STANDARDS FOR FOREIGN LANGUAGE LEARNING: DAY 5

Vocabulario en acción 1
Communication 1.1: Students engage in conversations, provide and obtain information, express feelings and emotions, and exchange opinions.
Communication 1.2: Students understand and interpret written and spoken language on a variety of topics.

Cultures 2.1: Students demonstrate an understanding of the relationship between the practices and perspectives of the culture studied.

CORE INSTRUCTION

Warm-Up
- (10 min.) Review **Vocabulario en acción 1**, pp. 86–91.

Vocabulario en acción 1
- (15 min.) Have students do Activity 10, p. 91.

Assess
- (20 min.) Give **Prueba: Vocabulario 1**.

Wrap-Up
- (5 min.) Preview **Gramática 1**, pp. 92–97.

OPTIONAL RESOURCES
- (5 min.) See Advanced Learners, p. 91. ▲

Practice Options
- *Lab Book,* pp. 19, 44 ▲ ● ■
- **Cuaderno de vocabulario y gramática,** pp. 29–31 ▲ ◆ ●
- *Activities for Communication,* pp. 25–26 ▲ ■
- **Cuaderno para hispanohablantes,** Chapter 7 ■
- *Teaching Transparencies:* **Vocabulario** 7.1, 7.2; **Vocabulario y gramática** Answers pp. 29–31 ▲ ◆ ●
- *Video Guide,* pp. 64–65, 66 ▲ ● ■
- *TPR Storytelling Book,* pp. 36–37 ▲ ●
- *Interactive Tutor* (Disc 2) or *DVD Tutor* (Disc 2) ▲ ● ■
- Online Practice, Chapter 7 (go.hrw.com, Keyword: EXP1B CH7)

Assessment Options
- *Assessment Program:* **Prueba: Vocabulario 1**, pp. 37–38
- *Assessment Program:* Alternative Assessment Guide, pp. 242, 250, 258 ▲ ● ■
- Test Generator

▲ = Advanced Learners   ◆ = Slower Pace Learners   ● = Special Learning Needs   ■ = Heritage Speakers

Holt Spanish 1B — Lesson Planner

Teacher's Name _____ Class _____ Date _____

Cuerpo sano, mente sana

CAPÍTULO 7

DAY 6 50-MINUTE LESSON PLAN

STANDARDS FOR FOREIGN LANGUAGE LEARNING: DAY 6

Gramática en acción 1

Communication 1.1: Students engage in conversations, provide and obtain information, express feelings and emotions, and exchange opinions.

Communication 1.2: Students understand and interpret written and spoken language on a variety of topics.

Communication 1.3: Students present information, concepts, and ideas to an audience of listeners or readers on a variety of topics.

Cultures 2.1: Students demonstrate an understanding of the relationship between the practices and perspectives of the culture studied.

CORE INSTRUCTION

Warm-Up
- (5 min.) Have students do Bell Work 7.2, p. 92.

Gramática en acción 1
- (20 min.) Present **Gramática:** *Verbs with reflexive pronouns,* p. 92 using Teaching **Gramática,** p. 92.
- (10 min.) Play Audio CD 7, Tr. 2 for Activity 11, p. 92.
- (10 min.) Have students do Activity 12, p. 93.

Wrap-Up
- (5 min.) Have students check answers to Activity 12 with a partner.

OPTIONAL RESOURCES
- (5 min.) See Slower Pace Learners, p. 93. ◆
- (5 min.) See Special Learning Needs, p. 93. ●

Practice Options
- *Lab Book,* pp. 19, 44 ▲ ● ■
- *Cuaderno de vocabulario y gramática,* pp. 29–31 ▲ ◆ ●
- *Activities for Communication,* pp. 25–26 ▲ ■
- *Cuaderno de actividades,* pp. 27–30 ▲ ● ■
- *Cuaderno para hispanohablantes,* Chapter 7 ■
- *Teaching Transparencies:* Bell Work 7.2; **Vocabulario** 7.1, 7.2; *Vocabulario y gramática* Answers pp. 29–31 ▲ ◆ ●
- *Video Guide,* pp. 64–65, 66 ▲ ● ■
- *TPR Storytelling Book,* pp. 36–37 ▲ ●
- *Grammar Tutor for Students of Spanish,* Chapter 7 ● ■
- *Interactive Tutor* (Disc 2) or *DVD Tutor* (Disc 2) ▲ ● ■
- Online Practice, Chapter 7 (go.hrw.com, Keyword: EXP1B CH7)

▲ = Advanced Learners   ◆ = Slower Pace Learners   ● = Special Learning Needs   ■ = Heritage Speakers

Holt Spanish 1B   Lesson Planner

Teacher's Name _____ Class _____ Date _____

Cuerpo sano, mente sana

CAPÍTULO 7

DAY 7 50-MINUTE LESSON PLAN

STANDARDS FOR FOREIGN LANGUAGE LEARNING: DAY 7

Gramática en acción 1

Communication 1.1: Students engage in conversations, provide and obtain information, express feelings and emotions, and exchange opinions.

Communication 1.2: Students understand and interpret written and spoken language on a variety of topics.

Communication 1.3: Students present information, concepts, and ideas to an audience of listeners or readers on a variety of topics.

Cultures 2.1: Students demonstrate an understanding of the relationship between the practices and perspectives of the culture studied.

CORE INSTRUCTION

Warm-Up
- (5 min.) Have students do Bell Work 7.3, p. 94.

Gramática en acción 1
- (10 min.) Show **GramaVisión 7,** Segment 1.
- (15 min.) Review verbs with reflexive pronouns, p. 92.
- (15 min.) Have students do Activities 13–14, p. 93.

Wrap-Up
- (5 min.) See Teacher to Teacher, p. 93.

OPTIONAL RESOURCES
- (10 min.) **Comunicación** (TE), p. 93

Practice Options
- *Lab Book,* p. 44 ▲ ● ■
- *Cuaderno de vocabulario y gramática,* pp. 32–34 ▲ ◆ ●
- *Cuaderno de actividades,* pp. 27–30 ▲ ● ■
- *Activities for Communication,* pp. 25–26 ▲ ■
- *Cuaderno para hispanohablantes,* Chapter 7 ■
- *Teaching Transparencies:* Bell Work 7.3; *Vocabulario y gramática* Answers pp. 32–34 ▲ ◆ ●
- *Video Guide,* pp. 64–65, 66 ▲ ● ■
- *Grammar Tutor for Students of Spanish,* Chapter 7 ● ■
- *Interactive Tutor* (Disc 2) or *DVD Tutor* (Disc 2) ▲ ● ■
- Online Practice, Chapter 7 (go.hrw.com, Keyword: EXP1B CH7)

▲ = Advanced Learners ◆ = Slower Pace Learners ● = Special Learning Needs ■ = Heritage Speakers

Holt Spanish 1B   Lesson Planner

Teacher's Name _____ Class _____ Date _____

Cuerpo sano, mente sana

CAPÍTULO 7

DAY 8 50-MINUTE LESSON PLAN

STANDARDS FOR FOREIGN LANGUAGE LEARNING: DAY 8

Gramática en acción 1
Communication 1.1: Students engage in conversations, provide and obtain information, express feelings and emotions, and exchange opinions.
Communication 1.2: Students understand and interpret written and spoken language on a variety of topics.

Communication 1.3: Students present information, concepts, and ideas to an audience of listeners or readers on a variety of topics.
Cultures 2.1: Students demonstrate an understanding of the relationship between the practices and perspectives of the culture studied.

CORE INSTRUCTION

Warm-Up
- (5 min.) Have students work with a partner to share sentences, Activity 13.

Gramática en acción 1
- (25 min.) Present **Gramática**: *Using infinitives*, p. 94 using Teaching **Gramática**, p. 94.
- (15 min.) Have students do Activities 15–17, p. 94–95.

Wrap-Up
- (5 min.) See Common Error Alert, p. 95.

OPTIONAL RESOURCES
- (5 min.) Circumlocution, p. 95
- (5 min.) Advanced Learners, p. 95 ▲

Practice Options
- *Lab Book*, p. 44 ▲ ● ■
- **Cuaderno de vocabulario y gramática,** pp. 32–34 ▲ ♦ ●
- **Cuaderno de actividades**, pp. 27–30 ▲ ● ■
- *Activities for Communication*, pp. 25–26 ▲ ■
- **Cuaderno para hispanohablantes,** Chapter 7 ■
- *Teaching Transparencies:* **Vocabulario y gramática** Answers pp. 32–34 ▲ ♦ ●
- *Video Guide*, pp. 64–65, 66 ▲ ● ■
- *Grammar Tutor for Students of Spanish*, Chapter 7 ● ■
- *Interactive Tutor* (Disc 2) or *DVD Tutor* (Disc 2) ▲ ● ■
- Online Practice, Chapter 7 (go.hrw.com, Keyword: EXP1B CH7)

▲ = Advanced Learners ♦ = Slower Pace Learners ● = Special Learning Needs ■ = Heritage Speakers

Holt Spanish 1B Lesson Planner

Teacher's Name _____ Class _____ Date _____

CAPÍTULO 7

Cuerpo sano, mente sana

DAY 9 50-MINUTE LESSON PLAN

STANDARDS FOR FOREIGN LANGUAGE LEARNING: DAY 9

Gramática en acción 1

Communication 1.1: Students engage in conversations, provide and obtain information, express feelings and emotions, and exchange opinions.

Communication 1.2: Students understand and interpret written and spoken language on a variety of topics.

Communication 1.3: Students present information, concepts, and ideas to an audience of listeners or readers on a variety of topics.

Cultures 2.1: Students demonstrate an understanding of the relationship between the practices and perspectives of the culture studied.

CORE INSTRUCTION

Warm-Up
- (5 min.) Review answers to Activity 15, p. 94.

Gramática en acción 1
- (10 min.) Review using infinitives, p. 94.
- (10 min.) Have students do Activity 18, p. 95.
- (20 min.) Present **Gramática: Repaso** *stem–changing verbs*, p. 96 using Teaching **Gramática**, p. 96.

Wrap-Up
- (5 min.) See **Comunicación** (TE), p. 95. Assign as homework.

OPTIONAL RESOURCES
- (5 min.) Multiple Intelligences, p. 95
- (10 min.) Show **GramaVisión 7**, Segment 2.

Practice Options
- *Lab Book,* p. 44 ▲ ● ■
- ***Cuaderno de vocabulario y gramática,*** pp. 32–34 ▲ ♦ ●
- ***Cuaderno de actividades***, pp. 27–30 ▲ ● ■
- *Activities for Communication,* pp. 25–26 ▲ ■
- ***Cuaderno para hispanohablantes,*** Chapter 7 ■
- *Teaching Transparencies:* ***Vocabulario y gramática*** Answers pp. 32–34 ▲ ♦ ●
- *Video Guide,* pp. 64–65, 66 ▲ ● ■
- *Grammar Tutor for Students of Spanish,* Chapter 7 ● ■
- *Interactive Tutor* (Disc 2) or *DVD Tutor* (Disc 2) ▲ ● ■
- Online Practice, Chapter 7 (go.hrw.com, Keyword: EXP1B CH7)

▲ = Advanced Learners ♦ = Slower Pace Learners ● = Special Learning Needs ■ = Heritage Speakers

Holt Spanish 1B — Lesson Planner

Teacher's Name _____ Class _____ Date _____

CAPÍTULO 7

Cuerpo sano, mente sana

DAY 10 50-MINUTE LESSON PLAN

STANDARDS FOR FOREIGN LANGUAGE LEARNING: DAY 10

Gramática en acción 1
Communication 1.1: Students engage in conversations, provide and obtain information, express feelings and emotions, and exchange opinions.
Communication 1.2: Students understand and interpret written and spoken language on a variety of topics.
Communication 1.3: Students present information, concepts, and ideas to an audience of listeners or readers on a variety of topics.

CORE INSTRUCTION

Warm-Up
- (5 min.) Review the stem–changing verbs in **¿Te acuerdas?**, p. 96.

Gramática en acción 1
- (10 min.) Review stem–changing verbs, p. 96.
- (10 min.) Play Audio CD 7, Tr. 3 for Activity 19, p. 96.
- (20 min.) Have students do Activities 20–23, pp. 96–97.

Wrap-Up
- (5 min.) Check answers to Activity 21. Remind students to study for **Prueba: Gramática 1**.

OPTIONAL RESOURCES
- (10 min.) **Comunicación** (TE), p. 97
- (5 min.) See Slower Pace Learners, p. 97. ◆
- (5 min.) See Special Learning Needs, p. 97. ●

Practice Options
- *Lab Book*, pp. 20, 44 ▲ ● ■
- **Cuaderno de vocabulario y gramática,** pp. 32–34 ▲ ◆ ●
- **Cuaderno de actividades**, pp. 27–30 ▲ ● ■
- *Activities for Communication,* pp. 25–26 ▲ ■
- **Cuaderno para hispanohablantes,** Chapter 7 ■
- *Teaching Transparencies:* **Vocabulario y gramática** Answers pp. 32–34 ▲ ◆ ●
- *Video Guide*, pp. 64–65, 66 ▲ ● ■
- *Grammar Tutor for Students of Spanish,* Chapter 7 ● ■
- *Interactive Tutor* (Disc 2) or *DVD Tutor* (Disc 2) ▲ ● ■
- Online Practice, Chapter 7 (go.hrw.com, Keyword: EXP1B CH7)

▲ = Advanced Learners   ◆ = Slower Pace Learners   ● = Special Learning Needs   ■ = Heritage Speakers

Holt Spanish 1B   Lesson Planner

Teacher's Name _____ Class _____ Date _____

CAPÍTULO 7

Cuerpo sano, mente sana

DAY 11 50-MINUTE LESSON PLAN

STANDARDS FOR FOREIGN LANGUAGE LEARNING: DAY 11

Gramática en acción 1

Communication 1.1: Students engage in conversations, provide and obtain information, express feelings and emotions, and exchange opinions.
Communication 1.2: Students understand and interpret written and spoken language on a variety of topics.
Communication 1.3: Students present information, concepts, and ideas to an audience of listeners or readers on a variety of topics.
Cultures 2.1: Students demonstrate an understanding of the relationship between the practices and perspectives of the culture studied.

Cultura

Communication 1.2: Students understand and interpret written and spoken language on a variety of topics.
Cultures 2.1: Students demonstrate an understanding of the relationship between the practices and perspectives of the culture studied.
Connections 3.1: Students reinforce and further their knowledge of other disciplines through the foreign language.
Comparisons 4.2: Students demonstrate understanding of the concept of culture through comparisons of the cultures studied and their own.
Communities 5.1: Students use the language both within and beyond the school setting.

CORE INSTRUCTION

Warm-Up
- (5 min.) Have students do Bell Work 7.5, p. 100.

Gramática en acción 1
- (10 min.) Review **Gramática en acción 1**, pp. 92–97.

Assess
- (20 min.) Give **Prueba: Gramática 1.**

Cultura
- (10 min.) Present **Comparaciones**, pp. 98–99. See Teaching **Cultura**, #1–2, p. 98.

Wrap-Up
- (5 min.) See Map Activities, p. 98.

OPTIONAL RESOURCES
- (5 min.) Slower Pace Learners, p. 99 ◆
- (5 min.) Special Learning Needs, p. 99 ●

Practice Options
- *Lab Book,* pp. 44–45 ▲ ● ■
- *Cuaderno de vocabulario y gramática,* pp. 32–34 ▲ ◆ ●
- *Cuaderno de actividades*, pp. 27–31 ▲ ● ■
- *Activities for Communication,* pp. 25–26 ▲ ■
- *Cuaderno para hispanohablantes,* pp. 53–60 ■
- *Teaching Transparencies:* Bell Work 7.5; Mapa 3; *Vocabulario y gramática* Answers pp. 32–34 ▲ ◆ ●
- *Video Guide,* pp. 64–65, 66, 67 ▲ ● ■
- *Grammar Tutor for Students of Spanish,* Chapter 7 ● ■
- *Interactive Tutor* (Disc 2) or *DVD Tutor* (Disc 2) ▲ ● ■
- Online Practice, Chapter 7 (go.hrw.com, Keyword: EXP1B CH7)

Assessment Options
- *Assessment Program*: **Prueba: Gramática 1**, pp. 39–40
- *Assessment Program*: **Prueba: Aplicación 1,** pp. 41–42
- *Assessment Program*: Alternative Assessment Guide, pp. 242, 250, 258 ▲ ● ■
- *Audio CD* 7, Tr. 16
- Test Generator

▲ = Advanced Learners   ◆ = Slower Pace Learners   ● = Special Learning Needs   ■ = Heritage Speakers

Holt Spanish 1B   Lesson Planner

Teacher's Name _____ Class _____ Date _____

Cuerpo sano, mente sana

CAPÍTULO **7**

DAY 12 50-MINUTE LESSON PLAN

STANDARDS FOR FOREIGN LANGUAGE LEARNING: DAY 12

Cultura

Communication 1.2: Students understand and interpret written and spoken language on a variety of topics.

Cultures 2.1: Students demonstrate an understanding of the relationship between the practices and perspectives of the culture studied.

Connections 3.1: Students reinforce and further their knowledge of other disciplines through the foreign language.

Comparisons 4.2: Students demonstrate understanding of the concept of culture through comparisons of the cultures studied and their own.

Communities 5.1: Students use the language both within and beyond the school setting.

Vocabulario en acción 2

Communication 1.2: Students understand and interpret written and spoken language on a variety of topics.

CORE INSTRUCTION

Warm-Up
- (5 min.) Have students re-read the interviews on pp. 98–99.

Cultura
- (10 min.) See Teaching **Cultura**, #3, p. 98.
- (10 min.) Present and assign **Comunidad**, p. 99.

Vocabulario en acción 2
- (20 min.) Present **Vocabulario en acción 2**, pp. 100–101 using Teaching **Vocabulario 2,** p. 100.

Wrap-Up
- (5 min.) Present Language Note and **También se puede decir**, p. 101.

OPTIONAL RESOURCES
- (5 min.) Interdisciplinary Link, p. 99
- (5 min.) Advanced Learners, p. 101 ▲
- (5 min.) Community Link, p. 99

Practice Options
- *Lab Book,* pp. 45, 46 ▲ ● ■
- ***Cuaderno de vocabulario y gramática,*** pp. 35–37 ▲ ◆ ●
- *Activities for Communication,* pp. 27–28 ▲ ■
- *Teaching Transparencies:* **Vocabulario** 7.3, 7.4; *Vocabulario y gramática* Answers pp. 35–37 ▲ ◆ ●
- *TPR Storytelling Book,* pp. 38–39 ▲ ●
- *Video Guide,* pp. 64–65, 67, 68 ▲ ● ■
- *Interactive Tutor* (Disc 2) or *DVD Tutor* (Disc 2) ▲ ● ■
- Online Practice, Chapter 7 (go.hrw.com, Keyword: EXP1B CH7)

▲ = Advanced Learners   ◆ = Slower Pace Learners   ● = Special Learning Needs   ■ = Heritage Speakers

Teacher's Name _____ Class _____ Date _____

CAPÍTULO 7

Cuerpo sano, mente sana

DAY 13 50-MINUTE LESSON PLAN

STANDARDS FOR FOREIGN LANGUAGE LEARNING: DAY 13

Vocabulario en acción 2

Communication 1.2: Students understand and interpret written and spoken language on a variety of topics.

Communication 1.3: Students present information, concepts, and ideas to an audience of listeners or readers on a variety of topics.

Cultures 2.1: Students demonstrate an understanding of the relationship between the practices and perspectives of the culture studied.

Comparisons 4.2: Students demonstrate understanding of the concept of culture through comparisons of the cultures studied and their own.

CORE INSTRUCTION

Warm-Up
- (5 min.) See Teacher to Teacher activity, p. 102.

Vocabulario en acción 2
- (10 min.) Show **ExpresaVisión,** Ch. 7.
- (15 min.) Review **Vocabulario 2** and **¡Exprésate!,** pp. 100–101.
- (5 min.) Present **Nota cultural,** p. 102.
- (10 min.) Have students do Activity 24–25, p. 102.

Wrap-Up
- (5 min.) Have students read the conversation in Activity 25 with a partner.

OPTIONAL RESOURCES
- (5 min.) TPR, p. 101
- (5 min.) Multiple Intelligences, p. 101
- (10 min.) Game, p. 102

Practice Options
- *Lab Book,* p. 46 ▲●■
- *Cuaderno de vocabulario y gramática,* pp. 35–37 ▲◆●
- *Activities for Communication,* pp. 27–28 ▲■
- *Teaching Transparencies:* **Vocabulario** 7.3, 7.4; *Vocabulario y gramática* Answers pp. 35–37 ▲◆●
- *TPR Storytelling Book,* pp. 38–39 ▲●
- *Video Guide,* pp. 64–65, 68 ▲●■
- *Interactive Tutor* (Disc 2) or *DVD Tutor* (Disc 2) ▲●■
- Online Practice, Chapter 7 (go.hrw.com, Keyword: EXP1B CH7)

▲ = Advanced Learners ◆ = Slower Pace Learners ● = Special Learning Needs ■ = Heritage Speakers

Holt Spanish 1B   Lesson Planner

Teacher's Name _____ Class _____ Date _____

Cuerpo sano, mente sana

CAPÍTULO 7

DAY 14 50-MINUTE LESSON PLAN

STANDARDS FOR FOREIGN LANGUAGE LEARNING: DAY 14

Vocabulario en acción 2

Communication 1.2: Students understand and interpret written and spoken language on a variety of topics.

Communication 1.3: Students present information, concepts, and ideas to an audience of listeners or readers on a variety of topics.

Cultures 2.1: Students demonstrate an understanding of the relationship between the practices and perspectives of the culture studied.

Comparisons 4.2: Students demonstrate understanding of the concept of culture through comparisons of the cultures studied and their own.

CORE INSTRUCTION

Warm-Up
- (5 min.) Read the statements from the first column of Activity 24, p. 102, and call on students to supply the correct response

Vocabulario en acción 2
- (20 min.) Have students do Activities 26–28, pp. 102–103.
- (15 min.) Present ¡Exprésate!, p. 104. See Teaching ¡Exprésate!, p. 104.
- (5 min.) Present Nota cultural, p. 104.

Wrap-Up
- (5 min.) See Extension, p. 103.

OPTIONAL RESOURCES
- (10 min.) Comunicación (TE), p. 103
- (5 min.) Advanced Learners, p. 103 ▲
- (5 min.) Special Learning Needs, p. 103 ●

Practice Options
- *Lab Book,* p. 46 ▲●■
- ***Cuaderno de vocabulario y gramática,*** pp. 35–37 ▲♦●
- *Activities for Communication,* pp. 27–28 ▲■
- *Teaching Transparencies:* **Vocabulario** 7.3, 7.4; ***Vocabulario y gramática*** Answers pp. 35–37 ▲♦●
- *TPR Storytelling Book,* pp. 38–39 ▲●
- *Video Guide,* pp. 64–65, 68 ▲●■
- *Interactive Tutor* (Disc 2) or *DVD Tutor* (Disc 2) ▲●■
- *Online Practice,* Chapter 7 (go.hrw.com, Keyword: EXP1B CH7)

▲ = Advanced Learners   ♦ = Slower Pace Learners   ● = Special Learning Needs   ■ = Heritage Speakers

Teacher's Name _____ Class _____ Date _____

CAPÍTULO 7

Cuerpo sano, mente sana

DAY 15 50-MINUTE LESSON PLAN

STANDARDS FOR FOREIGN LANGUAGE LEARNING: DAY 15

Vocabulario en acción 2

Communication 1.1: Students engage in conversations, provide and obtain information, express feelings and emotions, and exchange opinions.

Communication 1.2: Students understand and interpret written and spoken language on a variety of topics.

Communication 1.3: Students present information, concepts, and ideas to an audience of listeners or readers on a variety of topics.

Cultures 2.1: Students demonstrate an understanding of the relationship between the practices and perspectives of the culture studied.

Comparisons 4.2: Students demonstrate understanding of the concept of culture through comparisons of the cultures studied and their own.

CORE INSTRUCTION

Warm-Up
- (5 min.) Have students do Bell Work 7.6, p. 106.

Vocabulario en acción 2
- (10 min.) Review ¡Exprésate!, p. 104.
- (10 min.) Play Audio CD 7, Tr. 7 for Activity 29, p. 104.
- (20 min.) Have students do Activities 30–32, pp. 104–105.

Wrap-Up
- (5 min.) Do Activity 32 as an oral class activity. Remind students to study for **Prueba: Vocabulario 2.** ◆

OPTIONAL RESOURCES
- (10 min.) **Comunicación** (TE), p. 105
- (5 min.) See Slower Pace Learners, p. 105. ◆

Practice Options
- *Lab Book,* pp. 21, 46 ▲ ● ■
- ***Cuaderno de vocabulario y gramática,*** pp. 35–37 ▲ ◆ ●
- *Activities for Communication,* pp. 27–28 ▲ ■
- *Teaching Transparencies:* Bell Work 7.6; **Vocabulario** 7.3, 7.4; ***Vocabulario y gramática*** Answers, pp. 35–37 ▲ ● ■
- *TPR Storytelling Book,* pp. 38–39 ▲ ●
- *Video Guide,* pp. 64–65, 68 ▲ ● ■
- *Interactive Tutor* (Disc 2) or *DVD Tutor* (Disc 2) ▲ ● ■
- Online Practice, Chapter 7 (go.hrw.com, Keyword: EXP1B CH7)

▲ = Advanced Learners   ◆ = Slower Pace Learners   ● = Special Learning Needs   ■ = Heritage Speakers

Holt Spanish 1B   Lesson Planner

Teacher's Name _____ Class _____ Date _____

CAPÍTULO

Cuerpo sano, mente sana

DAY 16 50-MINUTE LESSON PLAN

STANDARDS FOR FOREIGN LANGUAGE LEARNING: DAY 16

Vocabulario en acción 2

Communication 1.1: Students engage in conversations, provide and obtain information, express feelings and emotions, and exchange opinions.
Communication 1.2: Students understand and interpret written and spoken language on a variety of topics.
Communication 1.3: Students present information, concepts, and ideas to an audience of listeners or readers on a variety of topics.

Cultures 2.1: Students demonstrate an understanding of the relationship between the practices and perspectives of the culture studied.
Comparisons 4.2: Students demonstrate understanding of the concept of culture through comparisons of the cultures studied and their own.

CORE INSTRUCTION

Warm-Up
- (5 min.) Ask a few students how they are feeling today.

Vocabulario en acción 2
- (10 min.) Have students do Activity 33, p. 105.
- (10 min.) Review **Vocabulario en acción 2**, pp. 100–105.

Assess
- (50 min.) Give **Prueba: Vocabulario 2**.

Wrap-Up
- (5 min.) Preview **Gramática en acción 2**, pp. 106–111.

OPTIONAL RESOURCES
- (10 min.) Multiple Intelligences, p. 105

Practice Options
- *Lab Book*, p. 46 ▲●■
- ***Cuaderno de vocabulario y gramática***, pp. 35–37 ▲◆●
- *Activities for Communication*, pp. 27–28 ▲■
- *Teaching Transparencies:* **Vocabulario** 7.3, 7.4; ***Vocabulario y gramática*** Answers pp. 35–37 ▲◆●
- *TPR Storytelling Book*, pp. 38–39 ▲●
- *Video Guide*, pp. 64–65, 68 ▲●■
- *Interactive Tutor* (Disc 2) or *DVD Tutor* (Disc 2) ▲●■
- Online Practice, Chapter 7 (go.hrw.com, Keyword: EXP1B CH7)

Assessment Options
- *Assessment Program*: **Prueba: Vocabulario 2**, pp. 43–44
- *Assessment Program*: Alternative Assessment Guide, pp. 242, 250, 258 ▲●■
- Test Generator

▲ = Advanced Learners ◆ = Slower Pace Learners ● = Special Learning Needs ■ = Heritage Speakers

Teacher's Name _____ Class _____ Date _____

CAPÍTULO 7

Cuerpo sano, mente sana

DAY 17 50-MINUTE LESSON PLAN

STANDARDS FOR FOREIGN LANGUAGE LEARNING: DAY 17

Gramática en acción 2
Communication 1.2: Students understand and interpret written and spoken language on a variety of topics.

CORE INSTRUCTION

Warm-Up
- (5 min.) Have students do Bell Work 7.6, p. 106.

Gramática en acción 2
- (20 min.) Present **Gramática: Estar, sentirse,** *and* **tener,** p. 106 using Teaching **Gramática,** p. 106.
- (10 min.) Play Audio CD 7, Tr. 8 for Activity 34, p. 106.
- (10 min.) Show **GramaVisión 7,** Segment 1.

Wrap-Up
- (5 min.) See Heritage Speakers, p. 107. ■

OPTIONAL RESOURCES
- (10 min.) See Special Learning Needs, p. 107.

Practice Options
- *Lab Book,* pp. 21, 46–47 ▲●■
- *Cuaderno de vocabulario y gramática,* pp. 38–40 ▲◆●
- *Cuaderno de actividades,* pp. 32–35 ▲●■
- *Activities for Communication,* pp. 27–28 ▲■
- *Cuaderno para hispanohablantes,* Chapter 7 ■
- *Teaching Transparencies: Vocabulario y gramática* Answers, pp. 38–40 ▲◆●
- *Video Guide,* pp. 64–65, 68 ▲●■
- *Grammar Tutor for Students of Spanish,* Chapter 7 ●■
- *Interactive Tutor* (Disc 2) or *DVD Tutor* (Disc 2) ▲●■
- Online Practice, Chapter 7 (go.hrw.com, Keyword: EXP1B CH7)

▲ = Advanced Learners   ◆ = Slower Pace Learners   ● = Special Learning Needs   ■ = Heritage Speakers

Holt Spanish 1B   Lesson Planner

Teacher's Name _____ Class _____ Date _____

Cuerpo sano, mente sana

CAPÍTULO 7

DAY 18 50-MINUTE LESSON PLAN

STANDARDS FOR FOREIGN LANGUAGE LEARNING: DAY 18

Gramática en acción 2
Communication 1.1: Students engage in conversations, provide and obtain information, express feelings and emotions, and exchange opinions.

Communication 1.2: Students understand and interpret written and spoken language on a variety of topics.

CORE INSTRUCTION

Warm-Up
- (5 min.) Ask volunteers to describe how the people pictured in Activity 34 are feeling.

Gramática en acción 2
- (15 min.) Review **estar, sentirse,** and **tener,** p. 106.
- (25 min.) Have students do Activities 35–37, p. 107.

Wrap-Up
- (5 min.) Review answers to Activity 36 as a class.

OPTIONAL RESOURCES
- (5 min.) Advanced Learners, p. 107 ▲
- (10 min.) **Comunicación** (TE), p. 107

Practice Options
- *Lab Book,* pp. 21, 46 ▲●■
- *Cuaderno de vocabulario y gramática,* pp. 38–40 ▲◆●
- *Cuaderno de actividades,* pp. 32–35 ▲●■
- *Activities for Communication,* pp. 27–28 ▲■
- *Cuaderno para hispanohablantes,* Chapter 7 ■
- *Teaching Transparencies: Vocabulario y gramática* Answers, pp. 38–40 ▲◆●
- *Video Guide,* pp. 64–65, 68 ▲●■
- *Grammar Tutor for Students of Spanish,* Chapter 7 ●■
- *Interactive Tutor* (Disc 2) or *DVD Tutor* (Disc 2) ▲●■
- Online Practice, Chapter 7 (go.hrw.com, Keyword: EXP1B CH7)

▲ = Advanced Learners ◆ = Slower Pace Learners ● = Special Learning Needs ■ = Heritage Speakers

Holt Spanish 1B   Lesson Planner

Teacher's Name _____ Class _____ Date _____

CAPÍTULO 7

Cuerpo sano, mente sana

DAY 19 50-MINUTE LESSON PLAN

STANDARDS FOR FOREIGN LANGUAGE LEARNING: DAY 19

Gramática en acción 2
Communication 1.1: Students engage in conversations, provide and obtain information, express feelings and emotions, and exchange opinions.
Communication 1.2: Students understand and interpret written and spoken language on a variety of topics.

Communication 1.3: Students present information, concepts, and ideas to an audience of listeners or readers on a variety of topics.

CORE INSTRUCTION

Warm-Up
- (5 min.) Have students do Bell Work 7.7, p. 108.

Gramática en acción 2
- (25 min.) Present **Gramática:** *Negative informal commands,* p. 108 using Teaching **Gramática,** p. 108.
- (15 min.) Have students do Activities 38–39, pp. 108–109.

Wrap-Up
- (5 min.) See Language to Language, p. 109.

OPTIONAL RESOURCES
- (10 min.) See **Comunicación** (TE), p. 109.

Practice Options
- *Lab Book,* pp. 46–47 ▲ ● ■
- *Cuaderno de vocabulario y gramática,* pp. 38–40 ▲ ◆ ●
- *Cuaderno de actividades,* pp. 32–35 ▲ ● ■
- *Activities for Communication,* pp. 27–28 ▲ ■
- *Cuaderno para hispanohablantes,* Chapter 7 ■
- *Teaching Transparencies:* Bell Work 7.7; *Vocabulario y gramática* Answers, pp. 38–40 ▲ ◆ ●
- *Video Guide,* pp. 64–65, 68 ▲ ● ■
- *Grammar Tutor for Students of Spanish,* Chapter 7 ● ■
- *Interactive Tutor* (Disc 2) or *DVD Tutor* (Disc 2) ▲ ● ■
- Online Practice, Chapter 7 (go.hrw.com, Keyword: EXP1B CH7)

▲ = Advanced Learners   ◆ = Slower Pace Learners   ● = Special Learning Needs   ■ = Heritage Speakers

Holt Spanish 1B — Lesson Planner

Teacher's Name _____ Class _____ Date _____

CAPÍTULO 7

Cuerpo sano, mente sana

DAY 20 50-MINUTE LESSON PLAN

STANDARDS FOR FOREIGN LANGUAGE LEARNING: DAY 20

Gramática en acción 2
Communication 1.1: Students engage in conversations, provide and obtain information, express feelings and emotions, and exchange opinions.
Communication 1.2: Students understand and interpret written and spoken language on a variety of topics.

Communication 1.3: Students present information, concepts, and ideas to an audience of listeners or readers on a variety of topics.

CORE INSTRUCTION

Warm-Up
- (5 min.) Review answers to Activity 39.

Gramática en acción 2
- (5 min.) Show **GramaVisión 7,** Segment 5.
- (15 min.) Review negative informal commands, p. 108.
- (10 min.) Have students do Activities 40–41, pp. 108–109.

Wrap-Up
- (5 min.) Do Activity 40 as a class activity.

OPTIONAL RESOURCES
- (10 min.) See Special Learning Needs, p. 109. ●
- (5 min.) See Advanced Learners, p. 109. ▲

Practice Options
- *Lab Book,* p. 46 ▲ ● ■
- ***Cuaderno de vocabulario y gramática,*** pp. 38–40 ▲ ♦ ●
- ***Cuaderno de actividades,*** pp. 32–35 ▲ ● ■
- *Activities for Communication,* pp. 27–28 ▲ ■
- ***Cuaderno para hispanohablantes,*** Chapter 7 ■
- *Teaching Transparencies:* ***Vocabulario y gramática*** Answers, pp. 38–40 ▲ ♦ ●
- *Video Guide,* pp. 64–65, 68 ▲ ● ■
- *Grammar Tutor for Students of Spanish,* Chapter 7 ● ■
- *Interactive Tutor* (Disc 2) or *DVD Tutor* (Disc 2) ▲ ● ■
- Online Practice, Chapter 7 (go.hrw.com, Keyword: EXP1B CH7)

▲ = Advanced Learners   ♦ = Slower Pace Learners   ● = Special Learning Needs   ■ = Heritage Speakers

Holt Spanish 1B   Lesson Planner

Teacher's Name _____ Class _____ Date _____

CAPÍTULO 7

Cuerpo sano, mente sana

DAY 21 50-MINUTE LESSON PLAN

STANDARDS FOR FOREIGN LANGUAGE LEARNING: DAY 21

Gramática en acción 2

Communication 1.1: Students engage in conversations, provide and obtain information, express feelings and emotions, and exchange opinions.

Communication 1.2: Students understand and interpret written and spoken language on a variety of topics.

Communication 1.3: Students present information, concepts, and ideas to an audience of listeners or readers on a variety of topics.

CORE INSTRUCTION

Warm-Up
- (5 min.) Have students do Bell Work 7.8, p. 110.

Gramática en acción 2
- (10 min.) Show **GramaVisión 7,** Segment 6.
- (15 min.) Present **Gramática:** *Objects and reflexive pronouns with commands,* p. 110 using Teaching **Gramática,** p. 110.
- (15 min.) Have students do Activities 42–43, pp. 110–111.

Wrap-Up
- (5 min.) Share class responses from Activity 43.

OPTIONAL RESOURCES
- (10 min.) See Slower Pace Learners, p. 111. ◆
- (10 min.) See Special Learning Needs, p. 111. ●

Practice Options
- *Lab Book,* p. 46 ▲●■
- ***Cuaderno de vocabulario y gramática,*** pp. 38–40 ▲◆●
- ***Cuaderno de actividades,*** pp. 32–35 ▲●■
- *Activities for Communication,* pp. 27–28 ▲■
- ***Cuaderno para hispanohablantes,*** Chapter 7 ■
- *Teaching Transparencies:* Bell Work 7.8; *Vocabulario y gramática* Answers, pp. 38–40 ▲◆●
- *Video Guide,* pp. 64–65, 68 ▲●■
- *Grammar Tutor for Students of Spanish,* Chapter 7 ●■
- *Interactive Tutor* (Disc 2) or *DVD Tutor* (Disc 2) ▲●■
- Online Practice, Chapter 7 (go.hrw.com, Keyword: EXP1B CH7)

▲ = Advanced Learners   ◆ = Slower Pace Learners   ● = Special Learning Needs   ■ = Heritage Speakers

Holt Spanish 1B   Lesson Planner

Teacher's Name _____ Class _____ Date _____

Cuerpo sano, mente sana

CAPÍTULO 7

DAY 22 50-MINUTE LESSON PLAN

STANDARDS FOR FOREIGN LANGUAGE LEARNING: DAY 22

Gramática en acción 2

Communication 1.1: Students engage in conversations, provide and obtain information, express feelings and emotions, and exchange opinions.

Communication 1.2: Students understand and interpret written and spoken language on a variety of topics.

Communication 1.3: Students present information, concepts, and ideas to an audience of listeners or readers on a variety of topics.

CORE INSTRUCTION

Warm-Up
- (5 min.) Have students work with partners to review answers to Activity 42, p. 110.

Gramática en acción 2
- (10 min.) Review object pronouns and informal commands, p. 110.
- (15 min.) Have students do Activities 44–45, p. 111.
- (15 min.) Review **Gramática en acción 2,** pp. 106–111.

Wrap-Up
- (5 min.) Have students help prepare index cards for the activity in **Comunicación**, p. 111. Remind students to study for **Prueba: Gramática 2**.

OPTIONAL RESOURCES
- (5 min.) See Slower Pace Learners, p. 111. ◆

Practice Options
- *Lab Book,* pp. 46 ▲ ● ■
- *Cuaderno de vocabulario y gramática,* pp. 38–40 ▲ ◆ ●
- *Cuaderno de actividades,* pp. 32–35 ▲ ● ■
- *Activities for Communication,* pp. 27–28 ▲ ■
- *Cuaderno para hispanohablantes,* Chapter 7 ■
- *Teaching Transparencies:* **Vocabulario y gramática** Answers, pp. 38–40 ▲ ◆ ●
- *Video Guide,* pp. 64–65, 68 ▲ ● ■
- *Grammar Tutor for Students of Spanish,* Chapter 7 ● ■
- *Interactive Tutor* (Disc 2) or *DVD Tutor* (Disc 2) ▲ ● ■
- Online Practice, Chapter 7 (go.hrw.com, Keyword: EXP1B CH7)

▲ = Advanced Learners ◆ = Slower Pace Learners ● = Special Learning Needs ■ = Heritage Speakers

Holt Spanish 1B Lesson Planner

Teacher's Name _____ Class _____ Date _____

Cuerpo sano, mente sana

CAPÍTULO 7

DAY 23 50-MINUTE LESSON PLAN

STANDARDS FOR FOREIGN LANGUAGE LEARNING: DAY 23

Gramática en acción 2

Communication 1.1: Students engage in conversations, provide and obtain information, express feelings and emotions, and exchange opinions.

Communication 1.2: Students understand and interpret written and spoken language on a variety of topics.

Communication 1.3: Students present information, concepts, and ideas to an audience of listeners or readers on a variety of topics.

Conexiones culturales

Communication 1.2: Students understand and interpret written and spoken language on a variety of topics.

Cultures 2.1: Students demonstrate an understanding of the relationship between the practices and perspectives of the culture studied.

Connections 3.2: Students acquire information and recognize the distinctive viewpoints that are only available through the foreign language and its cultures.

CORE INSTRUCTION

Warm-Up
- (5 min.) Have students ask and answer the questions they prepared on the index cards

Gramática en acción 2
- (10 min.) Review **Gramática en acción 2**, pp. 106–111.

Assess
- (20 min.) Give **Prueba: Gramática 2**.

Conexiones culturales
- (10 min.) Present **Conexiones culturales**, pp. 112–113 using Teaching **Conexiones culturales**, #1–2, p. 112.

Wrap-Up
- (5 min.) Do Cultures: Practices and Perspectives, p. 113, with students.

OPTIONAL RESOURCES
- (10 min.) Multiple Intelligences, p. 113
- (5 min.) Slower Pace Learners, p. 113 ◆

Practice Options
- Online Practice, Chapter 7 (go.hrw.com, Keyword: EXP1B CH7)

Assessment Options
- *Assessment Program*: **Prueba: Gramática 2**, pp. 45–46
- *Assessment Program*: **Prueba: Aplicación 2**, pp. 47–48
- *Assessment Program*: Alternative Assessment Guide, pp. 242, 250, 258 ▲ ● ■
- *Audio CD 7*, Tr. 17
- Test Generator

▲ = Advanced Learners   ◆ = Slower Pace Learners   ● = Special Learning Needs   ■ = Heritage Speakers

Holt Spanish 1B

Lesson Planner

Teacher's Name _____ Class _____ Date _____

Cuerpo sano, mente sana

CAPÍTULO 7

DAY 24 50-MINUTE LESSON PLAN

STANDARDS FOR FOREIGN LANGUAGE LEARNING: DAY 24

Conexiones culturales

Communication 1.2: Students understand and interpret written and spoken language on a variety of topics.

Cultures 2.1: Students demonstrate an understanding of the relationship between the practices and perspectives of the culture studied.

Connections 3.2: Students acquire information and recognize the distinctive viewpoints that are only available through the foreign language and its cultures.

Novela en video

Communication 1.1: Students engage in conversations, provide and obtain information, express feelings and emotions, and exchange opinions.

Communication 1.2: Students understand and interpret written and spoken language on a variety of topics.

Cultures 2.1: Students demonstrate an understanding of the relationship between the practices and perspectives of the culture studied.

Connections 3.2: Students acquire information and recognize the distinctive viewpoints that are only available through the foreign language and its cultures.

CORE INSTRUCTION

Warm-Up
- (5 min.) Play the "baseball game" from Slower Pace Learners, p. 113 again, using different vocabulary.

Conexiones culturales
- (20 min.) See Teaching **Conexiones culturales,** #3–5, p. 112.

Novela en video
- (20 min.) Present **Novela en video** using Teaching **Novela en video,** #1–3, p. 114. For a summary of the video, see **¿Quién será?,** p. 115.

Wrap-Up
- (5 min.) See Visual Learners, p. 114.

OPTIONAL RESOURCES
- (10 min.) Practices and Perspectives, p. 113
- (10 min.) Multiple Intelligences, p. 113
- (10 min.) Gestures, p. 115
- (10 min.) Special Learning Needs, p. 117 ●
- (10 min.) Culminating Project, p. 116

Practice Options
- *Lab Book,* p. 48 ▲ ● ■
- *Video Guide,* pp. 64–65, 69 ▲ ● ■
- *Interactive Tutor* (Disc 2) or *DVD Tutor* (Disc 2) ▲ ● ■
- Online Practice, Chapter 7 (go.hrw.com, Keyword: EXP1B CH7)

▲ = Advanced Learners ◆ = Slower Pace Learners ● = Special Learning Needs ■ = Heritage Speakers

Holt Spanish 1B — Lesson Planner

Teacher's Name _____ Class _____ Date _____

CAPÍTULO 7

Cuerpo sano, mente sana

DAY 25 50-MINUTE LESSON PLAN

STANDARDS FOR FOREIGN LANGUAGE LEARNING: DAY 25

Novela en video
Communication 1.1: Students engage in conversations, provide and obtain information, express feelings and emotions, and exchange opinions.
Communication 1.2: Students understand and interpret written and spoken language on a variety of topics.
Cultures 2.1: Students demonstrate an understanding of the relationship between the practices and perspectives of the culture studied.
Connections 3.2: Students acquire information and recognize the distinctive viewpoints that are only available through the foreign language and its cultures.

Leamos y escribamos
Communication 1.2: Students understand and interpret written and spoken language on a variety of topics.
Connections 3.2: Students acquire information and recognize the distinctive viewpoints that are only available through the foreign language and its cultures.

CORE INSTRUCTION

Warm-Up
- (5 min.) See Using the Strategy, p. 116.

Novela en video
- (10 min.) Show **VideoNovela**, Ch. 7.
- (15 min.) See Teaching **Novela en video,** #4, p. 114.

Leamos y escribamos
- (15 min.) Present ¡**En buena salud!** using Teaching **Leamos,** #1–3, p. 118.

Wrap-Up
- (5 min.) Have students do Activity C, p. 119.

OPTIONAL RESOURCES
- (5 min.) Practices and Perspectives, p. 114
- (10 min.) **Comunicación,** p. 117
- (5 min.) Advanced Learners, p. 117 ▲
- (5 min.) Applying the Strategies, p. 118

Practice Options
- *Lab Book*, p. 43 ▲ ● ■
- *Cuaderno de actividades*, p. 36 ▲ ● ■
- *Cuaderno para hispanohablantes*, pp. 53–60 ■
- *Reading Strategies and Skills Handbook*, Chapter 7 ▲ ● ■
- *¡Lee conmigo!* Level 1 reader ▲ ■
- *Video Guide*, pp. 64–65, 69 ▲ ● ■
- *Interactive Tutor* (Disc 2) or *DVD Tutor* (Disc 2) ▲ ● ■
- Online Practice, Chapter 7 (go.hrw.com, Keyword: EXP1B CH7)

▲ = Advanced Learners ◆ = Slower Pace Learners ● = Special Learning Needs ■ = Heritage Speakers

Holt Spanish 1B — Lesson Planner

Teacher's Name _____ Class _____ Date _____

CAPÍTULO 7

Cuerpo sano, mente sana

DAY 26 50-MINUTE LESSON PLAN

STANDARDS FOR FOREIGN LANGUAGE LEARNING: DAY 26

Leamos y escribamos
Communication 1.2: Students understand and interpret written and spoken language on a variety of topics.

Connections 3.2: Students acquire information and recognize the distinctive viewpoints that are only available through the foreign language and its cultures.

CORE INSTRUCTION

Warm-Up
- (5 min.) Have students skim **Leamos** text, p. 118.

Leamos y escribamos
- (10 min.) See Teaching **Leamos**, #4, p. 118.
- (30 min.) Present **Taller del escritor**, p. 119 using Teaching **Escribamos**, #1–3, p. 118.

Wrap-Up
- (5 min.) Make copies of the Writing Rubric, p. 119, discuss and hand out to students.

OPTIONAL RESOURCES
- (5 min.) Advanced Learners, p. 119 ▲
- (5 min.) Special Learning Needs, p. 119 ●

Practice Options
- *Cuaderno de actividades*, p. 36 ▲ ● ■
- *Cuaderno para hispanohablantes*, pp. 53–60 ■
- *Reading Strategies and Skills Handbook*, Chapter 7 ▲ ● ■
- *¡Lee conmigo!* Level 1 reader ▲ ■
- *Interactive Tutor* (Disc 2) or *DVD Tutor* (Disc 2) ▲ ● ■
- Online Practice, Chapter 7 (go.hrw.com, Keyword: EXP1B CH7)

▲ = Advanced Learners ◆ = Slower Pace Learners ● = Special Learning Needs ■ = Heritage Speakers

Holt Spanish 1B — Lesson Planner

Teacher's Name _____ Class _____ Date _____

CAPÍTULO 7

Cuerpo sano, mente sana

DAY 27 50-MINUTE LESSON PLAN

STANDARDS FOR FOREIGN LANGUAGE LEARNING: DAY 27

Leamos y escribamos

Communication 1.2: Students understand and interpret written and spoken language on a variety of topics.

Connections 3.2: Students acquire information and recognize the distinctive viewpoints that are only available through the foreign language and its cultures.

Repaso

Communication 1.2: Students understand and interpret written and spoken language on a variety of topics.

Communication 1.3: Students present information, concepts, and ideas to an audience of listeners or readers on a variety of topics.

Cultures 2.1: Students demonstrate an understanding of the relationship between the practices and perspectives of the culture studied.

Comparisons 4.1: Students demonstrate understanding of the nature of language through comparisons of the language studied and their own.

CORE INSTRUCTION

Warm-Up
- (5 min.) Have students in pairs think of a topic and develop a graphic organizer for it.

Leamos y escribamos
- (10 min.) Have students share work. See Teaching **Escribamos**, #4, p. 118.

Repaso
- (30 min.) Have students do Activities 1–4, pp. 120–121.

Wrap-Up
- (5 min.) See Fold-n-Learn, p. 120.

OPTIONAL RESOURCES
- (5 min.) Career Path, p. 120

Practice Options
- *Activities for Communication*, pp. 49, 67–68 ▲ ■
- *Teaching Transparencies:* **Situación, Capítulo 7**; Picture Stories, Chapter 7 ▲ ● ■
- *TPR Storytelling Book,* pp. 40–41 ▲ ●
- *Interactive Tutor* (Disc 2) or *DVD Tutor* (Disc 2) ▲ ● ■
- Online Practice, Chapter 7 (go.hrw.com, Keyword: EXP1B CH7)

▲ = Advanced Learners   ◆ = Slower Pace Learners   ● = Special Learning Needs   ■ = Heritage Speakers

Holt Spanish 1B

Teacher's Name _____ Class _____ Date _____

Cuerpo sano, mente sana

CAPÍTULO 7

DAY 28 50-MINUTE LESSON PLAN

STANDARDS FOR FOREIGN LANGUAGE LEARNING: DAY 28

Repaso

Communication 1.2: Students understand and interpret written and spoken language on a variety of topics.

Communication 1.3: Students present information, concepts, and ideas to an audience of listeners or readers on a variety of topics.

Cultures 2.1: Students demonstrate an understanding of the relationship between the practices and perspectives of the culture studied.

Comparisons 4.1: Students demonstrate understanding of the nature of language through comparisons of the language studied and their own.

CORE INSTRUCTION

Warm-Up
- (5 min.) Have students review Activity 4, with one person reading the statement, the other responding with advice.

Repaso
- (10 min.) Have students do Activity 5, p. 121.
- (10 min.) Play Audio CD 7, Tr. 11 for Activity 6, p. 121.
- (10 min.) Have students do Activity 7, p. 121.
- (10 min.) Play Audio CD 7, Tr. 12–14 for **Letra y sonido,** p. 122.

Wrap-Up
- (5 min.) Remind students of resources for review of the Chapter. See Chapter Review, p. 122.

OPTIONAL RESOURCES
- (10 min.) **Letra y sonido**, p. 122
- (10 min.) Game, p. 123

Practice Options
- *Lab Book,* pp. 22, 47
- *Activities for Communication,* pp. 49, 67–68 ▲ ■
- *Teaching Transparencies:* **Situación, Capítulo 7**; Picture Stories, Chapter 7 ▲ ● ■
- *Video Guide,* pp. 64–65, 70 ▲ ● ■
- *TPR Storytelling Book,* pp. 40–41 ▲ ●
- *Interactive Tutor* (Disc 2) or *DVD Tutor* (Disc 2) ▲ ● ■
- Online Practice, Chapter 7 (go.hrw.com, Keyword: EXP1B CH7)

▲ = Advanced Learners   ◆ = Slower Pace Learners   ● = Special Learning Needs   ■ = Heritage Speakers

Holt Spanish 1B   Lesson Planner

Teacher's Name _____ Class _____ Date _____

CAPÍTULO
7

Cuerpo sano, mente sana

DAY 29 50-MINUTE LESSON PLAN

STANDARDS FOR FOREIGN LANGUAGE LEARNING: DAY 29

Integración

Communication 1.1: Students engage in conversations, provide and obtain information, express feelings and emotions, and exchange opinions.

Communication 1.2: Students understand and interpret written and spoken language on a variety of topics.

Communication 1.3: Students present information, concepts, and ideas to an audience of listeners or readers on a variety of topics.

CORE INSTRUCTION

Warm-Up
- (5 min.) Review **Repaso de Gramática** 1 and 2, p. 122.

Integración
- (10 min.) Play Audio CD 7, Tr. 15 for Activity 1, p. 124.
- (30 min.) Have students do Activities 2–4, pp. 124–125.

Wrap-Up
- (5 min.) Answer general class questions about the Chapter Test. Remind students to study.

OPTIONAL RESOURCES
- (5 min.) Slower Pace Learners, p. 124 ◆
- (5 min.) Culture Project, p. 124
- (5 min.) Fine Art Connection, p. 125

Practice Options
- *Lab Book*, p. 22
- *Activities for Communication*, pp. 49, 67–68 ▲ ■
- *Cuaderno de actividades*, pp. 37–38 ▲ ● ■
- *Teaching Transparencies:* Fine Art, Chapter 7 ▲ ● ■
- *TPR Storytelling Book*, pp. 40–41 ▲ ●
- *Interactive Tutor* (Disc 2) or *DVD Tutor* (Disc 2) ▲ ● ■
- Online Practice, Chapter 7 (go.hrw.com, Keyword: EXP1B CH7)

▲ = Advanced Learners   ◆ = Slower Pace Learners   ● = Special Learning Needs   ■ = Heritage Speakers

Holt Spanish 1B   Lesson Planner

Teacher's Name _____ Class _____ Date _____

Cuerpo sano, mente sana

CAPÍTULO 7

DAY 30 50-MINUTE LESSON PLAN

CORE INSTRUCTION
Chapter Test

Assess
- (50 min.) Give Chapter Test.

OPTIONAL RESOURCES
- (10 min.) See **Cuaderno de actividades**, pp. 37–38, 80–81.

Practice Options
- *Grammar Tutor for Students of Spanish*, Chapter 7 ● ■
- *Interactive Tutor* (Disc 2) or *DVD Tutor* (Disc 2) ▲ ● ■
- Online Practice, Chapter 7 (go.hrw.com, Keyword: EXP1B CH7)

Assessment Options
- *Assessment Program:* **Examen: Capítulo 7**, pp. 145–155
- *Assessment Program:* **Examen oral: Capítulo 7**, p. 156
- *Assessment Program:* Alternative Assessment Guide, pp. 242, 250, 258 ▲ ● ■
- Audio CD 7, Tr. 18–19
- *Standardized Assessment Tutor*, Chapter 7
- Test Generator

▲ = Advanced Learners   ◆ = Slower Pace Learners   ● = Special Learning Needs   ■ = Heritage Speakers

Holt Spanish 1B   Lesson Planner

Teacher's Name _____ Class _____ Date _____

Vamos de compras

CAPÍTULO 8

DAY 1 50-MINUTE LESSON PLAN

STANDARDS FOR FOREIGN LANGUAGE LEARNING: DAY 1

Chapter Opener
Communication 1.2: Students understand and interpret written and spoken language on a variety of topics.

Vocabulario en acción 1
Communication 1.2: Students understand and interpret written and spoken language on a variety of topics.

Cultures 2.2: Students demonstrate an understanding of the relationship between the products and perspectives of the culture studied.

Comparisons 4.2: Students demonstrate understanding of the concept of culture through comparisons of the cultures studied and their own.

Before starting **Capítulo 8,** you may wish to teach **Geocultura: Florida,** pp. 126–129. For teaching suggestions, see pp. xv–xvi of this *Lesson Planner.*

CORE INSTRUCTION

Warm-Up
- (5 min.) See Learning Tips, p. 131.

Chapter Opener
- (5 min.) See Using the Photo and **Más vocabulario,** p. 130.
- (5 min.) See **Objetivos,** p. 130.

Vocabulario en acción 1
- (20 min.) Present **Vocabulario 1**, pp. 132–133 using Teaching **Vocabulario,** p. 132.
- (10 min.) Play Audio CD 8, Tr. 1 for Activity 1, p. 134.

Wrap-Up
- (5 min.) Present **También se puede decir** and Language Note, p. 133.

OPTIONAL RESOURCES
- (5 min.) Common Error Alert, p. 132
- (5 min.) Special Learning Needs, p. 133 ●
- (5 min.) **Más práctica,** p. 134

Practice Options
- *Lab Book,* pp. 23, 49, 50 ▲●■
- *Cuaderno de vocabulario y gramática,* pp. 41–43 ▲◆●
- *Activities for Communication,* pp. 29–30 ▲■
- *Cuaderno para hispanohablantes,* Chapter 8 ■
- *Teaching Transparencies:* Vocabulario 8.1, 8.2; *Vocabulario y gramática* Answers, pp. 41–43 ▲◆●
- *Video Guide,* pp. 72–72, 74–75, 76 ▲●■
- *TPR Storytelling Book,* pp. 42–43 ▲●
- *Interactive Tutor* (Disc 2) or *DVD Tutor* (Disc 2) ▲●■
- Online Practice, Chapter 8 (go.hrw.com, Keyword: EXP1B CH8)

▲ = Advanced Learners   ◆ = Slower Pace Learners   ● = Special Learning Needs   ■ = Heritage Speakers

Holt Spanish 1B   Lesson Planner

Teacher's Name _____ Class _____ Date _____

Vamos de compras

CAPÍTULO 8

DAY 2 50-MINUTE LESSON PLAN

STANDARDS FOR FOREIGN LANGUAGE LEARNING: DAY 2

Vocabulario en acción 1
Communication 1.2: Students understand and interpret written and spoken language on a variety of topics.
Cultures 2.2: Students demonstrate an understanding of the relationship between the products and perspectives of the culture studied.

Comparisons 4.2: Students demonstrate understanding of the concept of culture through comparisons of the cultures studied and their own.

CORE INSTRUCTION

Warm-Up
- (5 min.) Have students do Bell Work 8.1, p. 132.

Vocabulario en acción 1
- (10 min.) Show **ExpresaVisión,** Ch. 8.
- (10 min.) Review **Vocabulario 1** and **¡Exprésate!,** pp. 132–133.
- (5 min.) Present **Nota cultural,** p. 134.
- (15 min.) Have students do Activities 2–3, p. 134.

Wrap-Up
- (5 min.) See Practices and Perspectives, p. 134.

OPTIONAL RESOURCES
- (10 min.) TPR, p. 133
- (10 min.) Fold-n-Learn, p. 134
- (10 min.) Advanced Learners, pp. 133, 135 ▲

Practice Options
- *Lab Book,* p. 50 ▲ ● ■
- ***Cuaderno de vocabulario y gramática,*** pp. 41–43 ▲ ◆ ●
- *Activities for Communication,* pp. 29–30 ▲ ■
- ***Cuaderno para hispanohablantes,*** Chapter 8 ■
- *Teaching Transparencies:* Bell Work 8.1; Vocabulario 8.1, 8.2; ***Vocabulario y gramática*** Answers, pp. 41–43 ▲ ◆ ●
- *Video Guide,* pp. 74–75, 76 ▲ ● ■
- *TPR Storytelling Book,* pp. 42–43 ▲ ●
- *Interactive Tutor* (Disc 2) or *DVD Tutor* (Disc 2) ▲ ● ■
- Online Practice, Chapter 8 (go.hrw.com, Keyword: EXP1B CH8)

▲ = Advanced Learners   ◆ = Slower Pace Learners   ● = Special Learning Needs   ■ = Heritage Speakers

Holt Spanish 1B
Lesson Planner

Teacher's Name _____ Class _____ Date _____

Vamos de compras

CAPÍTULO 8

DAY 3 50-MINUTE LESSON PLAN

STANDARDS FOR FOREIGN LANGUAGE LEARNING: DAY 3

Vocabulario en acción 1
Communication 1.1: Students engage in conversations, provide and obtain information, express feelings and emotions, and exchange opinions.
Communication 1.2: Students understand and interpret written and spoken language on a variety of topics.

Cultures 2.2: Students demonstrate an understanding of the relationship between the products and perspectives of the culture studied.
Comparisons 4.2: Students demonstrate understanding of the concept of culture through comparisons of the cultures studied and their own.

CORE INSTRUCTION

Warm-Up
- (5 min.) Review answers to Activity 3 by having students read through the conversation with a partner.

Vocabulario en acción 1
- (25 min.) Have students do Activities 4–6, p. 135.
- (15 min.) Present **¡Exprésate!,** p. 136. See Teaching **¡Exprésate!,** p. 136.

Wrap-Up
- (5 min.) **Más práctica,** p. 135

OPTIONAL RESOURCES
- (5 min.) See Multiple Intelligences, p. 135.
- (10 min.) **Comunicación** (TE)**,** p. 135
- (10 min.) Teacher to Teacher, p. 137

Practice Options
- *Lab Book,* p. 50 ▲ ● ■
- *Cuaderno de vocabulario y gramática,* pp. 41–43 ▲ ● ■
- *Activities for Communication,* pp. 29–30 ▲ ■
- *Cuaderno para hispanohablantes,* Chapter 8 ■
- *Teaching Transparencies:* **Vocabulario** 8.1, 8.2; *Vocabulario y gramática* Answers, pp. 41–43 ▲ ◆ ●
- *Video Guide,* pp. 74–75, 76 ▲ ● ■
- *TPR Storytelling Book,* pp. 42–43 ▲ ●
- *Interactive Tutor* (Disc 2) or *DVD Tutor* (Disc 2) ▲ ● ■
- Online Practice, Chapter 8 (go.hrw.com, Keyword: EXP1B CH8)

▲ = Advanced Learners ◆ = Slower Pace Learners ● = Special Learning Needs ■ = Heritage Speakers

Holt Spanish 1B — Lesson Planner

Teacher's Name _____ Class _____ Date _____

Vamos de compras

CAPÍTULO **8**

DAY 4 50-MINUTE LESSON PLAN

STANDARDS FOR FOREIGN LANGUAGE LEARNING: DAY 4

Vocabulario en acción 1

Communication 1.1: Students engage in conversations, provide and obtain information, express feelings and emotions, and exchange opinions.

Communication 1.2: Students understand and interpret written and spoken language on a variety of topics.

Cultures 2.2: Students demonstrate an understanding of the relationship between the products and perspectives of the culture studied.

Connections 3.1: Students reinforce and further their knowledge of other disciplines through the foreign language.

Comparisons 4.2: Students demonstrate understanding of the concept of culture through comparisons of the cultures studied and their own.

CORE INSTRUCTION

Warm-Up
- (5 min.) Have students do Bell Work 8.2, p. 138.

Vocabulario en acción 1
- (10 min.) Review ¡Exprésate!, p. 136.
- (30 min.) Have students do Activities 7–10, pp. 136–137.

Wrap-Up
- (5 min.) See Math Link, p. 136. Remind students to study for **Prueba: Vocabulario 1.**

OPTIONAL RESOURCES
- (5 min.) Slower Pace Learners, p. 137 ◆
- (5 min.) Special Learning Needs, p. 137 ●

Practice Options
- *Lab Book,* p. 50 ▲ ● ■
- *Cuaderno de vocabulario y gramática,* pp. 41–43 ▲ ◆ ●
- *Activities for Communication,* pp. 29–30 ▲ ■
- *Cuaderno para hispanohablantes,* Chapter 8 ■
- *Teaching Transparencies:* Bell Work 8.2; Vocabulario 8.1, 8.2; *Vocabulario y gramática* Answers, pp. 41–43 ▲ ◆ ●
- *Video Guide,* pp. 74–75, 76 ▲ ● ■
- *TPR Storytelling Book,* pp. 42–43 ▲ ●
- *Interactive Tutor* (Disc 2) or *DVD Tutor* (Disc 2) ▲ ● ■
- Online Practice, Chapter 8 (go.hrw.com, Keyword: EXP1B CH8)

▲ = Advanced Learners   ◆ = Slower Pace Learners   ● = Special Learning Needs   ■ = Heritage Speakers

Holt Spanish 1B
Lesson Planner
Copyright © by Holt, Rinehart and Winston. All rights reserved.

Teacher's Name _____ Class _____ Date _____

Vamos de compras

CAPÍTULO 8

DAY 5 50-MINUTE LESSON PLAN

STANDARDS FOR FOREIGN LANGUAGE LEARNING: DAY 5

Vocabulario en acción 1

Communication 1.1: Students engage in conversations, provide and obtain information, express feelings and emotions, and exchange opinions.
Communication 1.2: Students understand and interpret written and spoken language on a variety of topics.
Cultures 2.2: Students demonstrate an understanding of the relationship between the products and perspectives of the culture studied.
Connections 3.1: Students reinforce and further their knowledge of other disciplines through the foreign language.
Comparisons 4.2: Students demonstrate understanding of the concept of culture through comparisons of the cultures studied and their own.

CORE INSTRUCTION

Warm-Up
- (5 min.) Bring some items of clothing to class and ask questions like those in **¡Exprésate!**, p. 133.

Vocabulario en acción 1
- (20 min.) Review **Vocabulario en acción 1,** pp. 132–137.

Assess
- (20 min.) Give **Prueba: Vocabulario 1**.

Wrap-Up
- (5 min.) Preview **Gramática en acción 1,** pp. 138–143.

OPTIONAL RESOURCES
- (10 min.) See **Comunicación** (TE), pp. 137.

Practice Options
- *Lab Book,* p. 50 ▲ ● ■
- *Cuaderno de vocabulario y gramática,* pp. 41–43 ▲ ◆ ●
- *Activities for Communication,* pp. 29–30 ▲ ■
- *Cuaderno para hispanohablantes,* Chapter 8 ■
- *Teaching Transparencies:* Vocabulario 8.1, 8.2; *Vocabulario y gramática* Answers, pp. 41–43 ▲ ◆ ●
- *Video Guide,* pp. 74–75, 76 ▲ ● ■
- *TPR Storytelling Book,* pp. 42–43 ▲ ●
- *Interactive Tutor* (Disc 2) or *DVD Tutor* (Disc 2) ▲ ● ■
- Online Practice, Chapter 8 (go.hrw.com, Keyword: EXP1B CH8)

Assessment Options
- *Assessment Program:* **Prueba: Vocabulario 1,** pp. 57–58
- *Assessment Program:* Alternative Assessment Guide, pp. 243, 251, 259 ▲ ● ■
- Test Generator

▲ = Advanced Learners   ◆ = Slower Pace Learners   ● = Special Learning Needs   ■ = Heritage Speakers

Holt Spanish 1B

Lesson Planner

Teacher's Name _____ Class _____ Date _____

CAPÍTULO **8**

Vamos de compras

DAY 6 50-MINUTE LESSON PLAN

STANDARDS FOR FOREIGN LANGUAGE LEARNING: DAY 6

Gramática en acción 1
Communication 1.1: Students engage in conversations, provide and obtain information, express feelings and emotions, and exchange opinions.
Communication 1.2: Students understand and interpret written and spoken language on a variety of topics.

Communication 1.3: Students present information, concepts, and ideas to an audience of listeners or readers on a variety of topics.
Cultures 2.1: Students demonstrate an understanding of the relationship between the practices and perspectives of the culture studied.

CORE INSTRUCTION

Warm-Up
- (5 min.) Have students look at the photo on p. 138 and say the numbers/prices they see.

Gramática en acción 1
- (20 min.) Present **Gramática: Costar**, *numbers to one million*, p. 138 using Teaching **Gramática**, p. 138.
- (10 min.) Play Audio CD 8, Tr. 2 for Activity 11, p. 138.
- (10 min.) Have students do Activity 12, p. 139.

Wrap-Up
- (5 min.) Have students do Activity 12, p. 139.

OPTIONAL RESOURCES
- (10 min.) Multiple Intelligences, p. 139
- (5 min.) See Slower Pace Learners, p. 139. ◆

Practice Options
- *Lab Book*, pp. 23, 50 ▲ ● ■
- ***Cuaderno de vocabulario y gramática,*** pp. 44–46 ▲ ◆ ●
- ***Cuaderno de actividades,*** pp. 39–42 ▲ ● ■
- *Activities for Communication*, pp. 29–30 ▲ ■
- *Cuaderno para hispanohablantes,* Chapter 8 ■
- *Teaching Transparencies:* **Vocabulario y gramática** Answers, pp. 44–46 ▲ ◆ ●
- *Video Guide*, pp. 74–75, 77 ▲ ● ■
- *Grammar Tutor for Students of Spanish*, Chapter 8 ● ■
- *Interactive Tutor* (Disc 2) or *DVD Tutor* (Disc 2) ▲ ● ■
- Online Practice, Chapter 8 (go.hrw.com, Keyword: EXP1B CH8)

▲ = Advanced Learners   ◆ = Slower Pace Learners   ● = Special Learning Needs   ■ = Heritage Speakers

Holt Spanish 1B   Lesson Planner

Teacher's Name _____ Class _____ Date _____

Vamos de compras

CAPÍTULO 8

DAY 7 50-MINUTE LESSON PLAN

STANDARDS FOR FOREIGN LANGUAGE LEARNING: DAY 7

Gramática en acción 1

Communication 1.1: Students engage in conversations, provide and obtain information, express feelings and emotions, and exchange opinions.

Communication 1.2: Students understand and interpret written and spoken language on a variety of topics.

Communication 1.3: Students present information, concepts, and ideas to an audience of listeners or readers on a variety of topics.

Cultures 2.1: Students demonstrate an understanding of the relationship between the practices and perspectives of the culture studied.

CORE INSTRUCTION

Warm-Up
- (5 min.) Have students do Bell Work 8.3, p. 140.

Gramática en acción 1
- (10 min.) Show **GramaVisión 1** Segment 1.
- (10 min.) Review **costar,** numbers to one million, p. 138.
- (15 min.) Have students do Activities 13–14, p. 139.

Wrap-Up
- (10 min.) See **Comunicación** (TE), p. 139.

OPTIONAL RESOURCES
- (10 min.) Teacher to Teacher, p. 139

Practice Options
- *Lab Book,* p. 50 ▲ ● ■
- *Cuaderno de vocabulario y gramática,* pp. 44–46 ▲ ◆ ●
- *Cuaderno de actividades*, pp. 39–42 ▲ ● ■
- *Activities for Communication,* pp. 29–30 ▲ ■
- *Cuaderno para hispanohablantes,* Chapter 8 ■
- *Teaching Transparencies:* Bell Work 8.3; *Vocabulario y gramática* Answers, pp. 44–46 ▲ ◆ ●
- *Video Guide,* pp. 74–75, 76 ▲ ● ■
- *Grammar Tutor for Students of Spanish,* Chapter 8 ● ■
- *Interactive Tutor* (Disc 2) or *DVD Tutor* (Disc 2) ▲ ● ■
- Online Practice, Chapter 8 (go.hrw.com, Keyword: EXP1B CH8)

▲ = Advanced Learners ◆ = Slower Pace Learners ● = Special Learning Needs ■ = Heritage Speakers

Holt Spanish 1B Lesson Planner

Teacher's Name _____ Class _____ Date _____

Vamos de compras

CAPÍTULO 8

DAY 8 50-MINUTE LESSON PLAN

STANDARDS FOR FOREIGN LANGUAGE LEARNING: DAY 8

Gramática en acción 1
Communication 1.1: Students engage in conversations, provide and obtain information, express feelings and emotions, and exchange opinions.
Communication 1.2: Students understand and interpret written and spoken language on a variety of topics.

Communication 1.3: Students present information, concepts, and ideas to an audience of listeners or readers on a variety of topics.
Cultures 2.1: Students demonstrate an understanding of the relationship between the practices and perspectives of the culture studied.

CORE INSTRUCTION

Warm-Up
- (5 min.) Have students work with a partner to say the numbers that are written in Activity 13, p. 139.

Gramática en acción 1
- (25 min.) Present **Gramática:** *Demonstrative adjectives and comparisons*, p. 140 using Teaching **Gramática,** p. 140.
- (10 min.) Play Audio CD 8, Tr. 3 for Activity 15, p. 140.
- (5 min.) Present **Nota cultural,** p. 140.

Wrap-Up
- (5 min.) See Common Error Alert, p. 141.

OPTIONAL RESOURCES
- (5 min.) **Comunicación** (TE), p. 141

Practice Options
- *Lab Book,* pp. 24, 50 ▲ ● ■
- *Cuaderno de vocabulario y gramática,* pp. 44–46 ▲ ◆ ●
- *Cuaderno de actividades,* pp. 39–42 ▲ ● ■
- *Activities for Communication,* pp. 29–30 ▲ ■
- *Cuaderno para hispanohablantes,* Chapter 8 ■
- *Teaching Transparencies:* **Vocabulario y gramática** Answers, pp. 44–46 ▲ ◆ ●
- *Video Guide,* pp. 74–75, 76 ▲ ● ■
- *Grammar Tutor for Students of Spanish,* Chapter 8 ● ■
- *Interactive Tutor* (Disc 2) or *DVD Tutor* (Disc 2) ▲ ● ■
- Online Practice, Chapter 8 (go.hrw.com, Keyword: EXP1B CH8)

▲ = Advanced Learners   ◆ = Slower Pace Learners   ● = Special Learning Needs   ■ = Heritage Speakers

Holt Spanish 1B
Lesson Planner

Teacher's Name _____ Class _____ Date _____

Vamos de compras

CAPÍTULO 8

DAY 9 50-MINUTE LESSON PLAN

STANDARDS FOR FOREIGN LANGUAGE LEARNING: DAY 9

Gramática en acción 1

Communication 1.1: Students engage in conversations, provide and obtain information, express feelings and emotions, and exchange opinions.

Communication 1.2: Students understand and interpret written and spoken language on a variety of topics.

Communication 1.3: Students present information, concepts, and ideas to an audience of listeners or readers on a variety of topics.

CORE INSTRUCTION

Warm-Up
- (5 min.) Review hint in Common Error Alert, p. 141.

Gramática en acción 1
- (10 min.) Show **GramaVisión 1,** Segment 20.
- (15 min.) Review demonstrative adjectives and comparisons, p. 140.
- (15 min.) Have students do Activities 16–18, p. 141

Wrap-Up
- (5 min.) Ask some students to share their comparisons from Activity 17.

OPTIONAL RESOURCES
- (5 min.) Advanced Learners, p. 141. ▲
- (5 min.) Special Learning Needs, p. 141 ●

Practice Options
- *Lab Book,* p. 50 ▲ ● ■
- ***Cuaderno de vocabulario y gramática,*** pp. 44–46 ▲ ◆ ●
- ***Cuaderno de actividades***, pp. 39–42 ▲ ● ■
- *Activities for Communication,* pp. 29–30 ▲ ■
- ***Cuaderno para hispanohablantes,*** Chapter 8 ■
- *Teaching Transparencies:* **Vocabulario y gramática** Answers, pp. 44–46 ▲ ◆ ●
- *Video Guide,* pp. 74–75, 76 ▲ ● ■
- *Grammar Tutor for Students of Spanish,* Chapter 8 ● ■
- *Interactive Tutor* (Disc 2) or *DVD Tutor* (Disc 2) ▲ ● ■
- Online Practice, Chapter 8 (go.hrw.com, Keyword: EXP1B CH8)

▲ = Advanced Learners   ◆ = Slower Pace Learners   ● = Special Learning Needs   ■ = Heritage Speakers

Holt Spanish 1B

Lesson Planner

Teacher's Name _____ Class _____ Date _____

Vamos de compras

CAPÍTULO 8

DAY 10 50-MINUTE LESSON PLAN

STANDARDS FOR FOREIGN LANGUAGE LEARNING: DAY 10

Gramática en acción 1
Communication 1.1: Students engage in conversations, provide and obtain information, express feelings and emotions, and exchange opinions.
Communication 1.2: Students understand and interpret written and spoken language on a variety of topics.

Communication 1.3: Students present information, concepts, and ideas to an audience of listeners or readers on a variety of topics.

CORE INSTRUCTION

Warm-Up
- (5 min.) Have students do Bell Work 8.4, p. 142.

Gramática en acción 1
- (15 min.) Present **Gramática: Quedar**, p. 142 using Teaching **Gramática,** p. 142.
- (25 min.) Have students do Activities 19–22, p. 142–143.

Wrap-Up
- (5 min.) Check answers to Activity 21, p. 143. Remind students to study for **Prueba: Gramática 1.**

OPTIONAL RESOURCES
- (5 min.) Multiple Intelligences, p. 143
- (10 min.) **Comunicación** (TE), p. 143

Practice Options
- *Lab Book,* p. 50 ▲●■
- ***Cuaderno de vocabulario y gramática,*** pp. 44–46 ▲◆●
- ***Cuaderno de actividades***, pp. 39–42 ▲●■
- *Activities for Communication,* pp. 29–30 ▲■
- ***Cuaderno para hispanohablantes,*** Chapter 8 ■
- *Teaching Transparencies:* Bell Work 8.4; *Vocabulario y gramática* Answers, pp. 44–46 ▲◆●
- *Video Guide,* pp. 75–75, 76 ▲●■
- *Grammar Tutor for Students of Spanish,* Chapter 8 ●■
- *Interactive Tutor* (Disc 2) or *DVD Tutor* (Disc 2) ▲●■
- Online Practice, Chapter 8 (go.hrw.com, Keyword: EXP1B CH8)

▲ = Advanced Learners   ◆ = Slower Pace Learners   ● = Special Learning Needs   ■ = Heritage Speakers

Holt Spanish 1B   Lesson Planner

Teacher's Name _____ Class _____ Date _____

CAPÍTULO 8

Vamos de compras

DAY 11 50-MINUTE LESSON PLAN

STANDARDS FOR FOREIGN LANGUAGE LEARNING: DAY 11

Gramática en acción 1

Communication 1.1: Students engage in conversations, provide and obtain information, express feelings and emotions, and exchange opinions.

Communication 1.2: Students understand and interpret written and spoken language on a variety of topics.

Communication 1.3: Students present information, concepts, and ideas to an audience of listeners or readers on a variety of topics.

Cultures 2.1: Students demonstrate an understanding of the relationship between the practices and perspectives of the culture studied.

CORE INSTRUCTION

Warm-Up
- (5 min.) Have pairs of students re-do one of the Bell work activities in this section (8.2, 8.3, or 8.4).

Gramática en acción 1

Assess
- (20 min.) Review **Gramática en acción 1,** pp. 138–143.
- (20 min.) Give **Prueba: Gramática 1.**

Wrap-Up
- (5 min.) Preview **Cultura** by assigning the Thinking Critically activity, p. 144, as homework.

OPTIONAL RESOURCES
- (10 min.) Re-present all 3 segments of **Gramavisión 1**.

Practice Options
- *Grammar Tutor for Students of Spanish,* Chapter 8 ● ■
- *Interactive Tutor* (Disc 2) or *DVD Tutor* (Disc 2) ▲ ● ■
- Online Practice, Chapter 8 (go.hrw.com, Keyword: EXP1B CH8)

Assessment Options
- *Assessment Program:* **Prueba: Gramática 1**, pp. 59–60
- *Assessment Program:* **Prueba: Aplicación 1,** pp. 61–62
- *Assessment Program:* Alternative Assessment Guide, pp. 243, 251, 259 ▲ ● ■
- *Audio CD* 8, Tr. 18
- Test Generator

▲ = Advanced Learners   ◆ = Slower Pace Learners   ● = Special Learning Needs   ■ = Heritage Speakers

Holt Spanish 1B   Lesson Planner

Teacher's Name _____ Class _____ Date _____

CAPÍTULO 8

Vamos de compras

DAY 12 50-MINUTE LESSON PLAN

STANDARDS FOR FOREIGN LANGUAGE LEARNING: DAY 12

Cultura
Communication 1.2: Students understand and interpret written and spoken language on a variety of topics.
Comparisons 4.2: Students demonstrate understanding of the concept of culture through comparisons of the cultures studied and their own.

Communities 5.2: Students show evidence of becoming life–long learners by using the language for personal enjoyment and enrichment.

CORE INSTRUCTION

Warm-Up
- (5 min.) Go over Thinking Critically activity, p. 144.

Cultura
- (35 min.) Present **Comparaciones,** pp. 144–145 using Teaching **Cultura,** #1–3, p. 144.
- (5 min.) Present and assign **Comunidad,** p. 145.

Wrap-Up
- (5 min.) See Map Activities, p. 144.

OPTIONAL RESOURCES
- (10 min.) Multiple Intelligences, p. 145
- (5 min.) Practices and Perspectives, p. 145
- (5 min.) Community Link, p. 145
- (10 min.) Teacher Note, p. 145
- (5 min.) See Slower Pace Learners, p. 145. ◆

Practice Options
- *Lab Book,* pp. 51 ▲ ● ■
- *Cuaderno de actividades,* p. 43 ▲ ● ■
- *Cuaderno para hispanohablantes,* pp. 61–68 ■
- *Teaching Transparencies:* Mapa 6 ▲ ● ■
- *Video Guide,* pp. 74–75, 77 ▲ ● ■
- *Interactive Tutor* (Disc 2) or *DVD Tutor* (Disc 2) ▲ ● ■
- Online Practice, Chapter 8 (go.hrw.com, Keyword: EXP1B CH8)

▲ = Advanced Learners   ◆ = Slower Pace Learners   ● = Special Learning Needs   ■ = Heritage Speakers

Holt Spanish 1B   Lesson Planner

Teacher's Name _____ Class _____ Date _____

Vamos de compras

CAPÍTULO 8

DAY 13 50-MINUTE LESSON PLAN

STANDARDS FOR FOREIGN LANGUAGE LEARNING: DAY 13

Vocabulario en acción 2
Communication 1.1: Students engage in conversations, provide and obtain information, express feelings and emotions, and exchange opinions.

Communication 1.2: Students understand and interpret written and spoken language on a variety of topics.

CORE INSTRUCTION

Warm-Up
- (5 min.) Have students do Bell Work 8.5, p. 146.

Vocabulario en acción 2
- (25 min.) Present **Vocabulario 2**, pp. 146–147 using Teaching **Vocabulario,** p. 146.
- (5 min.) Present **Nota cultural,** p. 148.
- (10 min.) Play Audio CD 8, Tr. 8 for Activity 23, p. 148.

Wrap-Up
- (5 min.) Present Language Note and **También se puede decir,** p. 147.

OPTIONAL RESOURCES
- (10 min.) Advanced Learners, p. 147 ▲
- (5 min.) Special Learning Needs, p. 147 ●

Practice Options
- *Lab Book,* p. 52 ▲●■
- ***Cuaderno de vocabulario y gramática,*** pp. 47–49 ▲◆●
- *Activities for Communication,* pp. 31–32 ▲■
- ***Cuaderno para hispanohablantes,*** Chapter 8 ■
- *Teaching Transparencies:* Bell Work 8.5; Vocabulario 8.3, 8.4; ***Vocabulario y gramática*** Answers, pp. 47–49 ▲◆●
- *Video Guide,* pp. 74–75, 78 ▲●■
- *TPR Storytelling Book,* pp. 44–45 ▲●
- *Interactive Tutor* (Disc 2) or *DVD Tutor* (Disc 2) ▲●■
- Online Practice, Chapter 8 (go.hrw.com, Keyword: EXP1B CH8)

▲ = Advanced Learners   ◆ = Slower Pace Learners   ● = Special Learning Needs   ■ = Heritage Speakers

Holt Spanish 1B   Lesson Planner

Teacher's Name _____ Class _____ Date _____

Vamos de compras

CAPÍTULO 8

DAY 14 50-MINUTE LESSON PLAN

STANDARDS FOR FOREIGN LANGUAGE LEARNING: DAY 14

Vocabulario en acción 2

Communication 1.1: Students engage in conversations, provide and obtain information, express feelings and emotions, and exchange opinions.

Communication 1.2: Students understand and interpret written and spoken language on a variety of topics.

Communication 1.3: Students present information, concepts, and ideas to an audience of listeners or readers on a variety of topics.

Cultures 2.2: Students demonstrate an understanding of the relationship between the products and perspectives of the culture studied.

CORE INSTRUCTION

Warm-Up
- (5 min.) Ask students questions from the **¡Exprésate!** box on page 147 and have them use the **Vocabulario** on pages 146–147 in their answers.

Vocabulario en acción 2
- (10 min.) Show **ExpresaVisión,** Ch. 8.
- (10 min.) Review **Vocabulario 2,** pp. 146–151.
- (20 min.) Have students do Activities 24–26, pp. 148–149.

Wrap-Up
- (5 min.) See Game, p. 148.

OPTIONAL RESOURCES
- (10 min.) TPR, p. 147
- (5 min.) Special Learning Needs, p. 149 ●
- (5 min.) Begin work on vocabulary mobiles, see Slower Pace Learners, p. 149. ◆

Practice Options
- *Lab Book,* p. 52 ▲ ● ■
- *Cuaderno de vocabulario y gramática,* pp. 47–49 ▲ ◆ ●
- *Activities for Communication,* pp. 31–32 ▲ ■
- *Cuaderno para hispanohablantes,* Chapter 8 ■
- *Teaching Transparencies:* Vocabulario 8.3, 8.4; *Vocabulario y gramática* Answers, pp. 47–49 ▲ ◆ ●
- *Video Guide,* pp. 74–75, 78 ▲ ● ■
- *TPR Storytelling Book,* pp. 44–45 ▲ ●
- *Interactive Tutor* (Disc 2) or *DVD Tutor* (Disc 2) ▲ ● ■
- Online Practice, Chapter 8 (go.hrw.com, Keyword: EXP1B CH8)

▲ = Advanced Learners ◆ = Slower Pace Learners ● = Special Learning Needs ■ = Heritage Speakers

Holt Spanish 1B   Lesson Planner

Teacher's Name _____ Class _____ Date _____

CAPÍTULO
8

Vamos de compras

DAY 15 50-MINUTE LESSON PLAN

STANDARDS FOR FOREIGN LANGUAGE LEARNING: DAY 15

Vocabulario en acción 2
Communication 1.1: Students engage in conversations, provide and obtain information, express feelings and emotions, and exchange opinions.
Communication 1.2: Students understand and interpret written and spoken language on a variety of topics.
Communication 1.3: Students present information, concepts, and ideas to an audience of listeners or readers on a variety of topics.
Cultures 2.2: Students demonstrate an understanding of the relationship between the products and perspectives of the culture studied.

CORE INSTRUCTION

Warm-Up
- (5 min.) Do circumlocution, p. 148 as a class activity.

Vocabulario en acción 2
- (10 min.) Have students do Activities 27–28, p. 149.
- (10 min.) Present **¡Exprésate!,** p. 150 using Teaching **¡Exprésate!,** p. 150.
- (20 min.) Have students do Activities 29–30, p. 150.

Wrap-Up
- (5 min.) Have pairs of students practice the conversation they created in Activity 29.

OPTIONAL RESOURCES
- (10 min.) **Comunicación** (TE), p. 149
- (10 min.) Slower Pace Learners, p. 149 ◆
- (10 min.) Heritage Speakers, p. 150 ■
- (5 min.) Continue work on mobiles, see Slower Pace Learners, p. 149. ◆

Practice Options
- *Lab Book,* p. 52 ▲ ● ■
- *Cuaderno de vocabulario y gramática,* pp. 47–49 ▲ ◆ ●
- *Activities for Communication,* pp. 31–32 ▲ ■
- *Cuaderno para hispanohablantes,* Chapter 8 ■
- *Teaching Transparencies:* Vocabulario 8.3, 8.4; *Vocabulario y gramática* Answers, pp. 47–49 ▲ ◆ ●
- *Video Guide,* pp. 74–75, 78 ▲ ● ■
- *TPR Storytelling Book,* pp. 44–45 ▲ ●
- *Interactive Tutor* (Disc 2) or *DVD Tutor* (Disc 2) ▲ ● ■
- Online Practice, Chapter 8 (go.hrw.com, Keyword: EXP1B CH8)

▲ = Advanced Learners   ◆ = Slower Pace Learners   ● = Special Learning Needs   ■ = Heritage Speakers

Holt Spanish 1B   Lesson Planner

Teacher's Name _____ Class _____ Date _____

Vamos de compras

CAPÍTULO 8

DAY 16 50-MINUTE LESSON PLAN

> **STANDARDS FOR FOREIGN LANGUAGE LEARNING: DAY 16**
>
> **Vocabulario en acción 2**
> **Communication 1.1:** Students engage in conversations, provide and obtain information, express feelings and emotions, and exchange opinions.
> **Communication 1.2:** Students understand and interpret written and spoken language on a variety of topics.
>
> **Communication 1.3:** Students present information, concepts, and ideas to an audience of listeners or readers on a variety of topics.
> **Cultures 2.2:** Students demonstrate an understanding of the relationship between the products and perspectives of the culture studied.

CORE INSTRUCTION

Warm-Up
- (5 min.) Have students do Bell Work 8.6, p. 152.

Vocabulario en acción 2
- (10 min.) Review ¡Exprésate!, p. 150.
- (20 min.) Have students do Activities 31–33, p. 151.
- (10 min.) Review **Vocabulario en acción 2**, pp. 146–151.

Wrap-Up
- (5 min.) Have students work with partners to act out the completed conversation in Activity 31. Remind students to study for **Prueba: Vocabulario 2**.

OPTIONAL RESOURCES
- (5 min.) **Más práctica,** p. 151
- (10 min.) **Comunicación** (TE), p. 151
- (5 min.) Advanced Learners, p. 151 ▲
- (5 min.) Special Learning Needs, p. 151 ●

Practice Options
- *Lab Book,* p. 52 ▲●■
- *Cuaderno de vocabulario y gramática,* pp. 47–49 ▲◆●
- *Activities for Communication,* pp. 31–32 ▲■
- *Cuaderno para hispanohablantes,* Chapter 8 ■
- *Teaching Transparencies:* Bell Work 8.6; Vocabulario 8.3, 8.4; *Vocabulario y gramática* Answers, pp. 47–49 ▲◆●
- *Video Guide,* pp. 74–75, 78 ▲●■
- *TPR Storytelling Book,* pp. 44–45 ▲●
- *Interactive Tutor* (Disc 2) or *DVD Tutor* (Disc 2) ▲●■
- Online Practice, Chapter 8 (go.hrw.com, Keyword: EXP1B CH8)

▲ = Advanced Learners   ◆ = Slower Pace Learners   ● = Special Learning Needs   ■ = Heritage Speakers

Holt Spanish 1B   Lesson Planner

Teacher's Name _____ Class _____ Date _____

CAPÍTULO
8

Vamos de compras

DAY 17 50-MINUTE LESSON PLAN

STANDARDS FOR FOREIGN LANGUAGE LEARNING: DAY 17

Vocabulario en acción 2
Communication 1.1: Students engage in conversations, provide and obtain information, express feelings and emotions, and exchange opinions.
Communication 1.2: Students understand and interpret written and spoken language on a variety of topics.
Communication 1.3: Students present information, concepts, and ideas to an audience of listeners or readers on a variety of topics.
Cultures 2.2: Students demonstrate an understanding of the relationship between the products and perspectives of the culture studied.

Gramática en acción 2
Communication 1.1: Students engage in conversations, provide and obtain information, express feelings and emotions, and exchange opinions.
Communication 1.2: Students understand and interpret written and spoken language on a variety of topics.
Communication 1.3: Students present information, concepts, and ideas to an audience of listeners or readers on a variety of topics.
Comparisons 4.2: Students demonstrate understanding of the concept of culture through comparisons of the cultures studied and their own.

CORE INSTRUCTION

Warm-Up
- (5 min.) Ask students questions based on Activity 27.

Vocabulario en acción 2
- (10 min.) Review **Vocabulario en acción 2**, pp. 146–151.

Assess
- (20 min.) Give **Prueba: Vocabulario 2**.

Gramática en acción 2
- (10 min.) Present **Gramática**: *Preterite of* **-ar** *verbs*, p. 152 using Teaching **Gramática**, #1–3, p. 152.

Wrap-Up
- (5 min.) See Common Error Alert, p. 153.

OPTIONAL RESOURCES
- (10 min.) Extension, p. 150

Practice Options
- *Lab Book*, p. 52 ▲ ● ■
- *Cuaderno de vocabulario y gramática,* pp. 50–52 ▲ ♦ ●
- *Cuaderno de actividades*, pp. 44–47 ▲ ● ■
- *Activities for Communication*, pp. 31–32 ▲ ■
- *Cuaderno para hispanohablantes,* Chapter 8 ■
- *Teaching Transparencies: Vocabulario y gramática* Answers pp. 50–52 ▲ ♦ ●
- *Video Guide*, pp. 74–75, 78 ▲ ● ■
- *Grammar Tutor for Students of Spanish*, Chapter 8 ● ■
- *Interactive Tutor* (Disc 2) or *DVD Tutor* (Disc 2) ▲ ● ■
- *Online Practice*, Chapter 8 (go.hrw.com, Keyword: EXP1B CH8)

Assessment Options
- *Assessment Program:* **Prueba: Vocabulario 2**, pp. 63–64
- *Assessment Program:* Alternative Assessment Guide, pp. 243, 251, 259 ▲ ● ■
- Test Generator

▲ = Advanced Learners   ♦ = Slower Pace Learners   ● = Special Learning Needs   ■ = Heritage Speakers

Holt Spanish 1B   Lesson Planner

Teacher's Name _____ Class _____ Date _____

Vamos de compras

CAPÍTULO **8**

DAY 18 50-MINUTE LESSON PLAN

STANDARDS FOR FOREIGN LANGUAGE LEARNING: DAY 18

Gramática en acción 2
Communication 1.1: Students engage in conversations, provide and obtain information, express feelings and emotions, and exchange opinions.
Communication 1.2: Students understand and interpret written and spoken language on a variety of topics.

Communication 1.3: Students present information, concepts, and ideas to an audience of listeners or readers on a variety of topics.
Comparisons 4.2: Students demonstrate understanding of the concept of culture through comparisons of the cultures studied and their own.

CORE INSTRUCTION

Warm-Up
- (5 min.) Review endings for regular preterite -ar verbs.

Gramática en acción 2
- (5 min.) Show **GramaVisión 2,** Segment 1.
- (10 min.) Present **Gramática:** *Preterite of* **-ar** *verbs,* p. 152 using Teaching **Gramática,** #4–5, p. 152.
- (10 min.) Play Audio CD 8, Tr. 9 for Activity 34, p. 152.
- (10 min.) Have students do Activities 35–36, pp. 152–153.

Wrap-Up
- (10 min.) See **Comunicación** (TE), p. 153.

OPTIONAL RESOURCES
- (10 min.) Special Learning Needs, p. 153 ●

Practice Options
- *Lab Book,* pp. 25, 52 ▲●■
- ***Cuaderno de vocabulario y gramática,*** pp. 50–52 ▲◆●
- ***Cuaderno de actividades***, pp. 44–47 ▲●■
- *Activities for Communication,* pp. 31–32 ▲■
- ***Cuaderno para hispanohablantes,*** Chapter 8 ■
- *Teaching Transparencies:* **Vocabulario y gramática** Answers pp. 50–52 ▲◆●
- *Video Guide,* pp. 74–75 ▲●■
- *Grammar Tutor for Students of Spanish,* Chapter 8 ●■
- *Interactive Tutor* (Disc 2) or *DVD Tutor* (Disc 2) ▲●■
- Online Practice, Chapter 8 (go.hrw.com, Keyword: EXP1B CH8)

▲ = Advanced Learners ◆ = Slower Pace Learners ● = Special Learning Needs ■ = Heritage Speakers

Holt Spanish 1B   Lesson Planner

Teacher's Name _____ Class _____ Date _____

Vamos de compras

CAPÍTULO 8

DAY 19 50-MINUTE LESSON PLAN

STANDARDS FOR FOREIGN LANGUAGE LEARNING: DAY 19

Gramática en acción 2
Communication 1.1: Students engage in conversations, provide and obtain information, express feelings and emotions, and exchange opinions.
Communication 1.2: Students understand and interpret written and spoken language on a variety of topics.
Communication 1.3: Students present information, concepts, and ideas to an audience of listeners or readers on a variety of topics.
Comparisons 4.2: Students demonstrate understanding of the concept of culture through comparisons of the cultures studied and their own.

CORE INSTRUCTION

Warm-Up
- (5 min.) Have students do Bell Work 8.7, p. 154.

Gramática en acción 2
- (10 min.) Have students do Activity 37, p. 153.
- (5 min.) Present **Nota cultural,** p. 152.
- (20 min.) Present **Gramática:** *Preterite of* **ir**, p. 154 using Teaching **Gramática**, #1–3, p. 154.

Wrap-Up
- (10 min.) Have students in pairs ask each other **¿A dónde fuiste...?**, using different times in the question and the vocabulary on pages 146–147 in their answers.

OPTIONAL RESOURCES
- (10 min.) See Advanced Learners, p. 153. ▲

Practice Options
- *Lab Book*, p. 52 ▲ ● ■
- *Cuaderno de vocabulario y gramática,* pp. 50–52 ▲ ◆ ●
- *Cuaderno de actividades*, pp. 44–47 ▲ ● ■
- *Activities for Communication*, pp. 31–32 ▲ ■
- *Cuaderno para hispanohablantes,* Chapter 8 ■
- *Teaching Transparencies:* Bell Work 8.7; *Vocabulario y gramática* Answers pp. 50–52 ▲ ◆ ●
- *Video Guide*, pp. 74–75, 78 ▲ ● ■
- *Grammar Tutor for Students of Spanish,* Chapter 8 ● ■
- *Interactive Tutor* (Disc 2) or *DVD Tutor* (Disc 2) ▲ ● ■
- Online Practice, Chapter 8 (go.hrw.com, Keyword: EXP1B CH8)

▲ = Advanced Learners   ◆ = Slower Pace Learners   ● = Special Learning Needs   ■ = Heritage Speakers

Holt Spanish 1B — Lesson Planner

Teacher's Name _____ Class _____ Date _____

Vamos de compras

CAPÍTULO **8**

DAY 20 50-MINUTE LESSON PLAN

STANDARDS FOR FOREIGN LANGUAGE LEARNING: DAY 20

Gramática en acción 2
Communication 1.1: Students engage in conversations, provide and obtain information, express feelings and emotions, and exchange opinions.
Communication 1.2: Students understand and interpret written and spoken language on a variety of topics.
Communication 1.3: Students present information, concepts, and ideas to an audience of listeners or readers on a variety of topics.
Comparisons 4.2: Students demonstrate understanding of the concept of culture through comparisons of the cultures studied and their own.

CORE INSTRUCTION

Warm-Up
- (5 min.) List **ir** and three **-ar** verbs on the board for students to conjugate in the preterite tense.

Gramática en acción 2
- (10 min.) Show **GramaVisión 2,** Segment 2.
- (10 min.) See Teaching **Gramática,** #4–5, p. 154.
- (20 min.) Have students do Activities 38–41, pp. 154–155.

Wrap-Up
- (5 min.) Have pairs of students ask each other the questions they wrote in Activity 40.

OPTIONAL RESOURCES
- (5 min.) See Advanced Learners, p. 155. ▲
- (5 min.) See Multiple Intelligences, p. 155.

Practice Options
- *Lab Book,* p. 52 ▲●■
- *Cuaderno de vocabulario y gramática,* pp. 50–52 ▲◆●
- *Cuaderno de actividades,* pp. 44–47 ▲●■
- *Activities for Communication,* pp. 31–32 ▲■
- *Cuaderno para hispanohablantes,* Chapter 8 ■
- *Teaching Transparencies: Vocabulario y gramática* Answers pp. 50–52 ▲◆●
- *Video Guide,* pp. 74–75, 78 ▲●■
- *Grammar Tutor for Students of Spanish,* Chapter 8 ●■
- *Interactive Tutor* (Disc 2) or *DVD Tutor* (Disc 2) ▲●■
- Online Practice, Chapter 8 (go.hrw.com, Keyword: EXP1B CH8)

▲ = Advanced Learners ◆ = Slower Pace Learners ● = Special Learning Needs ■ = Heritage Speakers

Holt Spanish 1B
Lesson Planner

Teacher's Name _____ Class _____ Date _____

CAPÍTULO 8

Vamos de compras

DAY 21 50-MINUTE LESSON PLAN

STANDARDS FOR FOREIGN LANGUAGE LEARNING: DAY 21

Gramática en acción 2

Communication 1.1: Students engage in conversations, provide and obtain information, express feelings and emotions, and exchange opinions.

Communication 1.2: Students understand and interpret written and spoken language on a variety of topics.

Communication 1.3: Students present information, concepts, and ideas to an audience of listeners or readers on a variety of topics.

Comparisons 4.2: Students demonstrate understanding of the concept of culture through comparisons of the cultures studied and their own.

CORE INSTRUCTION

Warm-Up
- (5 min.) Have students do Bell Work 8.8, p. 156.

Gramática en acción 2
- (10 min.) Have students do Activity 42, p. 155.
- (20 min.) Present **Gramática:** *The preterite of* **-ar** *verbs with reflexive pronouns*, p. 156 using Teaching **Gramática,** p. 156.
- (10 min.) Play Audio CD 8, Tr. 10 for Activity 43, p. 156.

Wrap-Up
- (5 min.) Have students work with a partner to tell three things they did this morning before school.

OPTIONAL RESOURCES
- (10 min.) **Comunicación** (TE), p. 155
- (5 min.) See Slower Pace Learners, p. 157. ●
- (5 min.) See Special Learning Needs, p. 157. ●

Practice Options
- *Lab Book,* pp. 25, 52 ▲ ● ■
- *Cuaderno de vocabulario y gramática,* pp. 50–52 ▲ ◆ ●
- *Cuaderno de actividades,* pp. 44–47 ▲ ● ■
- *Activities for Communication,* pp. 31–32 ▲ ■
- *Cuaderno para hispanohablantes,* Chapter 8 ■
- *Teaching Transparencies:* Bell Work 8.8; *Vocabulario y gramática* Answers pp. 50–52 ▲ ◆ ●
- *Video Guide,* pp. 74–75, 78 ▲ ● ■
- *Grammar Tutor for Students of Spanish,* Chapter 8 ● ■
- *Interactive Tutor* (Disc 2) or *DVD Tutor* (Disc 2) ▲ ● ■
- Online Practice, Chapter 8 (go.hrw.com, Keyword: EXP1B CH8)

▲ = Advanced Learners ◆ = Slower Pace Learners ● = Special Learning Needs ■ = Heritage Speakers

Holt Spanish 1B — Lesson Planner

Teacher's Name _____ Class _____ Date _____

Vamos de compras

CAPÍTULO 8

DAY 22 50-MINUTE LESSON PLAN

STANDARDS FOR FOREIGN LANGUAGE LEARNING: DAY 22

Gramática en acción 2
Communication 1.1: Students engage in conversations, provide and obtain information, express feelings and emotions, and exchange opinions.
Communication 1.2: Students understand and interpret written and spoken language on a variety of topics.
Communication 1.3: Students present information, concepts, and ideas to an audience of listeners or readers on a variety of topics.
Comparisons 4.2: Students demonstrate understanding of the concept of culture through comparisons of the cultures studied and their own.

CORE INSTRUCTION

Warm-Up
- (5 min.) Review Activity 43 by having students make statements about what is happening in each drawing.

Gramática en acción 2
- (5 min.) Show **GramaVisión 2,** Segment 6.
- (25 min.) Have students do Activities 44–46, p. 157.
- (10 min.) Review **Gramática en acción 2,** pp. 152–157.

Wrap-Up
- (5 min.) Review answers to Activity 44. Remind students to study for **Prueba: Gramática 2**.

OPTIONAL RESOURCES
- (10 min.) **Comunicación** (TE), p. 157

Practice Options
- *Lab Book,* p. 52 ▲●■
- ***Cuaderno de vocabulario y gramática,*** pp. 50–52 ▲◆●
- ***Cuaderno de actividades***, pp. 44–47 ▲●■
- *Activities for Communication*, pp. 31–32 ▲■
- ***Cuaderno para hispanohablantes,*** Chapter 8 ■
- *Teaching Transparencies:* ***Vocabulario y gramática*** Answers pp. 50–52 ▲◆●
- *Video Guide*, pp. 74–75, 78 ▲●■
- *Grammar Tutor for Students of Spanish*, Chapter 8 ●■
- *Interactive Tutor* (Disc 2) or *DVD Tutor* (Disc 2) ▲●■
- Online Practice, Chapter 8 (go.hrw.com, Keyword: EXP1B CH8)

▲ = Advanced Learners ◆ = Slower Pace Learners ● = Special Learning Needs ■ = Heritage Speakers

Holt Spanish 1B — Lesson Planner

Teacher's Name _____ Class _____ Date _____

CAPÍTULO 8

Vamos de compras

DAY 23 50-MINUTE LESSON PLAN

STANDARDS FOR FOREIGN LANGUAGE LEARNING: DAY 23

Gramática en acción 2
Communication 1.1: Students engage in conversations, provide and obtain information, express feelings and emotions, and exchange opinions.
Communication 1.2: Students understand and interpret written and spoken language on a variety of topics.
Communication 1.3: Students present information, concepts, and ideas to an audience of listeners or readers on a variety of topics.
Comparisons 4.2: Students demonstrate understanding of the concept of culture through comparisons of the cultures studied and their own.

Conexiones culturales
Communication 1.3: Students present information, concepts, and ideas to an audience of listeners or readers on a variety of topics.
Cultures 2.2: Students demonstrate an understanding of the relationship between the products and perspectives of the culture studied.
Connections 3.2: Students acquire information and recognize the distinctive viewpoints that are only available through the foreign language and its cultures.

CORE INSTRUCTION

Warm-Up
- (5 min.) Do Activity 39, p. 154 as a class activity.

Gramática en acción 2
- (10 min.) Review **Gramática en acción 2,** pp. 152–157.

Assess
- (20 min.) Give **Prueba: Gramática 2.**

Conexiones culturales
- (10 min.) Present **Conexiones culturales,** pp. 158–159. See Teaching **Conexiones culturales,** #1–3, p. 158.

Wrap-Up
- (5 min.) Encourage students to add any information they may have about people in the History Link, or about other currencies.

OPTIONAL RESOURCES
- (5 min.) See Connections, History Link, p. 159.
- (5 min.) See Connections, Thinking Critically, p. 159.

Practice Options
- *Interactive Tutor* (Disc 2) or *DVD Tutor* (Disc 2) ▲●■
- Online Practice, Chapter 8 (go.hrw.com, Keyword: EXP1B CH8)

Assessment Options
- *Assessment Program:* **Prueba: Gramática 2,** pp. 65–66
- *Assessment Program:* **Prueba: Aplicación 2,** pp. 67–68
- *Assessment Program:* Alternative Assessment Guide, pp. 243, 251, 259 ▲●■
- *Audio CD* 8, Tr. 19
- Test Generator

▲ = Advanced Learners ◆ = Slower Pace Learners ● = Special Learning Needs ■ = Heritage Speakers

Holt Spanish 1B   Lesson Planner

Teacher's Name _____ Class _____ Date _____

Vamos de compras

CAPÍTULO 8

DAY 24 50-MINUTE LESSON PLAN

STANDARDS FOR FOREIGN LANGUAGE LEARNING: DAY 24

Conexiones culturales
Communication 1.3: Students present information, concepts, and ideas to an audience of listeners or readers on a variety of topics.

Cultures 2.2: Students demonstrate an understanding of the relationship between the products and perspectives of the culture studied.

Connections 3.2: Students acquire information and recognize the distinctive viewpoints that are only available through the foreign language and its cultures.

Novela en video
Communication 1.2: Students understand and interpret written and spoken language on a variety of topics.

Cultures 2.1: Students demonstrate an understanding of the relationship between the practices and perspectives of the culture studied.

Connections 3.1: Students reinforce and further their knowledge of other disciplines through the foreign language.

Connections 3.2: Students acquire information and recognize the distinctive viewpoints that are only available through the foreign language and its cultures.

Comparisons 4.2: Students demonstrate understanding of the concept of culture through comparisons of the cultures studied and their own.

CORE INSTRUCTION

Warm-Up
- (5 min.) Have 1–2 pairs of students present their "currency" from Activity 2, p. 158.

Conexiones culturales
- (20 min.) See Teaching **Conexiones culturales**, #4–6, p. 158.

Novela en video
- (15 min.) Present **Novela en video**, pp. 160–163 using Teaching **Novela en video,** #1–2, p. 160.

Wrap-Up
- (5 min.) Discuss Gestures, p. 160.

OPTIONAL RESOURCES
- (5 min.) Advanced Learners, p. 159 ▲
- (5 min.) Multiple Intelligences, p. 159
- (10 min.) Culminating Project, p. 162
- (5 min.) See Visual Learners, p. 160.

Practice Options
- *Lab Book,* p. 54 ▲●■
- *Video Guide,* pp. 74–75, 79 ▲●■
- *Interactive Tutor* (Disc 2) or *DVD Tutor* (Disc 2) ▲●■
- Online Practice, Chapter 8 (go.hrw.com, Keyword: EXP1B CH8)

▲ = Advanced Learners ◆ = Slower Pace Learners ● = Special Learning Needs ■ = Heritage Speakers

Holt Spanish 1B — Lesson Planner

Teacher's Name _____ Class _____ Date _____

CAPÍTULO
8

Vamos de compras

DAY 25 50-MINUTE LESSON PLAN

STANDARDS FOR FOREIGN LANGUAGE LEARNING: DAY 25

Novela en video

Communication 1.2: Students understand and interpret written and spoken language on a variety of topics.

Cultures 2.1: Students demonstrate an understanding of the relationship between the practices and perspectives of the culture studied.

Connections 3.1: Students reinforce and further their knowledge of other disciplines through the foreign language.

Connections 3.2: Students acquire information and recognize the distinctive viewpoints that are only available through the foreign language and its cultures.

Comparisons 4.2: Students demonstrate understanding of the concept of culture through comparisons of the cultures studied and their own.

Leamos y escribamos

Communication 1.2: Students understand and interpret written and spoken language on a variety of topics.

Communication 1.3: Students present information, concepts, and ideas to an audience of listeners or readers on a variety of topics.

Cultures 2.1: Students demonstrate an understanding of the relationship between the practices and perspectives of the culture studied.

CORE INSTRUCTION

Warm-Up
- (5 min.) See Practices and Perspectives, p. 161.

Novela en video
- (20 min.) See Teaching **Novela en video,** #3–4, p. 160.

Leamos y escribamos
- (20 min.) Present **Una modeda de ¡Ay!,** p. 164 using Teaching **Leamos,** #1–2, p. 164.

Wrap-Up
- (5 min.) See Comparing and Contrasting, p. 162.

OPTIONAL RESOURCES
- (10 min.) **Comunicación** (TE)**,** p. 163
- (5 min.) Applying the Strategies, p. 164

Practice Options
- *Lab Book,* p. 54 ▲●■
- *Cuaderno de actividades*, p. 48 ▲●■
- *Cuaderno para hispanohablantes*, pp. 61–68 ■
- *Reading Strategies and Skills Handbook,* Chapter 8 ▲●■
- *¡Lee conmigo!* Level 1 reader ▲■
- *Video Guide,* pp. 74–75, 79 ▲●■
- *Interactive Tutor* (Disc 2) or *DVD Tutor* (Disc 2) ▲●■
- Online Practice, Chapter 8 (go.hrw.com, Keyword: EXP1B CH8)

▲ = Advanced Learners ◆ = Slower Pace Learners ● = Special Learning Needs ■ = Heritage Speakers

Holt Spanish 1B Lesson Planner

Teacher's Name _____ Class _____ Date _____

Vamos de compras

CAPÍTULO 8

DAY 26 50-MINUTE LESSON PLAN

STANDARDS FOR FOREIGN LANGUAGE LEARNING: DAY 26

Leamos y escribamos

Communication 1.2: Students understand and interpret written and spoken language on a variety of topics.

Communication 1.3: Students present information, concepts, and ideas to an audience of listeners or readers on a variety of topics.

Cultures 2.1: Students demonstrate an understanding of the relationship between the practices and perspectives of the culture studied.

CORE INSTRUCTION

Warm-Up
- (5 min.) Finish Activity A, p 164.

Leamos y escribamos
- (20 min.) See Teaching **Leamos**, #3–4, p. 164.
- (20 min.) Present **Taller del escritor**, p. 165 using Teaching **Escribamos**, #1–2, p. 165.

Wrap-Up
- (5 min.) Do the **Comprensión** questions, p. 165, as a class activity

OPTIONAL RESOURCES
- (5 min.) Heritage Speakers, p. 165 ■
- (5 min.) Multiple Intelligences, p. 165
- (5 min.) Additional Reading, pp. 270–271

Practice Options
- *Cuaderno de actividades*, p. 48 ▲●■
- *Cuaderno para hispanohablantes*, pp. 61–68 ■
- *Reading Strategies and Skills Handbook*, Chapter 8 ▲●■
- *¡Lee conmigo!* Level 1 reader ▲■
- *Interactive Tutor* (Disc 2) or *DVD Tutor* (Disc 2) ▲●■
- Online Practice, Chapter 8 (go.hrw.com, Keyword: EXP1B CH8)

▲ = Advanced Learners ◆ = Slower Pace Learners ● = Special Learning Needs ■ = Heritage Speakers

Teacher's Name _____ Class _____ Date _____

CAPÍTULO 8

Vamos de compras

DAY 27 50-MINUTE LESSON PLAN

STANDARDS FOR FOREIGN LANGUAGE LEARNING: DAY 27

Leamos y escribamos

Communication 1.2: Students understand and interpret written and spoken language on a variety of topics.

Communication 1.3: Students present information, concepts, and ideas to an audience of listeners or readers on a variety of topics.

Cultures 2.1: Students demonstrate an understanding of the relationship between the practices and perspectives of the culture studied.

Repaso

Communication 1.1: Students engage in conversations, provide and obtain information, express feelings and emotions, and exchange opinions.

Communication 1.2: Students understand and interpret written and spoken language on a variety of topics.

Communication 1.3: Students present information, concepts, and ideas to an audience of listeners or readers on a variety of topics.

Cultures 2.1: Students demonstrate an understanding of the relationship between the practices and perspectives of the culture studied.

Cultures 2.2: Students demonstrate an understanding of the relationship between the products and perspectives of the culture studied.

CORE INSTRUCTION

Warm-Up
- (5 min.) Review Writing Rubric you will use for this assignment.

Leamos y escribamos
- (10 min.) See Teaching **Escribamos**, #4, p. 164.

Repaso
- (30 min.) Have students do Activities 1–5, pp. 166–167.

Wrap-Up
- (5 min.) Present Fold-n-Learn, p. 166.

OPTIONAL RESOURCES
- (10 min.) Reteaching, p. 166
- (10 min.) Game, p. 166

Practice Options
- *Activities for Communication,* pp. 50, 69–70 ▲ ■
- *Cuaderno para hispanohablantes,* Chapter 8 ■
- *Teaching Transparencies:* **Situación, Capítulo 8**; Picture Stories, Chapter 8 ▲ ● ■
- *TPR Storytelling Book,* pp. 46–47 ▲ ●
- *Interactive Tutor* (Disc 2) or *DVD Tutor* (Disc 2) ▲ ● ■
- Online Practice, Chapter 8 (go.hrw.com, Keyword: EXP1B CH8)

▲ = Advanced Learners   ◆ = Slower Pace Learners   ● = Special Learning Needs   ■ = Heritage Speakers

Holt Spanish 1B   Lesson Planner

Teacher's Name _____ Class _____ Date _____

Vamos de compras

CAPÍTULO 8

DAY 28 50-MINUTE LESSON PLAN

STANDARDS FOR FOREIGN LANGUAGE LEARNING: DAY 28

Repaso

Communication 1.1: Students engage in conversations, provide and obtain information, express feelings and emotions, and exchange opinions.

Communication 1.2: Students understand and interpret written and spoken language on a variety of topics.

Communication 1.3: Students present information, concepts, and ideas to an audience of listeners or readers on a variety of topics.

Cultures 2.1: Students demonstrate an understanding of the relationship between the practices and perspectives of the culture studied.

Cultures 2.2: Students demonstrate an understanding of the relationship between the products and perspectives of the culture studied.

CORE INSTRUCTION

Warm-Up
- (5 min.) Review answers to Activity 3, p. 166.

Repaso
- (10 min.) Play Audio CD 8, Tr. 13 for Activity 6, p. 167.
- (10 min.) Have students do Activity 7, p. 167.
- (10 min.) Play Game, p. 166.
- (10 min.) Play Audio CD 8, Tr. 14–16 for **Letra y sonido,** p. 168.

Wrap-Up
- (5 min.) Remind students of Chapter Review resources, p. 168–169, and to study for Chapter Test.

OPTIONAL RESOURCES
- (10 min.) **Letra y sonido**, p. 168
- (10 min.) Teacher to Teacher, p. 169

Practice Options
- *Lab Book,* pp. 26, 53 ▲ ● ■
- *Activities for Communication,* pp. 50, 69–70 ▲ ■
- **Cuaderno para hispanohablantes,** Chapter 8 ■
- *Teaching Transparencies:* **Situación, Capítulo 8**; Picture Stories, Chapter 8 ▲ ● ■
- *Video Guide,* pp. 74–75, 80 ▲ ● ■
- *TPR Storytelling Book,* pp. 46–47 ▲ ●
- *Interactive Tutor* (Disc 2) or *DVD Tutor* (Disc 2) ▲ ● ■
- Online Practice, Chapter 8 (go.hrw.com, Keyword: EXP1B CH8)

▲ = Advanced Learners   ◆ = Slower Pace Learners   ● = Special Learning Needs   ■ = Heritage Speakers

Holt Spanish 1B — Lesson Planner

Teacher's Name _____ Class _____ Date _____

CAPÍTULO 8

Vamos de compras

DAY 29 50-MINUTE LESSON PLAN

STANDARDS FOR FOREIGN LANGUAGE LEARNING: DAY 29

Integración

Communication 1.1: Students engage in conversations, provide and obtain information, express feelings and emotions, and exchange opinions.

Communication 1.2: Students understand and interpret written and spoken language on a variety of topics.

Communication 1.3: Students present information, concepts, and ideas to an audience of listeners or readers on a variety of topics.

Connections 3.2: Students acquire information and recognize the distinctive viewpoints that are only available through the foreign language and its cultures.

CORE INSTRUCTION

Warm-Up
- (5 min.) See Fine Art Connection: Analyzing, p. 171.

Integración
- (10 min.) Play Audio CD 8, Tr. 17 for Activity 1, p. 170.
- (30 min.) Have students do Activities 2–4, pp. 170–171.

Wrap-Up
- (5 min.) Conduct a question/answer period in preparation for Chapter Test; remind students to study.

OPTIONAL RESOURCES
- (10 min.) Culture Project, p. 170
- (10 min.) Fine Art Connection, p. 171

Practice Options
- *Lab Book*, p. 26
- *Cuaderno de actividades*, pp. 49–50 ▲ ■
- *Teaching Transparencies:* Fine Art, Chapter 8 ▲ ● ■
- *Interactive Tutor* (Disc 2) or *DVD Tutor* (Disc 2) ▲ ● ■
- Online Practice, Chapter 8 (go.hrw.com, Keyword: EXP1B CH8)

▲ = Advanced Learners   ◆ = Slower Pace Learners   ● = Special Learning Needs   ■ = Heritage Speakers

Holt Spanish 1B   Lesson Planner

Teacher's Name _____ Class _____ Date _____

Vamos de compras

CAPÍTULO
8

DAY 30 50-MINUTE LESSON PLAN

CORE INSTRUCTION
Chapter Assessment

Assess
- (50 min.) Give Chapter 8 Test.

OPTIONAL RESOURCES
- (10 min.) Preview **Geocultura: La República Dominicana**, pp. 172–165.

Practice Options
- *Cuaderno de actividades*, pp. 49–50, 82–83 ▲ ● ■

Assessment Options
- *Assessment Program:* **Examen: Capítulo 8,** pp. 173–183
- *Assessment Program:* **Examen oral: Capítulo 8**, p. 184
- *Assessment Program:* Alternative Assessment Guide, pp. 243, 251, 259 ▲ ● ■
- Standardized Assessment Tutor, pp. 33–36
- *Audio CD* 8, Tr. 20–21
- Test Generator

▲ = Advanced Learners ◆ = Slower Pace Learners ● = Special Learning Needs ■ = Heritage Speakers

Holt Spanish 1B

Lesson Planner

Copyright © by Holt, Rinehart and Winston. All rights reserved.

Teacher's Name _____ Class _____ Date _____

CAPÍTULO
9

¡Festejemos!

DAY 1 50-MINUTE LESSON PLAN

> **STANDARDS FOR FOREIGN LANGUAGE LEARNING: DAY 1**
>
> **Chapter Opener**
> **Comparisons 4.2:** Students demonstrate understanding of the concept of culture through comparisons of the cultures studied and their own.
>
> **Vocabulario en acción 1**
> **Communication 1.2:** Students understand and interpret written and spoken language on a variety of topics.
>
> **Connections 3.1:** Students reinforce and further their knowledge of other disciplines through the foreign language.

Before starting **Capítulo 9,** you may wish to teach **Geocultura: La República Dominicana,** pp. 172–175. For teaching suggestions, see pp. xv–xvi of this *Lesson Planner.*

CORE INSTRUCTION

Warm-Up
- (5 min.) See Learning Tips. p.177.

Chapter Opener
- (5 min.) See Using the Photo and **Más vocabulario,** p. 176.
- (5 min.) See **Objetivos,** p. 176.

Vocabulario en acción 1
- (5 min.) See Bell Work 9.1, p. 178.
- (15 min.) Present **Vocabulario 1,** pp. 178–179 using Teaching **Vocabulario,** p. 178.
- (10 min.) Have students do Activity 1, p. 180.

Wrap-Up
- (5 min.) See **También se puede decir** and Language Note, p. 179.

OPTIONAL RESOURCES
- (5 min.) Common Error Alert, p. 178
- (5 min.) Advanced Learners, p. 179 ▲
- (5 min.) Special Learning Needs, p. 179 ●

Practice Options
- *Lab Book,* pp. 56–57
- *Cuaderno de vocabulario y gramática,* pp. 53–55
- *Activities for Communication,* pp. 33–34 ▲ ■
- *Cuaderno para hispanohablantes,* Chapter 9 ■
- *Teaching Transparencies:* Bell Work 9.1; **Vocabulario** 9.1, 9.2; *Vocabulario y gramática* Answers pp. 53–55 ▲ ● ■
- *Video Guide,* pp. 86–87 ▲ ● ■
- *TPR Storytelling Book,* pp. 48–49 ▲ ●
- *Interactive Tutor* (Disc 2) or *DVD Tutor* (Disc 2) ▲ ● ■
- Online Practice, Chapter 9 (go.hrw.com, Keyword: EXP1B CH9)

▲ = Advanced Learners   ◆ = Slower Pace Learners   ● = Special Learning Needs   ■ = Heritage Speakers

Holt Spanish 1B   Lesson Planner

Teacher's Name _____ Class _____ Date _____

¡Festejemos!

CAPÍTULO 9

DAY 2 50-MINUTE LESSON PLAN

> ### STANDARDS FOR FOREIGN LANGUAGE LEARNING: DAY 2
>
> **Vocabulario en acción 1**
>
> **Communication 1.1:** Students engage in conversations, provide and obtain information, express feelings and emotions, and exchange opinions.
>
> **Communication 1.2:** Students understand and interpret written and spoken language on a variety of topics.
>
> **Communication 1.3:** Students present information, concepts, and ideas to an audience of listeners or readers on a variety of topics.
>
> **Communities 5.1:** Students use the language both within and beyond the school setting.

CORE INSTRUCTION

Warm-Up
- (5 min.) Ask students questions about their plans for different holidays. Tell them to use vocabulary from p. 179 in their responses.

Vocabulario en acción 1
- (5 min.) Show **ExpresaVisión,** Ch. 9.
- (10 min.) Review **Vocabulario 1** and **¡Exprésate!,** pp. 178–179.
- (25 min.) Have students do Activities 2–4, pp. 180–181.

Wrap-Up
- (5 min.) See **Más práctica,** p. 181,

OPTIONAL RESOURCES
- (5 min.) **Más práctica,** p. 180
- (5 min.) Extension, p. 180
- (5 min.) Communities, p. 180
- (10 min.) Fold-n-Learn, p. 180

Practice Options
- *Lab Book,* pp. 56–57
- *Cuaderno de vocabulario y gramática,* pp. 53–55
- *Activities for Communication,* pp. 33–34 ▲ ■
- *Cuaderno para hispanohablantes,* Chapter 9 ■
- *Teaching Transparencies:* **Vocabulario** 9.1, 9.2; *Vocabulario y gramática* Answers pp. 53–55 ▲ ● ■
- *Video Guide,* pp. 86–87 ▲ ● ■
- *TPR Storytelling Book,* pp. 48–49 ▲ ●
- *Interactive Tutor* (Disc 2) or *DVD Tutor* (Disc 2) ▲ ● ■
- Online Practice, Chapter 9 (go.hrw.com, Keyword: EXP1B CH9)

▲ = Advanced Learners ◆ = Slower Pace Learners ● = Special Learning Needs ■ = Heritage Speakers

Teacher's Name _____ Class _____ Date _____

CAPÍTULO
9

¡Festejemos!

DAY 3 50-MINUTE LESSON PLAN

STANDARDS FOR FOREIGN LANGUAGE LEARNING: DAY 3

Vocabulario en acción 1
Communication 1.1: Students engage in conversations, provide and obtain information, express feelings and emotions, and exchange opinions.
Communication 1.2: Students understand and interpret written and spoken language on a variety of topics.
Communication 1.3: Students present information, concepts, and ideas to an audience of listeners or readers on a variety of topics.
Communities 5.1: Students use the language both within and beyond the school setting.

CORE INSTRUCTION

Warm-Up
- (5 min.) Have students share their various responses from Activity 3, p. 181.

Vocabulario en acción 1
- (15 min.) Have students do Activity 5, p. 181.
- (15 min.) See Teaching ¡Exprésate!, p. 182.
- (10 min.) Have students do Activities 6–7, p. 182.

Wrap-Up
- (5 min.) Have students work with a partner and read aloud the corrected conversation in Activity 7.

OPTIONAL RESOURCES
- (5 min.) Slower Pace Learners, p. 181 ◆
- (5 min.) Multiple Intelligences, p. 181
- (10 min.) **Comunicación** (TE), p. 181
- (10 min.) Teacher to Teacher, p. 182

Practice Options
- *Lab Book,* pp. 56–57
- ***Cuaderno de vocabulario y gramática,*** pp. 53–55
- *Activities for Communication,* pp. 33–34 ▲ ■
- ***Cuaderno para hispanohablantes,*** Chapter 9 ■
- *Teaching Transparencies:* **Vocabulario** 9.1, 9.2; ***Vocabulario y gramática*** Answers pp. 53–55 ▲ ● ■
- *Video Guide,* pp. 86–87 ▲ ● ■
- *TPR Storytelling Book,* pp. 48–49 ▲ ●
- *Interactive Tutor* (Disc 2) or *DVD Tutor* (Disc 2) ▲ ● ■
- Online Practice, Chapter 9 (go.hrw.com, Keyword: EXP1B CH9)

▲ = Advanced Learners ◆ = Slower Pace Learners ● = Special Learning Needs ■ = Heritage Speakers

Holt Spanish 1B — Lesson Planner

Teacher's Name _____ Class _____ Date _____

¡Festejemos!

CAPÍTULO 9

DAY 4 50-MINUTE LESSON PLAN

STANDARDS FOR FOREIGN LANGUAGE LEARNING: DAY 4

Vocabulario en acción 1

Communication 1.1: Students engage in conversations, provide and obtain information, express feelings and emotions, and exchange opinions.

Communication 1.2: Students understand and interpret written and spoken language on a variety of topics.

Communication 1.3: Students present information, concepts, and ideas to an audience of listeners or readers on a variety of topics.

Cultures 2.1: Students demonstrate an understanding of the relationship between the practices and perspectives of the culture studied.

Comparisons 4.2: Students demonstrate understanding of the concept of culture through comparisons of the cultures studied and their own.

CORE INSTRUCTION

Warm-Up
- (5 min.) Have students do Bell Work 9.2, p. 184.

Vocabulario en acción 1
- (5 min.) Review ¡Exprésate!, p. 182.
- (5 min.) Present Nota cultural, p. 183.
- (10 min.) Play Audio CD 9, Tr. 1 for Activity 8, p. 183.
- (20 min.) Have students do Activities 9–10, p. 183.

Wrap-Up
- (5 min.) Present Practices and Perspectives, p. 183. Remind students to study for **Prueba: Vocabulario 1**.

OPTIONAL RESOURCES
- (10 min.) **Comunicación** (TE), p. 183
- (5 min.) Advanced Learners, p. 183 ▲
- (5 min.) Multiple Intelligences, p. 183

Practice Options
- *Lab Book,* pp. 56–57
- **Cuaderno de vocabulario y gramática,** pp. 53–55
- *Activities for Communication,* pp. 33–34 ▲ ■
- **Cuaderno para hispanohablantes,** Chapter 9 ■
- *Teaching Transparencies:* Bell Work 9.2; **Vocabulario** 9.1, 9.2; **Vocabulario y gramática** Answers pp. 53–55 ▲ ● ■
- *Video Guide,* pp. 86–87 ▲ ● ■
- *TPR Storytelling Book,* pp. 48–49 ▲ ●
- *Interactive Tutor* (Disc 2) or *DVD Tutor* (Disc 2) ▲ ● ■
- Online Practice, Chapter 9 (go.hrw.com, Keyword: EXP1B CH9)

▲ = Advanced Learners ◆ = Slower Pace Learners ● = Special Learning Needs ■ = Heritage Speakers

Holt Spanish 1B — Lesson Planner

Teacher's Name _____ Class _____ Date _____

CAPÍTULO 9

¡Festejemos!

DAY 5 50-MINUTE LESSON PLAN

STANDARDS FOR FOREIGN LANGUAGE LEARNING: DAY 5

Vocabulario en acción 1

Communication 1.1: Students engage in conversations, provide and obtain information, express feelings and emotions, and exchange opinions.

Communication 1.2: Students understand and interpret written and spoken language on a variety of topics.

Communication 1.3: Students present information, concepts, and ideas to an audience of listeners or readers on a variety of topics.

Cultures 2.1: Students demonstrate an understanding of the relationship between the practices and perspectives of the culture studied.

Comparisons 4.2: Students demonstrate understanding of the concept of culture through comparisons of the cultures studied and their own.

Communities 5.1: Students use the language both within and beyond the school setting.

CORE INSTRUCTION

Vocabulario en acción 1

Warm-Up
- (20 min.) Review **Vocabulario en acción 1**, pp. 178–183.

Assess
- (20 min.) Give **Prueba: Vocabulario 1**.

Wrap-Up
- (5 min.) Preview **Gramática en acción 1**, pp. 184–189.

OPTIONAL RESOURCES
- (5 min.) Have students do TPR activity, p. 179.

Practice Options
- *Interactive Tutor* (Disc 2) or *DVD Tutor* (Disc 2) ▲●■
- Online Practice, Chapter 9 (go.hrw.com, Keyword: EXP1B CH9)

Assessment Options
- *Assessment Program:* **Prueba: Vocabulario 1**, pp. 77–78
- *Assessment Program:* Alternative Assessment Guide, pp. 244, 252, 260 ▲●■
- Test Generator

▲ = Advanced Learners   ◆ = Slower Pace Learners   ● = Special Learning Needs   ■ = Heritage Speakers

Holt Spanish 1B   Lesson Planner

Teacher's Name _____ Class _____ Date _____

¡Festejemos!

CAPÍTULO 9

DAY 6 50-MINUTE LESSON PLAN

STANDARDS FOR FOREIGN LANGUAGE LEARNING: DAY 6

Gramática en acción 1

Communication 1.1: Students engage in conversations, provide and obtain information, express feelings and emotions, and exchange opinions.

Communication 1.2: Students understand and interpret written and spoken language on a variety of topics.

Communication 1.3: Students present information, concepts, and ideas to an audience of listeners or readers on a variety of topics.

CORE INSTRUCTION

Warm-Up
- (5 min.) See Teaching **Gramática**, #1, p. 184.

Gramática en acción 1
- (20 min.) Present **Gramática**: *Preterite of* **-er** *and* **-ir** *verbs*, p. 184 using Teaching **Gramática**, #2–5, p. 184.
- (20 min.) Have students do Activities 11–13, pp. 184–185.

Wrap-Up
- (5 min.) Check answers to Activity 11.

OPTIONAL RESOURCES
- (10 min.) **Comunicación** (TE), p. 185

Practice Options
- *Lab Book*, pp. 56–57
- ***Cuaderno de vocabulario y gramática,*** pp. 56–58
- ***Cuaderno de actividades***, pp. 51–54 ▲ ● ■
- *Activities for Communication*, pp. 33–34 ▲ ■
- ***Cuaderno para hispanohablantes,*** Chapter 9 ■
- *Teaching Transparencies:* ***Vocabulario y gramática*** Answers, pp. 56–58 ▲ ● ■
- *Video Guide*, pp. 86–87 ▲ ● ■
- *Grammar Tutor for Students of Spanish*, Chapter 9 ● ■
- *Interactive Tutor* (Disc 2) or *DVD Tutor* (Disc 2) ▲ ● ■
- Online Practice, Chapter 9 (go.hrw.com, Keyword: EXP1B CH9)

▲ = Advanced Learners ◆ = Slower Pace Learners ● = Special Learning Needs ■ = Heritage Speakers

Holt Spanish 1B
Lesson Planner

Teacher's Name _____ Class _____ Date _____

CAPÍTULO 9

¡Festejemos!

DAY 7 50-MINUTE LESSON PLAN

STANDARDS FOR FOREIGN LANGUAGE LEARNING: DAY 7

Gramática en acción 1
Communication 1.1: Students engage in conversations, provide and obtain information, express feelings and emotions, and exchange opinions.
Communication 1.2: Students understand and interpret written and spoken language on a variety of topics.

Communication 1.3: Students present information, concepts, and ideas to an audience of listeners or readers on a variety of topics.

Warm-Up
- (5 min.) Have students do Bell Work 9.3, p. 186.

Gramática en acción 1
- (10 min.) Show **GramaVisión1,** Segment 1.
- (15 min.) Review preterite of **-er** and **-ir** verbs, p. 184.
- (15 min.) Have students do Activities 14–15, p. 185.

Wrap-Up
- (5 min.) Have students write preterite conjugation charts for **salir**, **asistir** and **comer**.

OPTIONAL RESOURCES
- (5 min.) See Slower Pace Learners, p. 185. ◆
- (5 min.) See Multiple Intelligences, p. 185. ◆

Practice Options
- *Lab Book,* pp. 56–57
- ***Cuaderno de vocabulario y gramática,*** pp. 56–58
- *Cuaderno de actividades,* pp. 51–54 ▲ ● ■
- *Activities for Communication,* pp. 33–34 ▲ ■
- *Cuaderno para hispanohablantes,* Chapter 9 ■
- *Teaching Transparencies:* Bell Work 9.3; *Vocabulario y gramática* Answers, pp. 56–58 ▲ ● ■
- *Video Guide,* pp. 86–87 ▲ ● ■
- *Grammar Tutor for Students of Spanish,* Chapter 9 ● ■
- *Interactive Tutor* (Disc 2) or *DVD Tutor* (Disc 2) ▲ ● ■
- Online Practice, Chapter 9 (go.hrw.com, Keyword: EXP1B CH9)

▲ = Advanced Learners   ◆ = Slower Pace Learners   ● = Special Learning Needs   ■ = Heritage Speakers

Holt Spanish 1B   Lesson Planner

Teacher's Name _____ Class _____ Date _____

¡Festejemos!

CAPÍTULO 9

DAY 8 50-MINUTE LESSON PLAN

STANDARDS FOR FOREIGN LANGUAGE LEARNING: DAY 8

Gramática en acción 1
Communication 1.1: Students engage in conversations, provide and obtain information, express feelings and emotions, and exchange opinions.
Communication 1.2: Students understand and interpret written and spoken language on a variety of topics.

Communication 1.3: Students present information, concepts, and ideas to an audience of listeners or readers on a variety of topics.

CORE INSTRUCTION

Warm-Up
- (5 min.) Have students use the phrases in Activity 13 to write sentences that tell whether or not they did those things last night.

Gramática en acción 1
- (5 min.) Show **GramaVisión 1,** Segment 2.
- (15 min.) Present **Gramática: Repaso,** *The preterite*, p. 186 using Teaching **Gramática,** p. 186.
- (10 min.) Play Audio CD 9, Tr. 2 for Activity 16, p. 186.
- (10 min.) Have students do Activities 17–18, pp. 186–187.

Wrap-Up
- (5 min.) Have pairs of students share the descriptions they wrote in Activity 18.

OPTIONAL RESOURCES
- (5 min.) See Advanced Learners, p. 187. ▲

Practice Options
- *Lab Book,* pp. 28, 56–57
- ***Cuaderno de vocabulario y gramática,*** pp. 56–58
- ***Cuaderno de actividades,*** pp. 51–54 ▲ ● ■
- *Activities for Communication,* pp. 33–34 ▲ ■
- ***Cuaderno para hispanohablantes,*** Chapter 9 ■
- *Teaching Transparencies:* **Vocabulario y gramática** Answers, pp. 56–58 ▲ ● ■
- *Video Guide,* pp. 86–87 ▲ ● ■
- *Grammar Tutor for Students of Spanish,* Chapter 9 ● ■
- *Interactive Tutor* (Disc 2) or *DVD Tutor* (Disc 2) ▲ ● ■
- Online Practice, Chapter 9 (go.hrw.com, Keyword: EXP1B CH9)

▲ = Advanced Learners ◆ = Slower Pace Learners ● = Special Learning Needs ■ = Heritage Speakers

Holt Spanish 1B — Lesson Planner

Teacher's Name _____ Class _____ Date _____

¡Festejemos!

CAPÍTULO 9

DAY 9 50-MINUTE LESSON PLAN

STANDARDS FOR FOREIGN LANGUAGE LEARNING: DAY 9

Gramática en acción 1

Communication 1.1: Students engage in conversations, provide and obtain information, express feelings and emotions, and exchange opinions.

Communication 1.2: Students understand and interpret written and spoken language on a variety of topics.

Communication 1.3: Students present information, concepts, and ideas to an audience of listeners or readers on a variety of topics.

CORE INSTRUCTION

Warm-Up
- (5 min.) Have students do Bell Work 9.4, p. 188.

Gramática en acción 1
- (10 min.) Review the preterite, p. 186.
- (10 min.) Have students do Activities 19–20, p. 187 using Special Learning Needs, p. 187. ●
- (10 min.) Show **GramaVisión 1,** Segment 3.
- (10 min.) Present **Gramática: pensar que** and **pensar** with infinitives, p. 188 using Teaching **Gramática,** p. 188.

Wrap-Up
- (5 min.) See Common Error Alert, p. 188.

OPTIONAL RESOURCES

Practice Options
- *Lab Book,* pp. 28, 56–57
- ***Cuaderno de vocabulario y gramática,*** pp. 56–58
- ***Cuaderno de actividades***, pp. 51–54 ▲ ● ■
- *Activities for Communication,* pp. 33–34 ▲ ■
- ***Cuaderno para hispanohablantes,*** Chapter 9 ■
- *Teaching Transparencies:* Bell Work 9.4; ***Vocabulario y gramática*** Answers, pp. 56–58 ▲ ● ■
- *Video Guide,* pp. 86–87 ▲ ● ■
- *Grammar Tutor for Students of Spanish,* Chapter 9 ● ■
- *Interactive Tutor* (Disc 2) or *DVD Tutor* (Disc 2) ▲ ● ■
- Online Practice, Chapter 9 (go.hrw.com, Keyword: EXP1B CH9)

▲ = Advanced Learners   ◆ = Slower Pace Learners   ● = Special Learning Needs   ■ = Heritage Speakers

Holt Spanish 1B   Lesson Planner

Teacher's Name _____ Class _____ Date _____

¡Festejemos!

CAPÍTULO 9

DAY 10 50-MINUTE LESSON PLAN

STANDARDS FOR FOREIGN LANGUAGE LEARNING: DAY 10

Gramática en acción 1

Communication 1.1: Students engage in conversations, provide and obtain information, express feelings and emotions, and exchange opinions.

Communication 1.2: Students understand and interpret written and spoken language on a variety of topics.

Communication 1.3: Students present information, concepts, and ideas to an audience of listeners or readers on a variety of topics.

Cultures 2.1: Students demonstrate an understanding of the relationship between the practices and perspectives of the culture studied.

Comparisons 4.2: Students demonstrate understanding of the concept of culture through comparisons of the cultures studied and their own.

CORE INSTRUCTION

Warm-Up
- (5 min.) Have students do Bell Work 9.5, p. 192.

Gramática en acción 1
- (10 min.) Review **pensar que** and **pensar** with infinitives, p. 188.
- (5 min.) Present **Nota cultural**, p. 188.
- (25 min.) Have students do Activities 21–23, pp. 188–189.

Wrap-Up
- (5 min.) Have students work with a partner to read aloud their responses to Activity 22. Remind students to study for **Prueba: Gramática 1**.

OPTIONAL RESOURCES
- (10 min.) Multiple Intelligences, p. 189
- (10 min.) **Comunicación** (TE), p. 189
- (5 min.) See Slower Pace Learners, p. 189. ◆

Practice Options
- *Lab Book,* pp. 56–57
- *Cuaderno de vocabulario y gramática,* pp. 56–58
- *Cuaderno de actividades,* pp. 51–54 ▲ ● ■
- *Activities for Communication,* pp. 33–34 ▲ ■
- *Cuaderno para hispanohablantes,* Chapter 9 ■
- *Teaching Transparencies:* Bell Work 9.5; *Vocabulario y gramática* Answers, pp. 56–58 ▲ ● ■
- *Video Guide,* pp. 86–87 ▲ ● ■
- *Grammar Tutor for Students of Spanish,* Chapter 9 ● ■
- *Interactive Tutor* (Disc 2) or *DVD Tutor* (Disc 2) ▲ ● ■
- Online Practice, Chapter 9 (go.hrw.com, Keyword: EXP1B CH9)

▲ = Advanced Learners   ◆ = Slower Pace Learners   ● = Special Learning Needs   ■ = Heritage Speakers

Holt Spanish 1B   Lesson Planner

Teacher's Name _____ Class _____ Date _____

¡Festejemos!

CAPÍTULO 9

DAY 11 50-MINUTE LESSON PLAN

STANDARDS FOR FOREIGN LANGUAGE LEARNING: DAY 11

Gramática en acción 1

Communication 1.1: Students engage in conversations, provide and obtain information, express feelings and emotions, and exchange opinions.
Communication 1.2: Students understand and interpret written and spoken language on a variety of topics.
Communication 1.3: Students present information, concepts, and ideas to an audience of listeners or readers on a variety of topics.

Cultures 2.1: Students demonstrate an understanding of the relationship between the practices and perspectives of the culture studied.
Comparisons 4.2: Students demonstrate understanding of the concept of culture through comparisons of the cultures studied and their own.

CORE INSTRUCTION

Warm-Up
- (20 min.) Review **Gramática en acción 1**, pp. 184–189.

Gramática en acción 1

Assess
- (20 min.) Give **Prueba: Gramática 1**.

OPTIONAL RESOURCES
- (10 min.) Preview **Cultura**, pp. 190–191.

Assessment Options
- *Assessment Program:* **Prueba: Gramática 1**, pp. 79–80
- *Assessment Program:* **Prueba: Aplicación 1**, pp. 81–82
- *Assessment Program:* Alternative Assessment Guide, pp. 244, 252, 260 ▲●■
- *Audio CD 9*, Tr. 15
- Test Generator
- Online Practice, Chapter 9 (go.hrw.com, Keyword: EXP1B CH9)

▲ = Advanced Learners   ◆ = Slower Pace Learners   ● = Special Learning Needs   ■ = Heritage Speakers

Holt Spanish 1B   Lesson Planner

Teacher's Name _____ Class _____ Date _____

¡Festejemos!

CAPÍTULO 9

DAY 12 50-MINUTE LESSON PLAN

STANDARDS FOR FOREIGN LANGUAGE LEARNING: DAY 12

Cultura

Communication 1.2: Students understand and interpret written and spoken language on a variety of topics.

Cultures 2.1: Students demonstrate an understanding of the relationship between the practices and perspectives of the culture studied.

Comparisons 4.1: Students demonstrate understanding of the nature of language through comparisons of the language studied and their own.

Comparisons 4.2: Students demonstrate understanding of the concept of culture through comparisons of the cultures studied and their own.

Communities 5.1: Students use the language both within and beyond the school setting.

CORE INSTRUCTION

Warm-Up
- (5 min.) See Slower Pace Learners, p. 191. ◆

Cultura
- (10 min.) See Map Activities, p. 190.
- (25 min.) Present **Comparaciones**, pp. 190–191. See Teaching **Cultura**, p. 190.
- (5 min.) Present and assign **Comunidad**, p. 191.

Wrap-Up
- (5 min.) See Heritage Speakers, p. 191. ■

OPTIONAL RESOURCES
- (5 min.) Comparing and Contrasting, p. 191
- (5 min.) Language to Language, p. 191
- (5 min.) Multiple Intelligences, p. 191

Practice Options
- *Lab Book,* p. 57
- ***Cuaderno de actividades,*** p. 55 ▲ ● ■
- ***Cuaderno para hispanohablantes,*** pp. 69–76 ■
- *Teaching Transparencies:* **Mapa** 4 ▲ ● ■
- *Video Guide,* pp. 83, 87 ▲ ● ■
- *Interactive Tutor* (Disc 2) or *DVD Tutor* (Disc 2) ▲ ● ■
- Online Practice, Chapter 9 (go.hrw.com, Keyword: EXP1B CH9)

▲ = Advanced Learners   ◆ = Slower Pace Learners   ● = Special Learning Needs   ■ = Heritage Speakers

Holt Spanish 1B   Lesson Planner

Teacher's Name _____ Class _____ Date _____

¡Festejemos!

CAPÍTULO 9

DAY 13 50-MINUTE LESSON PLAN

STANDARDS FOR FOREIGN LANGUAGE LEARNING: DAY 13

Vocabulario en acción 2
Communication 1.2: Students understand and interpret written and spoken language on a variety of topics.
Communication 1.3: Students present information, concepts, and ideas to an audience of listeners or readers on a variety of topics.

Comparisons 4.1: Students demonstrate understanding of the nature of language through comparisons of the language studied and their own.
Comparisons 4.2: Students demonstrate understanding of the concept of culture through comparisons of the cultures studied and their own.

CORE INSTRUCTION

Warm-Up
- (5 min.) Have students think of infinitives that might be useful to use with the pictures on pp. 192–193.

Vocabulario en acción 2
- (5 min.) Show **ExpresaVisión,** Ch. 9.
- (30 min.) Present **Vocabulario en acción 2,** pp. 192–193 using Teaching **Vocabulario,** p. 192.
- (5 min.) Present **Nota cultural,** p. 194.

Wrap-Up
- (5 min.) Present Language Note and **También se puede decir,** p. 193.

OPTIONAL RESOURCES
- (5 min.) TPR, p. 193
- (10 min.) Multiple Intelligences, p. 193
- (10 min.) Advanced Learners, p. 193 ▲

Practice Options
- *Lab Book,* pp. 58–59
- ***Cuaderno de vocabulario y gramática,*** pp. 59–61
- *Activities for Communication,* pp. 35–36 ▲ ■
- ***Cuaderno para hispanohablantes,*** Chapter 9 ■
- *Teaching Transparencies:* **Vocabulario** 9.3, 9.4; ***Vocabulario y gramática*** Answers, pp. 59–61 ▲ ● ■
- *Video Guide,* pp. 88–89 ▲ ● ■
- *TPR Storytelling Book,* pp. 50–51 ▲ ●
- *Interactive Tutor* (Disc 2) or *DVD Tutor* (Disc 2) ▲ ● ■
- Online Practice, Chapter 9 (go.hrw.com, Keyword: EXP1B CH9)

▲ = Advanced Learners   ◆ = Slower Pace Learners   ● = Special Learning Needs   ■ = Heritage Speakers

Holt Spanish 1B   Lesson Planner

Teacher's Name _____ Class _____ Date _____

¡Festejemos!

CAPÍTULO 9

DAY 14 50-MINUTE LESSON PLAN

STANDARDS FOR FOREIGN LANGUAGE LEARNING: DAY 14

Vocabulario en acción 2

Communication 1.2: Students understand and interpret written and spoken language on a variety of topics.

Communication 1.3: Students present information, concepts, and ideas to an audience of listeners or readers on a variety of topics.

Comparisons 4.1: Students demonstrate understanding of the nature of language through comparisons of the language studied and their own.

Comparisons 4.2: Students demonstrate understanding of the concept of culture through comparisons of the cultures studied and their own.

CORE INSTRUCTION

Warm-Up
- (5 min.) Present Products and Perspectives: **Piñatas**, p. 195.

Vocabulario en acción 2
- (15 min.) Review **Vocabulario 2** and **¡Exprésate!**, pp. 192–193.
- (25 min.) Have students do Activities 24–27, pp. 194–195.

Wrap-Up
- (5 min.) Check answers for Activity 26 and write them on the board, have students make corrections as needed.

OPTIONAL RESOURCES
- (5 min.) Multicultural Link, p. 194
- (5 min.) Heritage Speakers, p. 194 ■
- (10 min.) Game, p. 194
- (5 min.) Products and Perspectives, p. 195
- (10 min.) **Comunicación** (TE), p. 195
- (5 min.) Multiple Intelligences, p. 195

Practice Options
- *Lab Book,* pp. 58–59
- **Cuaderno de vocabulario y gramática,** pp. 59–61
- *Activities for Communication,* pp. 35–36 ▲ ■
- **Cuaderno para hispanohablantes,** Chapter 9 ■
- *Teaching Transparencies:* **Vocabulario** 9.3, 9.4; *Vocabulario y gramática* Answers, pp. 59–61 ▲ ● ■
- *Video Guide,* pp. 88–89 ▲ ● ■
- *TPR Storytelling Book,* pp. 50–51 ▲ ●
- *Interactive Tutor* (Disc 2) or *DVD Tutor* (Disc 2) ▲ ● ■
- Online Practice, Chapter 9 (go.hrw.com, Keyword: EXP1B CH9)

▲ = Advanced Learners   ◆ = Slower Pace Learners   ● = Special Learning Needs   ■ = Heritage Speakers

Holt Spanish 1B

Lesson Planner

Teacher's Name _____ Class _____ Date _____

¡Festejemos!

CAPÍTULO 9

DAY 15 50-MINUTE LESSON PLAN

> **STANDARDS FOR FOREIGN LANGUAGE LEARNING: DAY 15**
>
> **Vocabulario en acción 2**
> **Communication 1.2:** Students understand and interpret written and spoken language on a variety of topics.
>
> **Communication 1.3:** Students present information, concepts, and ideas to an audience of listeners or readers on a variety of topics.

CORE INSTRUCTION

Warm-Up
- (5 min.) Have students do Bell Work 9.6, p. 198.

Vocabulario en acción 2
- (15 min.) Have students do Activity 28, p. 195.
- (15 min.) See Teaching ¡Exprésate!, p. 196.
- (10 min.) Play Audio CD 9, Tr. 6 for Activity 29, p. 196.

OPTIONAL RESOURCES
- (5 min.) See Advanced Learners, p. 195. ▲
- (5 min.) Special Learning Needs, p. 197 ●
- (5 min.) Advanced Learners, p. 197 ▲

Practice Options
- *Lab Book,* pp. 25, 58–59
- **Cuaderno de vocabulario y gramática,** pp. 59–61
- *Activities for Communication,* pp. 35–36 ▲ ■
- **Cuaderno para hispanohablantes,** Chapter 9 ■
- *Teaching Transparencies:* Bell Work 9.6; **Vocabulario** 9.3, 9.4; **Vocabulario y gramática** Answers, pp. 59–61 ▲ ● ■
- *Video Guide,* pp. 88–89 ▲ ● ■
- *TPR Storytelling Book,* pp. 50–51 ▲ ●
- *Interactive Tutor* (Disc 2) or *DVD Tutor* (Disc 2) ▲ ● ■
- Online Practice, Chapter 9 (go.hrw.com, Keyword: EXP1B CH9)

▲ = Advanced Learners   ♦ = Slower Pace Learners   ● = Special Learning Needs   ■ = Heritage Speakers

Holt Spanish 1B

Lesson Planner

Teacher's Name _____ Class _____ Date _____

¡Festejemos!

CAPÍTULO 9

DAY 16 50-MINUTE LESSON PLAN

STANDARDS FOR FOREIGN LANGUAGE LEARNING: DAY 16

Vocabulario en acción 2

Communication 1.1: Students engage in conversations, provide and obtain information, express feelings and emotions, and exchange opinions.

Communication 1.2: Students understand and interpret written and spoken language on a variety of topics.

Communication 1.3: Students present information, concepts, and ideas to an audience of listeners or readers on a variety of topics.

CORE INSTRUCTION

Warm-Up
- (5 min.) Have students share the cards they created for the homework assignment.

Vocabulario en acción 2
- (10 min.) Review **¡Exprésate!,** p. 196.
- (30 min.) Have students do Activities 30–34, pp. 196–197.

Wrap-Up
- (5 min.) See **Más práctica,** p. 197. Remind students to study for **Prueba: Vocabulario 2.**

OPTIONAL RESOURCES
- (5 min.) Extension, p. 197
- (10 min.) **Comunicación** (TE), p. 197

Practice Options
- *Lab Book,* pp. 25, 58–59
- ***Cuaderno de vocabulario y gramática,*** pp. 59–61
- *Activities for Communication,* pp. 35–36 ▲ ■
- ***Cuaderno para hispanohablantes,*** Chapter 9 ■
- *Teaching Transparencies:* **Vocabulario** 9.3, 9.4; ***Vocabulario y gramática*** Answers, pp. 59–61 ▲ ● ■
- *Video Guide,* pp. 88–89 ▲ ● ■
- *TPR Storytelling Book,* pp. 50–51 ▲ ●
- *Interactive Tutor* (Disc 2) or *DVD Tutor* (Disc 2) ▲ ● ■
- Online Practice, Chapter 9 (go.hrw.com, Keyword: EXP1B CH9)

▲ = Advanced Learners ◆ = Slower Pace Learners ● = Special Learning Needs ■ = Heritage Speakers

Holt Spanish 1B   Lesson Planner

Teacher's Name _____ Class _____ Date _____

¡Festejemos!

CAPÍTULO 9

DAY 17 50-MINUTE LESSON PLAN

STANDARDS FOR FOREIGN LANGUAGE LEARNING: DAY 17

Vocabulario en acción 2

Communication 1.1: Students engage in conversations, provide and obtain information, express feelings and emotions, and exchange opinions.

Communication 1.2: Students understand and interpret written and spoken language on a variety of topics.

Communication 1.3: Students present information, concepts, and ideas to an audience of listeners or readers on a variety of topics.

Comparisons 4.1: Students demonstrate understanding of the nature of language through comparisons of the language studied and their own.

Comparisons 4.2: Students demonstrate understanding of the concept of culture through comparisons of the cultures studied and their own.

CORE INSTRUCTION

Warm-Up
- (20 min.) Review **Vocabulario en acción 2**, pp. 192–197.

Vocabulario en acción 2

Assess
- (20 min.) Give **Prueba: Vocabulario 2.**

OPTIONAL RESOURCES
- (10 min.) Preview **Gramática en acción 2**, pp. 198–203.

Assessment Options
- *Assessment Program:* **Prueba: Vocabulario 2**, pp. 83–84
- *Assessment Program:* Alternative Assessment Guide, pp. 244, 252, 260 ▲●■
- Test Generator
- Online Practice, Chapter 9 (go.hrw.com, Keyword: EXP1B CH9)

▲ = Advanced Learners   ◆ = Slower Pace Learners   ● = Special Learning Needs   ■ = Heritage Speakers

Holt Spanish 1B

Lesson Planner

Teacher's Name _____ Class _____ Date _____

¡Festejemos!

CAPÍTULO 9

DAY 18 50-MINUTE LESSON PLAN

STANDARDS FOR FOREIGN LANGUAGE LEARNING: DAY 18

Gramática en acción 2

Communication 1.1: Students engage in conversations, provide and obtain information, express feelings and emotions, and exchange opinions.

Communication 1.2: Students understand and interpret written and spoken language on a variety of topics.

Communication 1.3: Students present information, concepts, and ideas to an audience of listeners or readers on a variety of topics.

Communities 5.2: Students show evidence of becoming life–long learners by using the language for personal enjoyment and enrichment.

CORE INSTRUCTION

Warm-Up
- (5 min.) See Teaching **Gramática**, #1, p. 198.

Gramática en acción 2
- (5 min.) Show **GramaVisión 5,** Segment 4
- (20 min.) Present **Gramática:** *Direct object pronouns,* p. 198 using Teaching **Gramática,** #2–3 p. 198.
- (15 min.) Have students do Activities 35–37, pp. 198–199.

Wrap-Up
- (5 min.) Have students read through Activity 36 with a partner.

OPTIONAL RESOURCES
- (5 min.) Career Path, p. 199
- (5 min.) See Special Learning Needs, p. 199. ●
- (5 min.) See Slower Pace Learners, p. 199. ◆

Practice Options
- *Lab Book,* pp. 58–59
- *Cuaderno de vocabulario y gramática,* pp. 62–64
- *Cuaderno de actividades,* pp. 56–59 ▲ ● ■
- *Activities for Communication,* pp. 35–36 ▲ ■
- *Cuaderno para hispanohablantes,* Chapter 9 ■
- *Teaching Transparencies:* **Vocabulario y gramática** Answers, pp. 62–64 ▲ ● ■
- *Video Guide,* pp. 88–89 ▲ ● ■
- *Grammar Tutor for Students of Spanish,* Chapter 9 ● ■
- *Interactive Tutor* (Disc 2) or *DVD Tutor* (Disc 2) ▲ ● ■
- Online Practice, Chapter 9 (go.hrw.com, Keyword: EXP1B CH9)

▲ = Advanced Learners   ◆ = Slower Pace Learners   ● = Special Learning Needs   ■ = Heritage Speakers

Holt Spanish 1B   Lesson Planner

Teacher's Name _____ Class _____ Date _____

CAPÍTULO 9

¡Festejemos!

DAY 19 50-MINUTE LESSON PLAN

STANDARDS FOR FOREIGN LANGUAGE LEARNING: DAY 19

Gramática en acción 2

Communication 1.1: Students engage in conversations, provide and obtain information, express feelings and emotions, and exchange opinions.
Communication 1.2: Students understand and interpret written and spoken language on a variety of topics.
Communication 1.3: Students present information, concepts, and ideas to an audience of listeners or readers on a variety of topics.
Cultures 2.1: Students demonstrate an understanding of the relationship between the practices and perspectives of the culture studied.
Cultures 2.2: Students demonstrate an understanding of the relationship between the products and perspectives of the culture studied.
Comparisons 4.2: Students demonstrate understanding of the concept of culture through comparisons of the cultures studied and their own.
Communities 5.2: Students show evidence of becoming life–long learners by using the language for personal enjoyment and enrichment.

CORE INSTRUCTION

Warm-Up
- (5 min.) Have students do Bell Work 9.7, p. 200.

Gramática en acción 2
- (10 min.) Review direct object pronouns, p. 198.
- (10 min.) Have students do Activity 38, p. 199.
- (5 min.) Present **Nota cultural**, p. 199.
- (15 min.) Present **Gramática: conocer** and *personal* **a**, p. 200 using Teaching **Gramática**, p. 200.

Wrap-Up
- (5 min.) Ask students if they know certain people in the school. Have them respond using **conocer** and the direct object pronoun.

OPTIONAL RESOURCES
- (10 min.) **Comunicación** (TE), p. 199
- (5 min.) Slower Pace Learners, p. 199 ◆
- (5 min.) Multiple Intelligences, p. 201

Practice Options
- *Lab Book*, pp. 58–59
- *Cuaderno de vocabulario y gramática*, pp. 62–64
- *Cuaderno de actividades*, pp. 56–59 ▲ ● ■
- *Activities for Communication*, pp. 35–36 ▲ ■
- *Cuaderno para hispanohablantes*, Chapter 9 ■
- *Teaching Transparencies:* Bell Work 9.7; *Vocabulario y gramática* Answers, pp. 62–64 ▲ ● ■
- *Video Guide*, pp. 88–89 ▲ ● ■
- *Grammar Tutor for Students of Spanish*, Chapter 9 ● ■
- *Interactive Tutor* (Disc 2) or *DVD Tutor* (Disc 2) ▲ ● ■
- Online Practice, Chapter 9 (go.hrw.com, Keyword: EXP1B CH9)

▲ = Advanced Learners ◆ = Slower Pace Learners ● = Special Learning Needs ■ = Heritage Speakers

Holt Spanish 1B

Lesson Planner

Teacher's Name _____ Class _____ Date _____

¡Festejemos!

CAPÍTULO 9

DAY 20 50-MINUTE LESSON PLAN

STANDARDS FOR FOREIGN LANGUAGE LEARNING: DAY 20

Gramática en acción 2

Communication 1.1: Students engage in conversations, provide and obtain information, express feelings and emotions, and exchange opinions.

Communication 1.2: Students understand and interpret written and spoken language on a variety of topics.

Cultures 2.1: Students demonstrate an understanding of the relationship between the practices and perspectives of the culture studied.

Cultures 2.2: Students demonstrate an understanding of the relationship between the products and perspectives of the culture studied.

Comparisons 4.2: Students demonstrate understanding of the concept of culture through comparisons of the cultures studied and their own.

Communities 5.2: Students show evidence of becoming life–long learners by using the language for personal enjoyment and enrichment

CORE INSTRUCTION

Warm-Up
- (5 min.) Have students do Bell Work 9.8, p. 202.

Gramática en acción 2
- (10 min.) Show **GramaVisión 2,** Segment 5.
- (X min.) Review **Conocer** and personal **a,** p. 200.
- (20 min.) Have students do Activities 39–42, pp. 200–201.

Wrap-Up
- (5 min.) Have pairs of students practice the conversation they wrote in Activity 40.

OPTIONAL RESOURCES
- (5 min.) See Advanced Learners, p. 201. ▲

Practice Options
- *Lab Book,* pp. 58–59
- *Cuaderno de vocabulario y gramática,* pp. 62–64
- *Cuaderno de actividades,* pp. 56–59 ▲●■
- *Activities for Communication,* pp. 35–36 ▲■
- *Cuaderno para hispanohablantes,* Chapter 9 ■
- *Teaching Transparencies:* Bell Work 9.8; *Vocabulario y gramática* Answers, pp. 62–64 ▲●■
- *Video Guide,* pp. 88–89 ▲●■
- *Grammar Tutor for Students of Spanish,* Chapter 9 ●■
- *Interactive Tutor* (Disc 2) or *DVD Tutor* (Disc 2) ▲●■
- Online Practice, Chapter 9 (go.hrw.com, Keyword: EXP1B CH9)

▲ = Advanced Learners   ◆ = Slower Pace Learners   ● = Special Learning Needs   ■ = Heritage Speakers

Holt Spanish 1B   Lesson Planner

Teacher's Name _____ Class _____ Date _____

¡Festejemos!

CAPÍTULO 9

DAY 21 50-MINUTE LESSON PLAN

STANDARDS FOR FOREIGN LANGUAGE LEARNING: DAY 21

Gramática en acción 2
Communication 1.1: Students engage in conversations, provide and obtain information, express feelings and emotions, and exchange opinions.

Communication 1.2: Students understand and interpret written and spoken language on a variety of topics.

CORE INSTRUCTION

Warm-Up
- (5 min.) Review answers from Activity 41, p. 201.

Gramática en acción 2
- (10 min.) Show **GramaVisión 2,** Segment 6.
- (20 min.) Present **Gramática:** *Present progressive,* p. 202 using Teaching **Gramática,** p. 202.
- (10 min.) Play Audio CD 9, Tr. 7 for Activity 43, p. 202.

Wrap-Up
- (5 min.) Ask several students **¿Qué estás haciendo?** and have them answer using the present progressive.

OPTIONAL RESOURCES
- (10 min.) **Comunicación** (TE), p. 203

Practice Options
- *Lab Book,* pp. 58–59
- ***Cuaderno de vocabulario y gramática,*** pp. 62–64
- ***Cuaderno de actividades,*** pp. 56–59 ▲●■
- *Activities for Communication,* pp. 35–36 ▲■
- ***Cuaderno para hispanohablantes,*** Chapter 9 ■
- *Teaching Transparencies: **Vocabulario y gramática*** Answers, pp. 62–64 ▲●■
- *Video Guide,* pp. 88–89 ▲●■
- *Grammar Tutor for Students of Spanish,* Chapter 9 ●■
- *Interactive Tutor* (Disc 2) or *DVD Tutor* (Disc 2) ▲●■
- Online Practice, Chapter 9 (go.hrw.com, Keyword: EXP1B CH9)

▲ = Advanced Learners   ◆ = Slower Pace Learners   ● = Special Learning Needs   ■ = Heritage Speakers

Holt Spanish 1B   Lesson Planner

Teacher's Name _____ Class _____ Date _____

¡Festejemos!

CAPÍTULO 9

DAY 22 50-MINUTE LESSON PLAN

STANDARDS FOR FOREIGN LANGUAGE LEARNING: DAY 22

Gramática en acción 2
Communication 1.1: Students engage in conversations, provide and obtain information, express feelings and emotions, and exchange opinions.

Communication 1.2: Students understand and interpret written and spoken language on a variety of topics.

CORE INSTRUCTION

Warm-Up
- (5 min.) Have students look around the room and say what several people are doing, using the present progressive.

Gramática en acción 2
- (20 min.) Have students do Activities 44–46, p. 203.
- (20 min.) Review **Gramática en acción 2,** pp. 198–203.

Wrap-Up
- (5 min.) Have students check answers to Activity 44 with a partner. Remind students to study for **Prueba: Gramática 2.**

OPTIONAL RESOURCES
- (5 min.) Advanced Learners, p. 203 ▲
- (5 min.) Special Learning Needs, p. 203 ●

Practice Options
- *Lab Book,* pp. 58–59
- *Cuaderno de vocabulario y gramática,* pp. 62–64
- *Cuaderno de actividades,* pp. 56–59 ▲●■
- *Activities for Communication,* pp. 35–36 ▲■
- *Cuaderno para hispanohablantes,* Chapter 9 ■
- *Teaching Transparencies: Vocabulario y gramática* Answers, pp. 62–64 ▲●■
- *Video Guide,* pp. 88–89 ▲●■
- *Grammar Tutor for Students of Spanish,* Chapter 9 ●■
- *Interactive Tutor* (Disc 2) or *DVD Tutor* (Disc 2) ▲●■
- Online Practice, Chapter 9 (go.hrw.com, Keyword: EXP1B CH9)

▲ = Advanced Learners   ◆ = Slower Pace Learners   ● = Special Learning Needs   ■ = Heritage Speakers

Holt Spanish 1B — Lesson Planner

Teacher's Name _____ Class _____ Date _____

CAPÍTULO
9

¡Festejemos!

DAY 23 50-MINUTE LESSON PLAN

STANDARDS FOR FOREIGN LANGUAGE LEARNING: DAY 23

Gramática en acción 2

Communication 1.1: Students engage in conversations, provide and obtain information, express feelings and emotions, and exchange opinions.
Communication 1.2: Students understand and interpret written and spoken language on a variety of topics.
Cultures 2.1: Students demonstrate an understanding of the relationship between the practices and perspectives of the culture studied.
Cultures 2.2: Students demonstrate an understanding of the relationship between the products and perspectives of the culture studied.
Comparisons 4.2: Students demonstrate understanding of the concept of culture through comparisons of the cultures studied and their own.

Communities 5.2: Students show evidence of becoming life–long learners by using the language for personal enjoyment and enrichment

Conexiones culturales

Communication 1.2: Students understand and interpret written and spoken language on a variety of topics.
Cultures 2.1: Students demonstrate an understanding of the relationship between the practices and perspectives of the culture studied.
Comparisons 4.2: Students demonstrate understanding of the concept of culture through comparisons of the cultures studied and their own.

CORE INSTRUCTION

Warm-Up
- (5 min.) Review **Gramática en acción 2,** pp. 198–203.

Gramática en acción 2

Assess
- (20 min.) Give **Prueba: Gramática 2.**

Conexiones culturales
- (20 min.) Present **Conexiones culturales,** pp. 204–205 using Teaching **Conexiones culturales,** #1–2, p. 204.

Wrap-Up
- (5 min.) Have students share any personal experiences with environmental activities.

OPTIONAL RESOURCES
- (5 min.) Multiple Intelligences, p. 205

Practice Options
- *Interactive Tutor* (Disc 2) or *DVD Tutor* (Disc 2) ▲ ● ■
- Online Practice, Chapter 9 (go.hrw.com, Keyword: EXP1B CH9)

Assessment Options
- *Assessment Program:* **Prueba: Gramática 2,** pp. 85–86
- *Assessment Program:* **Prueba: Aplicación 2,** pp. 87–88
- *Assessment Program:* Alternative Assessment Guide, pp. 244, 252, 260 ▲ ● ■
- *Audio CD 9,* Tr. 16
- Test Generator

▲ = Advanced Learners   ◆ = Slower Pace Learners   ● = Special Learning Needs   ■ = Heritage Speakers

Teacher's Name _____ Class _____ Date _____

¡Festejemos!

CAPÍTULO 9

DAY 24 50-MINUTE LESSON PLAN

STANDARDS FOR FOREIGN LANGUAGE LEARNING: DAY 24

Conexiones culturales

Communication 1.2: Students understand and interpret written and spoken language on a variety of topics.
Cultures 2.1: Students demonstrate an understanding of the relationship between the practices and perspectives of the culture studied.
Comparisons 4.2: Students demonstrate understanding of the concept of culture through comparisons of the cultures studied and their own.

Novela en video

Communication 1.2: Students understand and interpret written and spoken language on a variety of topics.

Communication 1.3: Students present information, concepts, and ideas to an audience of listeners or readers on a variety of topics.
Connections 3.2: Students acquire information and recognize the distinctive viewpoints that are only available through the foreign language and its cultures.
Comparisons 4.2: Students demonstrate understanding of the concept of culture through comparisons of the cultures studied and their own.

CORE INSTRUCTION

Warm-Up
- (5 min.) See Teaching **Conexiones culturales**, #3, p. 204.

Conexiones culturales
- (20 min.) Present **Conexiones culturales**, pp. 204–205. See Teaching **Conexiones culturales**, #4–6, p. 204.

Novela en video
- (15 min.) See Teaching **Novela en video,** #1–2, p. 206.
- (5 min.) See Thinking Critically, p. 207.

Wrap-Up
- (5 min.) See Gestures, p. 206.

OPTIONAL RESOURCES
- (5 min.) Music Link, p. 205
- (5 min.) Advanced Learners, p. 205 ▲
- (5 min.) Visual Learners, p. 206
- (5 min.) Comparing and Contrasting, p. 207
- (5 min.) Culminating Project, p. 208

Practice Options
- *Lab Book,* p. 60
- *Video Guide,* pp. 84, 90 ▲ ● ■
- *Interactive Tutor* (Disc 2) or *DVD Tutor* (Disc 2) ▲ ● ■
- Online Practice, Chapter 9 (go.hrw.com, Keyword: EXP1B CH9)

▲ = Advanced Learners   ◆ = Slower Pace Learners   ● = Special Learning Needs   ■ = Heritage Speakers

Holt Spanish 1B — Lesson Planner

Teacher's Name _____ Class _____ Date _____

¡Festejemos!

CAPÍTULO 9

DAY 25 50-MINUTE LESSON PLAN

STANDARDS FOR FOREIGN LANGUAGE LEARNING: DAY 25

Novela en video

Communication 1.2: Students understand and interpret written and spoken language on a variety of topics.
Communication 1.3: Students present information, concepts, and ideas to an audience of listeners or readers on a variety of topics.
Connections 3.2: Students acquire information and recognize the distinctive viewpoints that are only available through the foreign language and its cultures.
Comparisons 4.2: Students demonstrate understanding of the concept of culture through comparisons of the cultures studied and their own.

Leamos y escribamos

Communication 1.1: Students engage in conversations, provide and obtain information, express feelings and emotions, and exchange opinions.

Communication 1.2: Students understand and interpret written and spoken language on a variety of topics.
Communication 1.3: Students present information, concepts, and ideas to an audience of listeners or readers on a variety of topics.
Cultures 2.1: Students demonstrate an understanding of the relationship between the practices and perspectives of the culture studied.
Connections 3.2: Students acquire information and recognize the distinctive viewpoints that are only available through the foreign language and its cultures.
Comparisons 4.2: Students demonstrate understanding of the concept of culture through comparisons of the cultures studied and their own.

CORE INSTRUCTION

Warm-Up
- (5 min.) See Thinking Critically, p. 208.

Novela en video
- (5 min.) Play **VideoNovela,** Ch. 9.
- (15 min.) See Teaching **Novela en video,** #3, p. 206.

Leamos y escribamos
- (20 min.) Present **Leamos y escribamos,** pp. 210–211 using Teaching **Leamos,** p. 210.

Wrap-Up
- (5 min.) See Activity C, p. 211.

OPTIONAL RESOURCES
- (5 min.) **Más práctica,** p. 209
- (5 min.) Slower Pace Learners, p. 209 ◆
- (10 min.) Multiple Intelligences, p. 209
- (5 min.) Applying the Strategies, p. 210
- (5 min.) Slower Pace Learners, p. 211 ◆
- (5 min.) Special Learning Needs, p. 211 ●

Practice Options
- *Cuaderno de actividades,* pp. 60 ▲ ● ■
- *Cuaderno para hispanohablantes,* pp. 69–76 ■
- Reading Strategies and Skills Handbook, Chapter 9 ▲ ● ■
- *¡Lee conmigo!* Level 1 Reader ▲ ■
- *Interactive Tutor* (Disc 2) or *DVD Tutor* (Disc 2) ▲ ● ■
- Online Practice, Chapter 9 (go.hrw.com, Keyword: EXP1B CH9)

▲ = Advanced Learners   ◆ = Slower Pace Learners   ● = Special Learning Needs   ■ = Heritage Speakers

Holt Spanish 1B   Lesson Planner

Teacher's Name _____ Class _____ Date _____

¡Festejemos!

CAPÍTULO 9

DAY 26 50-MINUTE LESSON PLAN

STANDARDS FOR FOREIGN LANGUAGE LEARNING: DAY 26

Leamos y escribamos
Communication 1.1: Students engage in conversations, provide and obtain information, express feelings and emotions, and exchange opinions.
Communication 1.2: Students understand and interpret written and spoken language on a variety of topics.
Communication 1.3: Students present information, concepts, and ideas to an audience of listeners or readers on a variety of topics.

Cultures 2.1: Students demonstrate an understanding of the relationship between the practices and perspectives of the culture studied.
Connections 3.2: Students acquire information and recognize the distinctive viewpoints that are only available through the foreign language and its cultures.
Comparisons 4.2: Students demonstrate understanding of the concept of culture through comparisons of the cultures studied and their own.

CORE INSTRUCTION

Warm-Up
- (5 min.) Show students the rubric you will use to assess the writing assignment.

Leamos y escribamos
- (40 min.) Present **Taller del escritor**, p. 211 using Teaching **Escribamos,** p. 210.

Wrap-Up
- (5 min.) See Process Writing, p. 211.

OPTIONAL RESOURCES
- (10 min.) See Slower Pace Learners, p. 211.
- (10 min.) See Special Learning Needs, p. 211.

Practice Options
- *Cuaderno de actividades*, pp. 60 ▲●■
- *Cuaderno para hispanohablantes,* pp. 69–765 ■
- Reading Strategies and Skills Handbook, Chapter 9 ▲●■
- *¡Lee conmigo!* Level 1 Reader ▲■
- *Interactive Tutor* (Disc 2) or *DVD Tutor* (Disc 2) ▲●■
- Online Practice, Chapter 9 (go.hrw.com, Keyword: EXP1B CH9)

▲ = Advanced Learners   ◆ = Slower Pace Learners   ● = Special Learning Needs   ■ = Heritage Speakers

Holt Spanish 1B   Lesson Planner

Teacher's Name _____ Class _____ Date _____

¡Festejemos!

CAPÍTULO 9

DAY 27 50-MINUTE LESSON PLAN

STANDARDS FOR FOREIGN LANGUAGE LEARNING: DAY 27

Repaso

Communication 1.2: Students understand and interpret written and spoken language on a variety of topics.

Communication 1.3: Students present information, concepts, and ideas to an audience of listeners or readers on a variety of topics.

Cultures 2.1: Students demonstrate an understanding of the relationship between the practices and perspectives of the culture studied.

Cultures 2.2: Students demonstrate an understanding of the relationship between the products and perspectives of the culture studied.

CORE INSTRUCTION

Warm-Up
- (15 min.) See Fold-n-Learn, p. 212.

Repaso
- (40 min.) Have students do Activities 1–5, pp. 212–213.

Wrap-Up
- (5 min.) Have students check answers to Activities 2 and 3 with a partner.

OPTIONAL RESOURCES
- (10 min.) Reteaching, p. 212

Practice Options
- *Lab Book*, pp. 30, 59
- *Activities for Communication*, pp. 51, 71–72 ▲ ■
- *Teaching Transparencies:* **Situación, Capítulo 9**; Picture Stories, Chapter 9 ▲ ● ■
- *Video Guide*, pp. 83, 89 ▲ ● ■
- *TPR Storytelling Book*, pp. 50–51 ▲ ●
- *Interactive Tutor* (Disc 2) or *DVD Tutor* (Disc 2) ▲ ● ■
- Online Practice, Chapter 9 (go.hrw.com, Keyword: EXP1B CH9)

▲ = Advanced Learners ◆ = Slower Pace Learners ● = Special Learning Needs ■ = Heritage Speakers

Holt Spanish 1B   Lesson Planner

Copyright © by Holt, Rinehart and Winston. All rights reserved.

Teacher's Name _____ Class _____ Date _____

¡Festejemos!

CAPÍTULO
9

DAY 28 50-MINUTE LESSON PLAN

STANDARDS FOR FOREIGN LANGUAGE LEARNING: DAY 28

Repaso

Communication 1.2: Students understand and interpret written and spoken language on a variety of topics.

Communication 1.3: Students present information, concepts, and ideas to an audience of listeners or readers on a variety of topics.

Cultures 2.1: Students demonstrate an understanding of the relationship between the practices and perspectives of the culture studied.

Cultures 2.2: Students demonstrate an understanding of the relationship between the products and perspectives of the culture studied.

CORE INSTRUCTION

Warm-Up
- (5 min.) Discuss answers to Activity 5, p. 213.

Repaso
- (10 min.) Play Audio CD 9, Tr. 10 for Activity 6, p. 213.
- (10 min.) Have students do Activity 7, p. 213.
- (10 min.) Play Game, p. 215.
- (10 min.) Play Audio CD 9, Tr. 11–13 for **Letra y sonido,** p. 214.

Wrap-Up
- (5 min.) Go over **Repaso de gramática** 1 and 2, p. 214. Remind students of upcoming Chapter Test.

OPTIONAL RESOURCES
- (5 min.) Teacher to Teacher, p. 214

Practice Options
- *Lab Book,* pp. 30, 59
- *Activities for Communication,* pp. 51, 71–72 ▲ ■
- *Teaching Transparencies:* **Situación, Capítulo 9;** Picture Stories, Chapter 9 ▲ ● ■
- *Video Guide,* pp. 83, 89 ▲ ● ■
- *TPR Storytelling Book,* pp. 50–51 ▲ ●
- *Interactive Tutor* (Disc 2) or *DVD Tutor* (Disc 2) ▲ ● ■
- Online Practice, Chapter 9 (go.hrw.com, Keyword: EXP1B CH9)

▲ = Advanced Learners ♦ = Slower Pace Learners ● = Special Learning Needs ■ = Heritage Speakers

Holt Spanish 1B Lesson Planner

Teacher's Name _____ Class _____ Date _____

¡Festejemos!

CAPÍTULO
9
DAY 29 50-MINUTE LESSON PLAN

> **STANDARDS FOR FOREIGN LANGUAGE LEARNING: DAY 29**
>
> **Integración**
> **Communication 1.1:** Students engage in conversations, provide and obtain information, express feelings and emotions, and exchange opinions.
> **Communication 1.2:** Students understand and interpret written and spoken language on a variety of topics.
> **Communication 1.3:** Students present information, concepts, and ideas to an audience of listeners or readers on a variety of topics.
>
> **Connections 3.1:** Students reinforce and further their knowledge of other disciplines through the foreign language.
> **Connections 3.2:** Students acquire information and recognize the distinctive viewpoints that are only available through the foreign language and its cultures.

CORE INSTRUCTION

Warm-Up
- (5 min.) See Fine Art Connection: Introduction, p. 217.

Integración
- (10 min.) Play Audio CD 9, Tr. 14 for Activity 1, p. 216.
- (30 min.) Have students do Activities 2–4, pp. 216–217.

Wrap-Up
- (5 min.) See Fine Art Connection: Analyzing, p. 217. Remind students to study for Chapter Test.

OPTIONAL RESOURCES
- (10 min.) Culture Project, p. 216

Practice Options
- *Lab Book,* p. 30
- *Cuaderno de actividades,* pp. 61–62
- *Teaching Transparencies:* Fine Art, Chapter 9 ▲ ● ■
- *Video Guide,* pp. ▲ ● ■
- *Interactive Tutor* (Disc 2) or *DVD Tutor* (Disc 2) ▲ ● ■
- Online Practice, Chapter 9 (go.hrw.com, Keyword: EXP1B CH9)

▲ = Advanced Learners   ◆ = Slower Pace Learners   ● = Special Learning Needs   ■ = Heritage Speakers

Holt Spanish 1B   Lesson Planner

Teacher's Name _____ Class _____ Date _____

¡Festejemos!

CAPÍTULO 9

DAY 30 50-MINUTE LESSON PLAN

CORE INSTRUCTION
Chapter Assessment

Assess
- (50 min.) Give Chapter 9 Test.

OPTIONAL RESOURCES
- (5 min.) Preview **Geocultura: Perú**, pp. 218–221.

Practice Options
- *Cuaderno de actividades,* pp. 84–85 ▲ ● ■
- Online Practice, Chapter 9 (go.hrw.com, Keyword: EXP1B CH9)

Assessment Options
- *Assessment Program:* **Examen: Capítulo 9**, pp. 185–195
- *Assessment Program:* **Examen oral: Capítulo 9**, p. 196
- *Assessment Program:* Alternative Assessment Guide, pp. 244, 252, 260 ▲ ● ■
- *Audio CD 9,* Tr. 17–18
- *Standardized Assessment Tutor,* Chapter 9
- Test Generator

▲ = Advanced Learners   ◆ = Slower Pace Learners   ● = Special Learning Needs   ■ = Heritage Speakers

Holt Spanish 1B   Lesson Planner

Teacher's Name _____ Class _____ Date _____

CAPÍTULO 10

¡A viajar!

DAY 1 50-MINUTE LESSON PLAN

STANDARDS FOR FOREIGN LANGUAGE LEARNING: DAY 1

Chapter Opener
Communication 1.2: Students understand and interpret written and spoken language on a variety of topics.

Vocabulario en acción 1
Communication 1.2: Students understand and interpret written and spoken language on a variety of topics.

Before starting **Capítulo 10,** you may wish to teach **Geocultura: Perú,** pp. 218–221. For teaching suggestions, see pp. xv–xvi of this *Lesson Planner.*

CORE INSTRUCTION

Warm-Up
- (5 min.) See Learning Tip, p. 233.

Chapter Opener
- (5 min.) See Using the Photo and **Más vocabulario,** p. 222.
- (5 min.) See **Objetivos,** p. 222.

Vocabulario en acción 1
- (5 min.) Show **ExpresaVisión,** Ch. 10.
- (20 min.) Present **Vocabulario 1**, pp. 224–225 using Teaching **Vocabulario,** p. 224.
- (5 min.) Present **¡Exprésate!,** p. 225.

Wrap-Up
- (5 min.) Present Language to Language, p. 225.

OPTIONAL RESOURCES
- (5 min.) TPR, p. 225
- (5 min.) Common Error Alert, p. 225
- (5 min.) **También se puede decir,** p. 225
- (10 min.) Advanced Learners, p. 225 ▲
- (10 min.) Multiple Intelligences, p. 225
- (5 min.) Bell Work 10.1, p. 224

Practice Options
- *Lab Book,* pp. 62–63
- *Cuaderno de vocabulario y gramática,* pp. 65–67
- *Activities for Communication,* pp. 37–38 ▲ ■
- *Cuaderno para hispanohablantes,* Chapter 10 ■
- *Teaching Transparencies:* Bell Work 10.1; **Vocabulario** 10.1, 10.2; *Vocabulario y gramática* Answers, pp. 65–67 ▲ ● ■
- *Video Guide,* pp. 96–97 ▲ ● ■
- *TPR Storytelling Book,* pp. 54–55 ▲ ●
- *Interactive Tutor* (Disc 2) or *DVD Tutor* (Disc 2) ▲ ● ■
- Online Practice, Chapter 10 (go.hrw.com, Keyword: EXP1B CH10)

▲ = Advanced Learners   ◆ = Slower Pace Learners   ● = Special Learning Needs   ■ = Heritage Speakers

Teacher's Name _____ Class _____ Date _____

¡A viajar!

CAPÍTULO 10

DAY 2 50-MINUTE LESSON PLAN

STANDARDS FOR FOREIGN LANGUAGE LEARNING: DAY 2

Vocabulario en acción 1
Communication 1.2: Students understand and interpret written and spoken language on a variety of topics.
Cultures 2.1: Students demonstrate an understanding of the relationship between the practices and perspectives of the culture studied.
Cultures 2.2: Students demonstrate an understanding of the relationship between the products and perspectives of the culture studied.
Connections 3.2: Students acquire information and recognize the distinctive viewpoints that are only available through the foreign language and its cultures.

CORE INSTRUCTION

Warm-Up
- (5 min.) Dictate five of the new **vocabulario** for students to write.

Vocabulario en acción 1
- (15 min.) Review **Vocabulario 1** and **¡Exprésate!**, pp. 224–225.
- (10 min.) Play Audio CD 10, Tr. 1 for Activity 1, p. 226.
- (5 min.) Have students do Activity 2, p. 226.
- (5 min.) Have students do Activity 3, p. 226.
- (5 min.) Present **Nota cultural,** p. 226.

Wrap-Up
- (5 min.) See **Más práctica**, p. 227.

OPTIONAL RESOURCES
- (5 min.) Social Studies Link, p. 226
- (10 min.) Fold-n-Learn, p. 226
- (5 min.) Variation, p. 227
- (10 min.) Special Learning Needs, p. 227 ●

Practice Options
- *Lab Book,* pp. 62–63
- ***Cuaderno de vocabulario y gramática,*** pp. 65–67
- *Activities for Communication,* pp. 37–38 ▲ ■
- ***Cuaderno para hispanohablantes,*** Chapter 10 ■
- *Teaching Transparencies:* **Vocabulario** 10.1, 10.2; ***Vocabulario y gramática*** Answers, pp. 65–67 ▲ ● ■
- *Video Guide,* pp. 96–97 ▲ ● ■
- *TPR Storytelling Book,* pp. 54–55 ▲ ●
- *Interactive Tutor* (Disc 2) or *DVD Tutor* (Disc 2) ▲ ● ■
- Online Practice, Chapter 10 (go.hrw.com, Keyword: EXP1B CH10)

▲ = Advanced Learners   ◆ = Slower Pace Learners   ● = Special Learning Needs   ■ = Heritage Speakers

Holt Spanish 1B
Lesson Planner

Teacher's Name _____ Class _____ Date _____

¡A viajar!

CAPÍTULO 10

DAY 3 50-MINUTE LESSON PLAN

STANDARDS FOR FOREIGN LANGUAGE LEARNING: DAY 3

Vocabulario en acción 1

Communication 1.2: Students understand and interpret written and spoken language on a variety of topics.

Communication 1.3: Students present information, concepts, and ideas to an audience of listeners or readers on a variety of topics.

Cultures 2.1: Students demonstrate an understanding of the relationship between the practices and perspectives of the culture studied.

Cultures 2.2: Students demonstrate an understanding of the relationship between the products and perspectives of the culture studied.

Connections 3.2: Students acquire information and recognize the distinctive viewpoints that are only available through the foreign language and its cultures.

CORE INSTRUCTION

Warm-Up
- (5 min.) Have students read aloud the completed sentences from Activity 2.

Vocabulario en acción 1
- (20 min.) Have students do Activities 4–6, p. 227.
- (15 min.) See Teaching **¡Exprésate!,** p. 228.
- (5 min.) Have students do Activity 7, p. 228.

Wrap-Up
- (5 min.) See **Más práctica,** p. 228.

OPTIONAL RESOURCES
- (10 min.) **Comunicación** (TE), p. 227
- (5 min.) Advanced Learners, p. 227 ▲
- (5 min.) Special Learning Needs, p. 227 ●

Practice Options
- *Lab Book,* pp. 31, 62–63
- **Cuaderno de vocabulario y gramática,** pp. 65–67
- *Activities for Communication,* pp. 37–38 ▲ ■
- **Cuaderno para hispanohablantes,** Chapter 10 ■
- *Teaching Transparencies:* **Vocabulario** 10.1, 10.2; *Vocabulario y gramática* Answers, pp. 65–67 ▲ ● ■
- *Video Guide,* pp. 96–97 ▲ ● ■
- *TPR Storytelling Book,* pp. 54–55 ▲ ●
- *Interactive Tutor* (Disc 2) or *DVD Tutor* (Disc 2) ▲ ● ■
- Online Practice, Chapter 10 (go.hrw.com, Keyword: EXP1B CH10)

▲ = Advanced Learners   ◆ = Slower Pace Learners   ● = Special Learning Needs   ■ = Heritage Speakers

Holt Spanish 1B — Lesson Planner

Teacher's Name _____ Class _____ Date _____

¡A viajar!

CAPÍTULO 10

DAY 4 50-MINUTE LESSON PLAN

> **STANDARDS FOR FOREIGN LANGUAGE LEARNING: DAY 4**
>
> **Vocabulario en acción 1**
> **Communication 1.1:** Students engage in conversations, provide and obtain information, express feelings and emotions, and exchange opinions.
> **Communication 1.2:** Students understand and interpret written and spoken language on a variety of topics.
>
> **Communication 1.3:** Students present information, concepts, and ideas to an audience of listeners or readers on a variety of topics.

CORE INSTRUCTION

Warm-Up
- (5 min.) Have students do Bell Work 10.2, p. 230.

Vocabulario en acción 1
- (10 min.) Review ¡Exprésate!, p. 228.
- (30 min.) Have students do Activities 8–11, pp. 228–229.

Wrap-Up
- (5 min.) Remind students to study for **Prueba: Vocabulario 1**.

OPTIONAL RESOURCES
- (10 min.) **Comunicación** (TE), p. 229
- (15 min.) Multiple Intelligences, p. 229
- (5 min.) Slower Pace Learners, p. 229. ◆

Practice Options
- *Lab Book*, pp. 31, 62–63
- *Cuaderno de vocabulario y gramática,* pp. 65–67
- *Activities for Communication*, pp. 37–38 ▲ ■
- *Cuaderno para hispanohablantes,* Chapter 10 ■
- *Teaching Transparencies:* Bell Work 10.2; **Vocabulario** 10.1, 10.2; *Vocabulario y gramática* Answers, pp. 65–67 ▲ ● ■
- *Video Guide*, pp. 96–97 ▲ ● ■
- *TPR Storytelling Book*, pp. 54–55 ▲ ●
- *Interactive Tutor* (Disc 2) or *DVD Tutor* (Disc 2) ▲ ● ■
- Online Practice, Chapter 10 (go.hrw.com, Keyword: EXP1B CH10)

▲ = Advanced Learners   ◆ = Slower Pace Learners   ● = Special Learning Needs   ■ = Heritage Speakers

Holt Spanish 1B

Lesson Planner

Teacher's Name _____ Class _____ Date _____

CAPÍTULO 10

¡A viajar!

DAY 5 50-MINUTE LESSON PLAN

STANDARDS FOR FOREIGN LANGUAGE LEARNING: DAY 5

Vocabulario en acción

Communication 1.1: Students engage in conversations, provide and obtain information, express feelings and emotions, and exchange opinions.

Communication 1.2: Students understand and interpret written and spoken language on a variety of topics.

Communication 1.3: Students present information, concepts, and ideas to an audience of listeners or readers on a variety of topics.

Cultures 2.1: Students demonstrate an understanding of the relationship between the practices and perspectives of the culture studied.

Cultures 2.2: Students demonstrate an understanding of the relationship between the products and perspectives of the culture studied.

Connections 3.2: Students acquire information and recognize the distinctive viewpoints that are only available through the foreign language and its cultures.

CORE INSTRUCTION

Warm-Up
- (20 min.) Review **Vocabulario en acción 1**, pp. 224–229.

Vocabulario en acción 1

Assess
- (20 min.) Give **Prueba: Vocabulario 1**.

OPTIONAL RESOURCES
- (10 min.) Preview **Gramática en acción 1**, pp. 230–235.

Practice Options
- *Interactive Tutor* (Disc 2) or *DVD Tutor* (Disc 2) ▲●■
- Online Practice, Chapter 10 (go.hrw.com, Keyword: EXP1B CH10)

Assessment Options
- *Assessment Program*: **Prueba: Vocabulario 1**, pp. 97–98
- *Assessment Program*: Alternative Assessment Guide, pp. 245, 253, 261 ▲●■
- Test Generator

▲ = Advanced Learners   ◆ = Slower Pace Learners   ● = Special Learning Needs   ■ = Heritage Speakers

Holt Spanish 1B — Lesson Planner

Teacher's Name _____ Class _____ Date _____

¡A viajar!

CAPÍTULO 10

DAY 6 50-MINUTE LESSON PLAN

STANDARDS FOR FOREIGN LANGUAGE LEARNING: DAY 6

Gramática en acción 1

Communication 1.2: Students understand and interpret written and spoken language on a variety of topics.

CORE INSTRUCTION

Warm-Up
- (5 min.) See Teaching **Gramática**, #1, p. 230.

Gramática en acción 1
- (20 min.) Present **Repaso**: the preterite, p. 230 using Teaching **Gramática,** #2–4, p. 230.
- (10 min.) Play Audio CD 10, Tr. 2 for Activity 12, p. 230.
- (10 min.) Have students do Activity 13, p. 231.

Wrap-Up
- (5 min.) Have students work with partners to review answers to Activity 13.

OPTIONAL RESOURCES
- (15 min.) Advanced Learners, p. 231 ▲
- (10 min.) Special Learning Needs, p. 231 ●

Practice Options
- *Lab Book,* pp. 31, 62–63
- *Cuaderno de vocabulario y gramática,* pp. 68–70
- *Cuaderno de actividades,* pp. 63–66 ▲ ● ■
- *Activities for Communication,* pp. 37–38 ▲ ■
- *Cuaderno para hispanohablantes,* Chapter 10 ■
- *Teaching Transparencies: Vocabulario y gramática* Answers, pp. 68–70 ▲ ● ■
- *Video Guide,* pp. 96–97 ▲ ● ■
- *Grammar Tutor for Students of Spanish,* Chapter 10 ● ■
- *Interactive Tutor* (Disc 2) or *DVD Tutor* (Disc 2) ▲ ● ■
- Online Practice, Chapter 10 (go.hrw.com, Keyword: EXP1B CH10)

▲ = Advanced Learners   ◆ = Slower Pace Learners   ● = Special Learning Needs   ■ = Heritage Speakers

Holt Spanish 1B — Lesson Planner

Teacher's Name _____ Class _____ Date _____

CAPÍTULO 10

¡A viajar!

DAY 7 50-MINUTE LESSON PLAN

STANDARDS FOR FOREIGN LANGUAGE LEARNING: DAY 7

Gramática en acción 1
Communication 1.2: Students understand and interpret written and spoken language on a variety of topics.

CORE INSTRUCTION

Warm-Up
- (5 min.) Have students do Bell Work 10.3, p. 232.

Gramática en acción 1
- (10 min.) Show **GramaVisión 1,** Segment 1.
- (20 min.) Review the preterite, p. 230.
- (10 min.) Have students do Activity 14, p. 231.

Wrap-Up
- (5 min.) See Teacher to Teacher, p. 231.

OPTIONAL RESOURCES
- (10 min.) **Comunicación** (TE), p. 231
- (10 min.) Special Learning Needs, p. 231 ●

Practice Options
- *Lab Book,* pp. 31, 62–63
- ***Cuaderno de vocabulario y gramática,*** pp. 68–70
- ***Cuaderno de actividades,*** pp. 63–66 ▲ ● ■
- *Activities for Communication,* pp. 37–38 ▲ ■
- ***Cuaderno para hispanohablantes,*** Chapter 10 ■
- *Teaching Transparencies:* Bell Work 10.3; **Vocabulario y gramática** Answers, pp. 68–70 ▲ ● ■
- *Video Guide,* pp. 96–97 ▲ ● ■
- *Grammar Tutor for Students of Spanish,* Chapter 10 ● ■
- *Interactive Tutor* (Disc 2) or *DVD Tutor* (Disc 2) ▲ ● ■
- Online Practice, Chapter 10 (go.hrw.com, Keyword: EXP1B CH10)

▲ = Advanced Learners   ◆ = Slower Pace Learners   ● = Special Learning Needs   ■ = Heritage Speakers

Holt Spanish 1B   Lesson Planner

Teacher's Name _____ Class _____ Date _____

¡A viajar!

CAPÍTULO 10

DAY 8 50-MINUTE LESSON PLAN

STANDARDS FOR FOREIGN LANGUAGE LEARNING: DAY 8

Gramática en acción 1

Communication 1.1: Students engage in conversations, provide and obtain information, express feelings and emotions, and exchange opinions.

Communication 1.2: Students understand and interpret written and spoken language on a variety of topics.

Communication 1.3: Students present information, concepts, and ideas to an audience of listeners or readers on a variety of topics.

Cultures 2.2: Students demonstrate an understanding of the relationship between the products and perspectives of the culture studied.

Communities 5.2: Students show evidence of becoming life–long learners by using the language for personal enjoyment and enrichment.

CORE INSTRUCTION

Warm-Up
- (5 min.) See Teaching **Gramática**, #1, p. 232.

Gramática en acción 1
- (20 min.) Present **Gramática**: Preterite of **-car, -gar, -zar** verbs using Teaching **Gramática**, #2–5, p. 232.
- (10 min.) Play Audio CD 10, Tr. 3 for Activity 15, p. 232.
- (10 min.) Have students do Activity 16, p. 232.

Wrap-Up
- (5 min.) See Career Path, p. 233.

OPTIONAL RESOURCES
- (5 min.) Slower Pace Learners, p. 233. ◆
- (5 min.) Special Learning Needs, p. 233. ●

Practice Options
- *Lab Book*, pp. 31, 62–63
- ***Cuaderno de vocabulario y gramática,*** pp. 68–70
- ***Cuaderno de actividades,*** pp. 63–66 ▲ ● ■
- *Activities for Communication*, pp. 37–38 ▲ ■
- ***Cuaderno para hispanohablantes,*** Chapter 10 ■
- *Teaching Transparencies:* ***Vocabulario y gramática*** Answers, pp. 68–70 ▲ ● ■
- *Video Guide*, pp. 96–97 ▲ ● ■
- *Grammar Tutor for Students of Spanish*, Chapter 10 ● ■
- *Interactive Tutor* (Disc 2) or *DVD Tutor* (Disc 2) ▲ ● ■
- Online Practice, Chapter 10 (go.hrw.com, Keyword: EXP1B CH10)

▲ = Advanced Learners ◆ = Slower Pace Learners ● = Special Learning Needs ■ = Heritage Speakers

Holt Spanish 1B — Lesson Planner

Teacher's Name _____ Class _____ Date _____

¡A viajar!

CAPÍTULO 10

DAY 9 50-MINUTE LESSON PLAN

STANDARDS FOR FOREIGN LANGUAGE LEARNING: DAY 9

Gramática en acción 1
Communication 1.1: Students engage in conversations, provide and obtain information, express feelings and emotions, and exchange opinions.
Communication 1.2: Students understand and interpret written and spoken language on a variety of topics.
Communication 1.3: Students present information, concepts, and ideas to an audience of listeners or readers on a variety of topics.

Cultures 2.2: Students demonstrate an understanding of the relationship between the products and perspectives of the culture studied.
Communities 5.2: Students show evidence of becoming life–long learners by using the language for personal enjoyment and enrichment.

CORE INSTRUCTION

Warm-Up
- (5 min.) Review the preterite of **-car, -gar, -zar** verbs, p. 232.

Gramática en acción 1
- (10 min.) Have students do Activities 17–18, pp. 232–233.
- (30 min.) Present **Gramática**: Preterite of **hacer**, p. 234 using Teaching **Gramática**, p. 234.

Wrap-Up
- (5 min.) Have students do Bell Work 10.4, p. 234.

OPTIONAL RESOURCES
- (5 min.) **Comunicación** (TE), p. 233

Practice Options
- *Lab Book,* pp. 62–63
- ***Cuaderno de vocabulario y gramática,*** pp. 68–70
- ***Cuaderno de actividades,*** pp. 63–66 ▲ ● ■
- *Activities for Communication,* pp. 37–38 ▲ ■
- ***Cuaderno para hispanohablantes,*** Chapter 10 ■
- *Teaching Transparencies:* Bell Work 10.4; ***Vocabulario y gramática*** Answers, pp. 68–70 ▲ ● ■
- *Video Guide,* pp. 96–97 ▲ ● ■
- *Grammar Tutor for Students of Spanish,* Chapter 10 ● ■
- *Interactive Tutor* (Disc 2) or *DVD Tutor* (Disc 2) ▲ ● ■
- Online Practice, Chapter 10 (go.hrw.com, Keyword: EXP1B CH10)

▲ = Advanced Learners   ◆ = Slower Pace Learners   ● = Special Learning Needs   ■ = Heritage Speakers

Holt Spanish 1B

Lesson Planner

Teacher's Name _____ Class _____ Date _____

¡A viajar!

CAPÍTULO 10

DAY 10 50-MINUTE LESSON PLAN

STANDARDS FOR FOREIGN LANGUAGE LEARNING: DAY 10

Gramática en acción 1
Communication 1.1: Students engage in conversations, provide and obtain information, express feelings and emotions, and exchange opinions.
Communication 1.2: Students understand and interpret written and spoken language on a variety of topics.

Communication 1.3: Students present information, concepts, and ideas to an audience of listeners or readers on a variety of topics.
Cultures 2.2: Students demonstrate an understanding of the relationship between the products and perspectives of the culture studied.

CORE INSTRUCTION

Warm-Up
- (5 min.) Have students do Bell Work 10.5, p. 238.

Gramática en acción 1
- (5 min.) Show **GramaVisión 1,** Segment 2.
- (10 min.) Review the preterite of **hacer,** p. 234.
- (5 min.) Present **Nota cultural,** p. 234.
- (20 min.) Have students do Activities 19–22, pp. 234–235.

Wrap-Up
- (5 min.) Remind students to study for **Prueba: Gramática 1**.

OPTIONAL RESOURCES
- (10 min.) **Comunicación** (TE), p. 235
- (10 min.) Multiple Intelligences, p. 235
- (5 min.) Slower Pace Learners, p. 235. ◆

Practice Options
- *Lab Book,* pp. 62–63
- ***Cuaderno de vocabulario y gramática,*** pp. 68–70
- ***Cuaderno de actividades,*** pp. 63–66 ▲ ● ■
- *Activities for Communication,* pp. 37–38 ▲ ■
- ***Cuaderno para hispanohablantes,*** Chapter 10 ■
- *Teaching Transparencies:* Bell Work 10.5; ***Vocabulario y gramática*** Answers, pp. 68–70 ▲ ● ■
- *Video Guide,* pp. 96–97 ▲ ● ■
- *Grammar Tutor for Students of Spanish,* Chapter 10 ● ■
- *Interactive Tutor* (Disc 2) or *DVD Tutor* (Disc 2) ▲ ● ■
- Online Practice, Chapter 10 (go.hrw.com, Keyword: EXP1B CH10)

▲ = Advanced Learners   ◆ = Slower Pace Learners   ● = Special Learning Needs   ■ = Heritage Speakers

Holt Spanish 1B

Lesson Planner

Teacher's Name _____ Class _____ Date _____

¡A viajar!

CAPÍTULO 10

DAY 11 50-MINUTE LESSON PLAN

STANDARDS FOR FOREIGN LANGUAGE LEARNING: DAY 11

Gramática en acción 1
Communication 1.1: Students engage in conversations, provide and obtain information, express feelings and emotions, and exchange opinions.
Communication 1.2: Students understand and interpret written and spoken language on a variety of topics.
Communication 1.3: Students present information, concepts, and ideas to an audience of listeners or readers on a variety of topics.
Cultures 2.2: Students demonstrate an understanding of the relationship between the products and perspectives of the culture studied.
Communities 5.2: Students show evidence of becoming life–long learners by using the language for personal enjoyment and enrichment.

Cultura
Communication 1.2: Students understand and interpret written and spoken language on a variety of topics.
Comparisons 4.2: Students demonstrate understanding of the concept of culture through comparisons of the cultures studied and their own.
Communities 5.1: Students use the language both within and beyond the school setting.
Communities 5.2: Students show evidence of becoming life–long learners by using the language for personal enjoyment and enrichment.

CORE INSTRUCTION

Warm-Up
- (10 min.) Review **Gramática en acción 1**, pp. 230–235.

Gramática en acción 1

Assess
- (20 min.) Give **Prueba: Gramática 1.**

Cultura
- (5 min.) Present **Cultura**, pp. 236–237 using Teaching **Cultura**, #1–2, p. 236.

Wrap-Up
- (5 min.) See Map Activities, p. 236.

OPTIONAL RESOURCES
- (10 min.) Advanced Learners, p. 237 ▲
- (5 min.) Special Learning Needs, p. 237 ●

Practice Options
- *Lab Book,* pp. 63
- ***Cuaderno de actividades,*** p. 67
- ***Cuaderno para hispanohablantes,*** pp. 77–84 ■
- *Video Guide,* pp. 93, 97 ▲ ● ■
- *Interactive Tutor* (Disc 2) or *DVD Tutor* (Disc 2) ▲ ● ■
- Online Practice, Chapter 10 (go.hrw.com, Keyword: EXP1B CH10)

Assessment Options
- *Assessment Program*: **Prueba: Gramática 1**, pp. 99–100
- *Assessment Program*: **Prueba: Aplicación 1,** pp. 101–102
- *Assessment Program*: Alternative Assessment Guide, pp. 245, 253, 261 ▲ ● ■
- Audio CD 10, Tr. 17
- Test Generator

▲ = Advanced Learners ◆ = Slower Pace Learners ● = Special Learning Needs ■ = Heritage Speakers

Holt Spanish 1B — Lesson Planner

Teacher's Name _____ Class _____ Date _____

¡A viajar!

CAPÍTULO 10

DAY 12 50-MINUTE LESSON PLAN

STANDARDS FOR FOREIGN LANGUAGE LEARNING: DAY 12

Cultura
Communication 1.2: Students understand and interpret written and spoken language on a variety of topics.
Comparisons 4.2: Students demonstrate understanding of the concept of culture through comparisons of the cultures studied and their own.
Communities 5.1: Students use the language both within and beyond the school setting.

Communities 5.2: Students show evidence of becoming life–long learners by using the language for personal enjoyment and enrichment.

Vocabulario en acción 2
Communication 1.2: Students understand and interpret written and spoken language on a variety of topics.

CORE INSTRUCTION

Warm-Up
- (5 min.) See Comparing and Contrasting, p. 237.

Cultura
- (10 min.) See Teaching **Cultura**, #3, p. 236.
- (5 min.) Present and assign **Comunidad**, p. 237.

Vocabulario en acción 2
- (25 min.) Present **Vocabulario 2**, pp. 238–239 using Teaching **Vocabulario**, p. 238.

Wrap-Up
- (5 min.) Present Language Note and **También se puede decir**, p. 239.

OPTIONAL RESOURCES
- (5 min.) Community Link, p. 237
- (10 min.) Multiple Intelligences, p. 239
- (10 min.) Advanced Learners, p. 239 ▲

Practice Options
- *Lab Book,* pp. 64–65
- *Cuaderno de vocabulario y gramática,* pp. 71–73
- *Cuaderno de actividades,* p. 67 ▲ ● ■
- *Activities for Communication,* pp. 39–40 ▲ ■
- *Cuaderno para hispanohablantes,* Chapter 10 ■
- *Teaching Transparencies:* **Vocabulario** 10.3, 10.4; *Vocabulario y gramática* Answers, pp. 71–73 ▲ ● ■
- *Video Guide,* pp. 98–99 ▲ ● ■
- *TPR Storytelling Book,* pp. 56–57 ▲ ●
- *Interactive Tutor* (Disc 2) or *DVD Tutor* (Disc 2) ▲ ● ■
- Online Practice, Chapter 10 (go.hrw.com, Keyword: EXP1B CH10)

▲ = Advanced Learners   ◆ = Slower Pace Learners   ● = Special Learning Needs   ■ = Heritage Speakers

Holt Spanish 1B Lesson Planner

Teacher's Name _____ Class _____ Date _____

¡A viajar!

CAPÍTULO 10

DAY 13 50-MINUTE LESSON PLAN

STANDARDS FOR FOREIGN LANGUAGE LEARNING: DAY 13

Vocabulario en acción 2
Communication 1.2: Students understand and interpret written and spoken language on a variety of topics.
Communication 1.3: Students present information, concepts, and ideas to an audience of listeners or readers on a variety of topics.
Cultures 2.2: Students demonstrate an understanding of the relationship between the products and perspectives of the culture studied.
Comparisons 4.2: Students demonstrate understanding of the concept of culture through comparisons of the cultures studied and their own.

CORE INSTRUCTION

Warm-Up
- (5 min.) See Game, p. 240.

Vocabulario en acción 2
- (10 min.) Show **ExpresaVisión,** Ch. 10.
- (20 min.) Review **Vocabulario 2** and **¡Exprésate!,** pp. 238–239.
- (5 min.) Present **Nota cultural,** p. 240.
- (5 min.) Play Audio CD 10, Tr. 7 for Activity 23, p. 240.

Wrap-Up
- (5 min.) See TPR Activity, p. 239.

OPTIONAL RESOURCES
- (10 min.) Practices and Perspectives, p. 240

Practice Options
- *Lab Book,* pp. 64–65
- *Cuaderno de vocabulario y gramática,* pp. 71–73
- *Cuaderno de actividades,* p. 67 ▲ ● ■
- *Activities for Communication,* pp. 39–40 ▲ ■
- *Cuaderno para hispanohablantes,* Chapter 10 ■
- *Teaching Transparencies:* **Vocabulario** 10.3, 10.4; *Vocabulario y gramática* Answers, pp. 71–73 ▲ ● ■
- *Video Guide,* pp. 98–99 ▲ ● ■
- *TPR Storytelling Book,* pp. 56–57 ▲ ●
- *Interactive Tutor* (Disc 2) or *DVD Tutor* (Disc 2) ▲ ● ■
- Online Practice, Chapter 10 (go.hrw.com, Keyword: EXP1B CH10)

▲ = Advanced Learners ◆ = Slower Pace Learners ● = Special Learning Needs ■ = Heritage Speakers

Holt Spanish 1B

Lesson Planner

Teacher's Name _____ Class _____ Date _____

¡A viajar!

CAPÍTULO 10

DAY 14 50-MINUTE LESSON PLAN

STANDARDS FOR FOREIGN LANGUAGE LEARNING: DAY 14

Vocabulario en acción 2

Communication 1.1: Students engage in conversations, provide and obtain information, express feelings and emotions, and exchange opinions.

Communication 1.2: Students understand and interpret written and spoken language on a variety of topics.

Communication 1.3: Students present information, concepts, and ideas to an audience of listeners or readers on a variety of topics.

Cultures 2.2: Students demonstrate an understanding of the relationship between the products and perspectives of the culture studied.

Comparisons 4.2: Students demonstrate understanding of the concept of culture through comparisons of the cultures studied and their own.

CORE INSTRUCTION

Warm-Up
- (5 min.) Have students do Bell Work 10.6, p. 244.

Vocabulario en acción 2
- (30 min.) Have students do Activities 24–26, pp. 240–241.
- (15 min.) See Teaching ¡Exprésate!, p. 242.

OPTIONAL RESOURCES
- (10 min.) **Más práctica,** p. 240, 241
- (10 min.) **Comunicación** (TE), p. 241
- (10 min.) Multiple Intelligences, p. 241
- (5 min.) Slower Pace Learners, p. 241. ◆

Practice Options
- *Lab Book,* pp. 64–65
- **Cuaderno de vocabulario y gramática,** pp. 71–73
- **Cuaderno de actividades,** p. 67 ▲ ● ■
- *Activities for Communication,* pp. 39–40 ▲ ■
- **Cuaderno para hispanohablantes,** Chapter 10 ■
- *Teaching Transparencies:* Bell Work 10.6; **Vocabulario** 10.3, 10.4; *Vocabulario y gramática* Answers, pp. 71–73 ▲ ● ■
- *Video Guide,* pp. 98–99 ▲ ● ■
- *TPR Storytelling Book,* pp. 56–57 ▲ ●
- *Interactive Tutor* (Disc 2) or *DVD Tutor* (Disc 2) ▲ ● ■
- Online Practice, Chapter 10 (go.hrw.com, Keyword: EXP1B CH10)

▲ = Advanced Learners ◆ = Slower Pace Learners ● = Special Learning Needs ■ = Heritage Speakers

Holt Spanish 1B   Lesson Planner

Teacher's Name _____ Class _____ Date _____

CAPÍTULO 10

¡A viajar!

DAY 15 50-MINUTE LESSON PLAN

STANDARDS FOR FOREIGN LANGUAGE LEARNING: DAY 15

Vocabulario en acción 2

Communication 1.1: Students engage in conversations, provide and obtain information, express feelings and emotions, and exchange opinions.

Communication 1.2: Students understand and interpret written and spoken language on a variety of topics.

Communication 1.3: Students present information, concepts, and ideas to an audience of listeners or readers on a variety of topics.

CORE INSTRUCTION

Warm-Up
- (5 min.) Have students review their sentences from Activity 25.

Vocabulario en acción 2
- (10 min.) Review ¡Exprésate!, p. 242.
- (30 min.) Have students do Activities 27–30, p. 195.

Wrap-Up
- (5 min.) Have students work with a partner to practice aloud the phrases in ¡Exprésate!, p. 242. They can replace the place names with ones of their own choosing. Remind students to study for **Prueba: Vocabulario 2**.

OPTIONAL RESOURCES
- (10 min.) Teacher to Teacher, p. 242
- (10 min.) **Comunicación** (TE), p. 243
- (5 min.) Advanced Learners, p. 243 ▲
- (5 min.) Multiple Intelligences, p. 243

Practice Options
- *Lab Book,* pp. 64–65
- ***Cuaderno de vocabulario y gramática,*** pp. 71–73
- ***Cuaderno de actividades,*** p. 67 ▲ ● ■
- *Activities for Communication,* pp. 39–40 ▲ ■
- ***Cuaderno para hispanohablantes,*** Chapter 10 ■
- *Teaching Transparencies:* **Vocabulario** 10.3, 10.4; ***Vocabulario y gramática*** Answers, pp. 71–73 ▲ ● ■
- *Video Guide,* pp. 98–99 ▲ ● ■
- *TPR Storytelling Book,* pp. 56–57 ▲ ●
- *Interactive Tutor* (Disc 2) or *DVD Tutor* (Disc 2) ▲ ● ■
- Online Practice, Chapter 10 (go.hrw.com, Keyword: EXP1B CH10)

▲ = Advanced Learners ◆ = Slower Pace Learners ● = Special Learning Needs ■ = Heritage Speakers

Holt Spanish 1B   Lesson Planner

Teacher's Name _____ Class _____ Date _____

¡A viajar!

CAPÍTULO 10

DAY 16 50-MINUTE LESSON PLAN

STANDARDS FOR FOREIGN LANGUAGE LEARNING: DAY 16

Vocabulario en acción 2

Communication 1.1: Students engage in conversations, provide and obtain information, express feelings and emotions, and exchange opinions.

Communication 1.2: Students understand and interpret written and spoken language on a variety of topics.

Communication 1.3: Students present information, concepts, and ideas to an audience of listeners or readers on a variety of topics.

Cultures 2.2: Students demonstrate an understanding of the relationship between the products and perspectives of the culture studied.

Comparisons 4.2: Students demonstrate understanding of the concept of culture through comparisons of the cultures studied and their own.

CORE INSTRUCTION

Warm-Up
- (20 min.) Review **Vocabulario en acción 2**, pp. 238–243.

Vocabulario en acción 2

Assess
- (20 min.) Give **Prueba: Vocabulario 2.**

OPTIONAL RESOURCES
- (10 min.) Preview **Gramática en acción 2**, pp. 244–249.

Practice Options
- *Interactive Tutor* (Disc 2) or *DVD Tutor* (Disc 2) ▲●■
- Online Practice, Chapter 10 (go.hrw.com, Keyword: EXP1B CH10)

Assessment Options
- *Assessment Program*: **Prueba: Vocabulario 2**, pp. 103–104
- *Assessment Program*: Alternative Assessment Guide, pp. 245, 253, 261 ▲●■
- Test Generator

▲ = Advanced Learners   ◆ = Slower Pace Learners   ● = Special Learning Needs   ■ = Heritage Speakers

Holt Spanish 1B — Lesson Planner

Teacher's Name _____ Class _____ Date _____

¡A viajar!

CAPÍTULO 10

DAY 17 50-MINUTE LESSON PLAN

STANDARDS FOR FOREIGN LANGUAGE LEARNING: DAY 17

Gramática en acción 2
Communication 1.2: Students understand and interpret written and spoken language on a variety of topics.

CORE INSTRUCTION

Warm-Up
- (5 min.) See Teaching **Gramática**, #1, p. 244.

Gramática en acción 2
- (10 min.) Show **GramaVisión 1,** Segment 4.

- (30 min.) Present **Gramática**: Informal commands of spelling-change and irregular verbs, p. 244 using Teaching **Gramática,** #2–5, p. 244.

Wrap-Up
- (5 min.) Give students time to make flash cards for the irregular verb forms.

OPTIONAL RESOURCES
- (5 min.) Special Learning Needs, p. 245. ●

Practice Options
- *Lab Book,* pp. 33, 64–65
- ***Cuaderno de vocabulario y gramática,*** pp. 74–76
- ***Cuaderno de actividades,*** pp. 68–71 ▲ ● ■
- *Activities for Communication,* pp. 39–40 ▲ ■
- ***Cuaderno para hispanohablantes,*** Chapter 10 ■
- *Teaching Transparencies:* ***Vocabulario y gramática*** Answers, pp. 74–76 ▲ ● ■
- *Video Guide,* pp. 98–99 ▲ ● ■
- *Grammar Tutor for Students of Spanish,* Chapter 10 ● ■
- *Interactive Tutor* (Disc 2) or *DVD Tutor* (Disc 2) ▲ ● ■
- Online Practice, Chapter 10 (go.hrw.com, Keyword: EXP1B CH10)

▲ = Advanced Learners   ◆ = Slower Pace Learners   ● = Special Learning Needs   ■ = Heritage Speakers

Holt Spanish 1B   Lesson Planner

Teacher's Name _____ Class _____ Date _____

¡A viajar!

CAPÍTULO 10

DAY 18 50-MINUTE LESSON PLAN

STANDARDS FOR FOREIGN LANGUAGE LEARNING: DAY 18

Gramática en acción 2

Communication 1.1: Students engage in conversations, provide and obtain information, express feelings and emotions, and exchange opinions.

Communication 1.2: Students understand and interpret written and spoken language on a variety of topics.

Communication 1.3: Students present information, concepts, and ideas to an audience of listeners or readers on a variety of topics.

CORE INSTRUCTION

Warm-Up
- (5 min.) Have students do Bell Work 10.7, p. 246.

Gramática en acción 2
- (10 min.) Review **Gramática,** p. 245.
- (10 min.) Play Audio CD 10, Tr. 8 for Activity 31, p. 245.
- (20 min.) Have students do Activities 32–33, p. 245.

Wrap-Up
- (5 min.) See **Comunicación** (TE), p. 245.

OPTIONAL RESOURCES
- (5 min.) Heritage Speakers, p. 245 ■
- (5 min.) Slower Pace Learners, p. 245 ◆

Practice Options
- *Lab Book,* pp. 33, 64–65
- *Cuaderno de vocabulario y gramática,* pp. 74–76
- *Cuaderno de actividades,* pp. 68–71 ▲ ● ■
- *Activities for Communication,* pp. 39–40 ▲ ■
- *Cuaderno para hispanohablantes,* Chapter 10 ■
- *Teaching Transparencies:* Bell Work 10.7; *Vocabulario y gramática* Answers, pp. 74–76 ▲ ● ■
- *Video Guide,* pp. 98–99 ▲ ● ■
- *Grammar Tutor for Students of Spanish,* Chapter 10 ● ■
- *Interactive Tutor* (Disc 2) or *DVD Tutor* (Disc 2) ▲ ● ■
- Online Practice, Chapter 10 (go.hrw.com, Keyword: EXP1B CH10)

▲ = Advanced Learners   ◆ = Slower Pace Learners   ● = Special Learning Needs   ■ = Heritage Speakers

Holt Spanish 1B   Lesson Planner

Teacher's Name _____ Class _____ Date _____

¡A viajar!

CAPÍTULO 10

DAY 19 50-MINUTE LESSON PLAN

STANDARDS FOR FOREIGN LANGUAGE LEARNING: DAY 19

Gramática en acción 2

Communication 1.1: Students engage in conversations, provide and obtain information, express feelings and emotions, and exchange opinions.

Communication 1.2: Students understand and interpret written and spoken language on a variety of topics.

Communication 1.3: Students present information, concepts, and ideas to an audience of listeners or readers on a variety of topics.

CORE INSTRUCTION

Warm-Up
- (5 min.) See Teaching **Gramática**, #1–2, p. 246.

Gramática en acción 2
- (25 min.) Present **Gramática: Repaso** direct object pronouns, p. 246 using Teaching **Gramática**, p. 246.
- (10 min.) Play Audio CD 10, Tr. 9 for Activity 34, p. 246.
- (5 min.) Have students do Activity 35, p. 246.

OPTIONAL RESOURCES
- (5 min.) Advanced Learners, p. 247. ▲

Practice Options
- *Lab Book,* pp. 33, 64–65
- **Cuaderno de vocabulario y gramática,** pp. 74–76
- **Cuaderno de actividades,** pp. 68–71 ▲ ● ■
- *Activities for Communication,* pp. 39–40 ▲ ■
- **Cuaderno para hispanohablantes,** Chapter 10 ■
- *Teaching Transparencies:* **Vocabulario y gramática** Answers, pp. 74–76 ▲ ● ■
- *Video Guide,* pp. 98–99 ▲ ● ■
- *Grammar Tutor for Students of Spanish,* Chapter 10 ● ■
- *Interactive Tutor* (Disc 2) or *DVD Tutor* (Disc 2) ▲ ● ■
- Online Practice, Chapter 10 (go.hrw.com, Keyword: EXP1B CH10)

▲ = Advanced Learners   ◆ = Slower Pace Learners   ● = Special Learning Needs   ■ = Heritage Speakers

Holt Spanish 1B   Lesson Planner

Teacher's Name _____ Class _____ Date _____

¡A viajar!

CAPÍTULO 10

DAY 20 50-MINUTE LESSON PLAN

STANDARDS FOR FOREIGN LANGUAGE LEARNING: DAY 20

Gramática en acción 2
Communication 1.1: Students engage in conversations, provide and obtain information, express feelings and emotions, and exchange opinions.
Communication 1.2: Students understand and interpret written and spoken language on a variety of topics.
Communication 1.3: Students present information, concepts, and ideas to an audience of listeners or readers on a variety of topics.
Cultures 2.1: Students demonstrate an understanding of the relationship between the practices and perspectives of the culture studied.

CORE INSTRUCTION

Warm-Up
- (5 min.) Have students do Bell Work 10.8, p. 248.

Gramática en acción 2
- (5 min.) Show **GramaVisión 1,** Segment 5.
- (10 min.) Review direct object pronouns, p. 246.
- (10 min.) Have students do Activities 36–37, p. 247.
- (5 min.) Present **Nota cultural,** p. 247.
- (10 min.) Have students do Activity 38, p. 247.

Wrap-Up
- (5 min.) See **Comunicación** (TE), p. 247. Assign as homework.

OPTIONAL RESOURCES
- (15 min.) Multiple Intelligences, p. 247

Practice Options
- *Lab Book,* pp. 33, 64–65
- *Cuaderno de vocabulario y gramática,* pp. 74–76
- *Cuaderno de actividades,* pp. 68–71 ▲●■
- *Activities for Communication,* pp. 39–40 ▲■
- *Cuaderno para hispanohablantes,* Chapter 10 ■
- *Teaching Transparencies:* Bell Work 10.8; *Vocabulario y gramática* Answers, pp. 74–76 ▲●■
- *Video Guide,* pp. 98–99 ▲●■
- *Grammar Tutor for Students of Spanish,* Chapter 10 ●■
- *Interactive Tutor* (Disc 2) or *DVD Tutor* (Disc 2) ▲●■
- Online Practice, Chapter 10 (go.hrw.com, Keyword: EXP1B CH10)

▲ = Advanced Learners   ◆ = Slower Pace Learners   ● = Special Learning Needs   ■ = Heritage Speakers

Holt Spanish 1B   Lesson Planner

Teacher's Name _____ Class _____ Date _____

CAPÍTULO 10

¡A viajar!

DAY 21 50-MINUTE LESSON PLAN

STANDARDS FOR FOREIGN LANGUAGE LEARNING: DAY 21

Gramática en acción 2
Communication 1.1: Students engage in conversations, provide and obtain information, express feelings and emotions, and exchange opinions.

Communication 1.2: Students understand and interpret written and spoken language on a variety of topics.

CORE INSTRUCTION

Warm-Up
- (5 min.) Review homework assignment from **Comunicación** (TE), p. 247.

Gramática en acción 2
- (10 min.) Show **GramaVisión 1,** Segment 6.
- (20 min.) Present **Gramática: Repaso** verbs followed by infinitives, p. 248 using Teaching **Gramática,** p. 248.
- (10 min.) Have students do Activities 39–41, pp. 248–249.

Wrap-Up
- (5 min.) Review answers to Activity 40, p. 248.

OPTIONAL RESOURCES
- (5 min.) Slower Pace Learners, p. 249. ◆

Practice Options
- *Lab Book,* pp. 33, 64–65
- *Cuaderno de vocabulario y gramática,* pp. 74–76
- *Cuaderno de actividades,* pp. 68–71 ▲ ● ■
- *Activities for Communication,* pp. 39–40 ▲ ■
- *Cuaderno para hispanohablantes,* Chapter 10 ■
- *Teaching Transparencies: Vocabulario y gramática* Answers, pp. 74–76 ▲ ● ■
- *Video Guide,* pp. 98–99 ▲ ● ■
- *Grammar Tutor for Students of Spanish,* Chapter 10 ● ■
- *Interactive Tutor* (Disc 2) or *DVD Tutor* (Disc 2) ▲ ● ■
- Online Practice, Chapter 10 (go.hrw.com, Keyword: EXP1B CH10)

▲ = Advanced Learners ◆ = Slower Pace Learners ● = Special Learning Needs ■ = Heritage Speakers

Holt Spanish 1B   Lesson Planner

Teacher's Name _____ Class _____ Date _____

¡A viajar!

CAPÍTULO 10

DAY 22 50-MINUTE LESSON PLAN

> **STANDARDS FOR FOREIGN LANGUAGE LEARNING: DAY 22**
>
> **Gramática en acción 2**
> **Communication 1.1:** Students engage in conversations, provide and obtain information, express feelings and emotions, and exchange opinions.
>
> **Communication 1.2:** Students understand and interpret written and spoken language on a variety of topics.

CORE INSTRUCTION

Warm-Up
- (5 min.) Use phrases from **Gramática** and ask students questions about what they hope to do, want to do, and so on, for this weekend.

Gramática en acción 2
- (10 min.) Review verbs followed by infinitives, p. 248.
- (20 min.) Have students do Activities 42–43, p. 249.
- (10 min.) Review **Gramática en acción 2**, pp. 244–249.

Wrap-Up
- (5 min.) Review for **Prueba: Gramática 2.**

OPTIONAL RESOURCES
- (10 min.) **Comunicación** (TE), p. 249
- (5 min.) Special Learning Needs, p. 249 ●

Practice Options
- *Lab Book,* pp. 33, 64–65
- **Cuaderno de vocabulario y gramática,** pp. 74–76
- **Cuaderno de actividades,** pp. 68–71 ▲ ● ■
- *Activities for Communication,* pp. 39–40 ▲ ■
- **Cuaderno para hispanohablantes,** Chapter 10 ■
- *Teaching Transparencies: Vocabulario y gramática* Answers, pp. 74–76 ▲ ● ■
- *Video Guide,* pp. 98–99 ▲ ● ■
- *Grammar Tutor for Students of Spanish,* Chapter 10 ● ■
- *Interactive Tutor* (Disc 2) or *DVD Tutor* (Disc 2) ▲ ● ■
- Online Practice, Chapter 10 (go.hrw.com, Keyword: EXP1B CH10)

▲ = Advanced Learners ◆ = Slower Pace Learners ● = Special Learning Needs ■ = Heritage Speakers

Holt Spanish 1B — Lesson Planner

Teacher's Name _____ Class _____ Date _____

CAPÍTULO 10

¡A viajar!

DAY 23 50-MINUTE LESSON PLAN

STANDARDS FOR FOREIGN LANGUAGE LEARNING: DAY 23

Gramática en acción 2

Communication 1.1: Students engage in conversations, provide and obtain information, express feelings and emotions, and exchange opinions.

Communication 1.2: Students understand and interpret written and spoken language on a variety of topics.

Communication 1.3: Students present information, concepts, and ideas to an audience of listeners or readers on a variety of topics.

Cultures 2.1: Students demonstrate an understanding of the relationship between the practices and perspectives of the culture studied.

Conexiones culturales

Connections 3.1: Students reinforce and further their knowledge of other disciplines through the foreign language.

Comparisons 4.1: Students demonstrate understanding of the nature of language through comparisons of the language studied and their own.

CORE INSTRUCTION

Warm-Up
- (10 min.) Review **Gramática en acción 2,** pp. 244–249.

Gramática en acción 2
Assess
- (20 min.) Give Prueba: Gramática 2.

Conexiones culturales
- (15 min.) Present **Conexiones culturales,** pp. 250–251 using **Conexiones culturales,** #1–3, p. 250.

Wrap-Up
- (5 min.) Ask students to share any personal experiences with viewing phosphorescence in the ocean.

OPTIONAL RESOURCES
- (15 min.) Advanced Learners, p. 251. ▲

Practice Options
- Online Practice, Chapter 10 (go.hrw.com, Keyword: EXP1B CH10)

Assessment Options
- *Assessment Program*: **Prueba: Gramática 2,** pp. 105–106
- *Assessment Program*: **Prueba: Aplicación 2,** pp. 107–108
- *Assessment Program*: Alternative Assessment Guide, pp. 245, 253, 261 ▲●■
- Audio CD 10, Tr. 18
- Test Generator

▲ = Advanced Learners   ◆ = Slower Pace Learners   ● = Special Learning Needs   ■ = Heritage Speakers

Holt Spanish 1B

Lesson Planner

Teacher's Name _____ Class _____ Date _____

¡A viajar!

CAPÍTULO 10

DAY 24 50-MINUTE LESSON PLAN

STANDARDS FOR FOREIGN LANGUAGE LEARNING: DAY 24

Conexiones culturales
Connections 3.1: Students reinforce and further their knowledge of other disciplines through the foreign language.
Comparisons 4.1: Students demonstrate understanding of the nature of language through comparisons of the language studied and their own.

Novela en video
Communication 1.1: Students engage in conversations, provide and obtain information, express feelings and emotions, and exchange opinions.
Communication 1.2: Students understand and interpret written and spoken language on a variety of topics.

Cultures 2.1: Students demonstrate an understanding of the relationship between the practices and perspectives of the culture studied.
Connections 3.2: Students acquire information and recognize the distinctive viewpoints that are only available through the foreign language and its cultures.
Comparisons 4.2: Students demonstrate understanding of the concept of culture through comparisons of the cultures studied and their own.
Communities 5.1: Students use the language both within and beyond the school setting.

CORE INSTRUCTION

Warm-Up
- (5 min.) See Multiple Intelligences, p. 251.

Conexiones culturales
- (20 min.) See Teaching **Conexiones culturales,** #4–6, p. 250.

Novela en video
- (15 min.) See Teaching **Novela en video,** #1, p. 252.
- (5 min.) See Gestures, p. 254.

Wrap-Up
- (5 min.) See Visual Learners, p. 252.

OPTIONAL RESOURCES
- (5 min.) Comparing and Contrasting, p. 253
- (10 min.) **Comunicación** (TE), p. 253
- (15 min.) Culminating Project, p. 254

Practice Options
- *Lab Book,* p. 66
- *Video Guide,* pp. 94, 100 ▲●■
- Online Practice, Chapter 10 (go.hrw.com, Keyword: EXP1B CH10)

▲ = Advanced Learners   ◆ = Slower Pace Learners   ● = Special Learning Needs   ■ = Heritage Speakers

Holt Spanish 1B — Lesson Planner

Teacher's Name _____ Class _____ Date _____

¡A viajar!

CAPÍTULO 10

DAY 25 50-MINUTE LESSON PLAN

> ### STANDARDS FOR FOREIGN LANGUAGE LEARNING: DAY 25
>
> **Novela en video**
> **Communication 1.1:** Students engage in conversations, provide and obtain information, express feelings and emotions, and exchange opinions.
> **Communication 1.2:** Students understand and interpret written and spoken language on a variety of topics.
> **Cultures 2.1:** Students demonstrate an understanding of the relationship between the practices and perspectives of the culture studied.
> **Connections 3.2:** Students acquire information and recognize the distinctive viewpoints that are only available through the foreign language and its cultures.
> **Comparisons 4.2:** Students demonstrate understanding of the concept of culture through comparisons of the cultures studied and their own.
> **Communities 5.1:** Students use the language both within and beyond the school setting.
>
> **Leamos y escribamos**
> **Communication 1.1:** Students engage in conversations, provide and obtain information, express feelings and emotions, and exchange opinions.
> **Communication 1.2:** Students understand and interpret written and spoken language on a variety of topics.
> **Communication 1.3:** Students present information, concepts, and ideas to an audience of listeners or readers on a variety of topics.
> **Cultures 2.1:** Students demonstrate an understanding of the relationship between the practices and perspectives of the culture studied.
> **Connections 3.2:** Students acquire information and recognize the distinctive viewpoints that are only available through the foreign language and its cultures.
> **Comparisons 4.2:** Students demonstrate understanding of the concept of culture through comparisons of the cultures studied and their own.

CORE INSTRUCTION

Warm-Up
- (5 min.) Summarize video action with students' help.

Novela en video
- (15 min.) See Teaching **Novela en video,** #2–3, p. 252.

Leamos y escribamos
- (20 min.) See Teaching **Leamos,** p. 256.

Wrap-Up
- (10 min.) Have students do Activities 1–3, p. 255.

OPTIONAL RESOURCES
- (10 min.) Community Link, p. 254
- (10 min.) **Comunicación** (TE), p. 255
- (10 min.) Advanced Learners, p. 255 ▲
- (5 min.) Special Learning Needs, p. 255 ●
- (5 min.) Applying the Strategies, p. 256
- (5 min.) Advanced Learners, p. 257 ▲

Practice Options
- *Cuaderno de actividades,* p. 72 ▲ ● ■
- *Cuaderno para hispanohablantes,* Chapter 10 ■
- Reading Strategies and Skills Handbook, Chapter 10 ▲ ● ■
- *¡Lee conmigo!* Level 1 Reader ▲ ■
- Online Practice, Chapter 10 (go.hrw.com, Keyword: EXP1B CH10)

▲ = Advanced Learners   ◆ = Slower Pace Learners   ● = Special Learning Needs   ■ = Heritage Speakers

Holt Spanish 1B

Lesson Planner

Teacher's Name _____ Class _____ Date _____

¡A viajar!

CAPÍTULO
10

DAY 26 50-MINUTE LESSON PLAN

STANDARDS FOR FOREIGN LANGUAGE LEARNING: DAY 26

Leamos y escribamos

Communication 1.1: Students engage in conversations, provide and obtain information, express feelings and emotions, and exchange opinions.

Communication 1.2: Students understand and interpret written and spoken language on a variety of topics.

Communication 1.3: Students present information, concepts, and ideas to an audience of listeners or readers on a variety of topics.

Cultures 2.1: Students demonstrate an understanding of the relationship between the practices and perspectives of the culture studied.

Connections 3.2: Students acquire information and recognize the distinctive viewpoints that are only available through the foreign language and its cultures.

Comparisons 4.2: Students demonstrate understanding of the concept of culture through comparisons of the cultures studied and their own.

CORE INSTRUCTION

Warm-Up
- (5 min.) See Process Writing, p. 257.

Leamos y escribamos
- (45 min.) Present **Taller del escritor**, p. 257. See Teaching **Escribamos,** p. 256.

Wrap-Up
- (5 min.) Remind students of upcoming Chapter Test.

OPTIONAL RESOURCES
- (5 min.) Special Learning Needs, p. 257. ●

Practice Options
- *Cuaderno de actividades*, p. 72 ▲ ● ■
- *Cuaderno para hispanohablantes,* Chapter 10 ■
- Reading Strategies and Skills Handbook, Chapter 10 ▲ ● ■
- *¡Lee conmigo!* Level 1 Reader ▲ ■
- Online Practice, Chapter 10 (go.hrw.com, Keyword: EXP1B CH10)

▲ = Advanced Learners   ◆ = Slower Pace Learners   ● = Special Learning Needs   ■ = Heritage Speakers

Holt Spanish 1B

Lesson Planner

Teacher's Name _____ Class _____ Date _____

CAPÍTULO 10

¡A viajar!

DAY 27 50-MINUTE LESSON PLAN

STANDARDS FOR FOREIGN LANGUAGE LEARNING: DAY 27

Repaso

Communication 1.1: Students engage in conversations, provide and obtain information, express feelings and emotions, and exchange opinions.

Communication 1.2: Students understand and interpret written and spoken language on a variety of topics.

Communication 1.3: Students present information, concepts, and ideas to an audience of listeners or readers on a variety of topics.

Cultures 2.1: Students demonstrate an understanding of the relationship between the practices and perspectives of the culture studied.

Cultures 2.2: Students demonstrate an understanding of the relationship between the products and perspectives of the culture studied.

CORE INSTRUCTION

Warm-Up
- (5 min.) Before doing Activity 1, have students look at the pictures and say something in Spanish about each one.

Repaso
- (40 min.) Have students do Activities 1–5, pp. 258–259.

Wrap-Up
- (5 min.) See Fold-n-Learn, p. 258.

OPTIONAL RESOURCES
- (10 min.) Game Bank, pp. T60–T63

Practice Options
- *Lab Book,* pp. 34, 59
- *Activities for Communication,* pp. 52, 73–74 ▲ ■
- *Teaching Transparencies:* **Situación, Capítulo 10**; Picture Stories, Chapter 10 ▲ ● ■
- *Video Guide,* pp. 94, 99 ▲ ● ■
- *TPR Storytelling Book,* pp. 58–59 ▲ ●
- *Interactive Tutor* (Disc 2) or *DVD Tutor* (Disc 2) ▲ ● ■
- Online Practice, Chapter 10 (go.hrw.com, Keyword: EXP1B CH10)

▲ = Advanced Learners ◆ = Slower Pace Learners ● = Special Learning Needs ■ = Heritage Speakers

Holt Spanish 1B   Lesson Planner

Teacher's Name _____ Class _____ Date _____

¡A viajar!

CAPÍTULO 10

DAY 28 50-MINUTE LESSON PLAN

STANDARDS FOR FOREIGN LANGUAGE LEARNING: DAY 28

Repaso

Communication 1.1: Students engage in conversations, provide and obtain information, express feelings and emotions, and exchange opinions.

Communication 1.2: Students understand and interpret written and spoken language on a variety of topics.

Communication 1.3: Students present information, concepts, and ideas to an audience of listeners or readers on a variety of topics.

Cultures 2.1: Students demonstrate an understanding of the relationship between the practices and perspectives of the culture studied.

Cultures 2.2: Students demonstrate an understanding of the relationship between the products and perspectives of the culture studied.

CORE INSTRUCTION

Warm-Up
- (5 min.) Review answers to Activities 3–4.

Repaso
- (10 min.) Play Audio CD 10, Tr. 12 for Activity 6, p. 259.
- (5 min.) Have students do Activity 7, p. 259.
- (15 min.) See Circumlocution, p. 261.
- (10 min.) Play Audio CD 10, Tr. 13–15 for **Letra y sonido,** p. 260.

Wrap-Up
- (5 min.) Go over **Repaso de gramática** 1 and 2, p. 260. Remind students to study for the Chapter Test.

OPTIONAL RESOURCES
- (10 min.) Game Bank, pp. T60–T63

Practice Options
- *Lab Book,* pp. 34, 59
- *Activities for Communication,* pp. 52, 73–74 ▲ ■
- *Teaching Transparencies:* **Situación, Capítulo 10**; Picture Stories, Chapter 10 ▲ ● ■
- *Video Guide,* pp. 94, 99 ▲ ● ■
- *TPR Storytelling Book,* pp. 58–59 ▲ ●
- *Interactive Tutor* (Disc 2) or *DVD Tutor* (Disc 2) ▲ ● ■
- Online Practice, Chapter 10 (go.hrw.com, Keyword: EXP1B CH10)

▲ = Advanced Learners ◆ = Slower Pace Learners ● = Special Learning Needs ■ = Heritage Speakers

Holt Spanish 1B — Lesson Planner

Teacher's Name _____ Class _____ Date _____

¡A viajar!

CAPÍTULO 10

DAY 29 50-MINUTE LESSON PLAN

STANDARDS FOR FOREIGN LANGUAGE LEARNING: DAY 29

Integración

Communication 1.1: Students engage in conversations, provide and obtain information, express feelings and emotions, and exchange opinions.

Communication 1.2: Students understand and interpret written and spoken language on a variety of topics.

Communication 1.3: Students present information, concepts, and ideas to an audience of listeners or readers on a variety of topics.

Connections 3.1: Students reinforce and further their knowledge of other disciplines through the foreign language.

Connections 3.2: Students acquire information and recognize the distinctive viewpoints that are only available through the foreign language and its cultures.

CORE INSTRUCTION

Warm-Up
- (5 min.) See Find Art Connection: Introduction, p. 263.

Integración
- (10 min.) Play Audio CD 10, Tr. 16 for Activity 1, p. 262.
- (30 min.) Have students do Activities 2–4, pp. 262–263.

Wrap-Up
- (5 min.) See Fine Art Connection: Analyzing, p. 263. Remind students to study for the Chapter Test.

OPTIONAL RESOURCES
- (5 min.) Additional Practice, p. 262
- (10 min.) Culture Project, p. 262
- (10 min.) Fine Art Connection, p. 263

Practice Options
- *Teaching Transparencies*: Fine Art, Chapter 10 ▲ ● ■
- *Interactive Tutor* (Disc 2) or *DVD Tutor* (Disc 2) ▲ ● ■
- Online Practice, Chapter 10 (go.hrw.com, Keyword: EXP1B CH10)

▲ = Advanced Learners   ◆ = Slower Pace Learners   ● = Special Learning Needs   ■ = Heritage Speakers

Holt Spanish 1B   Lesson Planner

Teacher's Name _____ Class _____ Date _____

¡A viajar!

CAPÍTULO 10

DAY 30 50-MINUTE LESSON PLAN

CORE INSTRUCTION

Chapter Assessment

Assess
- (50 min.) Give Chapter 10 Test.

OPTIONAL RESOURCES
- (50 min.) You may also choose from other modes of assessment listed in the box below.

Assessment Options
- *Assessment Program*: **Examen: Capítulo 10,** pp. 197–207
- *Assessment Program*: **Examen oral: Capítulo 10,** pp. 208
- *Assessment Program*: Alternative Assessment Guide, pp. 245, 253, 261 ▲ ● ■
- *Assessment Program*: **Examen final,** pp. 209–223
- Audio CD 10, Tr. 19–20, 21–23
- *Standardized Assessment Tutor*, Chapter 10
- Test Generator
- Online Practice, Chapter 10 (go.hrw.com, Keyword: EXP1B CH10)

▲ = Advanced Learners   ◆ = Slower Pace Learners   ● = Special Learning Needs   ■ = Heritage Speakers

Holt Spanish 1B   Lesson Planner

90-Minute Block Lesson Plans

Teacher's Name _____ Class _____ Date _____

Capítulo puente

CAPÍTULO P

BLOCK 1 90-MINUTE LESSON PLAN

STANDARDS FOR FOREIGN LANGUAGE LEARNING: BLOCK 1

Chapter Opener
Communication 1.2: Students understand and interpret written and spoken language on a variety of topics.

Vocabulario en acción 1
Communication 1.1: Students engage in conversations, provide and obtain information, express feelings and emotions, and exchange opinions.
Communication 1.2: Students understand and interpret written and spoken language on a variety of topics.
Cultures 2.1: Students demonstrate an understanding of the relationship between the practices and perspectives of the culture studied.

Comparisons 4.1: Students demonstrate understanding of the nature of language through comparisons of the language studied and their own.

Gramática en acción 1
Communication 1.1: Students engage in conversations, provide and obtain information, express feelings and emotions, and exchange opinions.
Communication 1.2: Students understand and interpret written and spoken language on a variety of topics.
Communication 1.3: Students present information, concepts, and ideas to an audience of listeners or readers on a variety of topics.

CORE INSTRUCTION

Warm-Up
- (5 min.) Present **Objetivos**, p. T74.

Chapter Opener
- (5 min.) See Using the Photo, p. T74.

Vocabulario en acción 1
- (15 min.) Present **Vocabulario 1**, pp. 2–3 using Teaching **Vocabulario**, p. 2.
- (10 min.) Play Audio CD 6, Tr. 1 for Activity 1, p. 4.
- (15 min.) Have students do Activities 2, 3, 4 and 5, pp. 4–5.

Gramática en acción 1
- (5 min.) Have students do Bell Work CP. 2, p. 6.
- (15 min.) Present **Gramática:** *The verbs* **ser** *and* **estar**, p. 6 using Teaching **Gramática**, p. 6.
- (10 min.) Have students do Activities 6–9, p. 7.
- (5 min.) Assign **Comunicación**, p. 7.

Wrap-Up
- (5 min.) Have students ask and answer questions about the pictures in Activity 5 (¿Quién es...?, ¿Cómo es...?) Remind students to prepare for **Prueba: Vocabulario 1**.

OPTIONAL RESOURCES
- (5 min.) Learning Tip, p. 1
- (5 min.) TPR, p. 3
- (5 min.) Slower Pace Learners, p. 3 ◆
- (5 min.) Special Learning Needs, pp. 3, 7 ●
- (5 min.) Slower Pace Learners, p. 7 ◆

▲ = Advanced Learners   ◆ = Slower Pace Learners   ● = Special Learning Needs   ■ = Heritage Speakers

Holt Spanish 1B   Lesson Planner

Teacher's Name _____ Class _____ Date _____

CAPÍTULO P

BLOCK 1 90-MINUTE LESSON PLAN

Practice Options
- **GramaVisión,** Level 1A, Ch. 2, 5
- *Lab Book,* pp. 9–10
- ***Cuaderno de vocabulario y gramática,*** pp. 1–5
- *Teaching Transparencies:* Bell Work CP.1, CP.2; ***Vocabulario y gramática*** Answers, pp. 1–5 ▲ ● ■
- *Interactive Tutor* (Disc 1) or *DVD Tutor* (Disc 1) ▲ ● ■
- Online Practice, **Capítulo puente** (go.hrw.com, Keyword: EXP1B CHP)

▲ = Advanced Learners   ◆ = Slower Pace Learners   ● = Special Learning Needs   ■ = Heritage Speakers

Holt Spanish 1B   Lesson Planner

Teacher's Name _____ Class _____ Date _____

Capítulo puente

CAPÍTULO P

BLOCK 2 90-MINUTE LESSON PLAN

STANDARDS FOR FOREIGN LANGUAGE LEARNING: BLOCK 2

Gramática en acción 1
Communication 1.1: Students engage in conversations, provide and obtain information, express feelings and emotions, and exchange opinions.
Communication 1.2: Students understand and interpret written and spoken language on a variety of topics.

Vocabulario en acción 2
Communication 1.1: Students engage in conversations, provide and obtain information, express feelings and emotions, and exchange opinions.

Communication 1.2: Students understand and interpret written and spoken language on a variety of topics.
Communication 1.3: Students present information, concepts, and ideas to an audience of listeners or readers on a variety of topics.
Comparisons 4.1: Students demonstrate understanding of the nature of language through comparisons of the language studied and their own.

CORE INSTRUCTION

Vocabulario en acción 1

Warm-Up
- (5 min.) Have students do Bell Work CP.1, p. 2.

Assess
- (10 min.) Give **Prueba: Vocabulario 1.**

Gramática en acción 1
- (10 min.) Present **Gramática:** *The verbs* **gustar** *and* **tener**, p. 8 using Teaching **Gramática**, p. 8.
- (5 min.) Have students do Activity 10, p. 8.
- (5 min.) Play Audio CD 6, Tr. 2 for Activity 11, p. 9.
- (10 min.) Have students do Activities 12–13, p. 9.
- (10 min.) **Comunicación** (TE), p. 9

Vocabulario en acción 2
- (10 min.) Present **Vocabulario 2**, pp. 12–14 using Teaching **Vocabulario**, p. 12.
- (5 min.) Play Audio CD 6, Tr. 3 for Activity 14, p. 14.
- (10 min.) Have students do Activity 15, p. 14.
- (10 min.) Have students do Activities 16–18, p. 15.

Wrap-Up
- (5 min.) Have students pretend to have a phone conversation using the dialog they wrote in Activity 16, p. 15. Remind students to prepare for **Prueba: Gramática 1.**

OPTIONAL RESOURCES
- (5 min.) Advanced Learners, p. 9 ▲
- (5 min.) Multiple Intelligences, p. 9
- (5 min.) TPR, p. 13
- (5 min.) Slower Pace Learners, p. 13 ◆
- (5 min.) Special Learning Needs, pp. 13 ●
- (5 min.) **También se puede decir…**, p. 13

▲ = Advanced Learners ◆ = Slower Pace Learners ● = Special Learning Needs ■ = Heritage Speakers

Holt Spanish 1B
Lesson Planner

Teacher's Name _____ Class _____ Date _____

CAPÍTULO P

BLOCK 2 90-MINUTE LESSON PLAN

Practice Options
- *Lab Book,* pp. 9–12
- ***Cuaderno de vocabulario y gramática,*** pp. 1–10
- ***Cuaderno de actividades,*** pp. 1–4 ▲ ● ■
- *Teaching Transparencies:* Bell Work CP.3, CP.4; ***Vocabulario y gramática*** Answers, pp. 1–10 ▲ ● ■
- *Interactive Tutor* (Disc 1) or *DVD Tutor* (Disc 1) ▲ ● ■
- Online Practice, **Capítulo puente** (go.hrw.com, Keyword: EXP1B CHP)

Assessment Options
- *Assessment Program:* **Prueba: Vocabulario 1**, pp. 1–2
- Test Generator

▲ = Advanced Learners ◆ = Slower Pace Learners ● = Special Learning Needs ■ = Heritage Speakers

Holt Spanish 1B — Lesson Planner

Teacher's Name _____ Class _____ Date _____

Capítulo puente

CAPÍTULO P

BLOCK 3 90-MINUTE LESSON PLAN

STANDARDS FOR FOREIGN LANGUAGE LEARNING: BLOCK 3

Gramática en acción 1

Communication 1.1: Students engage in conversations, provide and obtain information, express feelings and emotions, and exchange opinions.

Communication 1.2: Students understand and interpret written and spoken language on a variety of topics.

Gramática en acción 2

Communication 1.1: Students engage in conversations, provide and obtain information, express feelings and emotions, and exchange opinions.

Communication 1.2: Students understand and interpret written and spoken language on a variety of topics.

Communication 1.3: Students present information, concepts, and ideas to an audience of listeners or readers on a variety of topics.

CORE INSTRUCTION

Warm-Up
- (5 min.) Have students do Bell Work CP. 5, p. 16.

Gramática en acción 1
- (15 min.) Give **Prueba: Gramática 1**.

Gramática en acción 2
- (10 min.) Present **Gramática: querer, ir a + infinitive**, p. 16 using Teaching **Gramática**, #1–2, p. 16.
- (5 min.) Play Audio CD 6, Tr. 4 for Activity 19, p. 16
- (10 min.) Have students do Activities 20–22, p. 17.
- (10 min.) Do **Comunicación** (TE), p.17.
- (10 min.) See Teaching **Gramática**, #1–2, p. 18.
- (5 min.) Have students do Activities 23, p. 18.
- (15 min.) Have students do Activities 24–26, p. 19. See **Comunicación** (TE), p. 19.

Wrap-Up
- (5 min.) Read Activity 23 aloud as a class. Remind students to prepare for **Prueba: Gramática 2**.

OPTIONAL RESOURCES
- (5 min.) Slower Pace Learners, p. 17 ◆
- (5 min.) Advanced Learners, p. 19 ▲
- (5 min.) Special Learning Needs, p. 17. ●
- (5 min.) Special Learning Needs, p. 19 ●

▲ = Advanced Learners ◆ = Slower Pace Learners ● = Special Learning Needs ■ = Heritage Speakers

Teacher's Name _____ Class _____ Date _____

CAPÍTULO P

BLOCK 3 90-MINUTE LESSON PLAN

Practice Options
- *Lab Book,* pp. 11–12, 13–14
- ***Cuaderno de vocabulario y gramática,*** pp. 6–10
- ***Cuaderno de actividades,*** pp. 5–8 ▲ ● ■
- *Teaching Transparencies:* Bell Work CP.5, CP.6; ***Vocabulario y gramática*** Answers, pp. 6–10 ▲ ● ■
- *Interactive Tutor* (Disc 1) or *DVD Tutor* (Disc 1) ▲ ● ■
- Online Practice, **Capítulo puente** (go.hrw.com, Keyword: EXP1B CHP)

Assessment Options
- *Assessment Program*: **Prueba: Gramática 1**, pp. 3–4
- Test Generator

▲ = Advanced Learners   ◆ = Slower Pace Learners   ● = Special Learning Needs   ■ = Heritage Speakers

Holt Spanish 1B   Lesson Planner

Teacher's Name _____ Class _____ Date _____

Capítulo puente

CAPÍTULO P

BLOCK 4 90-MINUTE LESSON PLAN

STANDARDS FOR FOREIGN LANGUAGE LEARNING: BLOCK 4

Vocabulario en acción 3
Communication 1.2: Students understand and interpret written and spoken language on a variety of topics.
Cultures 2.1: Students demonstrate an understanding of the relationship between the practices and perspectives of the culture studied.

Gramática en acción 3
Communication 1.1: Students engage in conversations, provide and obtain information, express feelings and emotions, and exchange opinions.

Communication 1.2: Students understand and interpret written and spoken language on a variety of topics.
Communication 1.3: Students present information, concepts, and ideas to an audience of listeners or readers on a variety of topics.

CORE INSTRUCTION

Gramática en acción 2

Warm-Up
- (5 min.) Have students do Bell Work CP. 7, p. 22.

Assess
- (15 min.) Give **Prueba: Gramática 2.**

Vocabulario en acción 3
- (10 min.) Present **Vocabulario 3**, pp. 22–23 using Teaching **Vocabulario**, p. 22.
- (10 min.) Have students do Activities 27 and 28, p. 24.
- (5 min.) Play Audio CD 6, Tr. 5 for Activity 29, p. 25.

Gramática en acción 3
- (5 min.) Have students do Bell Work CP.8, p. 26.
- (10 min.) Have students do Activities 30 and 31, p. 25.
- (10 min.) Present **Gramática:** *The present tense of* **-er** *and* **-ir** *verbs*, p. 26 using Teaching **Gramática**, #1–2, p. 26.
- (5 min.) Have students do Activities 32 and 33, pp. 26–27.
- (5 min.) Have students do Activities 34–35, p. 27.
- (5 min.) Do **Comunicación** (TE), p. 27.

Wrap-Up
- (5 min.) Have students check answers to Activity 32 with a partner. Remind students to prepare for the Chapter Test. Assign **Prueba: Vocabulario 3** as a take–home quiz.

OPTIONAL RESOURCES
- (5 min.) TPR, p. 23
- (5 min.) Practices and Perspectives, p. 24
- (5 min.) Slower Pace Learners, p. 23 ◆
- (5 min.) Multiple Intelligences, p. 27
- (5 min.) Slower Pace Learners, p. 27. ◆

▲ = Advanced Learners   ◆ = Slower Pace Learners   ● = Special Learning Needs   ■ = Heritage Speakers

Holt Spanish 1B
Lesson Planner

Teacher's Name _____ Class _____ Date _____

CAPÍTULO
P

BLOCK 4 90-MINUTE LESSON PLAN

Practice Options
- *Lab Book,* pp. 13–14
- *Cuaderno de vocabulario y gramática,* pp. 11–15
- *Cuaderno de actividades,* pp. 9–12 ▲●■
- *Teaching Transparencies:* Bell Work CP.7, CP.8; *Vocabulario y gramática* Answers, pp. 11–15 ▲●■
- *Interactive Tutor* (Disc 1) or *DVD Tutor* (Disc 1) ▲●■
- Online Practice, **Capítulo puente** (go.hrw.com, Keyword: EXP1B CHP)

Assessment Options
- *Assessment Program*: **Prueba: Gramática 2**, pp. 7–8
- *Assessment Program*: **Prueba: Vocabulario 3**, pp. 9–10
- Test Generator

▲ = Advanced Learners   ◆ = Slower Pace Learners   ● = Special Learning Needs   ■ = Heritage Speakers

Holt Spanish 1B   Lesson Planner

Teacher's Name _____ Class _____ Date _____

Capítulo puente

CAPÍTULO P

BLOCK 5 90-MINUTE LESSON PLAN

> **STANDARDS FOR FOREIGN LANGUAGE LEARNING: BLOCK 5**
>
> **Gramática en acción 3**
> **Communication 1.1:** Students engage in conversations, provide and obtain information, express feelings and emotions, and exchange opinions.
> **Communication 1.2:** Students understand and interpret written and spoken language on a variety of topics.
>
> **Communication 1.3:** Students present information, concepts, and ideas to an audience of listeners or readers on a variety of topics.
> **Communities 5.2:** Students show evidence of becoming life–long learners by using the language for personal enjoyment and enrichment.

CORE INSTRUCTION

Warm-Up
- (5 min.) Have students do Bell Work CP. 9, p. 28.

Gramática en acción 3
- (10 min.) Present **Gramática**: *Stem–changing verbs*, p. 28 using Teaching **Gramática**, p. 28.
- (10 min.) Play Audio CD 6, Tr. 6 for Activity 36, p. 28.
- (10 min.) Have students do Activities 37–39, p. 29.
- (5 min.) Do **Comunicación**, p. 29.

Chapter Assessment

Assess
- (50 min.) Give the Chapter Test.

OPTIONAL RESOURCES
- (10 min.) Advanced Learners, p. 29 ▲
- (5 min.) Special Learning Needs, p. 29 ●
- (10 min.) **Repaso: El mundo hispanohablante,** pp. 30–31.
- (10 min.) **¿Quién eres?,** pp. 32–33.
- (5 min.) Preview **Geocultura: México,** pp. 34–37.

▲ = Advanced Learners ◆ = Slower Pace Learners ● = Special Learning Needs ■ = Heritage Speakers

Holt Spanish 1B

Lesson Planner

Teacher's Name _____ Class _____ Date _____

CAPÍTULO P

BLOCK 5 90-MINUTE LESSON PLAN

Practice Options
- *Lab Book,* pp. 13–14
- ***Cuaderno de vocabulario y gramática,*** pp. 11–15
- ***Cuaderno de actividades***, p. 13 ▲ ● ■
- *Teaching Transparencies:* Bell Work CP.9; ***Vocabulario y gramática*** Answers, pp. 11–15 ▲ ● ■
- *Interactive Tutor* (Disc 1) or *DVD Tutor* (Disc 1) ▲ ● ■
- Online Practice, **Capítulo puente** (go.hrw.com, Keyword: EXP1B CHP)

Assessment Options
- *Assessment Program*: **Examen: Capítulo puente,** pp. 121–131
- *Assessment Program*: **Examen oral: Capítulo puente,** p. 132
- Test Generator

▲ = Advanced Learners   ◆ = Slower Pace Learners   ● = Special Learning Needs   ■ = Heritage Speakers

Holt Spanish 1B   Lesson Planner

Teacher's Name _____ Class _____ Date _____

¡A comer!

CAPÍTULO 6

BLOCK 1 90-MINUTE LESSON PLAN

STANDARDS FOR FOREIGN LANGUAGE LEARNING: BLOCK 1

Chapter Opener
Communication 1.2: Students understand and interpret written and spoken language on a variety of topics.

Vocabulario en acción 1
Communication 1.2: Students understand and interpret written and spoken language on a variety of topics.

Cultures 2.1: Students demonstrate an understanding of the relationship between the practices and perspectives of the culture studied.
Connections 3.1: Students reinforce and further their knowledge of other disciplines through the foreign language.
Comparisons 4.2: Students demonstrate understanding of the concept of culture through comparisons of the cultures studied and their own.

Before starting **Capítulo 6,** you may wish to teach **Geocultura: México,** pp. 34–37. For teaching suggestions, see pp. xv–xvi of this *Lesson Planner*.

CORE INSTRUCTION

Warm-Up
- (5 min.) See Learning Tips, p. 39.

Chapter Opener
- (5 min.) See Using the Photo and **Más vocabulario,** p. 38.
- (5 min.) See **Objetivos,** p. 38.

Vocabulario en acción 1
- (10 min.) Show **ExpresaVisión,** Ch. 6.
- (30 min.) See Teaching **Vocabulario,** p. 40.
- (10 min.) Present other expressions from **¡Exprésate!,** p. 41.
- (5 min.) Present **Nota cultural,** p. 42.
- (5 min.) Have students do Activity 1, p. 42.
- (10 min.) Play Audio CD 6, Tr. 1 for Activity 2, p. 42.

Wrap-Up
- (5 min.) See Game, p. 42.

OPTIONAL RESOURCES
- (5 min.) Common Error Alert, pp. 40, 41
- (5 min.) Advanced Learners, p. 41 ▲
- (5 min.) Multiple Intelligences, p. 41
- (5 min.) TPR, p. 41
- (5 min.) **También se puede decir,** p. 41
- (5 min.) **Más práctica,** p. 42
- (5 min.) Fold-N-Learn, p. 42

▲ = Advanced Learners ◆ = Slower Pace Learners ● = Special Learning Needs ■ = Heritage Speakers

Holt Spanish 1B Lesson Planner

Teacher's Name _____ Class _____ Date _____

CAPÍTULO 6

BLOCK 1 90-MINUTE LESSON PLAN

Practice Options
- *Lab Book,* pp. 38–39
- ***Cuaderno de vocabulario y gramática,*** pp. 17–19
- *Activities for Communication,* pp. 21–22 ▲ ■
- ***Cuaderno para hispanohablantes,*** Chapter 6 ■
- *Teaching Transparencies:* **Vocabulario** 6.1, 6.2; ***Vocabulario y gramática*** Answers, pp. 17–19 ▲ ● ■
- *Video Guide,* pp. 56–57 ▲ ● ■
- *TPR Storytelling Book,* pp. 30–31 ▲ ●
- *Interactive Tutor* (Disc 2) or *DVD Tutor* (Disc 2) ▲ ● ■
- Online Practice, Chapter 6 (go.hrw.com, Keyword: EXP1B CH6)

▲ = Advanced Learners ◆ = Slower Pace Learners ● = Special Learning Needs ■ = Heritage Speakers

Holt Spanish 1B — Lesson Planner

Teacher's Name _____ Class _____ Date _____

¡A comer!

CAPÍTULO 6

BLOCK 2 90-MINUTE LESSON PLAN

STANDARDS FOR FOREIGN LANGUAGE LEARNING: BLOCK 2

Vocabulario en acción 1

Communication 1.1: Students engage in conversations, provide and obtain information, express feelings and emotions, and exchange opinions.

Communication 1.2: Students understand and interpret written and spoken language on a variety of topics.

Communication 1.3: Students present information, concepts, and ideas to an audience of listeners or readers on a variety of topics.

Cultures 2.1: Students demonstrate an understanding of the relationship between the practices and perspectives of the culture studied.

Connections 3.1: Students reinforce and further their knowledge of other disciplines through the foreign language.

Comparisons 4.2: Students demonstrate understanding of the concept of culture through comparisons of the cultures studied and their own.

CORE INSTRUCTION

Warm-Up
- (5 min.) Have students do Bell Work 6.1, p. 40.

Vocabulario en acción 1
- (15 min.) Review **Vocabulario 1** and **¡Exprésate!**, pp. 40–41.
- (25 min.) Have students do Activities 3–6, pp. 42–43.
- (15 min.) See Teaching **¡Exprésate!**, p. 44.
- (25 min.) Have students do Activities 7–10, pp. 44–45.

Wrap-Up
- (5 min.) Have students do Bell Work 6.2, p. 46. Remind students to study for **Prueba: Vocabulario 1.**

OPTIONAL RESOURCES
- (5 min.) Game, p. 42
- (5 min.) Slower Pace Learners, p. 43 ◆
- (5 min.) Special Learning Needs, p. 43 ●
- (10 min.) **Comunicación** (TE), p. 43
- (5 min.) Language Note, p. 45
- (5 min.) Extension, p. 44
- (5 min.) Advanced Learners, p. 45 ▲
- (5 min.) Multiple Intelligences, p. 45
- (10 min.) **Comunicación** (TE), p. 45

▲ = Advanced Learners   ◆ = Slower Pace Learners   ● = Special Learning Needs   ■ = Heritage Speakers

Holt Spanish 1B   Lesson Planner

Teacher's Name _____ Class _____ Date _____

CAPÍTULO 6

BLOCK 2 90-MINUTE LESSON PLAN

Practice Options
- *Lab Book,* pp. 38–39
- ***Cuaderno de vocabulario y gramática,*** pp. 17–19
- *Activities for Communication,* pp. 21–22 ▲ ■
- ***Cuaderno para hispanohablantes,*** Chapter 6 ■
- *Teaching Transparencies:* Bell Work 6.1, 6.2; **Vocabulario** 6.1, 6.2; ***Vocabulario y gramática*** Answers, pp. 17–19 ▲ ● ■
- *Video Guide,* pp. 56–57 ▲ ● ■
- *TPR Storytelling Book,* pp. 30–31 ▲ ●
- *Interactive Tutor* (Disc 2) or *DVD Tutor* (Disc 2) ▲ ● ■
- Online Practice, Chapter 6 (go.hrw.com, Keyword: EXP1B CH6)

▲ = Advanced Learners   ◆ = Slower Pace Learners   ● = Special Learning Needs   ■ = Heritage Speakers

Holt Spanish 1B   Lesson Planner

Teacher's Name _____ Class _____ Date _____

¡A comer!

CAPÍTULO 6

BLOCK 3 90-MINUTE LESSON PLAN

STANDARDS FOR FOREIGN LANGUAGE LEARNING: BLOCK 3

Vocabulario en acción 1

Communication 1.1: Students engage in conversations, provide and obtain information, express feelings and emotions, and exchange opinions.

Communication 1.2: Students understand and interpret written and spoken language on a variety of topics.

Communication 1.3: Students present information, concepts, and ideas to an audience of listeners or readers on a variety of topics.

Cultures 2.1: Students demonstrate an understanding of the relationship between the practices and perspectives of the culture studied.

Connections 3.1: Students reinforce and further their knowledge of other disciplines through the foreign language.

Comparisons 4.2: Students demonstrate understanding of the concept of culture through comparisons of the cultures studied and their own.

Gramática en acción 1

Communication 1.1: Students engage in conversations, provide and obtain information, express feelings and emotions, and exchange opinions.

Communication 1.2: Students understand and interpret written and spoken language on a variety of topics.

CORE INSTRUCTION

Warm-Up
- (20 min.) Review **Vocabulario en acción 1**, pp. 40–45.

Vocabulario en acción 1

Assess
- (20 min.) Give **Prueba: Vocabulario 1**.
- (20 min.) Ask students to give examples of how they have used **estar** and **ser** in previous lessons.

Gramática en acción 1
- (30 min.) Present **Gramática: ser** and **estar**, p. 46. See Teaching **Gramática**, p. 46.
- (10 min.) Have students do Activity 11, p. 46.
- (5 min.) Present **Nota cultural**, p. 46. See Special Learning Needs, p. 47. ●

OPTIONAL RESOURCES
- (5 min.) See Career Path, p. 47.

▲ = Advanced Learners   ◆ = Slower Pace Learners   ● = Special Learning Needs   ■ = Heritage Speakers

Holt Spanish 1B
Lesson Planner
Copyright © by Holt, Rinehart and Winston. All rights reserved.

Teacher's Name _____ Class _____ Date _____

CAPÍTULO 6

BLOCK 3 90-MINUTE LESSON PLAN

Practice Options
- *Lab Book,* pp. 38–39
- ***Cuaderno de vocabulario y gramática,*** pp. 20–22
- ***Cuaderno de actividades,*** pp. 15–18 ▲●■
- *Activities for Communication,* pp. 21–22 ▲■
- ***Cuaderno para hispanohablantes,*** Chapter 6 ■
- *Teaching Transparencies:* ***Vocabulario y gramática*** Answers, pp. 20–22 ▲●■
- *Video Guide,* pp. 56–57 ▲●■
- *Grammar Tutor for Students of Spanish,* Chapter 6 ●■
- *Interactive Tutor* (Disc 2) or *DVD Tutor* (Disc 2) ▲●■
- Online Practice, Chapter 6 (go.hrw.com, Keyword: EXP1B CH6)

Assessment Options
- *Assessment Program*: **Prueba: Vocabulario 1**, pp. 17–18
- *Assessment Program*: Alternative Assessment Guide, pp. 241, 249, 257 ▲●■
- Test Generator

▲ = Advanced Learners ◆ = Slower Pace Learners ● = Special Learning Needs ■ = Heritage Speakers

Holt Spanish 1B   Lesson Planner

Teacher's Name _____ Class _____ Date _____

¡A comer!

CAPÍTULO 6

BLOCK 4 90-MINUTE LESSON PLAN

STANDARDS FOR FOREIGN LANGUAGE LEARNING: BLOCK 4

Gramática en acción 1

Communication 1.1: Students engage in conversations, provide and obtain information, express feelings and emotions, and exchange opinions.

Communication 1.2: Students understand and interpret written and spoken language on a variety of topics.

Communication 1.3: Students present information, concepts, and ideas to an audience of listeners or readers on a variety of topics.

Cultures 2.2: Students demonstrate an understanding of the relationship between the products and perspectives of the culture studied.

Communities 5.2: Students show evidence of becoming life–long learners by using the language for personal enjoyment and enrichment.

CORE INSTRUCTION

Warm-Up
- (5 min.) Have students do Bell Work 6.3, p. 48.

Gramática en acción 1
- (10 min.) Review **ser** and **estar**, p. 46.
- (25 min.) Have students do Activities 12–15, p. 47.
- (30 min.) Present **Gramática: pedir** and **servir**, p. 48 using Teaching **Gramática**, p. 48.
- (10 min.) Play Audio CD 6, Tr. 2 for Activity 16, p. 48.
- (5 min.) Have students do Activity 17, p. 48.

Wrap-Up
- (5 min.) Have students do Bell Work 6.4, p. 50.

OPTIONAL RESOURCES
- (10 min.) **Comunicación** (TE), **pp.** 47, 49
- (5 min.) Practices and Perspectives, p. 49
- (5 min.) Slower Pace Learners, p. 47. ◆

▲ = Advanced Learners   ◆ = Slower Pace Learners   ● = Special Learning Needs   ■ = Heritage Speakers

Holt Spanish 1B

Lesson Planner

Teacher's Name _____ Class _____ Date _____

CAPÍTULO 6

BLOCK 4 90-MINUTE LESSON PLAN

Practice Options
- *Lab Book,* pp. 38–39
- ***Cuaderno de vocabulario y gramática,*** pp. 20–22
- ***Cuaderno de actividades,*** pp. 15–18 ▲ ● ■
- *Activities for Communication,* pp. 21–22 ▲ ■
- ***Cuaderno para hispanohablantes,*** Chapter 6 ■
- *Teaching Transparencies:* Bell Work 6.3, 6.4; ***Vocabulario y gramática*** Answers, pp. 20–22 ▲ ● ■
- *Video Guide,* pp. 56–57 ▲ ● ■
- *Grammar Tutor for Students of Spanish,* Chapter 6 ● ■
- *Interactive Tutor* (Disc 2) or *DVD Tutor* (Disc 2) ▲ ● ■
- Online Practice, Chapter 6 (go.hrw.com, Keyword: EXP1B CH6)

▲ = Advanced Learners ◆ = Slower Pace Learners ● = Special Learning Needs ■ = Heritage Speakers

Holt Spanish 1B   Lesson Planner

Teacher's Name _____ Class _____ Date _____

¡A comer!

CAPÍTULO 6

BLOCK 5 90-MINUTE LESSON PLAN

STANDARDS FOR FOREIGN LANGUAGE LEARNING: BLOCK 5

Gramática en acción 1

Communication 1.1: Students engage in conversations, provide and obtain information, express feelings and emotions, and exchange opinions.

Communication 1.2: Students understand and interpret written and spoken language on a variety of topics.

Communication 1.3: Students present information, concepts, and ideas to an audience of listeners or readers on a variety of topics.

Cultures 2.1: Students demonstrate an understanding of the relationship between the practices and perspectives of the culture studied.

CORE INSTRUCTION

Warm-Up
- (5 min.) Review answers to Activity 17 as a class.

Gramática en acción 1
- (20 min.) Have students do Activities 18–20, p. 49.
- (10 min.) Show **GramaVisión 1,** Segment 3.
- (20 min.) Present **Gramática: preferir, poder** and **probar**, p. 50 using Teaching **Gramática**, p. 50.
- (30 min.) Have students do Activities 21–24, pp. 50–51.

Wrap-Up
- (5 min.) Have students do Bell Work 6.5, p. 54. Remind students to study for **Prueba: Gramática 1.**

OPTIONAL RESOURCES
- (10 min.) Advanced Learners, p. 49 ▲
- (10 min.) **Comunicación** (TE), p. 51
- (5 min.) Multiple Intelligences, p. 49
- (5 min.) Slower Pace Learners, p. 51 ◆
- (5 min.) Special Learning Needs, p. 51 ●

▲ = Advanced Learners ◆ = Slower Pace Learners ● = Special Learning Needs ■ = Heritage Speakers

Holt Spanish 1B — Lesson Planner

Teacher's Name _____ Class _____ Date _____

CAPÍTULO 6

BLOCK 5 90-MINUTE LESSON PLAN

Practice Options
- *Lab Book,* pp. 38–39
- ***Cuaderno de vocabulario y gramática,*** pp. 20–22
- ***Cuaderno de actividades***, pp. 15–18 ▲ ● ■
- *Activities for Communication,* pp. 21–22 ▲ ■
- ***Cuaderno para hispanohablantes,*** Chapter 6 ■
- *Teaching Transparencies:* Bell Work, 6.5; ***Vocabulario y gramática*** Answers, pp. 20–22 ▲ ● ■
- *Video Guide,* pp. 56–57 ▲ ● ■
- *Grammar Tutor for Students of Spanish,* Chapter 6 ● ■
- *Interactive Tutor* (Disc 2) or *DVD Tutor* (Disc 2) ▲ ● ■
- Online Practice, Chapter 6 (go.hrw.com, Keyword: EXP1B CH6)

▲ = Advanced Learners ◆ = Slower Pace Learners ● = Special Learning Needs ■ = Heritage Speakers

Holt Spanish 1B — Lesson Planner

Teacher's Name _____ Class _____ Date _____

¡A comer!

CAPÍTULO 6

BLOCK 6 90-MINUTE LESSON PLAN

STANDARDS FOR FOREIGN LANGUAGE LEARNING: BLOCK 6

Gramática en acción 1
Communication 1.1: Students engage in conversations, provide and obtain information, express feelings and emotions, and exchange opinions.
Communication 1.2: Students understand and interpret written and spoken language on a variety of topics.
Communication 1.3: Students present information, concepts, and ideas to an audience of listeners or readers on a variety of topics.

Cultura
Communication 1.2: Students understand and interpret written and spoken language on a variety of topics.
Cultures 2.2: Students demonstrate an understanding of the relationship between the products and perspectives of the culture studied.

Comparisons 4.2: Students demonstrate understanding of the concept of culture through comparisons of the cultures studied and their own.
Communities 5.1: Students use the language both within and beyond the school setting.
Communities 5.2: Students show evidence of becoming life–long learners by using the language for personal enjoyment and enrichment.

Vocabulario en acción 2
Communication 1.2: Students understand and interpret written and spoken language on a variety of topics.
Comparisons 4.1: Students demonstrate understanding of the nature of language through comparisons of the language studied and their own.

CORE INSTRUCTION

Warm-Up
- (10 min.) Review **Gramática en acción 1**, pp. 46–51.

Gramática en acción 1
Assess
- (20 min.) Give **Prueba: Gramática 1.**

Cultura
- (30 min.) See Teaching **Cultura,** p. 52.
- (5 min.) Present and assign **Comunidad,** p. 53.

Vocabulario en acción 2
- (20 min.) Present **Vocabulario 2,** pp. 54–55 using Teaching **Vocabulario,** p. 54.

Wrap-Up
- (5 min.) Present Language Note and **También se puede decir,** p. 55.

OPTIONAL RESOURCES
- (5 min.) Heritage Speakers, p. 52 ■
- (5 min.) Map Activities, p. 52
- (5 min.) Special Learning Needs, p. 53 ●
- (10 min.) Advanced Learners, p. 53 ▲
- (10 min.) **Comunidad** (TE), p. 53
- (5 min.) Products and Perspectives, p. 53
- (10 min.) Community Link, p. 53
- (5 min.) Special Learning Needs, p. 55 ●

▲ = Advanced Learners ◆ = Slower Pace Learners ● = Special Learning Needs ■ = Heritage Speakers

Holt Spanish 1B Lesson Planner

Teacher's Name _____ Class _____ Date _____

CAPÍTULO 6

BLOCK 6 90-MINUTE LESSON PLAN

Practice Options
- *Lab Book*, p. 39–41
- ***Cuaderno de vocabulario y gramática,*** pp. 23–25
- ***Cuaderno de actividades***, p. 19 ▲ ● ■
- *Activities for Communication*, pp. 21–24 ▲ ■
- *Teaching Transparencies:* **Vocabulario** 6.3, 6.4; ***Vocabulario y gramática*** Answers, pp. 23–25 ▲ ● ■
- *TPR Storytelling Book*, pp. 32–33 ▲ ●
- *Video Guide*, pp. 53, 57–59 ▲ ● ■
- *Interactive Tutor* (Disc 2) or *DVD Tutor* (Disc 2) ▲ ● ■
- Online Practice, Chapter 6 (go.hrw.com, Keyword: EXP1B CH6)

Assessment Options
- *Assessment Program*: **Prueba: Gramática 1**, pp. 19–20
- *Assessment Program*: **Prueba: Aplicacíon 1**, pp. 21–22
- *Assessment Program*: Alternative Assessment Guide, pp. 241, 249, 257 ▲ ● ■
- *Audio CD 6*, Tr. 15
- Test Generator

▲ = Advanced Learners ◆ = Slower Pace Learners ● = Special Learning Needs ■ = Heritage Speakers

Teacher's Name _____ Class _____ Date _____

¡A comer!

CAPÍTULO 6

BLOCK 7 90-MINUTE LESSON PLAN

STANDARDS FOR FOREIGN LANGUAGE LEARNING: BLOCK 7

Vocabulario en acción 2

Communication 1.1: Students engage in conversations, provide and obtain information, express feelings and emotions, and exchange opinions.

Communication 1.2: Students understand and interpret written and spoken language on a variety of topics.

Communication 1.3: Students present information, concepts, and ideas to an audience of listeners or readers on a variety of topics.

Cultures 2.1: Students demonstrate an understanding of the relationship between the practices and perspectives of the culture studied.

Comparisons 4.1: Students demonstrate understanding of the nature of language through comparisons of the language studied and their own.

CORE INSTRUCTION

Warm-Up
- (5 min.) Have students ask a partner the questions from **¡Exprésate!**, p. 55.

Vocabulario en acción 2
- (10 min.) Show **ExpresaVisión,** Ch. 6.
- (10 min.) Review **Vocabulario 2,** pp. 54–59.
- (5 min.) Present **Nota cultural,** p. 56.
- (40 min.) Have students do Activities 25–31, pp. 56–57.
- (15 min.) See Teaching **¡Exprésate!,** p. 58.

Wrap-Up
- (5 min.) Have students do Bell Work 6.6, p. 60.

OPTIONAL RESOURCES
- (5 min.) TPR activity, p. 55
- (10 min.) Advanced Learners, p. 55 ▲
- (5 min.) Practices and Perspectives, p. 56
- (5 min.) Game, p. 56
- (5 min.) Slower Pace Learners, p. 57 ◆
- (5 min.) Multiple Intelligences, p. 57
- (10 min.) **Comunicación** (TE), p. 57
- (5 min.) Language Note, p. 57

▲ = Advanced Learners   ◆ = Slower Pace Learners   ● = Special Learning Needs   ■ = Heritage Speakers

Holt Spanish 1B   Lesson Planner

Teacher's Name _____ Class _____ Date _____

CAPÍTULO 6

BLOCK 7 90-MINUTE LESSON PLAN

Practice Options
- *Lab Book,* pp. 40–41
- ***Cuaderno de vocabulario y gramática,*** pp. 23–25
- *Activities for Communication,* pp. 23–24 ▲ ■
- ***Cuaderno para hispanohablantes,*** Chapter 6 ■
- *Teaching Transparencies:* Bell Work 6.6; **Vocabulario** 6.3, 6.4; ***Vocabulario y gramática*** Answers, pp. 23–25 ▲ ● ■
- *Video Guide,* pp. 58–59 ▲ ● ■
- *TPR Storytelling Book,* pp. 32–33 ▲ ●
- *Interactive Tutor* (Disc 2) or *DVD Tutor* (Disc 2) ▲ ● ■
- Online Practice, Chapter 6 (go.hrw.com, Keyword: EXP1B CH6)

▲ = Advanced Learners   ◆ = Slower Pace Learners   ● = Special Learning Needs   ■ = Heritage Speakers

Holt Spanish 1B   Lesson Planner

Teacher's Name _____ Class _____ Date _____

¡A comer!

CAPÍTULO 6

BLOCK 8 90-MINUTE LESSON PLAN

STANDARDS FOR FOREIGN LANGUAGE LEARNING: BLOCK 8

Vocabulario en acción 2

Communication 1.1: Students engage in conversations, provide and obtain information, express feelings and emotions, and exchange opinions.
Communication 1.2: Students understand and interpret written and spoken language on a variety of topics.
Communication 1.3: Students present information, concepts, and ideas to an audience of listeners or readers on a variety of topics.
Cultures 2.1: Students demonstrate an understanding of the relationship between the practices and perspectives of the culture studied.

Comparisons 4.1: Students demonstrate understanding of the nature of language through comparisons of the language studied and their own.

Gramática en acción 2

Communication 1.1: Students engage in conversations, provide and obtain information, express feelings and emotions, and exchange opinions.
Communication 1.2: Students understand and interpret written and spoken language on a variety of topics.
Communication 1.3: Students present information, concepts, and ideas to an audience of listeners or readers on a variety of topics.

CORE INSTRUCTION

Warm-Up
- (5 min.) Review **¡Exprésate!,** p. 58.

Vocabulario en acción 2
- (10 min.) Play Audio CD 6, Tr. 6 for Activity 32, p. 58.
- (30 min.) Have students do Activities 33–36, pp. 58–59.

Gramática en acción 2
- (25 min.) Present **Gramática:** Direct objects and direct object pronouns, p. 60 using Teaching **Gramática,** p. 60.
- (15 min.) Have students do Activities 37–38, pp. 60–61.

Wrap-Up
- (5 min.) See Common Error Alert, p. 60. Remind students to study for **Prueba: Vocabulario 2**.

OPTIONAL RESOURCES
- (5 min.) Language to Language, p. 58
- (5 min.) Extension, p. 59
- (10 min.) Special Learning Needs, p. 59 ●
- (10 min.) **Comunicación** (TE), p. 59
- (5 min.) Slower Pace Learners, p. 59 ◆

▲ = Advanced Learners   ◆ = Slower Pace Learners   ● = Special Learning Needs   ■ = Heritage Speakers

Holt Spanish 1B

Lesson Planner

Teacher's Name _____ Class _____ Date _____

CAPÍTULO 6

BLOCK 8 90-MINUTE LESSON PLAN

Practice Options
- *Lab Book,* pp. 17, 40–41
- **Cuaderno de vocabulario y gramática,** pp. 23–28
- **Cuaderno de actividades**, p. 20–23 ▲ ● ■
- *Activities for Communication,* pp. 23–24 ▲ ■
- **Cuaderno para hispanohablantes,** Chapter 6 ■
- *Teaching Transparencies:* **Vocabulario** 6.3, 6.4; **Vocabulario y gramática** Answers, pp. 23–28 ▲ ● ■
- *Video Guide,* pp. 58–59 ▲ ● ■
- *TPR Storytelling Book,* pp. 32–33 ▲ ●
- *Interactive Tutor* (Disc 2) or *DVD Tutor* (Disc 2) ▲ ● ■
- Online Practice, Chapter 6 (go.hrw.com, Keyword: EXP1B CH6)

▲ = Advanced Learners   ◆ = Slower Pace Learners   ● = Special Learning Needs   ■ = Heritage Speakers

Holt Spanish 1B   Lesson Planner

Teacher's Name _____ Class _____ Date _____

¡A comer!

CAPÍTULO 6

BLOCK 9 90-MINUTE LESSON PLAN

STANDARDS FOR FOREIGN LANGUAGE LEARNING: BLOCK 9

Vocabulario en acción 2
Communication 1.1: Students engage in conversations, provide and obtain information, express feelings and emotions, and exchange opinions.
Communication 1.2: Students understand and interpret written and spoken language on a variety of topics.
Communication 1.3: Students present information, concepts, and ideas to an audience of listeners or readers on a variety of topics.
Cultures 2.1: Students demonstrate an understanding of the relationship between the practices and perspectives of the culture studied.
Comparisons 4.1: Students demonstrate understanding of the nature of language through comparisons of the language studied and their own.

Gramática en acción 2
Communication 1.1: Students engage in conversations, provide and obtain information, express feelings and emotions, and exchange opinions.
Communication 1.2: Students understand and interpret written and spoken language on a variety of topics.
Communication 1.3: Students present information, concepts, and ideas to an audience of listeners or readers on a variety of topics.
Cultures 2.1: Students demonstrate an understanding of the relationship between the practices and perspectives of the culture studied.
Comparisons 4.2: Students demonstrate understanding of the concept of culture through comparisons of the cultures studied and their own.

CORE INSTRUCTION

Warm-Up
- (10 min.) Review **Vocabulario en acción 2**, pp. 54–59.

Vocabulario en acción 2

Assess
- (20 min.) Give **Prueba: Vocabulario 2**.

Gramática en acción 2
- (10 min.) Review direct objects and direct object pronouns, p. 60.
- (15 min.) Have students do Activities 39–40, pp. 60–61.
- (30 min.) Present **Gramática**: Affirmative informal commands, p. 62 using Teaching **Gramática,** p. 62.

Wrap-Up
- (5 min.) Have students do Bell Work 6.7, p. 62.

OPTIONAL RESOURCES
- (10 min.) **Comunicación** (TE)**,** p. 61
- (5 min.) Teacher to Teacher, p. 61
- (5 min.) Slower Pace Learners, p. 61 ◆
- (5 min.) Multiple Intelligences, p. 61 ◆

▲ = Advanced Learners ◆ = Slower Pace Learners ● = Special Learning Needs ■ = Heritage Speakers

Holt Spanish 1B — Lesson Planner

Teacher's Name _____ Class _____ Date _____

CAPÍTULO 6

BLOCK 9 90-MINUTE LESSON PLAN

Practice Options
- *Lab Book*, pp. 40–41
- ***Cuaderno de vocabulario y gramática,*** pp. 26–28
- *Activities for Communication*, pp. 23–24 ▲ ■
- ***Cuaderno de actividades***, pp. 20–23 ▲ ● ■
- ***Cuaderno para hispanohablantes,*** Chapter 6 ■
- *Teaching Transparencies:* Bell Work 6.7; **Vocabulario y gramática** Answers, pp. 26–28 ▲ ● ■
- *Grammar Tutor for Students of Spanish*, Chapter 6 ● ■
- *Video Guide*, pp. 58–59 ▲ ● ■
- *Interactive Tutor* (Disc 2) or *DVD Tutor* (Disc 2) ▲ ● ■
- Online Practice, Chapter 6 (go.hrw.com, Keyword: EXP1B CH6)

Assessment Options
- *Assessment Program*: **Prueba: Vocabulario 2**, pp. 23–24
- *Assessment Program*: Alternative Assessment Guide, pp. 241, 249, 257 ▲ ● ■
- Test Generator

▲ = Advanced Learners ♦ = Slower Pace Learners ● = Special Learning Needs ■ = Heritage Speakers

Holt Spanish 1B　　　　　　　　　　　　　　　　　　　　　　　　　　　　Lesson Planner

Teacher's Name _____ Class _____ Date _____

¡A comer!

CAPÍTULO 6

BLOCK 10 90-MINUTE LESSON PLAN

STANDARDS FOR FOREIGN LANGUAGE LEARNING: BLOCK 10

Gramática en acción 2

Communication 1.1: Students engage in conversations, provide and obtain information, express feelings and emotions, and exchange opinions.

Communication 1.2: Students understand and interpret written and spoken language on a variety of topics.

Communication 1.3: Students present information, concepts, and ideas to an audience of listeners or readers on a variety of topics.

Cultures 2.1: Students demonstrate an understanding of the relationship between the practices and perspectives of the culture studied.

Comparisons 4.2: Students demonstrate understanding of the concept of culture through comparisons of the cultures studied and their own.

CORE INSTRUCTION

Warm-Up
- (5 min.) Give students a few informal commands that they can act out.

Gramática en acción 2
- (5 min.) Review affirmative informal commands, p. 62.
- (5 min.) Present **Nota cultural**, p. 62.
- (20 min.) Have students do Activities 41–44, pp. 62–63. See Special Learning Needs, p. 63. ●
- (10 min.) Show **GramaVisión 1,** Segment 6.
- (20 min.) Present **Gramática:** Affirmative informal commands with pronouns, p. 64 using Teaching **Gramática,** p. 64.
- (15 min.) Have students do Activities 45–46, p. 64.
- (5 min.) Play Audio CD 6, Tr. 7 for Activity 47, p. 65.

Wrap-Up
- (5 min.) Have students do Bell Work 6.8, p. 64. Remind students to study for **Prueba: Gramática 2.**

OPTIONAL RESOURCES
- (5 min.) Teacher to Teacher, p. 63
- (10 min.) Advanced Learners, p. 63 ▲
- (10 min.) **Comunicación** (TE), p. 63

▲ = Advanced Learners   ◆ = Slower Pace Learners   ● = Special Learning Needs   ■ = Heritage Speakers

Holt Spanish 1B   Lesson Planner

Teacher's Name _____ Class _____ Date _____

CAPÍTULO 6

BLOCK 10 90-MINUTE LESSON PLAN

Practice Options
- *Lab Book,* pp. 40–41
- **Cuaderno de vocabulario y gramática,** pp. 26–28
- *Activities for Communication,* pp. 23–24 ▲ ■
- **Cuaderno de actividades,** pp. 20–23 ▲ ● ■
- **Cuaderno para hispanohablantes,** Chapter 6 ■
- *Teaching Transparencies:* Bell Work 6.8; **Vocabulario y gramática** Answers, pp. 26–28 ▲ ● ■
- *Grammar Tutor for Students of Spanish,* Chapter 6 ● ■
- *Video Guide,* pp. 58–59 ▲ ● ■
- *Interactive Tutor* (Disc 2) or *DVD Tutor* (Disc 2) ▲ ● ■
- Online Practice, Chapter 6 (go.hrw.com, Keyword: EXP1B CH6)

▲ = Advanced Learners ◆ = Slower Pace Learners ● = Special Learning Needs ■ = Heritage Speakers

Holt Spanish 1B — Lesson Planner

Teacher's Name _____ Class _____ Date _____

¡A comer!

CAPÍTULO 6

BLOCK 11 90-MINUTE LESSON PLAN

STANDARDS FOR FOREIGN LANGUAGE LEARNING: BLOCK 11

Gramática en acción 2
Communication 1.1: Students engage in conversations, provide and obtain information, express feelings and emotions, and exchange opinions.
Communication 1.2: Students understand and interpret written and spoken language on a variety of topics.
Communication 1.3: Students present information, concepts, and ideas to an audience of listeners or readers on a variety of topics.
Cultures 2.1: Students demonstrate an understanding of the relationship between the practices and perspectives of the culture studied.
Comparisons 4.2: Students demonstrate understanding of the concept of culture through comparisons of the cultures studied and their own.

Conexiones culturales
Communication 1.1: Students engage in conversations, provide and obtain information, express feelings and emotions, and exchange opinions.
Cultures 2.1: Students demonstrate an understanding of the relationship between the practices and perspectives of the culture studied.
Cultures 2.2: Students demonstrate an understanding of the relationship between the products and perspectives of the culture studied.
Connections 3.1: Students reinforce and further their knowledge of other disciplines through the foreign language.
Comparisons 4.2: Students demonstrate understanding of the concept of culture through comparisons of the cultures studied and their own.

CORE INSTRUCTION

Warm-Up
- (5 min.) Review class answers to Activities 45–46, p. 64.

Gramática en acción 2
- (10 min.) Have students do Activities 48–49, p. 65.
- (15 min.) Review **Gramática en acción 2,** pp. 60–65.

Assess
- (20 min.) Give **Prueba: Gramática 2.**

Conexiones culturales
- (40 min.) See Teaching **Conexiones culturales,** #1–6, p. 66.

OPTIONAL RESOURCES
- (10 min.) Multiple Intelligences, pp. 65, 67
- (5 min.) Practices and Perspectives, p. 67
- (5 min.) Suggestion, p. 67
- (5 min.) **Conexiones culturales,** Activity 3, p. 67
- (5 min.) Advanced Learners, p. 67. ▲
- (5 min.) Slower Pace Learners, p. 65. ◆●

▲ = Advanced Learners   ◆ = Slower Pace Learners   ● = Special Learning Needs   ■ = Heritage Speakers

Holt Spanish 1B   Lesson Planner

Teacher's Name _____ Class _____ Date _____

CAPÍTULO
6

BLOCK 11 90-MINUTE LESSON PLAN

Practice Options
- *Lab Book*, pp. 40–41
- **Cuaderno de vocabulario y gramática,** pp. 26–28
- *Activities for Communication*, pp. 23–24 ▲ ■
- **Cuaderno de actividades**, pp. 20–23 ▲ ● ■
- **Cuaderno para hispanohablantes,** Chapter 6 ■
- *Teaching Transparencies:* **Vocabulario y gramática** Answers, pp. 26–28 ▲ ● ■
- *Grammar Tutor for Students of Spanish*, Chapter 6 ● ■
- *Video Guide*, pp. 58–59 ▲ ● ■
- *Interactive Tutor* (Disc 2) or *DVD Tutor* (Disc 2) ▲ ● ■
- Online Practice, Chapter 6 (go.hrw.com, Keyword: EXP1B CH6)

Assessment Options
- *Assessment Program*: **Prueba: Gramática 2**, pp. 25–26
- *Assessment Program*: **Prueba: Aplicacíon 2**, pp. 27–28
- *Audio CD 6*, Tr. 16
- *Assessment Program*: Alternative Assessment Guide, pp. 241, 249, 257 ▲ ● ■
- Test Generator

▲ = Advanced Learners ◆ = Slower Pace Learners ● = Special Learning Needs ■ = Heritage Speakers

Holt Spanish 1B Lesson Planner

Teacher's Name _____ Class _____ Date _____

¡A comer!

CAPÍTULO 6

BLOCK 12 90-MINUTE LESSON PLAN

STANDARDS FOR FOREIGN LANGUAGE LEARNING: BLOCK 12

Novela en video
Communication 1.1: Students engage in conversations, provide and obtain information, express feelings and emotions, and exchange opinions.
Communication 1.2: Students understand and interpret written and spoken language on a variety of topics.
Cultures 2.1: Students demonstrate an understanding of the relationship between the practices and perspectives of the culture studied.
Connections 3.2: Students acquire information and recognize the distinctive viewpoints that are only available through the foreign language and its cultures.
Comparisons 4.2: Students demonstrate understanding of the concept of culture through comparisons of the cultures studied and their own.

Leamos y escribamos
Communication 1.3: Students present information, concepts, and ideas to an audience of listeners or readers on a variety of topics.
Connections 3.1: Students reinforce and further their knowledge of other disciplines through the foreign language.
Connections 3.2: Students acquire information and recognize the distinctive viewpoints that are only available through the foreign language and its cultures.
Comparisons 4.2: Students demonstrate understanding of the concept of culture through comparisons of the cultures studied and their own.
Communities 5.1: Students use the language both within and beyond the school setting.

CORE INSTRUCTION

Warm-Up
- (5 min.) See Visual Learners, p. 68.

Novela en video
- (35 min.) See Teaching **Novela en video**, p. 68.

Leamos y escribamos
- (30 min.) See Teaching **Leamos**, p. 72.
- (10 min.) Present **Taller del escritor**, p. 73 using Teaching **Escribamos**, #1–2, p. 72.
- (5 min.) Have students begin **Taller del escritor**, step 1, p. 73. Assign the rest as homework.

Wrap-Up
- (5 min.) Read the recipe for **Salsa**, p. 73, and make sure all students understand the ingredients and instructions.

OPTIONAL RESOURCES
- (5 min.) Gestures, p. 68
- (5 min.) Comparing and Contrasting, p. 69
- (10 min.) Culminating Project, p. 70
- (5 min.) Language Note, p. 70
- (5 min.) **Más práctica**, p. 71
- (5 min.) Applying the Strategies, p. 72
- (10 min.) Additional Reading, pp. 266–267
- (5 min.) Special Learning Needs, p. 73 ●

▲ = Advanced Learners ◆ = Slower Pace Learners ● = Special Learning Needs ■ = Heritage Speakers

Holt Spanish 1B

Lesson Planner

Teacher's Name _____ Class _____ Date _____

CAPÍTULO 6

BLOCK 12 90-MINUTE LESSON PLAN

Practice Options
- *Lab Book,* pp. 42
- ***Cuaderno de actividades,*** p. 24 ▲ ● ■
- ***Cuaderno para hispanohablantes,*** pp. 45–52 ■
- *Reading Strategies and Skills Handbook,* Chapter 6 ▲ ● ■
- ***¡Lee conmigo!*** Level 1 Reader ▲ ■
- *Video Guide,* pp. 54, 60 ▲ ● ■
- *Interactive Tutor* (Disc 2) or *DVD Tutor* (Disc 2) ▲ ● ■
- Online Practice, Chapter 6 (go.hrw.com, Keyword: EXP1B CH6)

▲ = Advanced Learners ◆ = Slower Pace Learners ● = Special Learning Needs ■ = Heritage Speakers

Teacher's Name _____ Class _____ Date _____

CAPÍTULO 6

¡A comer!

BLOCK 13 90-MINUTE LESSON PLAN

STANDARDS FOR FOREIGN LANGUAGE LEARNING: BLOCK 13

Leamos y escribamos

Communication 1.3: Students present information, concepts, and ideas to an audience of listeners or readers on a variety of topics.

Connections 3.1: Students reinforce and further their knowledge of other disciplines through the foreign language.

Connections 3.2: Students acquire information and recognize the distinctive viewpoints that are only available through the foreign language and its cultures.

Comparisons 4.2: Students demonstrate understanding of the concept of culture through comparisons of the cultures studied and their own.

Communities 5.1: Students use the language both within and beyond the school setting.

Repaso

Communication 1.2: Students understand and interpret written and spoken language on a variety of topics.

Communication 1.3: Students present information, concepts, and ideas to an audience of listeners or readers on a variety of topics.

Cultures 2.1: Students demonstrate an understanding of the relationship between the practices and perspectives of the culture studied.

Cultures 2.2: Students demonstrate an understanding of the relationship between the products and perspectives of the culture studied.

CORE INSTRUCTION

Leamos y escribamos

Warm-Up
- (5 min.) Review the writing rubric you will use to assess this assignment.
- (30 min.) See Teaching **Escribamos,** #3, p. 72.

Repaso
- (25 min.) Have students do Activities 1–5, pp. 74–75.
- (5 min.) Play Audio CD 6, Tr. 10 for Activity 6, p. 75.
- (5 min.) Have students do Activity 7, p. 75.
- (10 min.) Play Audio CD 6, Tr. 11–13 for **Letra y sonido,** p. 76.

Wrap-Up
- (10 min.) See Game, p. 77. Remind students to study for Chapter Test.

OPTIONAL RESOURCES
- (10 min.) Advanced Learners, p. 73 ▲
- (10 min.) Special Learning Needs, p. 73 ●
- (5 min.) Fold-n-Learn, p. 74
- (5 min.) Reteaching, p. 74
- (5 min.) **Letra y sonido,** p. 76

▲ = Advanced Learners ◆ = Slower Pace Learners ● = Special Learning Needs ■ = Heritage Speakers

Holt Spanish 1B — Lesson Planner

Teacher's Name _____ Class _____ Date _____

CAPÍTULO 6

BLOCK 13 90-MINUTE LESSON PLAN

Practice Options
- *Lab Book,* pp. 18, 41
- *Activities for Communication,* pp. 48, 65–66 ▲■
- **Cuaderno para hispanohablantes,** Chapter 6 ■
- *Teaching Transparencies:* **Situación, Capítulo 6**; Picture Stories, Chapter 6 ▲●■
- *Video Guide,* pp. 54, 59 ▲●■
- *TPR Storytelling Book,* pp. 34–35 ▲●
- *Grammar Tutor for Students of Spanish,* Chapter 6 ●■
- *Interactive Tutor* (Disc 2) or *DVD Tutor* (Disc 2) ▲●■
- Online Practice, Chapter 6 (go.hrw.com, Keyword: EXP1B CH6)

▲ = Advanced Learners   ◆ = Slower Pace Learners   ● = Special Learning Needs   ■ = Heritage Speakers

Holt Spanish 1B   Lesson Planner

Teacher's Name _____ Class _____ Date _____

¡A comer!

CAPÍTULO 6

BLOCK 14 90-MINUTE LESSON PLAN

STANDARDS FOR FOREIGN LANGUAGE LEARNING: BLOCK 14

Integración

Communication 1.1: Students engage in conversations, provide and obtain information, express feelings and emotions, and exchange opinions.

Communication 1.2: Students understand and interpret written and spoken language on a variety of topics.

Communication 1.3: Students present information, concepts, and ideas to an audience of listeners or readers on a variety of topics.

Communities 5.1: Students use the language both within and beyond the school setting.

CORE INSTRUCTION

Chapter Assessment

Assess
- (50 min.) Give Chapter Test.

Warm-Up
- (5 min.) See Fine Art Connection, Introduction, p. 79.

Integración
- (10 min.) Play Audio CD 6, Tr. 14 for Activity 1, p. 78.
- (20 min.) Have students do Activities 2–4, pp. 78–79.

Wrap-Up
- (5 min.) Preview **Geocultura: Argentina**, pp. 80–83.

OPTIONAL RESOURCES
- (10 min.) **Más práctica,** p. 78
- (10 min.) Culture Project, p. 78

▲ = Advanced Learners ◆ = Slower Pace Learners ● = Special Learning Needs ■ = Heritage Speakers

Holt Spanish 1B

Lesson Planner

Teacher's Name _____ Class _____ Date _____

CAPÍTULO 6

BLOCK 14 90-MINUTE LESSON PLAN

Practice Options
- *Lab Book,* pp. 18, 41
- ***Cuaderno de actividades***, pp. 25–26 ▲ ● ■
- *Teaching Transparencies:* Fine Art, Chapter 6 ▲ ● ■
- *Interactive Tutor* (Disc 2) or *DVD Tutor* (Disc 2) ▲ ● ■
- Online Practice, Chapter 6 (go.hrw.com, Keyword: EXP1B CH6)

Assessment Options
- *Assessment Program*: **Examen, Capítulo 6,** pp. 133–143
- *Assessment Program*: **Examen oral: Capítulo 6,** p. 144
- *Audio CD* 6, Tr. 17–18
- *Assessment Program*: Alternative Assessment Guide, pp. 241, 249, 257 ▲ ● ■
- *Standardized Assessment Tutor,* Chapter 6
- Test Generator
- Online Practice, Chapter 6 (go.hrw.com, Keyword: EXP1B CH6)

▲ = Advanced Learners   ◆ = Slower Pace Learners   ● = Special Learning Needs   ■ = Heritage Speakers

Holt Spanish 1B — Lesson Planner

Teacher's Name _____ Class _____ Date _____

Cuerpo sano, mente sana

CAPÍTULO 7

BLOCK 1 90-MINUTE LESSON PLAN

STANDARDS FOR FOREIGN LANGUAGE LEARNING: BLOCK 1

Chapter Opener
Communication 1.2: Students understand and interpret written and spoken language on a variety of topics.

Vocabulario en acción 1
Communication 1.2: Students understand and interpret written and spoken language on a variety of topics.

Before starting **Capítulo 7,** you may wish to teach **Geocultura: Argentina,** pp. 80–83. For teaching suggestions, see pp. xv–xvi of this *Lesson Planner*.

CORE INSTRUCTION

Warm-Up
- (5 min.) See Learning Tips, p. 85.

Chapter Opener
- (5 min.) See Using the Photo and **Más vocabulario,** p. 84.
- (5 min.) See **Objetivos,** p. 84.

Vocabulario en acción 1, pp. 86–91
- (35 min.) Introduce **Vocabulario en acción 1,** pp. 86–87 using Teaching **Vocabulario,** p. 86.
- (35 min.) Have students do Activities 1–5, pp. 88–89.

Wrap-Up
- (5 min.) Have students practice pronunciation of all new vocabulary words.

OPTIONAL RESOURCES
- (5 min.) Common Error Alert, p. 87
- (5 min.) **También se puede decir,** p. 87
- (10 min.) Advanced Learners, p. 87 ▲
- (5 min.) Multiple Intelligences, p. 87
- (5 min.) Bell Work 7.1, p. 86
- (5 min.) **Más práctica,** p. 88
- (10 min.) **Comunicación** (TE), p. 89
- (10 min.) Slower Pace Learners, p. 89 ◆

▲ = Advanced Learners   ◆ = Slower Pace Learners   ● = Special Learning Needs   ■ = Heritage Speakers

Holt Spanish 1B

Teacher's Name _____ Class _____ Date _____

CAPÍTULO 7

BLOCK 1 90-MINUTE LESSON PLAN

Practice Options
- *Lab Book,* pp. 44–45
- **Cuaderno de vocabulario y gramática,** pp. 29–31
- *Activities for Communication,* pp. 25–26 ▲ ■
- **Cuaderno para hispanohablantes,** Chapter 7 ■
- *Teaching Transparencies:* Bell Work 7.1; Vocabulario 7.1, 7.2; **Vocabulario y gramática** Answers pp. 29–31 ▲ ● ■
- *Video Guide,* pp. 66–67 ▲ ● ■
- *TPR Storytelling Book,* pp. 36–37 ▲ ●
- *Interactive Tutor* (Disc 2) or *DVD Tutor* (Disc 2) ▲ ● ■
- Online Practice, Chapter 7 (go.hrw.com, Keyword: EXP1B CH7)

▲ = Advanced Learners   ◆ = Slower Pace Learners   ● = Special Learning Needs   ■ = Heritage Speakers

Holt Spanish 1B — Lesson Planner

Teacher's Name _____ Class _____ Date _____

Cuerpo sano, mente sana

CAPÍTULO 7

BLOCK 2 90-MINUTE LESSON PLAN

STANDARDS FOR FOREIGN LANGUAGE LEARNING: BLOCK 2

Vocabulario en acción 1

Communication 1.1: Students engage in conversations, provide and obtain information, express feelings and emotions, and exchange opinions.

Communication 1.2: Students understand and interpret written and spoken language on a variety of topics.

Cultures 2.1: Students demonstrate an understanding of the relationship between the Practices and Perspectives of the culture studied.

CORE INSTRUCTION

Warm-Up
- (5 min.) Point to parts of the body and review the vocabulary.

Vocabulario en acción 1
- (5 min.) Show **ExpresaVisión,** Ch. 7.
- (10 min.) Review **Vocabulario 1** and **¡Exprésate!,** pp. 86–87.
- (20 min.) Present **¡Exprésate!,** p. 90 using Teaching **¡Exprésate!,** p. 90.
- (10 min.) Play Audio CD 7, Tr. 1 for Activity 6, p. 90.
- (5 min.) Present **Nota cultural,** p. 90.
- (30 min.) Have students do Activities 7–10, pp. 90–91.

Wrap-Up
- (5 min.) Have students work with a partner to check answers to Activity 7. Remind students to study for **Prueba: Vocabulario 1**.

OPTIONAL RESOURCES
- (5 min.) TPR, p. 87
- (10 min.) Fold-n-Learn, p. 88
- (10 min.) Multiple Intelligences, p. 89
- (10 min.) Science Link, p. 90
- (5 min.) Geography Link, p. 90
- (5 min.) **Comunicación** (TE), p. 91
- (10 min.) Advanced Learners, p. 91 ▲
- (5 min.) Special Learning Needs, p. 91. ●

▲ = Advanced Learners   ◆ = Slower Pace Learners   ● = Special Learning Needs   ■ = Heritage Speakers

Holt Spanish 1B

Lesson Planner

Copyright © by Holt, Rinehart and Winston. All rights reserved.

Teacher's Name _____ Class _____ Date _____

CAPÍTULO 7

BLOCK 2 90-MINUTE LESSON PLAN

Practice Options
- *Lab Book,* pp. 44–45
- ***Cuaderno de vocabulario y gramática,*** pp. 29–31
- *Activities for Communication,* pp. 25–26 ▲ ■
- ***Cuaderno para hispanohablantes,*** Chapter 7 ■
- *Teaching Transparencies:* Vocabulario 7.1, 7.2; ***Vocabulario y gramática*** Answers pp. 29–31 ▲ ● ■
- *Video Guide,* pp. 66–67 ▲ ● ■
- *TPR Storytelling Book,* pp. 36–37 ▲ ●
- *Interactive Tutor* (Disc 2) or *DVD Tutor* (Disc 2) ▲ ● ■
- Online Practice, Chapter 7 (go.hrw.com, Keyword: EXP1B CH7)

▲ = Advanced Learners   ◆ = Slower Pace Learners   ● = Special Learning Needs   ■ = Heritage Speakers

Holt Spanish 1B   Lesson Planner

Teacher's Name _____ Class _____ Date _____

Cuerpo sano, mente sana

CAPÍTULO 7

BLOCK 3 90-MINUTE LESSON PLAN

STANDARDS FOR FOREIGN LANGUAGE LEARNING: BLOCK 3

Vocabulario en acción 1

Communication 1.1: Students engage in conversations, provide and obtain information, express feelings and emotions, and exchange opinions.
Communication 1.2: Students understand and interpret written and spoken language on a variety of topics.
Cultures 2.1: Students demonstrate an understanding of the relationship between the Practices and Perspectives of the culture studied.

Gramática en acción 1

Communication 1.1: Students engage in conversations, provide and obtain information, express feelings and emotions, and exchange opinions.
Communication 1.2: Students understand and interpret written and spoken language on a variety of topics.
Communication 1.3: Students present information, concepts, and ideas to an audience of listeners or readers on a variety of topics.
Cultures 2.1: Students demonstrate an understanding of the relationship between the Practices and Perspectives of the culture studied.

CORE INSTRUCTION

Warm-Up
- (20 min.) Review **Vocabulario en acción 1**, pp. 86–91.

Assess
- (20 min.) Give **Prueba: Vocabulario 1**.

Gramática en acción 1
- (30 min.) Present **Gramática:** Verbs with reflexive pronouns, p. 92 using Teaching **Gramática**, p. 92.
- (5 min.) Play Audio CD 7, Tr. 2 for Activity 11, p. 92.
- (10 min.) Have students do Activity 12, p. 93.

Wrap-Up
- (5 min.) Have students check answers to Activity 12 with a partner.

OPTIONAL RESOURCES
- (5 min.) Special Learning Needs, p. 93 ●
- (5 min.) Bell Work 7.2, p. 92
- (10 min.) *Lab Book,* pp. 20, 44–45
- (5 min.) Slower Pace Learners, p. 93. ◆

▲ = Advanced Learners   ◆ = Slower Pace Learners   ● = Special Learning Needs   ■ = Heritage Speakers

Holt Spanish 1B   Lesson Planner

Teacher's Name _____ Class _____ Date _____

CAPÍTULO 7

BLOCK 3 90-MINUTE LESSON PLAN

Practice Options
- *Cuaderno de vocabulario y gramática,* pp. 32–34
- *Cuaderno de actividades*, pp. 27–30 ▲●■
- *Activities for Communication,* pp. 25–26 ▲■
- *Cuaderno para hispanohablantes,* Chapter 7 ■
- *Teaching Transparencies:* Bell Work 7.2; **Vocabulario y gramática** Answers pp. 32–34 ▲●■
- *Video Guide,* pp. 66–67 ▲●■
- *Grammar Tutor for Students of Spanish,* Chapter 7 ●■
- *Interactive Tutor* (Disc 2) or *DVD Tutor* (Disc 2) ▲●■
- Online Practice, Chapter 7 (go.hrw.com, Keyword: EXP1B CH7)

Assessment Options
- *Assessment Program*: **Prueba: Vocabulario 1**, pp. 37–38
- *Assessment Program*: Alternative Assessment Guide, pp. 242, 250, 258 ▲●■
- Test Generator

▲ = Advanced Learners   ◆ = Slower Pace Learners   ● = Special Learning Needs   ■ = Heritage Speakers

Holt Spanish 1B   Lesson Planner

Teacher's Name _____ Class _____ Date _____

Cuerpo sano, mente sana

CAPÍTULO
7

BLOCK 4 90-MINUTE LESSON PLAN

STANDARDS FOR FOREIGN LANGUAGE LEARNING: BLOCK 4

Gramática en acción 1

Communication 1.1: Students engage in conversations, provide and obtain information, express feelings and emotions, and exchange opinions.

Communication 1.2: Students understand and interpret written and spoken language on a variety of topics.

Communication 1.3: Students present information, concepts, and ideas to an audience of listeners or readers on a variety of topics.

Cultures 2.1: Students demonstrate an understanding of the relationship between the Practices and Perspectives of the culture studied.

CORE INSTRUCTION

Warm-Up
- (5 min.) Have students do Bell Work 7.3, p. 94.

Gramática en acción 1
- (10 min.) Show **GramaVisión 1,** Segment 1.
- (20 min.) Review verbs with reflexive pronouns, p. 92.
- (15 min.) Have students do Activities 13–14, p. 93.
- (35 min.) Present **Gramática**: Using infinitives, p. 94 using Teaching **Gramática,** p. 94.

Wrap-Up
- (5 min.) See Teacher to Teacher, p. 93.

OPTIONAL RESOURCES
- (10 min.) **Comunicación** (TE), p. 93
- (5 min.) Common Error Alert, p. 95

▲ = Advanced Learners   ◆ = Slower Pace Learners   ● = Special Learning Needs   ■ = Heritage Speakers

Holt Spanish 1B   Lesson Planner

Teacher's Name _____ Class _____ Date _____

CAPÍTULO 7

BLOCK 4 90-MINUTE LESSON PLAN

Practice Options
- *Lab Book,* pp. 20, 44–45
- ***Cuaderno de vocabulario y gramática,*** pp. 32–34
- ***Cuaderno de actividades****,* pp. 27–30 ▲ ● ■
- *Activities for Communication,* pp. 25–26 ▲ ■
- ***Cuaderno para hispanohablantes,*** Chapter 7 ■
- *Teaching Transparencies:* Bell Work 7.3; ***Vocabulario y gramática*** Answers pp. 32–34 ▲ ● ■
- *Video Guide,* pp. 66–67 ▲ ● ■
- *Grammar Tutor for Students of Spanish,* Chapter 7 ● ■
- *Interactive Tutor* (Disc 2) or *DVD Tutor* (Disc 2) ▲ ● ■
- Online Practice, Chapter 7 (go.hrw.com, Keyword: EXP1B CH7)

▲ = Advanced Learners   ◆ = Slower Pace Learners   ● = Special Learning Needs   ■ = Heritage Speakers

Holt Spanish 1B   Lesson Planner

Teacher's Name _____ Class _____ Date _____

Cuerpo sano, mente sana

CAPÍTULO 7

BLOCK 5 90-MINUTE LESSON PLAN

STANDARDS FOR FOREIGN LANGUAGE LEARNING: BLOCK 5

Gramática en acción 1
Communication 1.1: Students engage in conversations, provide and obtain information, express feelings and emotions, and exchange opinions.
Communication 1.2: Students understand and interpret written and spoken language on a variety of topics.
Communication 1.3: Students present information, concepts, and ideas to an audience of listeners or readers on a variety of topics.
Cultures 2.1: Students demonstrate an understanding of the relationship between the Practices and Perspectives of the culture studied.

CORE INSTRUCTION

Warm-Up
- (5 min.) Have students compare sentences from Activity 13, p. 93.

Gramática en acción 1
- (5 min.) Review using infinitives, p. 94.
- (25 min.) Have students do Activities 15–18, p. 94–95.
- (25 min.) Present **Gramática: Repaso** stem–changing verbs, p. 96 using Teaching **Gramática,** p. 96.
- (5 min.) Play Audio CD 7, Tr. 3 for Activity 19, p. 96.
- (20 min.) Have students do Activities 20–22, pp. 96–97.

Wrap-Up
- (5 min.) Check answers to Activity 21. Remind students to study for **Prueba: Gramática 1**.

OPTIONAL RESOURCES
- (5 min.) Circumlocution, p. 95
- (10 min.) **Comunicación** (TE), p. 95
- (10 min.) Multiple Intelligences, p. 95
- (5 min.) Advanced Learners, p. 95 ▲
- (5 min.) Slower Pace Learners, p. 97. ◆

▲ = Advanced Learners   ◆ = Slower Pace Learners   ● = Special Learning Needs   ■ = Heritage Speakers

Holt Spanish 1B   Lesson Planner

Teacher's Name _____ Class _____ Date _____

CAPÍTULO 7

BLOCK 5 90-MINUTE LESSON PLAN

Practice Options
- *Lab Book,* pp. 44–45
- ***Cuaderno de vocabulario y gramática,*** pp. 32–34
- ***Cuaderno de actividades***, pp. 27–30 ▲ ● ■
- *Activities for Communication,* pp. 25–26 ▲ ■
- ***Cuaderno para hispanohablantes,*** Chapter 7 ■
- *Teaching Transparencies:* ***Vocabulario y gramática*** Answers pp. 32–34 ▲ ● ■
- *Video Guide,* pp. 66–67 ▲ ● ■
- *Grammar Tutor for Students of Spanish,* Chapter 7 ● ■
- *Interactive Tutor* (Disc 2) or *DVD Tutor* (Disc 2) ▲ ● ■
- Online Practice, Chapter 7 (go.hrw.com, Keyword: EXP1B CH7)

▲ = Advanced Learners ◆ = Slower Pace Learners ● = Special Learning Needs ■ = Heritage Speakers

Holt Spanish 1B   Lesson Planner

Teacher's Name _____ Class _____ Date _____

Cuerpo sano, mente sana

CAPÍTULO 7

BLOCK 6 90-MINUTE LESSON PLAN

STANDARDS FOR FOREIGN LANGUAGE LEARNING: BLOCK 6

Gramática en acción 1
Communication 1.1: Students engage in conversations, provide and obtain information, express feelings and emotions, and exchange opinions.
Communication 1.2: Students understand and interpret written and spoken language on a variety of topics.
Communication 1.3: Students present information, concepts, and ideas to an audience of listeners or readers on a variety of topics.
Cultures 2.1: Students demonstrate an understanding of the relationship between the Practices and Perspectives of the culture studied.

Cultura
Communication 1.2: Students understand and interpret written and spoken language on a variety of topics.

Cultures 2.1: Students demonstrate an understanding of the relationship between the Practices and Perspectives of the culture studied.
Connections 3.1: Students reinforce and further their knowledge of other disciplines through the foreign language.
Comparisons 4.2: Students demonstrate understanding of the concept of culture through comparisons of the cultures studied and their own.
Communities 5.1: Students use the language both within and beyond the school setting.

Vocabulario en acción 2
Communication 1.2: Students understand and interpret written and spoken language on a variety of topics.

CORE INSTRUCTION

Warm-Up
- (5 min.) Have students do Bell Work 7.5, p. 100.

Gramática en acción 1
- (5 min.) Have students do Activity 23, p. 97.

Assess
- (10 min.) Review **Gramática en acción 1**, pp. 92–97.
- (20 min.) Give **Prueba: Gramática 1**.

Cultura
- (30 min.) Present **Comparaciones**, pp. 98–99 using Teaching **Cultura**, p. 98.
- (5 min.) Present and assign **Comunidad**, p. 99.

Vocabulario en acción 2
- (10 min.) Present **Vocabulario en acción 2**, pp. 100–101 using Teaching **Vocabulario**, #1, p. 100.

Wrap-Up
- (5 min.) Present Language Note and **También se puede decir**, p. 101.

OPTIONAL RESOURCES
- (10 min.) **Comunicación** (TE), p. 97
- (5 min.) Map Activities, p. 98
- (5 min.) Interdisciplinary Link, p. 99
- (5 min.) Slower Pace Learners, p. 99 ◆
- (5 min.) Special Learning Needs, p. 99 ●
- (5 min.) Community Link, p. 99
- (5 min.) Special Learning Needs, p. 97. ●

▲ = Advanced Learners ◆ = Slower Pace Learners ● = Special Learning Needs ■ = Heritage Speakers

Holt Spanish 1B — Lesson Planner

Teacher's Name _____ Class _____ Date _____

CAPÍTULO 7

BLOCK 6 90-MINUTE LESSON PLAN

Practice Options
- *Lab Book*, pp. 46–47
- *Cuaderno de vocabulario y gramática,* pp. 35–37
- *Cuaderno de actividades*, p. 31 ▲●■
- *Activities for Communication,* pp. 27–28 ▲■
- *Teaching Transparencies:* Bell Work 7.5; Vocabulario 7.3, 7.4; *Vocabulario y gramática* Answers pp. 35–37 ▲●■
- *TPR Storytelling Book*, pp. 38–39 ▲●
- *Video Guide*, pp. 68–69 ▲●■
- *Interactive Tutor* (Disc 2) or *DVD Tutor* (Disc 2) ▲●■
- Online Practice, Chapter 7 (go.hrw.com, Keyword: EXP1B CH7)

Assessment Options
- *Assessment Program*: **Prueba: Gramática 1**, pp. 39–40
- *Assessment Program*: **Prueba: Aplicación 1,** pp. 41–42
- *Assessment Program*: Alternative Assessment Guide, pp. 242, 250, 258 ▲●■
- Audio CD 7, Tr. 16
- Test Generator

▲ = Advanced Learners   ◆ = Slower Pace Learners   ● = Special Learning Needs   ■ = Heritage Speakers

Holt Spanish 1B — Lesson Planner

Teacher's Name _____ Class _____ Date _____

Cuerpo sano, mente sana

CAPÍTULO
7

BLOCK 7 90-MINUTE LESSON PLAN

STANDARDS FOR FOREIGN LANGUAGE LEARNING: BLOCK 7

Vocabulario en acción 2
Communication 1.2: Students understand and interpret written and spoken language on a variety of topics.
Communication 1.3: Students present information, concepts, and ideas to an audience of listeners or readers on a variety of topics.

Cultures 2.1: Students demonstrate an understanding of the relationship between the Practices and Perspectives of the culture studied.
Comparisons 4.2: Students demonstrate understanding of the concept of culture through comparisons of the cultures studied and their own.

CORE INSTRUCTION

Warm-Up
- (5 min.) See Teacher to Teacher activity, p. 102.

Vocabulario en acción 2
- (5 min.) Show **ExpresaVisión,** Ch. 7.
- (10 min.) Review **Vocabulario 2,** pp. 100–101.
- (15 min.) See Teaching **Vocabulario,** #2–3, p. 100.
- (5 min.) Present **Nota cultural,** p. 102.
- (25 min.) Have students do Activity 24–28, pp 102–103.
- (15 min.) Present **¡Exprésate!,** p. 104 using Teaching **¡Exprésate!,** p. 104.
- (5 min.) Present **Nota cultural,** p. 104.

Wrap-Up
- (5 min.) See Extension, p. 103.

OPTIONAL RESOURCES
- (5 min.) **TPR,** p. 101
- (5 min.) Multiple Intelligences, p. 101
- (5 min.) Advanced Learners, p. 101 ▲
- (5 min.) **Community Link,** p. 99
- (10 min.) **Comunicación** (TE), p. 103
- (5 min.) Advanced Learners, p. 103 ▲
- (5 min.) Special Learning Needs, p. 103 ●

▲ = Advanced Learners   ◆ = Slower Pace Learners   ● = Special Learning Needs   ■ = Heritage Speakers

Holt Spanish 1B   Lesson Planner

Teacher's Name _____ Class _____ Date _____

CAPÍTULO 7

BLOCK 7 90-MINUTE LESSON PLAN

Practice Options
- *Lab Book,* pp. 46–47
- ***Cuaderno de vocabulario y gramática,*** pp. 35–37
- *Activities for Communication,* pp. 27–28 ▲ ■
- *Teaching Transparencies:* Vocabulario 7.3, 7.4; ***Vocabulario y gramática*** Answers pp. 35–37 ▲ ● ■
- *TPR Storytelling Book,* pp. 38–39 ▲ ●
- *Video Guide,* pp. 68–69 ▲ ● ■
- *Interactive Tutor* (Disc 2) or *DVD Tutor* (Disc 2) ▲ ● ■
- *Online Edition,* Chapter 7 (www.go.hrw.com

▲ = Advanced Learners   ◆ = Slower Pace Learners   ● = Special Learning Needs   ■ = Heritage Speakers

Holt Spanish 1B — Lesson Planner

Teacher's Name _____ Class _____ Date _____

CAPÍTULO

Cuerpo sano, mente sana

BLOCK 8 90-MINUTE LESSON PLAN

STANDARDS FOR FOREIGN LANGUAGE LEARNING: BLOCK 8

Vocabulario en acción 2

Communication 1.1: Students engage in conversations, provide and obtain information, express feelings and emotions, and exchange opinions.

Communication 1.2: Students understand and interpret written and spoken language on a variety of topics.

Communication 1.3: Students present information, concepts, and ideas to an audience of listeners or readers on a variety of topics.

Cultures 2.1: Students demonstrate an understanding of the relationship between the Practices and Perspectives of the culture studied.

Comparisons 4.2: Students demonstrate understanding of the concept of culture through comparisons of the cultures studied and their own.

Gramática en acción 2

Communication 1.2: Students understand and interpret written and spoken language on a variety of topics

CORE INSTRUCTION

Warm-Up
- (5 min.) Have students do Bell Work 7.6, p. 106.

Vocabulario en acción 2
- (15 min.) Review **Vocabulario 2** and **¡Exprésate!**, pp. 100–104.
- (5 min.) Play Audio CD 7, Tr. 7 for Activity 29, p. 104.
- (25 min.) Have students do Activities 30–33, pp. 104–105.

Gramática en acción 2
- (30 min.) Present **Gramática: Estar, sentirse,** and **tener**, p. 106 using Teaching **Gramática,** p. 106.
- (5 min.) Play Audio CD 7, Tr. 8 for Activity 34, p. 106.

Wrap-Up
- (5 min.) Remind students to study for **Prueba: Vocabulario 2.**

OPTIONAL RESOURCES
- (10 min.) **Comunicación** (TE), p. 105
- (5 min.) *Lab Book,* pp. 21, 46–47
- (5 min.) See Heritage Speakers, p. 107 ■

▲ = Advanced Learners   ◆ = Slower Pace Learners   ● = Special Learning Needs   ■ = Heritage Speakers

Teacher's Name _____ Class _____ Date _____

CAPÍTULO 7

BLOCK 8 90-MINUTE LESSON PLAN

Practice Options
- *Cuaderno de vocabulario y gramática,* pp. 35–40
- *Cuaderno de actividades*, pp. 32–35 ▲ ● ■
- *Activities for Communication,* pp. 27–28 ▲ ■
- *Teaching Transparencies:* Bell Work 7.6; Vocabulario 7.3, 7.4; **Vocabulario y gramática** Answers pp. 35–40 ▲ ● ■
- *TPR Storytelling Book,* pp. 38–39 ▲ ●
- *Video Guide,* pp. 68–69 ▲ ● ■
- *Grammar Tutor for Students of Spanish,* Chapter 7 ● ■
- *Interactive Tutor* (Disc 2) or *DVD Tutor* (Disc 2) ▲ ● ■
- Online Practice, Chapter 7 (go.hrw.com, Keyword: EXP1B CH7)

▲ = Advanced Learners ◆ = Slower Pace Learners ● = Special Learning Needs ■ = Heritage Speakers

Holt Spanish 1B — Lesson Planner

Teacher's Name _____ Class _____ Date _____

Cuerpo sano, mente sana

CAPÍTULO 7

BLOCK 9 90-MINUTE LESSON PLAN

STANDARDS FOR FOREIGN LANGUAGE LEARNING: BLOCK 9

Vocabulario en acción 2
Communication 1.1: Students engage in conversations, provide and obtain information, express feelings and emotions, and exchange opinions.
Communication 1.2: Students understand and interpret written and spoken language on a variety of topics.
Communication 1.3: Students present information, concepts, and ideas to an audience of listeners or readers on a variety of topics.
Cultures 2.1: Students demonstrate an understanding of the relationship between the Practices and Perspectives of the culture studied.
Comparisons 4.2: Students demonstrate understanding of the concept of culture through comparisons of the cultures studied and their own.

Gramática en acción 2
Communication 1.1: Students engage in conversations, provide and obtain information, express feelings and emotions, and exchange opinions.
Communication 1.2: Students understand and interpret written and spoken language on a variety of topics.
Communication 1.3: Students present information, concepts, and ideas to an audience of listeners or readers on a variety of topics.

CORE INSTRUCTION

Warm-Up
- (10 min.) Review **Vocabulario en acción 2,** pp. 100–105.

Vocabulario en acción 2
Assess
- (20 min.) Give **Prueba: Vocabulario 2.**

Gramática en acción 2
- (10 min.) Review **estar, sentirse,** and **tener,** p. 106.
- (25 min.) Have students do Activities 35–37, p. 107.
- (20 min.) Present **Gramática:** Negative informal commands, p. 108 using Teaching **Gramática,** p. 108.

Wrap-Up
- (5 min.) Review answers to Activity 36 as a class.

OPTIONAL RESOURCES
- (10 min.) Advanced Learners, p. 107 ▲
- (10 min.) **Comunicación** (TE), p. 107
- (5 min.) Special Learning Needs, p. 107. ●

▲ = Advanced Learners   ◆ = Slower Pace Learners   ● = Special Learning Needs   ■ = Heritage Speakers

Holt Spanish 1B — Lesson Planner

Teacher's Name _____ Class _____ Date _____

CAPÍTULO 7

BLOCK 9 90-MINUTE LESSON PLAN

Practice Options
- *Lab Book,* pp. 21, 46–47
- **Cuaderno de vocabulario y gramática,** pp. 38–40
- **Cuaderno de actividades**, pp. 32–35 ▲ ● ■
- *Activities for Communication,* pp. 27–28 ▲ ■
- **Cuaderno para hispanohablantes,** Chapter 7 ■
- *Teaching Transparencies:* **Vocabulario y gramática** Answers, pp. 38–40 ▲ ● ■
- *Video Guide,* pp. 68–69 ▲ ● ■
- *Grammar Tutor for Students of Spanish,* Chapter 7 ● ■
- *Interactive Tutor* (Disc 2) or *DVD Tutor* (Disc 2) ▲ ● ■
- Online Practice, Chapter 7 (go.hrw.com, Keyword: EXP1B CH7)

Assessment Options
- *Assessment Program*: **Prueba: Vocabulario 2**, pp. 43–44
- *Assessment Program*: Alternative Assessment Guide, pp. 242, 250, 258 ▲ ● ■
- Test Generator

▲ = Advanced Learners ◆ = Slower Pace Learners ● = Special Learning Needs ■ = Heritage Speakers

Holt Spanish 1B — Lesson Planner

Teacher's Name _____ Class _____ Date _____

CAPÍTULO 7

Cuerpo sano, mente sana

BLOCK 10 90-MINUTE LESSON PLAN

STANDARDS FOR FOREIGN LANGUAGE LEARNING: BLOCK 10

Gramática en acción 2

Communication 1.1: Students engage in conversations, provide and obtain information, express feelings and emotions, and exchange opinions.

Communication 1.2: Students understand and interpret written and spoken language on a variety of topics.

Communication 1.3: Students present information, concepts, and ideas to an audience of listeners or readers on a variety of topics.

CORE INSTRUCTION

Warm-Up
- (5 min.) Have students do Bell Work 7.8, p. 110.

Gramática en acción 2
- (5 min.) Show **GramaVisión 1,** Segment 5.
- (10 min.) Review negative informal commands, p. 108.
- (25 min.) Have students do Activities 38–41, pp. 108–109.
- (20 min.) Present **Gramática:** *Objects and reflexive pronouns with commands*, p. 110 using Teaching **Gramática,** p. 110.
- (20 min.) Have students do Activities 42–43, pp. 110–111.

Wrap-Up
- (5 min.) Share class responses from Activity 43. Remind students to study for **Prueba: Gramática 2.**

OPTIONAL RESOURCES
- (10 min.) **Comunicación** (TE), p. 109
- (5 min.) Language to Language, p. 109
- (5 min.) Advanced Learners, p. 109 ▲
- (5 min.) Special Learning Needs, p. 109. ●
- (5 min.) Slower Pace Learners, p. 111 ◆
- (5 min.) Special Learning Needs, p. 111. ●

▲ = Advanced Learners ◆ = Slower Pace Learners ● = Special Learning Needs ■ = Heritage Speakers

Holt Spanish 1B — Lesson Planner

Teacher's Name _____ Class _____ Date _____

CAPÍTULO 7

BLOCK 10 90-MINUTE LESSON PLAN

Practice Options
- *Lab Book,* pp. 46–47
- **Cuaderno de vocabulario y gramática,** pp. 38–40
- **Cuaderno de actividades**, pp. 32–35 ▲ ● ■
- *Activities for Communication,* pp. 27–28 ▲ ■
- **Cuaderno para hispanohablantes,** Chapter 7 ■
- *Teaching Transparencies:* Bell Work 7.8; **Vocabulario y gramática** Answers, pp. 38–40 ▲ ● ■
- *Video Guide,* pp. 68–69 ▲ ● ■
- *Grammar Tutor for Students of Spanish,* Chapter 7 ● ■
- *Interactive Tutor* (Disc 2) or *DVD Tutor* (Disc 2) ▲ ● ■
- Online Practice, Chapter 7 (go.hrw.com, Keyword: EXP1B CH7)

▲ = Advanced Learners ◆ = Slower Pace Learners ● = Special Learning Needs ■ = Heritage Speakers

Holt Spanish 1B — Lesson Planner

Teacher's Name _____ Class _____ Date _____

Cuerpo sano, mente sana

CAPÍTULO 7

BLOCK 11 90-MINUTE LESSON PLAN

STANDARDS FOR FOREIGN LANGUAGE LEARNING: BLOCK 11

Gramática en acción 2
Communication 1.1: Students engage in conversations, provide and obtain information, express feelings and emotions, and exchange opinions.
Communication 1.2: Students understand and interpret written and spoken language on a variety of topics.
Communication 1.3: Students present information, concepts, and ideas to an audience of listeners or readers on a variety of topics.

Conexiones culturales
Communication 1.2: Students understand and interpret written and spoken language on a variety of topics.
Cultures 2.1: Students demonstrate an understanding of the relationship between the Practices and Perspectives of the culture studied.
Connections 3.2: Students acquire information and recognize the distinctive viewpoints that are only available through the foreign language and its cultures.

CORE INSTRUCTION

Warm-Up
- (5 min.) Do Activity 42, p. 110 as a class activity.

Gramática en acción 2
- (10 min.) Have students do Activities 44–45, p. 111.
- (25 min.) Review **Gramática en acción 2,** pp. 106–111.

Assess
- (20 min.) Give **Prueba: Gramática 2.**

Conexiones culturales
- (25 min.) Present **Conexiones culturales,** pp. 112–113 using Teaching **Conexiones culturales,** #1–3, p. 112.

Wrap-Up
- (10 min.) **Comunicación** (TE), p. 111

OPTIONAL RESOURCES
- (10 min.) Multiple Intelligences, p. 113
- (5 min.) Slower Pace Learners, p. 113 ◆
- (5 min.) Slower Pace Learners, p. 111. ◆

▲ = Advanced Learners ◆ = Slower Pace Learners ● = Special Learning Needs ■ = Heritage Speakers

Holt Spanish 1B — Lesson Planner

Teacher's Name _____ Class _____ Date _____

CAPÍTULO 7

BLOCK 11 90-MINUTE LESSON PLAN

Practice Options
- Online Practice, Chapter 7 (go.hrw.com, Keyword: EXP1B CH7)

Assessment Options
- *Assessment Program*: **Prueba: Gramática 2**, pp. 45–46
- *Assessment Program*: **Prueba: Aplicación 2,** pp. 47–48
- *Assessment Program*: Alternative Assessment Guide, pp. 242, 250, 258 ▲ ● ■
- *Audio CD* 7, Tr. 17
- Test Generator

▲ = Advanced Learners   ◆ = Slower Pace Learners   ● = Special Learning Needs   ■ = Heritage Speakers

Teacher's Name _____ Class _____ Date _____

Cuerpo sano, mente sana

CAPÍTULO 7

BLOCK 12 90-MINUTE LESSON PLAN

STANDARDS FOR FOREIGN LANGUAGE LEARNING: BLOCK 12

Conexiones culturales
Communication 1.2: Students understand and interpret written and spoken language on a variety of topics.
Cultures 2.1: Students demonstrate an understanding of the relationship between the Practices and Perspectives of the culture studied.
Connections 3.2: Students acquire information and recognize the distinctive viewpoints that are only available through the foreign language and its cultures.

Novela en video
Communication 1.1: Students engage in conversations, provide and obtain information, express feelings and emotions, and exchange opinions.
Communication 1.2: Students understand and interpret written and spoken language on a variety of topics.

Cultures 2.1: Students demonstrate an understanding of the relationship between the Practices and Perspectives of the culture studied.
Connections 3.2: Students acquire information and recognize the distinctive viewpoints that are only available through the foreign language and its cultures.

Leamos y escribamos
Communication 1.2: Students understand and interpret written and spoken language on a variety of topics.
Connections 3.2: Students acquire information and recognize the distinctive viewpoints that are only available through the foreign language and its cultures.

CORE INSTRUCTION

Warm-Up
- (5 min.) Have students do **Comunicación** (TE), p. 111 again, using different index cards.

Conexiones culturales
- (20 min.) See Teaching **Conexiones culturales**, #4–5, p. 112.

Novela en video
- (35 min.) See Teaching **Novela en video**, #1–3, p. 114.

Leamos y escribamos
- (30 min.) Present **¡En buena salud!**, p. 118 using Teaching **Leamos**, p. 118.

Wrap-Up
- (5 min.) Have students do Activity C, p. 119.

OPTIONAL RESOURCES
- (5 min.) Practices and Perspectives, p. 113, 115
- (5 min.) Multiple Intelligences, p. 113
- (5 min.) Gestures, p. 114
- (5 min.) Visual Learners, p. 114
- (10 min.) Culminating Project, p. 116
- (5 min.) Special Learning Needs, p. 117 ●
- (10 min.) **Comunicación** (TE), p. 117
- (10 min.) Advanced Learners, pp. 117, 119 ▲

▲ = Advanced Learners   ◆ = Slower Pace Learners   ● = Special Learning Needs   ■ = Heritage Speakers

Holt Spanish 1B   Lesson Planner

Teacher's Name _____ Class _____ Date _____

CAPÍTULO 7

BLOCK 12 90-MINUTE LESSON PLAN

Practice Options
- *Lab Book,* p. 43
- ***Cuaderno de actividades***, p. 36 ▲ ● ■
- ***Cuaderno para hispanohablantes***, pp. 53–60 ■
- *Reading Strategies and Skills Handbook*, Chapter 7 ▲ ● ■
- *¡Lee conmigo!* Level 1 Reader ▲ ■
- *Video Guide,* pp. 64, 70 ▲ ● ■
- *Interactive Tutor* (Disc 2) or *DVD Tutor* (Disc 2) ▲ ● ■
- Online Practice, Chapter 7 (go.hrw.com, Keyword: EXP1B CH7)

▲ = Advanced Learners ◆ = Slower Pace Learners ● = Special Learning Needs ■ = Heritage Speakers

Holt Spanish 1B   Lesson Planner

Teacher's Name _____ Class _____ Date _____

Cuerpo sano, mente sana

CAPÍTULO 7

BLOCK 13 90-MINUTE LESSON PLAN

STANDARDS FOR FOREIGN LANGUAGE LEARNING: BLOCK 13

Leamos y escribamos

Communication 1.2: Students understand and interpret written and spoken language on a variety of topics.

Connections 3.2: Students acquire information and recognize the distinctive viewpoints that are only available through the foreign language and its cultures.

Repaso

Communication 1.2: Students understand and interpret written and spoken language on a variety of topics.

Communication 1.3: Students present information, concepts, and ideas to an audience of listeners or readers on a variety of topics.

Cultures 2.1: Students demonstrate an understanding of the relationship between the Practices and Perspectives of the culture studied.

Comparisons 4.1: Students demonstrate understanding of the nature of language through comparisons of the language studied and their own.

CORE INSTRUCTION

Warm-Up
- (5 min.) Do the "Anticipation Guide" strategy, p.118 with students as a class activity.

Leamos y escribamos
- (25 min.) Present **Taller del escritor**, p. 119 using Teaching **Escribamos,** #1–3, p. 118.

Repaso
- (30 min.) Have students do Activities 1–5, pp. 120–121.
- (5 min.) Play Audio CD 7, Tr. 11 for Activity 6, p. 121.
- (10 min.) Have students do Activity 7, p. 121.
- (10 min.) Play Audio CD 7, Tr. 12–14 for **Letra y sonido,** p. 122.

Wrap-Up
- (5 min.) See Fold-N-Learn, p. 120. Remind students to study for Chapter Test.

OPTIONAL RESOURCES
- (5 min.) Special Learning Needs, p. 119 ●
- (5 min.) Career Path, p. 120
- (5 min.) Letra y sonido, p. 122
- (5 min.) Game, p. 123

▲ = Advanced Learners   ◆ = Slower Pace Learners   ● = Special Learning Needs   ■ = Heritage Speakers

Teacher's Name _____ Class _____ Date _____

CAPÍTULO 7

BLOCK 13 90-MINUTE LESSON PLAN

Practice Options
- *Lab Book*, p. 22, 43, 47
- *Activities for Communication*, pp. 49, 67–68 ▲ ■
- **Cuaderno de actividades**, p. 36 ▲ ● ■
- **Cuaderno para hispanohablantes**, pp. 53–60 ■
- *Reading Strategies and Skills Handbook*, Chapter 7 ▲ ● ■
- *¡Lee conmigo!* Level 1 reader ▲ ■
- *Teaching Transparencies:* **Situación, Capítulo 7**; Picture Stories, Chapter 7 ▲ ● ■
- *Video Guide*, pp. 63, 69 ▲ ● ■
- *TPR Storytelling Book*, pp. 40–41 ▲ ●
- *Interactive Tutor* (Disc 2) or *DVD Tutor* (Disc 2) ▲ ● ■
- Online Practice, Chapter 7 (go.hrw.com, Keyword: EXP1B CH7)

▲ = Advanced Learners ◆ = Slower Pace Learners ● = Special Learning Needs ■ = Heritage Speakers

Teacher's Name _____ Class _____ Date _____

CAPÍTULO 7

Cuerpo sano, mente sana

BLOCK 14 90-MINUTE LESSON PLAN

STANDARDS FOR FOREIGN LANGUAGE LEARNING: BLOCK 14

Leamos y escribamos
Communication 1.2: Students understand and interpret written and spoken language on a variety of topics.
Connections 3.2: Students acquire information and recognize the distinctive viewpoints that are only available through the foreign language and its cultures.

Integración
Communication 1.1: Students engage in conversations, provide and obtain information, express feelings and emotions, and exchange opinions.
Communication 1.2: Students understand and interpret written and spoken language on a variety of topics.
Communication 1.3: Students present information, concepts, and ideas to an audience of listeners or readers on a variety of topics.

CORE INSTRUCTION

Chapter Test

Assess
- (50 min.) Give Chapter Test.

Leamos y escribamos
- (10 min.) See Teaching **Escribamos**, #4, p. 118.

Integración
- (5 min.) Play Audio CD 7, Tr. 15 for Activity 1, p. 124.
- (20 min.) Have students do Activities 2–4, pp. 124–125.

Wrap-Up
- (5 min.) Preview **Geocultura**: Florida, pp. 126–129.

OPTIONAL RESOURCES
- (5 min.) Slower Pace Learners, p. 124 ◆
- (10 min.) Culture Project, p. 124
- (5 min.) Fine Art Connection, p. 125

▲ = Advanced Learners   ◆ = Slower Pace Learners   ● = Special Learning Needs   ■ = Heritage Speakers

Holt Spanish 1B   Lesson Planner

Teacher's Name _____ Class _____ Date _____

CAPÍTULO 7

BLOCK 14 90-MINUTE LESSON PLAN

Practice Options
- *Lab Book,* pp. 22
- ***Cuaderno de actividades***, pp. 37–38, 80–81
- *Activities for Communication,* pp. 49, 67–68 ▲ ■
- *Teaching Transparencies:* **Situación, Capítulo 7**; Picture Stories, Chapter 7; Fine Art, Chapter 7 ▲ ● ■
- *Video Guide,* pp. 63, 69 ▲ ● ■
- *TPR Storytelling Book,* pp. 40–41 ▲ ●
- *Interactive Tutor* (Disc 2) or *DVD Tutor* (Disc 2) ▲ ● ■
- Online Practice, Chapter 7 (go.hrw.com, Keyword: EXP1B CH7)

Assessment Options
- *Assessment Program:* **Examen: Capítulo 7**, pp. 145–155
- *Assessment Program:* **Examen oral: Capítulo 7**, p. 156
- *Assessment Program:* Alternative Assessment Guide, pp. 242, 250, 258 ▲ ● ■
- *Audio CD 7,* Tr. 18–19
- *Standardized Assessment Tutor,* Chapter 7
- Test Generator

▲ = Advanced Learners   ◆ = Slower Pace Learners   ● = Special Learning Needs   ■ = Heritage Speakers

Holt Spanish 1B — Lesson Planner

Teacher's Name _____ Class _____ Date _____

Vamos de compras

CAPÍTULO 8

BLOCK 1 90-MINUTE LESSON PLAN

STANDARDS FOR FOREIGN LANGUAGE LEARNING: BLOCK 1

Chapter Opener
Communication 1.2: Students understand and interpret written and spoken language on a variety of topics.

Vocabulario en acción 1
Communication 1.2: Students understand and interpret written and spoken language on a variety of topics.

Cultures 2.2: Students demonstrate an understanding of the relationship between the products and perspectives of the culture studied.

Comparisons 4.2: Students demonstrate understanding of the concept of culture through comparisons of the cultures studied and their own.

Before starting **Capítulo 8,** you may wish to teach **Geocultura: Florida,** pp. 126–129. For teaching suggestions, see pp. xv–xvi of this *Lesson Planner.*

CORE INSTRUCTION

Warm-Up
- (5 min.) See Learning Tips, p. 131.

Chapter Opener
- (5 min.) See Using the Photo and **Más vocabulario,** p. 130.
- (5 min.) See **Objetivos,** p. 130.

Vocabulario en acción 1
- (10 min.) Show **ExpresaVisión,** Ch. 8.
- (25 min.) Present **Vocabulario 1,** pp. 132–133 using Teaching **Vocabulario,** p. 132.
- (10 min.) Present **Nota cultural,** p. 134.
- (10 min.) Play Audio CD 8, Tr. 1 for Activity 1, p. 134.
- (15 min.) Have students do Activities 2–4, p. 135.

Wrap-Up
- (5 min.) Present **También se puede decir** and Language Note, p. 133.

OPTIONAL RESOURCES
- (5 min.) Common Error Alert, p. 132
- (5 min.) Special Learning Needs, p. 133 ●
- (5 min.) **Más práctica,** p. 134
- (10 min.) Fold-n-Learn, p. 134
- (5 min.) Practices and Perspectives, p. 134
- (10 min.) Advanced Learners, p. 135 ▲

▲ = Advanced Learners   ◆ = Slower Pace Learners   ● = Special Learning Needs   ■ = Heritage Speakers

Holt Spanish 1B   Lesson Planner

Teacher's Name _____ Class _____ Date _____

CAPÍTULO 8

BLOCK 1 90-MINUTE LESSON PLAN

Practice Options
- *Lab Book,* pp. 50–51
- ***Cuaderno de vocabulario y gramática,*** pp. 41–43
- *Activities for Communication,* pp. 29–30 ▲ ■
- ***Cuaderno para hispanohablantes,*** Chapter 8 ■
- *Teaching Transparencies:* Vocabulario 8.1, 8.2; ***Vocabulario y gramática*** Answers, pp. 41–43 ▲ ● ■
- *Video Guide,* pp. 76–77 ▲ ● ■
- *TPR Storytelling Book,* pp. 42–43 ▲ ●
- *Interactive Tutor* (Disc 2) or *DVD Tutor* (Disc 2) ▲ ● ■
- Online Practice, Chapter 8 (go.hrw.com, Keyword: EXP1B CH8)

▲ = Advanced Learners   ◆ = Slower Pace Learners   ● = Special Learning Needs   ■ = Heritage Speakers

Holt Spanish 1B   Lesson Planner

Teacher's Name _____ Class _____ Date _____

Vamos de compras

CAPÍTULO 8

BLOCK 2 90-MINUTE LESSON PLAN

STANDARDS FOR FOREIGN LANGUAGE LEARNING: BLOCK 2

Vocabulario en acción 1

Communication 1.1: Students engage in conversations, provide and obtain information, express feelings and emotions, and exchange opinions.

Communication 1.2: Students understand and interpret written and spoken language on a variety of topics.

Cultures 2.2: Students demonstrate an understanding of the relationship between the products and perspectives of the culture studied.

Comparisons 4.2: Students demonstrate understanding of the concept of culture through comparisons of the cultures studied and their own.

CORE INSTRUCTION

Warm-Up
- (5 min.) Have students do Bell Work 8.1, p. 132.

Vocabulario en acción 1
- (20 min.) Review **Vocabulario 1** and **¡Exprésate!**, pp. 132–133.
- (20 min.) Have students do Activities 5–6, p. 135.
- (20 min.) Present **¡Exprésate!**, p. 136 using Teaching **¡Exprésate!**, p. 136.
- (20 min.) Have students do Activities 7–9, pp. 136–137. See **Más práctica**, p. 137.

Wrap-Up
- (5 min.) See Math Link, p. 136. Remind students to study for **Prueba: Vocabulario 1**.

OPTIONAL RESOURCES
- (10 min.) TPR, p. 133
- (10 min.) Advanced Learners, p. 133 ▲
- (5 min.) Multiple Intelligences, p. 135
- (5 min.) **Más práctica**, p. 135
- (10 min.) Special Learning Needs, p. 137 ●

▲ = Advanced Learners ◆ = Slower Pace Learners ● = Special Learning Needs ■ = Heritage Speakers

Teacher's Name _____ Class _____ Date _____

CAPÍTULO 8

BLOCK 2 90-MINUTE LESSON PLAN

Practice Options
- *Lab Book,* pp. 50–51
- *Cuaderno de vocabulario y gramática,* pp. 41–43
- *Activities for Communication,* pp. 29–30 ▲ ■
- *Cuaderno para hispanohablantes,* Chapter 8 ■
- *Teaching Transparencies:* Bell Work 8.1; Vocabulario 8.1, 8.2; *Vocabulario y gramática* Answers, pp. 41–43 ▲ ● ■
- *Video Guide,* pp. 76–77 ▲ ● ■
- *TPR Storytelling Book,* pp. 42–43 ▲ ●
- *Interactive Tutor* (Disc 2) or *DVD Tutor* (Disc 2) ▲ ● ■
- Online Practice, Chapter 8 (go.hrw.com, Keyword: EXP1B CH8)

▲ = Advanced Learners   ◆ = Slower Pace Learners   ● = Special Learning Needs   ■ = Heritage Speakers

Holt Spanish 1B   Lesson Planner

Teacher's Name _____ Class _____ Date _____

Vamos de compras

CAPÍTULO 8

BLOCK 3 90-MINUTE LESSON PLAN

STANDARDS FOR FOREIGN LANGUAGE LEARNING: BLOCK 3

Vocabulario en acción 1

Communication 1.1: Students engage in conversations, provide and obtain information, express feelings and emotions, and exchange opinions.
Communication 1.2: Students understand and interpret written and spoken language on a variety of topics.
Cultures 2.2: Students demonstrate an understanding of the relationship between the products and perspectives of the culture studied.
Connections 3.1: Students reinforce and further their knowledge of other disciplines through the foreign language.
Comparisons 4.2: Students demonstrate understanding of the concept of culture through comparisons of the cultures studied and their own.

Gramática en acción 1

Communication 1.1: Students engage in conversations, provide and obtain information, express feelings and emotions, and exchange opinions.
Communication 1.2: Students understand and interpret written and spoken language on a variety of topics.
Communication 1.3: Students present information, concepts, and ideas to an audience of listeners or readers on a variety of topics.
Cultures 2.1: Students demonstrate an understanding of the relationship between the practices and perspectives of the culture studied.

CORE INSTRUCTION

Warm-Up
- (5 min.) Have students do Bell Work 8.2, p. 138.

Vocabulario en acción 1
- (10 min.) Have students do Activity 10, p. 137.
- (15 min.) Review **Vocabulario en acción 1,** pp. 132–137.

Assess
- (20 min.) Give **Prueba: Vocabulario 1**.

Gramática en acción 1
- (25 min.) Present **Gramática: Costar**, numbers to one million, p. 138 using Teaching **Gramática,** p. 138.
- (10 min.) Play Audio CD 8, Tr. 2 for Activity 11, p. 138.

Wrap-Up
- (5 min.) Ask students the questions in Activity 10.

OPTIONAL RESOURCES
- (5 min.) Teacher to Teacher, p. 137
- (5 min.) Slower Pace Learners, p. 137 ◆
- (10 min.) **Comunicación** (TE), p. 137
- (5 min.) Multiple Intelligences, p. 139
- (5 min.) Slower Pace Learners, p. 139 ◆

▲ = Advanced Learners   ◆ = Slower Pace Learners   ● = Special Learning Needs   ■ = Heritage Speakers

Holt Spanish 1B

Lesson Planner

Teacher's Name _____ Class _____ Date _____

CAPÍTULO
8

BLOCK 3 90-MINUTE LESSON PLAN

Practice Options
- *Lab Book,* pp. 23, 50–51
- ***Cuaderno de vocabulario y gramática,*** pp. 41–46
- ***Cuaderno de actividades***, pp. 39–42 ▲ ● ■
- *Activities for Communication,* pp. 29–30 ▲ ■
- ***Cuaderno para hispanohablantes,*** Chapter 8 ■
- *Teaching Transparencies:* Bell Work 8.2; Vocabulario 8.1, 8.2; ***Vocabulario y gramática*** Answers, pp. 41–46 ▲ ● ■
- *Video Guide,* pp. 76–77 ▲ ● ■
- *Grammar Tutor for Students of Spanish,* Chapter 8 ● ■
- *TPR Storytelling Book,* pp. 42–43 ▲ ●
- *Interactive Tutor* (Disc 2) or *DVD Tutor* (Disc 2) ▲ ● ■
- Online Practice, Chapter 8 (go.hrw.com, Keyword: EXP1B CH8)

Assessment Options
- *Assessment Program:* **Prueba: Vocabulario 1**, pp. 57–58
- *Assessment Program:* Alternative Assessment Guide, pp. 243, 251, 259 ▲ ● ■
- Test Generator

▲ = Advanced Learners   ◆ = Slower Pace Learners   ● = Special Learning Needs   ■ = Heritage Speakers

Holt Spanish 1B   Lesson Planner

Teacher's Name _____ Class _____ Date _____

Vamos de compras

CAPÍTULO **8**

BLOCK 4 90-MINUTE LESSON PLAN

STANDARDS FOR FOREIGN LANGUAGE LEARNING: BLOCK 4

Gramática en acción 1

Communication 1.1: Students engage in conversations, provide and obtain information, express feelings and emotions, and exchange opinions.

Communication 1.2: Students understand and interpret written and spoken language on a variety of topics.

Communication 1.3: Students present information, concepts, and ideas to an audience of listeners or readers on a variety of topics.

Cultures 2.1: Students demonstrate an understanding of the relationship between the practices and perspectives of the culture studied.

CORE INSTRUCTION

Warm-Up
- (5 min.) Have students do Bell Work 8.3, p. 140.

Gramática en acción 1
- (5 min.) Show **GramaVisión 1,** Segment 1.
- (10 min.) Review **costar,** numbers to one million, p. 138.
- (20 min.) Have students do Activities 12–14, p. 139.
- (30 min.) Present **Gramática**: Demonstrative adjectives and comparisons, p. 140 using Teaching **Gramática,** p. 140.
- (10 min.) Play Audio CD 8, Tr. 3 for Activity 15, p. 140.
- (5 min.) Present **Nota cultural,** p. 140.

Wrap-Up
- (5 min.) See Common Error Alert, p. 141.

OPTIONAL RESOURCES
- (10 min.) Teacher to Teacher, p. 139
- (10 min.) **Comunicación** (TE)**,** pp. 139, 141

▲ = Advanced Learners   ◆ = Slower Pace Learners   ● = Special Learning Needs   ■ = Heritage Speakers

Teacher's Name _____ Class _____ Date _____

CAPÍTULO 8

BLOCK 4 90-MINUTE LESSON PLAN

Practice Options
- *Lab Book,* pp. 24, 50–51
- **Cuaderno de vocabulario y gramática,** pp. 44–46
- **Cuaderno de actividades**, pp. 39–42 ▲ ● ■
- *Activities for Communication,* pp. 29–30 ▲ ■
- **Cuaderno para hispanohablantes,** Chapter 8 ■
- *Teaching Transparencies:* Bell Work 8.3; **Vocabulario y gramática** Answers, pp. 44–46 ▲ ● ■
- *Video Guide,* pp. 76–77 ▲ ● ■
- *Grammar Tutor for Students of Spanish,* Chapter 8 ● ■
- *Interactive Tutor* (Disc 2) or *DVD Tutor* (Disc 2) ▲ ● ■
- Online Practice, Chapter 8 (go.hrw.com, Keyword: EXP1B CH8)

▲ = Advanced Learners ◆ = Slower Pace Learners ● = Special Learning Needs ■ = Heritage Speakers

Holt Spanish 1B   Lesson Planner

Teacher's Name _____ Class _____ Date _____

Vamos de compras

CAPÍTULO 8

BLOCK 5 90-MINUTE LESSON PLAN

STANDARDS FOR FOREIGN LANGUAGE LEARNING: BLOCK 5

Gramática en acción 1

Communication 1.1: Students engage in conversations, provide and obtain information, express feelings and emotions, and exchange opinions.

Communication 1.2: Students understand and interpret written and spoken language on a variety of topics.

Communication 1.3: Students present information, concepts, and ideas to an audience of listeners or readers on a variety of topics.

CORE INSTRUCTION

Warm-Up
- (5 min.) Have students do Bell Work 8.4, p. 142.

Gramática en acción 1
- (5 min.) Show **GramaVisión1,** Segment 2.
- (15 min.) Review demonstrative adjectives and comparisons, p. 140.
- (20 min.) Have students do Activities 16–18, p. 141.
- (20 min.) Present **Gramática: Quedar**, p. 142 using Teaching **Gramática,** p. 142.
- (20 min.) Have students do Activities 19–22, p. 142–143.

Wrap-Up
- (5 min.) Check answers to Activity 21, p. 143. Remind students to study for **Prueba: Gramática 1**.

OPTIONAL RESOURCES
- (5 min.) Multiple Intelligences, p. 143
- (5 min.) **Comunicación** (TE)**,** p. 143
- (5 min.) Slower Pace Learners, p. 143 ◆
- (5 min.) Advanced Learners, p. 141 ▲
- (5 min.) Special Learning Needs, p. 141 ●

▲ = Advanced Learners   ◆ = Slower Pace Learners   ● = Special Learning Needs   ■ = Heritage Speakers

Holt Spanish 1B · Lesson Planner

Teacher's Name _____ Class _____ Date _____

CAPÍTULO 8

BLOCK 5 90-MINUTE LESSON PLAN

Practice Options
- *Lab Book,* pp. 24, 50–51
- ***Cuaderno de vocabulario y gramática,*** pp. 44–46
- ***Cuaderno de actividades***, pp. 39–42 ▲ ● ■
- *Activities for Communication,* pp. 29–30 ▲ ■
- ***Cuaderno para hispanohablantes,*** Chapter 8 ■
- *Teaching Transparencies:* Bell Work 8.4; ***Vocabulario y gramática*** Answers, pp. 44–46 ▲ ● ■
- *Video Guide,* pp. 76–77 ▲ ● ■
- *Grammar Tutor for Students of Spanish,* Chapter 8 ● ■
- *Interactive Tutor* (Disc 2) or *DVD Tutor* (Disc 2) ▲ ● ■
- Online Practice, Chapter 8 (go.hrw.com, Keyword: EXP1B CH8)

▲ = Advanced Learners ◆ = Slower Pace Learners ● = Special Learning Needs ■ = Heritage Speakers

Holt Spanish 1B   Lesson Planner

Teacher's Name _____ Class _____ Date _____

Vamos de compras

CAPÍTULO 8

BLOCK 6 90-MINUTE LESSON PLAN

STANDARDS FOR FOREIGN LANGUAGE LEARNING: BLOCK 6

Gramática en acción 1
Communication 1.1: Students engage in conversations, provide and obtain information, express feelings and emotions, and exchange opinions.
Communication 1.2: Students understand and interpret written and spoken language on a variety of topics.
Communication 1.3: Students present information, concepts, and ideas to an audience of listeners or readers on a variety of topics.
Cultures 2.1: Students demonstrate an understanding of the relationship between the practices and perspectives of the culture studied.

Cultura
Communication 1.2: Students understand and interpret written and spoken language on a variety of topics.
Comparisons 4.2: Students demonstrate understanding of the concept of culture through comparisons of the cultures studied and their own.
Communities 5.2: Students show evidence of becoming life–long learners by using the language for personal enjoyment and enrichment.

CORE INSTRUCTION

Warm-Up
- (5 min.) Have students do Bell Work 8.5, p. 146.

Gramática en acción 1
- (20 min.) Review **Gramática en acción 1,** pp. 138–143.

Assess
- (20 min.) Give **Prueba: Gramática 1.**

Cultura
- (30 min.) Present **Comparaciones,** pp. 144–145 using Teaching **Cultura,** #1–3, p. 144.
- (10 min.) Present and assign **Comunidad,** p. 145.

Wrap-Up
- (5 min.) See Map Activities, p. 144.

OPTIONAL RESOURCES
- (5 min.) Thinking Critically, p. 144
- (5 min.) Practices and Perspectives, p. 145
- (5 min.) Multiple Intelligences, p. 145
- (5 min.) Community Link, p. 145
- (5 min.) Teacher Note, p. 145
- (5 min.) Slower Pace Learners, p. 145. ◆

▲ = Advanced Learners   ◆ = Slower Pace Learners   ● = Special Learning Needs   ■ = Heritage Speakers

Teacher's Name _____ Class _____ Date _____

CAPÍTULO 8

BLOCK 6 90-MINUTE LESSON PLAN

Practice Options
- *Lab Book,* pp. 51
- ***Cuaderno de actividades,*** p. 43 ▲ ● ■
- ***Cuaderno para hispanohablantes,*** pp. 61–68 ■
- *Teaching Transparencies:* Bell Work 8.5; Mapa 6 ▲ ● ■
- *Video Guide,* pp. 73, 77 ▲ ● ■
- *Grammar Tutor for Students of Spanish,* Chapter 8 ● ■
- *Interactive Tutor* (Disc 2) or *DVD Tutor* (Disc 2) ▲ ● ■
- Online Practice, Chapter 8 (go.hrw.com, Keyword: EXP1B CH8)

Assessment Options
- *Assessment Program:* **Prueba: Gramática 1**, pp. 59–60
- *Assessment Program:* **Prueba: Aplicación 1,** pp. 61–62
- *Assessment Program:* Alternative Assessment Guide, pp. 243, 251, 259 ▲ ● ■
- *Audio CD* 8, Tr. 18
- Test Generator

▲ = Advanced Learners   ◆ = Slower Pace Learners   ● = Special Learning Needs   ■ = Heritage Speakers

Holt Spanish 1B   Lesson Planner

Teacher's Name _____ Class _____ Date _____

Vamos de compras

CAPÍTULO **8**

BLOCK 7 90-MINUTE LESSON PLAN

STANDARDS FOR FOREIGN LANGUAGE LEARNING: BLOCK 7

Vocabulario en acción 2
Communication 1.1: Students engage in conversations, provide and obtain information, express feelings and emotions, and exchange opinions.
Communication 1.2: Students understand and interpret written and spoken language on a variety of topics.
Communication 1.3: Students present information, concepts, and ideas to an audience of listeners or readers on a variety of topics.
Cultures 2.2: Students demonstrate an understanding of the relationship between the products and perspectives of the culture studied.

CORE INSTRUCTION

Warm-Up
- (5 min.) Have students do Bell Work 8.5, p. 146.

Vocabulario en acción 2
- (5 min.) Show **ExpresaVisión,** Ch. 8.
- (25 min.) Present **Vocabulario 2**, pp. 146–147 using Teaching **Vocabulario,** p. 146.
- (10 min.) Present **Nota cultural,** p. 148.
- (10 min.) Play Audio CD 8, Tr. 8 for Activity 23, p. 148.
- (30 min.) Have students do Activities 24–28, pp. 148–149.

Wrap-Up
- (5 min.) Present Language Note and **También se puede decir,** p. 147.

OPTIONAL RESOURCES
- (10 min.) Advanced Learners, p. 147 ▲
- (5 min.) Special Learning Needs, p. 147 ●
- (5 min.) TPR, p. 147
- (10 min.) Game, p. 148
- (5 min.) Special Learning Needs, p. 149 ●

▲ = Advanced Learners   ◆ = Slower Pace Learners   ● = Special Learning Needs   ■ = Heritage Speakers

Teacher's Name _____ Class _____ Date _____

CAPÍTULO 8

BLOCK 7 90-MINUTE LESSON PLAN

Practice Options
- *Lab Book,* pp. 52–53
- **Cuaderno de vocabulario y gramática,** pp. 47–49
- *Activities for Communication,* pp. 31–32 ▲ ■
- **Cuaderno para hispanohablantes,** Chapter 8 ■
- *Teaching Transparencies:* Bell Work 8.5; Vocabulario 8.3, 8.4; **Vocabulario y gramática** Answers, pp. 47–49 ▲ ● ■
- *Video Guide,* pp. 78–79 ▲ ● ■
- *TPR Storytelling Book,* pp. 44–45 ▲ ●
- *Interactive Tutor* (Disc 2) or *DVD Tutor* (Disc 2) ▲ ● ■
- Online Practice, Chapter 8 (go.hrw.com, Keyword: EXP1B CH8)

▲ = Advanced Learners   ◆ = Slower Pace Learners   ● = Special Learning Needs   ■ = Heritage Speakers

Holt Spanish 1B   Lesson Planner

Teacher's Name _____ Class _____ Date _____

Vamos de compras

CAPÍTULO **8**

BLOCK 8 90-MINUTE LESSON PLAN

STANDARDS FOR FOREIGN LANGUAGE LEARNING: BLOCK 8

Vocabulario en acción 2
Communication 1.1: Students engage in conversations, provide and obtain information, express feelings and emotions, and exchange opinions.
Communication 1.2: Students understand and interpret written and spoken language on a variety of topics.
Communication 1.3: Students present information, concepts, and ideas to an audience of listeners or readers on a variety of topics.
Cultures 2.2: Students demonstrate an understanding of the relationship between the products and perspectives of the culture studied.

Gramática en acción 2
Communication 1.1: Students engage in conversations, provide and obtain information, express feelings and emotions, and exchange opinions.
Communication 1.2: Students understand and interpret written and spoken language on a variety of topics.
Communication 1.3: Students present information, concepts, and ideas to an audience of listeners or readers on a variety of topics.
Comparisons 4.2: Students demonstrate understanding of the concept of culture through comparisons of the cultures studied and their own.

CORE INSTRUCTION

Warm-Up
- (5 min.) Have students do Bell Work 8.6, p. 152.

Vocabulario en acción 2
- (20 min.) Review **Vocabulario 2** and **¡Exprésate!**, pp. 146–151.
- (15 min.) Present **¡Exprésate!**, p. 150 using Teaching **¡Exprésate!**, p. 150.
- (30 min.) Have students do Activities 29–33, pp. 150–151.

Gramática en acción 2
- (15 min.) Present **Gramática:** *Preterite of* **-ar** *verbs*, p. 152 using Teaching **Gramática**, #1–3, p. 152.

Wrap-Up
- (5 min.) See Common Error Alert, p. 153. Remind students to study for **Prueba: Vocabulario 2**.

OPTIONAL RESOURCES
- (10 min.) **Comunicación** (TE), p. 149
- (5 min.) Slower Pace Learners, p. 149 ◆
- (5 min.) Extension, p. 150
- (5 min.) Heritage Speakers, p. 150 ■
- (5 min.) **Más práctica,** p. 151
- (10 min.) **Comunicación** (TE), p. 151
- (5 min.) Advanced Learners, p. 151 ▲
- (5 min.) Special Learning Needs, p. 151 ●
- (5 min.) Circumlocution, p. 150

▲ = Advanced Learners ◆ = Slower Pace Learners ● = Special Learning Needs ■ = Heritage Speakers

Holt Spanish 1B — Lesson Planner

Teacher's Name _____ Class _____ Date _____

CAPÍTULO
8

BLOCK 8 90-MINUTE LESSON PLAN

Practice Options
- *Lab Book,* pp. 52–53
- ***Cuaderno de vocabulario y gramática,*** pp. 47–49
- *Activities for Communication,* pp. 31–32 ▲ ■
- ***Cuaderno para hispanohablantes,*** Chapter 8 ■
- *Teaching Transparencies:* Bell Work 8.6; Vocabulario 8.3, 8.4; ***Vocabulario y gramática*** Answers, pp. 47–49 ▲ ● ■
- *Video Guide,* pp. 78–79 ▲ ● ■
- *TPR Storytelling Book,* pp. 44–45 ▲ ●
- *Interactive Tutor* (Disc 2) or *DVD Tutor* (Disc 2) ▲ ● ■
- Online Practice, Chapter 8 (go.hrw.com, Keyword: EXP1B CH8)

▲ = Advanced Learners ◆ = Slower Pace Learners ● = Special Learning Needs ■ = Heritage Speakers

Holt Spanish 1B Lesson Planner

Teacher's Name _____ Class _____ Date _____

CAPÍTULO **8**

Vamos de compras

BLOCK 9 90-MINUTE LESSON PLAN

STANDARDS FOR FOREIGN LANGUAGE LEARNING: BLOCK 9

Vocabulario en acción 2
Communication 1.1: Students engage in conversations, provide and obtain information, express feelings and emotions, and exchange opinions.
Communication 1.2: Students understand and interpret written and spoken language on a variety of topics.
Communication 1.3: Students present information, concepts, and ideas to an audience of listeners or readers on a variety of topics.
Cultures 2.2: Students demonstrate an understanding of the relationship between the products and perspectives of the culture studied.

Gramática en acción 2
Communication 1.1: Students engage in conversations, provide and obtain information, express feelings and emotions, and exchange opinions.
Communication 1.2: Students understand and interpret written and spoken language on a variety of topics.
Communication 1.3: Students present information, concepts, and ideas to an audience of listeners or readers on a variety of topics.
Comparisons 4.2: Students demonstrate understanding of the concept of culture through comparisons of the cultures studied and their own.

CORE INSTRUCTION

Warm-Up
- (5 min.) Have pairs of students ask and answer questions based on the **¡Exprésate!** box, p. 147.

Vocabulario en acción 2
- (15 min.) Review **Vocabulario en acción 2**, pp. 146–151.

Assess
- (20 min.) Give **Prueba: Vocabulario 2**.

Gramática en acción 2
- (15 min.) Present **Gramática:** *Preterite of -ar verbs*, p. 152 using Teaching **Gramática**, #4–5, p. 152.

- (5 min.) Present **Nota cultural**, p. 152.
- (10 min.) Play Audio CD 8, Tr. 9 for Activity 34, p. 152.
- (10 min.) Have students do Activities 35–37, pp. 152–153.

Wrap-Up
- (10 min.) See **Comunicación** (TE), p. 153.

OPTIONAL RESOURCES
- (5 min.) Special Learning Needs, p. 153 ●
- (5 min.) Advanced Learners, p. 153 ▲

Teacher's Name _____ Class _____ Date _____

CAPÍTULO 8

BLOCK 9 90-MINUTE LESSON PLAN

Practice Options
- *Lab Book,* pp. 25, 52–53
- **Cuaderno de vocabulario y gramática,** pp. 50–52
- **Cuaderno de actividades**, pp. 44–47 ▲ ● ■
- *Activities for Communication,* pp. 31–32 ▲ ■
- **Cuaderno para hispanohablantes,** Chapter 8 ■
- *Teaching Transparencies:* **Vocabulario y gramática** Answers pp. 50–52 ▲ ● ■
- *Video Guide,* pp. 78–79 ▲ ● ■
- *Grammar Tutor for Students of Spanish,* Chapter 8 ● ■
- *Interactive Tutor* (Disc 2) or *DVD Tutor* (Disc 2) ▲ ● ■
- Online Practice, Chapter 8 (go.hrw.com, Keyword: EXP1B CH8)

Assessment Options
- *Assessment Program:* **Prueba: Vocabulario 2**, pp. 63–64
- *Assessment Program:* Alternative Assessment Guide, pp. 243, 251, 259 ▲ ● ■
- Test Generator

▲ = Advanced Learners   ◆ = Slower Pace Learners   ● = Special Learning Needs   ■ = Heritage Speakers

Teacher's Name _____ Class _____ Date _____

Vamos de compras

CAPÍTULO 8

BLOCK 10 90-MINUTE LESSON PLAN

STANDARDS FOR FOREIGN LANGUAGE LEARNING: BLOCK 10

Gramática en acción 2
Communication 1.1: Students engage in conversations, provide and obtain information, express feelings and emotions, and exchange opinions.
Communication 1.2: Students understand and interpret written and spoken language on a variety of topics.
Communication 1.3: Students present information, concepts, and ideas to an audience of listeners or readers on a variety of topics.
Comparisons 4.2: Students demonstrate understanding of the concept of culture through comparisons of the cultures studied and their own.

CORE INSTRUCTION

Warm-Up
- (5 min.) Have students do Bell Work 8.7, p. 154.

Gramática en acción 2
- (20 min.) Present **Gramática**: *Preterite of* **ir**, p. 154 using Teaching **Gramática,** p. 154.
- (30 min.) Have students do Activities 38–42, pp. 154–155.
- (25 min.) Present **Gramática**: The *preterite of* **-ar** *verbs with reflexive pronouns*, p. 156 using Teaching **Gramática,** p. 156.

Wrap-Up
- (10 min.) **Comunicación** (TE)**,** p. 155

OPTIONAL RESOURCES
- (10 min.) Advanced Learners, p. 155. ▲
- (10 min.) Multiple Intelligences, p. 155.

▲ = Advanced Learners   ◆ = Slower Pace Learners   ● = Special Learning Needs   ■ = Heritage Speakers

Holt Spanish 1B

Lesson Planner

Copyright © by Holt, Rinehart and Winston. All rights reserved.

Teacher's Name _____ Class _____ Date _____

CAPÍTULO 8

BLOCK 10 90-MINUTE LESSON PLAN

Practice Options
- *Lab Book,* pp. 25, 52–53
- **Cuaderno de vocabulario y gramática,** pp. 50–52
- **Cuaderno de actividades,** pp. 44–47 ▲ ● ■
- *Activities for Communication,* pp. 31–32 ▲ ■
- *Cuaderno para hispanohablantes,* Chapter 8 ■
- *Teaching Transparencies:* Bell Work 8.7; **Vocabulario y gramática** Answers pp. 50–52 ▲ ● ■
- *Video Guide,* pp. 78–79 ▲ ● ■
- *Grammar Tutor for Students of Spanish,* Chapter 8 ● ■
- *Interactive Tutor* (Disc 2) or *DVD Tutor* (Disc 2) ▲ ● ■
- Online Practice, Chapter 8 (go.hrw.com, Keyword: EXP1B CH8)

▲ = Advanced Learners   ◆ = Slower Pace Learners   ● = Special Learning Needs   ■ = Heritage Speakers

Holt Spanish 1B   Lesson Planner

Teacher's Name _____ Class _____ Date _____

Vamos de compras

CAPÍTULO 8

BLOCK 11 90-MINUTE LESSON PLAN

STANDARDS FOR FOREIGN LANGUAGE LEARNING: BLOCK 11

Gramática en acción 2
Communication 1.1: Students engage in conversations, provide and obtain information, express feelings and emotions, and exchange opinions.
Communication 1.2: Students understand and interpret written and spoken language on a variety of topics.
Communication 1.3: Students present information, concepts, and ideas to an audience of listeners or readers on a variety of topics.
Comparisons 4.2: Students demonstrate understanding of the concept of culture through comparisons of the cultures studied and their own.

Conexiones culturales
Communication 1.3: Students present information, concepts, and ideas to an audience of listeners or readers on a variety of topics.
Cultures 2.2: Students demonstrate an understanding of the relationship between the products and perspectives of the culture studied.
Connections 3.2: Students acquire information and recognize the distinctive viewpoints that are only available through the foreign language and its cultures.

CORE INSTRUCTION

Warm-Up
- (5 min.) Have students do Bell Work 8.8, p. 156.

Gramática en acción 2
- (10 min.) Show **GramaVisión 2,** Segment 6.
- (10 min.) Play Audio CD 8, Tr. 10 for Activity 43, p.156.
- (30 min.) Have students do Activities 44–46, p. 157.

Conexiones culturales
- (30 min.) Present **Conexiones culturales**, pp. 158–159 using Teaching **Conexiones culturales,** p. 158.

Wrap-Up
- (5 min.) Encourage students to add any information they may have about people in the History Link, or about other currencies. Remind students to study for **Prueba: Gramática 2**.

OPTIONAL RESOURCES
- (10 min.) **Comunicación** (TE)**,** p. 157
- (5 min.) Thinking Critically, p. 159
- (5 min.) Advanced Learners, p. 159 ▲
- (5 min.) Multiple Intelligences, p. 159
- (5 min.) Slower Pace Learners, p. 157 ◆
- (5 min.) Special Learning Needs, p. 157. ●

▲ = Advanced Learners   ◆ = Slower Pace Learners   ● = Special Learning Needs   ■ = Heritage Speakers

Holt Spanish 1B — Lesson Planner

Teacher's Name _____ Class _____ Date _____

CAPÍTULO 8

BLOCK 11 90-MINUTE LESSON PLAN

Practice Options
- *Lab Book,* pp. 25, 52–53
- **Cuaderno de vocabulario y gramática,** pp. 50–52
- **Cuaderno de actividades**, pp. 44–47 ▲●■
- *Activities for Communication,* pp. 31–32 ▲■
- **Cuaderno para hispanohablantes,** Chapter 8 ■
- *Teaching Transparencies:* Bell Work 8.8; **Vocabulario y gramática** Answers pp. 50–52 ▲●■
- *Video Guide,* pp. 78–79 ▲●■
- *Grammar Tutor for Students of Spanish,* Chapter 8 ●■
- *Interactive Tutor* (Disc 2) or *DVD Tutor* (Disc 2) ▲●■
- Online Practice, Chapter 8 (go.hrw.com, Keyword: EXP1B CH8)

▲ = Advanced Learners   ◆ = Slower Pace Learners   ● = Special Learning Needs   ■ = Heritage Speakers

Holt Spanish 1B   Lesson Planner

Teacher's Name _____ Class _____ Date _____

CAPÍTULO
8

Vamos de compras

BLOCK 12 90-MINUTE LESSON PLAN

STANDARDS FOR FOREIGN LANGUAGE LEARNING: BLOCK 12

Gramática en acción 2
Communication 1.1: Students engage in conversations, provide and obtain information, express feelings and emotions, and exchange opinions.
Communication 1.2: Students understand and interpret written and spoken language on a variety of topics.
Communication 1.3: Students present information, concepts, and ideas to an audience of listeners or readers on a variety of topics.
Comparisons 4.2: Students demonstrate understanding of the concept of culture through comparisons of the cultures studied and their own.

Novela en video
Communication 1.2: Students understand and interpret written and spoken language on a variety of topics.
Cultures 2.1: Students demonstrate an understanding of the relationship between the practices and perspectives of the culture studied.

Connections 3.1: Students reinforce and further their knowledge of other disciplines through the foreign language.
Connections 3.2: Students acquire information and recognize the distinctive viewpoints that are only available through the foreign language and its cultures.
Comparisons 4.2: Students demonstrate understanding of the concept of culture through comparisons of the cultures studied and their own.

Leamos y escribamos
Communication 1.2: Students understand and interpret written and spoken language on a variety of topics.
Communication 1.3: Students present information, concepts, and ideas to an audience of listeners or readers on a variety of topics.
Cultures 2.1: Students demonstrate an understanding of the relationship between the practices and perspectives of the culture studied.

CORE INSTRUCTION

Warm-Up
- (5 min.) Have pairs of students ask each other questions based on Activity 31.

Gramática en acción 2
- (10 min.) Review **Gramática en acción 2**, pp. 152–157.

Assess
- (20 min.) Give **Prueba: Gramática 2**.

Novela en video
- (30 min.) Present **Novela en video**, pp. 160–163 using Teaching **Novela en video,** #1–2, p. 160.

Leamos y escribamos
- (20 min.) Present **Una modeda de ¡Ay!**, p. 164 using Teaching **Leamos**, #1–2, p. 164.

Wrap-Up
- (5 min.) See Comparing and Contrasting, p. 162.

OPTIONAL RESOURCES
- (5 min.) Gestures, p. 160.
- (5 min.) Visual Learners, p. 160
- (5 min.) Practices and Perspectives, p. 161
- (5 min.) Culminating Project, p. 162
- (5 min.) Applying the Strategies, p. 164
- (10 min.) **Comunicación** (TE), p. 163

▲ = Advanced Learners   ◆ = Slower Pace Learners   ● = Special Learning Needs   ■ = Heritage Speakers

Holt Spanish 1B   Lesson Planner

Teacher's Name _____ Class _____ Date _____

CAPÍTULO 8

BLOCK 12 90-MINUTE LESSON PLAN

Practice Options
- *Lab Book,* pp. 25, 52–54
- ***Cuaderno de actividades***, p. 48 ▲ ● ■
- ***Cuaderno para hispanohablantes***, pp. 61–68 ■
- *Reading Strategies and Skills Handbook,* Chapter 8 ▲ ● ■
- *¡Lee conmigo!* Level 1 reader ▲ ■
- *Video Guide,* pp. 74, 80 ▲ ● ■
- *Interactive Tutor* (Disc 2) or *DVD Tutor* (Disc 2) ▲ ● ■
- Online Practice, Chapter 8 (go.hrw.com, Keyword: EXP1B CH8)

Assessment Options
- *Assessment Program:* **Prueba: Gramática 2**, pp. 65–66
- *Assessment Program:* **Prueba: Aplicación 2,** pp. 67–68
- *Assessment Program:* Alternative Assessment Guide, pp. 243, 251, 259 ▲ ● ■
- *Audio CD 8*, Tr. 19
- Test Generator

▲ = Advanced Learners   ◆ = Slower Pace Learners   ● = Special Learning Needs   ■ = Heritage Speakers

Holt Spanish 1B — Lesson Planner

Teacher's Name _____ Class _____ Date _____

Vamos de compras

CAPÍTULO 8

BLOCK 13 90-MINUTE LESSON PLAN

STANDARDS FOR FOREIGN LANGUAGE LEARNING: BLOCK 13

Leamos y escribamos
Communication 1.2: Students understand and interpret written and spoken language on a variety of topics.
Communication 1.3: Students present information, concepts, and ideas to an audience of listeners or readers on a variety of topics.
Cultures 2.1: Students demonstrate an understanding of the relationship between the practices and perspectives of the culture studied.

Repaso
Communication 1.1: Students engage in conversations, provide and obtain information, express feelings and emotions, and exchange opinions.

Communication 1.2: Students understand and interpret written and spoken language on a variety of topics.
Communication 1.3: Students present information, concepts, and ideas to an audience of listeners or readers on a variety of topics.
Cultures 2.1: Students demonstrate an understanding of the relationship between the practices and perspectives of the culture studied.
Cultures 2.2: Students demonstrate an understanding of the relationship between the products and perspectives of the culture studied.

CORE INSTRUCTION

Warm-Up
- (5 min.) Review Writing Rubric you will use for this project.

Leamos y escribamos
- (20 min.) See Teaching **Leamos,** #3–4, p. 164.
- (30 min.) Present **Taller del escritor,** p. 165 using Teaching **Escribamos,** #3–4, p. 164.

Repaso
- (10 min.) Have students do Activities 1–5, pp. 166–167.
- (10 min.) Play Audio CD 8, Tr. 13 for Activity 6, p.167.
- (5 min.) Have students do Activity 7, p. 167.

Wrap-Up
- (10 min.) Present Fold-N-Learn, p. 166. Remind students to study for Chapter Test.

OPTIONAL RESOURCES
- (5 min.) Heritage Speakers, p. 165 ■
- (5 min.) Advanced Learners, p. 165 ▲
- (5 min.) Multiple Intelligences, p. 165
- (5 min.) Reteaching, p. 166
- (10 min.) Game, p. 166
- (10 min.) Teacher to Teacher, p. 169
- (5 min.) Additional Reading, pp. 270–271

▲ = Advanced Learners ◆ = Slower Pace Learners ● = Special Learning Needs ■ = Heritage Speakers

Holt Spanish 1B — Lesson Planner

Teacher's Name _____ Class _____ Date _____

CAPÍTULO 8

BLOCK 13 90-MINUTE LESSON PLAN

Practice Options
- *Lab Book*, pp. 26, 53
- ***Cuaderno de actividades***, p. 48 ▲ ● ■
- *Activities for Communication*, pp. 50, 69–70 ▲ ■
- ***Cuaderno para hispanohablantes***, pp. 61–68 ■
- *Reading Strategies and Skills Handbook*, Chapter 8 ▲ ● ■
- *¡Lee conmigo!* Level 1 reader ▲ ■
- *Teaching Transparencies:* **Situación, Capítulo 8**; Picture Stories, Chapter 8 ▲ ● ■
- *Video Guide*, pp. 73, 79 ▲ ● ■
- *TPR Storytelling Book*, pp. 46–47 ▲ ●
- *Interactive Tutor* (Disc 2) or *DVD Tutor* (Disc 2) ▲ ● ■
- Online Practice, Chapter 8 (go.hrw.com, Keyword: EXP1B CH8)

▲ = Advanced Learners   ◆ = Slower Pace Learners   ● = Special Learning Needs   ■ = Heritage Speakers

Holt Spanish 1B   Lesson Planner

Teacher's Name _____ Class _____ Date _____

Vamos de compras

CAPÍTULO **8**

BLOCK 14 90-MINUTE LESSON PLAN

STANDARDS FOR FOREIGN LANGUAGE LEARNING: BLOCK 14

Integración

Communication 1.1: Students engage in conversations, provide and obtain information, express feelings and emotions, and exchange opinions.

Communication 1.2: Students understand and interpret written and spoken language on a variety of topics.

Communication 1.3: Students present information, concepts, and ideas to an audience of listeners or readers on a variety of topics.

Connections 3.2: Students acquire information and recognize the distinctive viewpoints that are only available through the foreign language and its cultures.

CORE INSTRUCTION

Chapter Assessment

Assess
- (50 min.) Give Chapter 8 Test.

Integración
- (10 min.) Play Audio CD 8, Tr. 14–16 for **Letra y sonido,** p. 168.
- (10 min.) Play Audio CD 8, Tr. 17 for Activity 1, p.170.
- (10 min.) Have students do Activities 2–4, pp. 170–171.

Wrap-Up
- (10 min.) Preview **Geocultura: : La República Dominicana,** pp. 172–165.

OPTIONAL RESOURCES
- (10 min.) Teaching Escribamos, #4, p. 164
- (10 min.) **Letra y sonido,** p. 168
- (10 min.) Culture Project, p. 170
- (10 min.) Fine Art Connection, p. 171

▲ = Advanced Learners ◆ = Slower Pace Learners ● = Special Learning Needs ■ = Heritage Speakers

Teacher's Name _____ Class _____ Date _____

CAPÍTULO 8

BLOCK 14 90-MINUTE LESSON PLAN

Practice Options
- *Interactive Tutor* (Disc 2) or *DVD Tutor* (Disc 2) ▲●■
- Online Practice, Chapter 8 (go.hrw.com, Keyword: EXP1B CH8)

Assessment Options
- *Assessment Program:* **Examen: Capítulo 8,** pp. 173–183
- *Assessment Program:* **Examen oral: Capítulo 8**, p. 184
- *Assessment Program:* Alternative Assessment Guide, pp. 243, 251, 259 ▲●■
- Standardized Assessment Tutor, pp. 33–36
- *Audio CD* 8, Tr. 20–21
- Test Generator

▲ = Advanced Learners   ◆ = Slower Pace Learners   ● = Special Learning Needs   ■ = Heritage Speakers

Teacher's Name _____ Class _____ Date _____

¡Festejemos!

CAPÍTULO 9

BLOCK 1 90-MINUTE LESSON PLAN

STANDARDS FOR FOREIGN LANGUAGE LEARNING: BLOCK 1

Chapter Opener
Comparisons 4.2: Students demonstrate understanding of the concept of culture through comparisons of the cultures studied and their own.

Vocabulario en acción 1
Communication 1.1: Students engage in conversations, provide and obtain information, express feelings and emotions, and exchange opinions.

Communication 1.2: Students understand and interpret written and spoken language on a variety of topics.

Communication 1.3: Students present information, concepts, and ideas to an audience of listeners or readers on a variety of topics.

Communities 5.1: Students use the language both within and beyond the school setting.

Before starting **Capítulo 9,** you may wish to teach **Geocultura: La República Dominicana,** pp. 172–175. For teaching suggestions, see pp. xv–xvi of this *Lesson Planner*.

CORE INSTRUCTION

Warm-Up
- (5 min.) See Learning Tips, p.177.

Chapter Opener
- (5 min.) See Using the Photo and **Más vocabulario,** p. 176.
- (5 min.) See **Objetivos,** p. 176.

Vocabulario en acción 1
- (5 min.) Bell Work 9.1, p. 178
- (5 min.) Show **ExpresaVisión,** Ch. 9.
- (30 min.) Present **Vocabulario 1**, pp. 178–179 using Teaching **Vocabulario,** p. 178.
- (20 min.) Have students do Activity 1–5, pp. 180–181.

Wrap-Up
- (5 min.) See **También se puede decir** and Language Note, p. 179.

OPTIONAL RESOURCES
- (5 min.) Common Error Alert, p. 178
- (5 min.) Advanced Learners, p. 179
- (5 min.) Special Learning Needs, p. 179 ●
- (5 min.) **Más práctica,** p. 180
- (10 min.) Extension, p. 180
- (10 min.) Communities, p. 180
- (10 min.) Fold-n-Learn, p. 180
- (5 min.) **Más práctica,** p. 181
- (5 min.) Slower Pace Learners, p. 181 ◆
- (5 min.) Multiple Intelligences, p. 181
- (10 min.) **Comunicación** (TE), p. 181

▲ = Advanced Learners   ◆ = Slower Pace Learners   ● = Special Learning Needs   ■ = Heritage Speakers

Holt Spanish 1R

Teacher's Name _____ Class _____ Date _____

CAPÍTULO 9

BLOCK 1 90-MINUTE LESSON PLAN

Practice Options
- *Lab Book,* pp. 56–57
- ***Cuaderno de vocabulario y gramática,*** pp. 53–55
- *Activities for Communication,* pp. 33–34 ▲ ■
- ***Cuaderno para hispanohablantes,*** Chapter 9 ■
- *Teaching Transparencies:* Bell Work 9.1; Vocabulario 9.1, 9.2; ***Vocabulario y gramática*** Answers pp. 53–55 ▲ ● ■
- *Video Guide,* pp. 86–87 ▲ ● ■
- *TPR Storytelling Book,* pp. 48–49 ▲ ●
- *Interactive Tutor* (Disc 2) or *DVD Tutor* (Disc 2) ▲ ● ■
- Online Practice, Chapter 9 (go.hrw.com, Keyword: EXP1B CH9)

▲ = Advanced Learners ◆ = Slower Pace Learners ● = Special Learning Needs ■ = Heritage Speakers

Holt Spanish 1B

Lesson Planner

Teacher's Name _____ Class _____ Date _____

¡Festejemos!

CAPÍTULO 9

BLOCK 2 90-MINUTE LESSON PLAN

STANDARDS FOR FOREIGN LANGUAGE LEARNING: BLOCK 2

Vocabulario en acción 1

Communication 1.1: Students engage in conversations, provide and obtain information, express feelings and emotions, and exchange opinions.

Communication 1.2: Students understand and interpret written and spoken language on a variety of topics.

Communication 1.3: Students present information, concepts, and ideas to an audience of listeners or readers on a variety of topics.

Cultures 2.1: Students demonstrate an understanding of the relationship between the practices and perspectives of the culture studied.

Comparisons 4.2: Students demonstrate understanding of the concept of culture through comparisons of the cultures studied and their own.

Communities 5.1: Students use the language both within and beyond the school setting.

CORE INSTRUCTION

Warm-Up
- (5 min.) Have students do Bell Work 9.2, p. 184.

Vocabulario en acción 1
- (15 min.) Review **Vocabulario 1** and **¡Exprésate!**, pp. 178–179.
- (15 min.) See Teaching **¡Exprésate!**, p. 182.
- (15 min.) Have students do Activities 6–7, p. 182.
- (10 min.) Present **Nota cultural,** p. 183.
- (10 min.) Play Audio CD 9, Tr. 1 for Activity 8, p. 183.
- (15 min.) Have students do Activities 9–10, p. 183.

Wrap-Up
- (5 min.) Present Practices and Perspectives, p. 183. Remind students to study for **Prueba: Vocabulario 1**.

OPTIONAL RESOURCES
- (10 min.) TPR, p. 179
- (10 min.) Teacher to Teacher, p. 182
- (10 min.) **Comunicación** (TE), p. 183
- (5 min.) Advanced Learners, p. 183
- (10 min.) Multiple Intelligences, p. 183

▲ = Advanced Learners   ◆ = Slower Pace Learners   ● = Special Learning Needs   ■ = Heritage Speakers

Teacher's Name _____ Class _____ Date _____

CAPÍTULO 9

BLOCK 2 90-MINUTE LESSON PLAN

Practice Options
- *Lab Book,* pp. 56–57
- ***Cuaderno de vocabulario y gramática,*** pp. 53–55
- *Activities for Communication,* pp. 33–34 ▲ ■
- ***Cuaderno para hispanohablantes,*** Chapter 9 ■
- *Teaching Transparencies:* Bell Work 9.2; **Vocabulario** 9.1, 9.2; ***Vocabulario y gramática*** Answers pp. 53–55 ▲ ● ■
- *Video Guide,* pp. 86–87 ▲ ● ■
- *TPR Storytelling Book,* pp. 48–49 ▲ ●
- *Interactive Tutor* (Disc 2) or *DVD Tutor* (Disc 2) ▲ ● ■
- Online Practice, Chapter 9 (go.hrw.com, Keyword: EXP1B CH9)

▲ = Advanced Learners   ◆ = Slower Pace Learners   ● = Special Learning Needs   ■ = Heritage Speakers

Holt Spanish 1B   Lesson Planner

Teacher's Name _____ Class _____ Date _____

¡Festejemos!

CAPÍTULO 9

BLOCK 3 90-MINUTE LESSON PLAN

STANDARDS FOR FOREIGN LANGUAGE LEARNING: BLOCK 3

Vocabulario en acción 1

Communication 1.1: Students engage in conversations, provide and obtain information, express feelings and emotions, and exchange opinions.

Communication 1.2: Students understand and interpret written and spoken language on a variety of topics.

Communication 1.3: Students present information, concepts, and ideas to an audience of listeners or readers on a variety of topics.

Cultures 2.1: Students demonstrate an understanding of the relationship between the practices and perspectives of the culture studied.

Comparisons 4.2: Students demonstrate understanding of the concept of culture through comparisons of the cultures studied and their own.

Communities 5.1: Students use the language both within and beyond the school setting.

Gramática en acción 1

Communication 1.1: Students engage in conversations, provide and obtain information, express feelings and emotions, and exchange opinions.

Communication 1.2: Students understand and interpret written and spoken language on a variety of topics.

Communication 1.3: Students present information, concepts, and ideas to an audience of listeners or readers on a variety of topics.

CORE INSTRUCTION

Warm-Up
- (15 min.) Review **Vocabulario en acción 1**, pp. 178–183.

Vocabulario en acción 1

Assess
- (20 min.) Give **Prueba: Vocabulario 1**.

Gramática en acción 1
- (25 min.) Present **Gramática**: *Preterite of* **-er** *and* **-ir** *verbs*, p. 184 using Teaching **Gramática**, p. 184.
- (25 min.) Have students do Activities 11–13, pp. 184–185.

Wrap-Up
- (5 min.) Check answers to Activity 11.

OPTIONAL RESOURCES
- (10 min.) **Comunicación** (TE), p. 185

▲ = Advanced Learners ◆ = Slower Pace Learners ● = Special Learning Needs ■ = Heritage Speakers

Holt Spanish 1B   Lesson Planner

Teacher's Name _____ Class _____ Date _____

CAPÍTULO 9

BLOCK 3 90-MINUTE LESSON PLAN

Practice Options
- *Lab Book,* pp. 56–57
- **Cuaderno de vocabulario y gramática,** pp. 56–58
- **Cuaderno de actividades**, pp. 51–54 ▲ ● ■
- *Activities for Communication,* pp. 33–34 ▲ ■
- **Cuaderno para hispanohablantes,** Chapter 9 ■
- *Teaching Transparencies:* **Vocabulario y gramática** Answers, pp. 56–58 ▲ ● ■
- *Video Guide,* pp. 86–87 ▲ ● ■
- *Grammar Tutor for Students of Spanish,* Chapter 9 ● ■
- *Interactive Tutor* (Disc 2) or *DVD Tutor* (Disc 2) ▲ ● ■
- Online Practice, Chapter 9 (go.hrw.com, Keyword: EXP1B CH9)

Assessment Options
- *Assessment Program:* **Prueba: Vocabulario 1**, pp. 77–78
- *Assessment Program:* Alternative Assessment Guide, pp. 244, 252, 260 ▲ ● ■
- Test Generator

▲ = Advanced Learners   ◆ = Slower Pace Learners   ● = Special Learning Needs   ■ = Heritage Speakers

Holt Spanish 1B — Lesson Planner

Teacher's Name _____ Class _____ Date _____

¡Festejemos!

CAPÍTULO 9

BLOCK 4 90-MINUTE LESSON PLAN

STANDARDS FOR FOREIGN LANGUAGE LEARNING: BLOCK 4

Gramática en acción 1

Communication 1.1: Students engage in conversations, provide and obtain information, express feelings and emotions, and exchange opinions.

Communication 1.2: Students understand and interpret written and spoken language on a variety of topics.

Communication 1.3: Students present information, concepts, and ideas to an audience of listeners or readers on a variety of topics.

Warm-Up
- (5 min.) Have students do Bell Work 9.3, p. 186.

Gramática en acción 1
- (5 min.) Show **GramaVisión,** Ch. 9.
- (15 min.) Review preterite of **-er** and **-ir** verbs, p. 184.
- (20 min.) Have students do Activities 14–15, p. 185.
- (20 min.) Present **Gramática: Repaso,** *The preterite,* p. 186 using Teaching **Gramática,** p. 186.
- (10 min.) Play Audio CD 9, Tr. 2 for Activity 16, p. 186.
- (15 min.) Have students do Activities 17–18, pp. 186–187.

Wrap-Up
- (5 min.) See Advanced Learners, p. 187.

OPTIONAL RESOURCES
- (5 min.) Slower Pace Learners, p. 185. ◆
- (5 min.) Multiple Intelligences, p. 185. ◆

▲ = Advanced Learners   ◆ = Slower Pace Learners   ● = Special Learning Needs   ■ = Heritage Speakers

Holt Spanish 1B — Lesson Planner

Teacher's Name _____ Class _____ Date _____

CAPÍTULO 9

BLOCK 4 90-MINUTE LESSON PLAN

Practice Options
- *Lab Book,* pp. 28, 56–57
- **Cuaderno de vocabulario y gramática,** pp. 56–58
- **Cuaderno de actividades**, pp. 51–54 ▲ ● ■
- *Activities for Communication,* pp. 33–34 ▲ ■
- **Cuaderno para hispanohablantes,** Chapter 9 ■
- *Teaching Transparencies:* Bell Work 9.3; **Vocabulario y gramática** Answers, pp. 56–58 ▲ ● ■
- *Video Guide,* pp. 86–87 ▲ ● ■
- *Grammar Tutor for Students of Spanish,* Chapter 9 ● ■
- *Interactive Tutor* (Disc 2) or *DVD Tutor* (Disc 2) ▲ ● ■
- Online Practice, Chapter 9 (go.hrw.com, Keyword: EXP1B CH9)

▲ = Advanced Learners   ◆ = Slower Pace Learners   ● = Special Learning Needs   ■ = Heritage Speakers

Holt Spanish 1B   Lesson Planner

Teacher's Name _____ Class _____ Date _____

¡Festejemos!

CAPÍTULO 9

BLOCK 5 90-MINUTE LESSON PLAN

STANDARDS FOR FOREIGN LANGUAGE LEARNING: BLOCK 5

Gramática en acción 1

Communication 1.1: Students engage in conversations, provide and obtain information, express feelings and emotions, and exchange opinions.
Communication 1.2: Students understand and interpret written and spoken language on a variety of topics.
Communication 1.3: Students present information, concepts, and ideas to an audience of listeners or readers on a variety of topics.

Cultures 2.1: Students demonstrate an understanding of the relationship between the practices and perspectives of the culture studied.
Comparisons 4.2: Students demonstrate understanding of the concept of culture through comparisons of the cultures studied and their own.

CORE INSTRUCTION

Warm-Up
- (5 min.) Have students do Bell Work 9.4, p. 188.

Gramática en acción 1
- (10 min.) Review the preterite, p. 186.
- (15 min.) Have students do Activities 19–20, p. 187.
- (10 min.) Show **GramaVisión 1,** Segment 2.
- (15 min.) Present **Gramática: Pensar que** and **pensar** with infinitives, p. 188 using Teaching **Gramática,** p. 188.
- (10 min.) Present **Nota cultural,** p. 188.
- (20 min.) Have students do Activities 21–23, pp. 188–189.

Wrap-Up
- (5 min.) Have students work with a partner to read aloud their responses to Activity 22. Remind students to study for **Prueba: Gramática 1**.

OPTIONAL RESOURCES
- (5 min.) Common Error Alert, p. 188
- (10 min.) Multiple Intelligences, p. 189
- (10 min.) **Comunicación** (TE), pp. 187, 189
- (5 min.) Special Learning Needs, p. 187. ●
- (5 min.) Slower Pace Learners, p. 189. ◆

▲ = Advanced Learners ◆ = Slower Pace Learners ● = Special Learning Needs ■ = Heritage Speakers

Holt Spanish 1B

Lesson Planner

Teacher's Name _____ Class _____ Date _____

CAPÍTULO 9

BLOCK 5 90-MINUTE LESSON PLAN

Practice Options
- *Lab Book,* pp. 28, 56–57
- ***Cuaderno de vocabulario y gramática,*** pp. 56–58
- ***Cuaderno de actividades***, pp. 51–54 ▲ ● ■
- *Activities for Communication,* pp. 33–34 ▲ ■
- ***Cuaderno para hispanohablantes,*** Chapter 9 ■
- *Teaching Transparencies:* Bell Work 9.4; ***Vocabulario y gramática*** Answers, pp. 56–58 ▲ ● ■
- *Video Guide,* pp. 86–87 ▲ ● ■
- *Grammar Tutor for Students of Spanish,* Chapter 9 ● ■
- *Interactive Tutor* (Disc 2) or *DVD Tutor* (Disc 2) ▲ ● ■
- Online Practice, Chapter 9 (go.hrw.com, Keyword: EXP1B CH9)

▲ = Advanced Learners   ◆ = Slower Pace Learners   ● = Special Learning Needs   ■ = Heritage Speakers

Holt Spanish 1B — Lesson Planner

Teacher's Name _____ Class _____ Date _____

¡Festejemos!

CAPÍTULO 9

BLOCK 6 90-MINUTE LESSON PLAN

STANDARDS FOR FOREIGN LANGUAGE LEARNING: BLOCK 6

Gramática en acción 1
Communication 1.1: Students engage in conversations, provide and obtain information, express feelings and emotions, and exchange opinions.
Communication 1.2: Students understand and interpret written and spoken language on a variety of topics.
Communication 1.3: Students present information, concepts, and ideas to an audience of listeners or readers on a variety of topics.
Cultures 2.1: Students demonstrate an understanding of the relationship between the practices and perspectives of the culture studied.
Comparisons 4.2: Students demonstrate understanding of the concept of culture through comparisons of the cultures studied and their own.

Cultura
Communication 1.2: Students understand and interpret written and spoken language on a variety of topics.
Cultures 2.1: Students demonstrate an understanding of the relationship between the practices and perspectives of the culture studied.

Comparisons 4.1: Students demonstrate understanding of the nature of language through comparisons of the language studied and their own.
Comparisons 4.2: Students demonstrate understanding of the concept of culture through comparisons of the cultures studied and their own.
Communities 5.1: Students use the language both within and beyond the school setting.

Vocabulario en acción 2
Communication 1.2: Students understand and interpret written and spoken language on a variety of topics.
Communication 1.3: Students present information, concepts, and ideas to an audience of listeners or readers on a variety of topics.
Comparisons 4.1: Students demonstrate understanding of the nature of language through comparisons of the language studied and their own.
Comparisons 4.2: Students demonstrate understanding of the concept of culture through comparisons of the cultures studied and their own.

CORE INSTRUCTION

Warm-Up
- (5 min.) Have pairs of students read to each other the paragraph they created in Activity 11.

Gramática en acción 1

Assess
- (10 min.) Review **Gramática en acción 1**, pp. 184–189.
- (20 min.) Give **Prueba: Gramática 1.**

Cultura
- (35 min.) Present **Comparaciones**, pp. 190–191 using Teaching **Cultura**, p. 190.
- (5 min.) Present and assign **Comunidad**, p. 191.

Vocabulario en acción 2
- (15 min.) Present **Vocabulario 2**, pp. 192–193 using Teaching **Vocabulario**, #1, p. 192.

Wrap-Up
- (5 min.) Present Language Note and **También se puede decir**, p. 193.

OPTIONAL RESOURCES
- (5 min.) Map Activities, p. 190
- (5 min.) Heritage Speakers, p. 191 ■
- (5 min.) Comparing and Contrasting, p. 191
- (5 min.) Language to Language, p. 191
- (5 min.) Slower Pace Learners, p. 191 ◆
- (5 min.) Multiple Intelligences, pp. 191, 193

▲ = Advanced Learners ◆ = Slower Pace Learners ● = Special Learning Needs ■ = Heritage Speakers

Holt Spanish 1B

Lesson Planner

Teacher's Name _____ Class _____ Date _____

CAPÍTULO 9

BLOCK 6 90-MINUTE LESSON PLAN

Practice Options
- *Lab Book,* p. 57–59
- ***Cuaderno de vocabulario y gramática,*** pp. 59–61
- *Activities for Communication,* pp. 35–36 ▲ ■
- ***Cuaderno de actividades***, p. 55 ▲ ● ■
- ***Cuaderno para hispanohablantes,*** pp. 69–76 ■
- *Teaching Transparencies:* **Mapa** 4; **Vocabulario** 9.3, 9.4; ***Vocabulario y gramática*** Answers, pp. 59–61 ▲ ● ■
- *Video Guide,* pp. 83, 87–89 ▲ ● ■
- *Interactive Tutor* (Disc 2) or *DVD Tutor* (Disc 2) ▲ ● ■
- Online Practice, Chapter 9 (go.hrw.com, Keyword: EXP1B CH9)

Assessment Options
- *Assessment Program:* **Prueba: Gramática 1**, pp. 79–80
- *Assessment Program:* **Prueba: Aplicación 1,** pp. 81–82
- *Assessment Program:* Alternative Assessment Guide, pp. 244, 252, 260 ▲ ● ■
- *Audio CD 9,* Tr. 15
- Test Generator

▲ = Advanced Learners ◆ = Slower Pace Learners ● = Special Learning Needs ■ = Heritage Speakers

Holt Spanish 1B — Lesson Planner

Teacher's Name _____ Class _____ Date _____

¡Festejemos!

CAPÍTULO 9

BLOCK 7 90-MINUTE LESSON PLAN

STANDARDS FOR FOREIGN LANGUAGE LEARNING: BLOCK 7

Vocabulario en acción 2

Communication 1.2: Students understand and interpret written and spoken language on a variety of topics.

Communication 1.3: Students present information, concepts, and ideas to an audience of listeners or readers on a variety of topics.

Comparisons 4.1: Students demonstrate understanding of the nature of language through comparisons of the language studied and their own.

Comparisons 4.2: Students demonstrate understanding of the concept of culture through comparisons of the cultures studied and their own.

CORE INSTRUCTION

Warm-Up
- (5 min.) Have students do Bell Work 9.5, p. 192.

Vocabulario en acción 2
- (15 min.) Review **Vocabulario 2,** pp. 192–193.
- (10 min.) See Teaching Vocabulario, #2–3, p. 192.
- (5 min.) Present **Nota cultural**, p. 194.
- (35 min.) Have students do Activities 24–28, pp. 194–195.
- (15 min.) See Teaching **¡Exprésate!,** p. 196.

Wrap-Up
- (10 min.) Products and Perspectives, p. 195 Assign as homework.

OPTIONAL RESOURCES
- (5 min.) TPR, p. 193
- (5 min.) Advanced Learners, p. 193
- (5 min.) Multicultural Link, p. 194
- (5 min.) Heritage Speakers, p. 194 ■
- (10 min.) Game, p. 194
- (5 min.) Advanced Learners, p. 195.
- (5 min.) Products and Perspectives, p. 195
- (10 min.) **Comunicación** (TE), p. 195
- (5 min.) Multiple Intelligences, p. 195

▲ = Advanced Learners   ◆ = Slower Pace Learners   ● = Special Learning Needs   ■ = Heritage Speakers

Holt Spanish 1B   Lesson Planner

Teacher's Name _____ Class _____ Date _____

CAPÍTULO 9

BLOCK 7 90-MINUTE LESSON PLAN

Practice Options
- *Lab Book,* pp. 58–59
- ***Cuaderno de vocabulario y gramática,*** pp. 59–61
- *Activities for Communication,* pp. 35–36 ▲ ■
- ***Cuaderno para hispanohablantes,*** Chapter 9 ■
- *Teaching Transparencies:* Bell Work 9.5; **Vocabulario** 9.3, 9.4; ***Vocabulario y gramática*** Answers, pp. 59–61 ▲ ● ■
- *Video Guide,* pp. 88–89 ▲ ● ■
- *TPR Storytelling Book,* pp. 50–51 ▲ ●
- *Interactive Tutor* (Disc 2) or *DVD Tutor* (Disc 2) ▲ ● ■
- Online Practice, Chapter 9 (go.hrw.com, Keyword: EXP1B CH9)

▲ = Advanced Learners   ◆ = Slower Pace Learners   ● = Special Learning Needs   ■ = Heritage Speakers

Holt Spanish 1B   Lesson Planner

Teacher's Name _____ Class _____ Date _____

¡Festejemos!

CAPÍTULO 9

BLOCK 8 90-MINUTE LESSON PLAN

STANDARDS FOR FOREIGN LANGUAGE LEARNING: BLOCK 8

Vocabulario en acción 2
Communication 1.1: Students engage in conversations, provide and obtain information, express feelings and emotions, and exchange opinions.
Communication 1.2: Students understand and interpret written and spoken language on a variety of topics.
Communication 1.3: Students present information, concepts, and ideas to an audience of listeners or readers on a variety of topics.
Comparisons 4.1: Students demonstrate understanding of the nature of language through comparisons of the language studied and their own.
Comparisons 4.2: Students demonstrate understanding of the concept of culture through comparisons of the cultures studied and their own.

Gramática en acción 2
Communication 1.1: Students engage in conversations, provide and obtain information, express feelings and emotions, and exchange opinions.
Communication 1.2: Students understand and interpret written and spoken language on a variety of topics.
Communication 1.3: Students present information, concepts, and ideas to an audience of listeners or readers on a variety of topics.
Communities 5.2: Students show evidence of becoming life–long learners by using the language for personal enjoyment and enrichment.

CORE INSTRUCTION

Warm-Up
- (5 min.) Have students do Bell Work 9.6, p. 198.

Vocabulario en acción 2
- (10 min.) Review **¡Exprésate!,** p. 196.
- (10 min.) Play Audio CD 9, Tr. 6 for Activity 29, p. 196.
- (35 min.) Have students do Activities 30–34, pp. 196–197.

Gramática en acción 2
- (25 min.) Present **Gramática:** *Direct object pronouns*, p. 198 using Teaching **Gramática,** p. 198.

Wrap-Up
- (5 min.) See **Más práctica,** p. 197. Remind students to study for **Prueba: Vocabulario 2.**

OPTIONAL RESOURCES
- (5 min.) Extension, p. 197
- (10 min.) **Comunicación** (TE), p. 197
- (5 min.) Special Learning Needs, p. 197 ●
- (5 min.) Advanced Learners, p. 197
- (5 min.) Special Learning Needs, p. 199. ●

▲ = Advanced Learners ◆ = Slower Pace Learners ● = Special Learning Needs ■ = Heritage Speakers

Holt Spanish 1B   Lesson Planner

Teacher's Name _____ Class _____ Date _____

CAPÍTULO 9

BLOCK 8 90-MINUTE LESSON PLAN

Practice Options
- *Lab Book,* pp. 58–59
- ***Cuaderno de vocabulario y gramática,*** pp. 62–64
- *Activities for Communication,* pp. 35–36 ▲ ■
- ***Cuaderno para hispanohablantes,*** Chapter 9 ■
- *Teaching Transparencies:* Bell Work 9.6; ***Vocabulario y gramática*** Answers, pp. 62–64 ▲ ● ■
- *Video Guide,* pp. 88–89 ▲ ● ■
- *Grammar Tutor for Students of Spanish,* Chapter 9 ● ■
- *Interactive Tutor* (Disc 2) or *DVD Tutor* (Disc 2) ▲ ● ■
- Online Practice, Chapter 9 (go.hrw.com, Keyword: EXP1B CH9)

▲ = Advanced Learners   ◆ = Slower Pace Learners   ● = Special Learning Needs   ■ = Heritage Speakers

Holt Spanish 1B   Lesson Planner

Teacher's Name _____ Class _____ Date _____

¡Festejemos!

CAPÍTULO 9

BLOCK 9 90-MINUTE LESSON PLAN

STANDARDS FOR FOREIGN LANGUAGE LEARNING: BLOCK 9

Vocabulario en acción 2
Communication 1.1: Students engage in conversations, provide and obtain information, express feelings and emotions, and exchange opinions.
Communication 1.2: Students understand and interpret written and spoken language on a variety of topics.
Communication 1.3: Students present information, concepts, and ideas to an audience of listeners or readers on a variety of topics.
Comparisons 4.1: Students demonstrate understanding of the nature of language through comparisons of the language studied and their own.
Comparisons 4.2: Students demonstrate understanding of the concept of culture through comparisons of the cultures studied and their own.

Gramática en acción 2
Communication 1.1: Students engage in conversations, provide and obtain information, express feelings and emotions, and exchange opinions.
Communication 1.2: Students understand and interpret written and spoken language on a variety of topics.
Communication 1.3: Students present information, concepts, and ideas to an audience of listeners or readers on a variety of topics.
Communities 5.2: Students show evidence of becoming life–long learners by using the language for personal enjoyment and enrichment.

CORE INSTRUCTION

Warm-Up
- (5 min.) Have students in pairs ask and answer the questions in Activity 26.

Vocabulario en acción 2
- (15 min.) Review **Vocabulario en acción 2,** pp. 192–197.

Assess
- (20 min.) Give **Prueba: Vocabulario 2.**

Gramática en acción 2
- (5 min.) Show **GramaVisión 2,** Segment 4.
- (15 min.) Review direct object pronouns, p. 198.
- (20 min.) Have students do Activities 35–38, pp. 198–199.
- (5 min.) Present **Nota cultural,** p. 199.

Wrap-Up
- (5 min.) Have students read through Activity 36 with a partner.

OPTIONAL RESOURCES
- (5 min.) Career Path, p. 199

▲ = Advanced Learners   ◆ = Slower Pace Learners   ● = Special Learning Needs   ■ = Heritage Speakers

Holt Spanish 1B   Lesson Planner

Teacher's Name _____ Class _____ Date _____

CAPÍTULO 9

BLOCK 9 90-MINUTE LESSON PLAN

Practice Options
- *Lab Book,* pp. 58–59
- ***Cuaderno de vocabulario y gramática,*** pp. 62–64
- ***Cuaderno de actividades,*** pp. 56–59 ▲●■
- *Activities for Communication,* pp. 35–36 ▲■
- ***Cuaderno para hispanohablantes,*** Chapter 9 ■
- *Teaching Transparencies: **Vocabulario y gramática*** Answers, pp. 62–64 ▲●■
- *Video Guide,* pp. 88–89 ▲●■
- *Grammar Tutor for Students of Spanish,* Chapter 9 ●■
- *Interactive Tutor* (Disc 2) or *DVD Tutor* (Disc 2) ▲●■
- Online Practice, Chapter 9 (go.hrw.com, Keyword: EXP1B CH9)

Assessment Options
- *Assessment Program:* **Prueba: Vocabulario 2**, pp. 83–84
- *Assessment Program:* Alternative Assessment Guide, pp. 244, 252, 260 ▲●■
- Test Generator

▲ = Advanced Learners   ◆ = Slower Pace Learners   ● = Special Learning Needs   ■ = Heritage Speakers

Holt Spanish 1B   Lesson Planner

Teacher's Name _____ Class _____ Date _____

¡Festejemos!

CAPÍTULO **9**

BLOCK 10 90-MINUTE LESSON PLAN

STANDARDS FOR FOREIGN LANGUAGE LEARNING: BLOCK 10

Gramática en acción 2

Communication 1.1: Students engage in conversations, provide and obtain information, express feelings and emotions, and exchange opinions.

Communication 1.2: Students understand and interpret written and spoken language on a variety of topics.

Communication 1.3: Students present information, concepts, and ideas to an audience of listeners or readers on a variety of topics.

Cultures 2.1: Students demonstrate an understanding of the relationship between the practices and perspectives of the culture studied.

Cultures 2.2: Students demonstrate an understanding of the relationship between the products and perspectives of the culture studied.

Comparisons 4.2: Students demonstrate understanding of the concept of culture through comparisons of the cultures studied and their own.

Communities 5.2: Students show evidence of becoming life–long learners by using the language for personal enjoyment and enrichment.

CORE INSTRUCTION

Warm-Up
- (5 min.) Have students do Bell Work 9.7, p. 200.

Gramática en acción 2
- (15 min.) Present **Gramática:** *conocer* and *personal* **a**, p. 200 using Teaching **Gramática,** p. 200.
- (20 min.) Have students do Activities 39–42, pp. 200–201.
- (35 min.) Present **Gramática:** *Present progressive,* p. 202 using Teaching **Gramática,** p. 202.
- (10 min.) Play Audio CD 9, Tr. 7 for Activity 43, p. 202.

Wrap-Up
- (5 min.) Have students do Bell Work 9.8, p. 202. Remind students to study for **Prueba: Gramática 2**.

OPTIONAL RESOURCES
- (5 min.) Multiple Intelligences, p. 201
- (5 min.) Advanced Learners, p. 201
- (10 min.) **Comunicación** (TE), p. 201

▲ = Advanced Learners ◆ = Slower Pace Learners ● = Special Learning Needs ■ = Heritage Speakers

Holt Spanish 1B   Lesson Planner

Teacher's Name _____ Class _____ Date _____

CAPÍTULO 9

BLOCK 10 90-MINUTE LESSON PLAN

Practice Options
- *Lab Book*, pp. 58–59
- ***Cuaderno de vocabulario y gramática,*** pp. 62–64
- ***Cuaderno de actividades,*** pp. 56–59 ▲●■
- *Activities for Communication*, pp. 35–36 ▲■
- ***Cuaderno para hispanohablantes,*** Chapter 9 ■
- *Teaching Transparencies:* Bell Work 9.7, 9.8; ***Vocabulario y gramática*** Answers, pp. 62–64 ▲●■
- *Video Guide*, pp. 88–89 ▲●■
- *Grammar Tutor for Students of Spanish*, Chapter 9 ●■
- *Interactive Tutor* (Disc 2) or *DVD Tutor* (Disc 2) ▲●■
- Online Practice, Chapter 9 (go.hrw.com, Keyword: EXP1B CH9)

▲ = Advanced Learners ◆ = Slower Pace Learners ● = Special Learning Needs ■ = Heritage Speakers

Holt Spanish 1B — Lesson Planner

Teacher's Name _____ Class _____ Date _____

¡Festejemos!

CAPÍTULO 9

BLOCK 11 90-MINUTE LESSON PLAN

STANDARDS FOR FOREIGN LANGUAGE LEARNING: BLOCK 11

Gramática en acción 2
Communication 1.1: Students engage in conversations, provide and obtain information, express feelings and emotions, and exchange opinions.
Communication 1.2: Students understand and interpret written and spoken language on a variety of topics.
Communication 1.3: Students present information, concepts, and ideas to an audience of listeners or readers on a variety of topics.
Cultures 2.1: Students demonstrate an understanding of the relationship between the practices and perspectives of the culture studied.
Cultures 2.2: Students demonstrate an understanding of the relationship between the products and perspectives of the culture studied.

Comparisons 4.2: Students demonstrate understanding of the concept of culture through comparisons of the cultures studied and their own.
Communities 5.2: Students show evidence of becoming life–long learners by using the language for personal enjoyment and enrichment.

Conexiones culturales
Communication 1.2: Students understand and interpret written and spoken language on a variety of topics.
Cultures 2.1: Students demonstrate an understanding of the relationship between the practices and perspectives of the culture studied.
Comparisons 4.2: Students demonstrate understanding of the concept of culture through comparisons of the cultures studied and their own.

CORE INSTRUCTION

Warm-Up
- (10 min.) Review the present progressive, p. 202.

Gramática en acción 2
- (20 min.) Have students do Activities 44–46, p. 203.

Assess
- (20 min.) Review **Gramática en acción 2**, pp. 198–203.
- (20 min.) Give **Prueba: Gramática 2**.

Conexiones culturales
- (15 min.) Present **Conexiones culturales**, pp. 204–205 using Teaching **Conexiones culturales**, #1–2, p. 204.

Wrap-Up
- (5 min.) Have students share any personal experiences with environmental activities.

OPTIONAL RESOURCES
- (10 min.) **Comunicación** (TE), p. 203
- (5 min.) Advanced Learners, p. 203
- (5 min.) Special Learning Needs, p. 203 ●
- (5 min.) Multiple Intelligences, p. 205

▲ = Advanced Learners ◆ = Slower Pace Learners ● = Special Learning Needs ■ = Heritage Speakers

Holt Spanish 1B

Lesson Planner

Teacher's Name _____ Class _____ Date _____

CAPÍTULO 9

BLOCK 11 90-MINUTE LESSON PLAN

Practice Options
- *Interactive Tutor* (Disc 2) or *DVD Tutor* (Disc 2) ▲●■
- Online Practice, Chapter 9 (go.hrw.com, Keyword: EXP1B CH9)

Assessment Options
- *Assessment Program:* **Prueba: Gramática 2**, pp. 85–86
- *Assessment Program:* **Prueba: Aplicación 2,** pp. 87–88
- *Assessment Program:* Alternative Assessment Guide, pp. 244, 252, 260 ▲●■
- *Audio CD 9*, Tr. 16
- Test Generator

▲ = Advanced Learners ◆ = Slower Pace Learners ● = Special Learning Needs ■ = Heritage Speakers

Holt Spanish 1B — Lesson Planner

Teacher's Name _____ Class _____ Date _____

¡Festejemos!

CAPÍTULO 9

BLOCK 12 90-MINUTE LESSON PLAN

STANDARDS FOR FOREIGN LANGUAGE LEARNING: BLOCK 12

Conexiones culturales
Communication 1.2: Students understand and interpret written and spoken language on a variety of topics.
Cultures 2.1: Students demonstrate an understanding of the relationship between the practices and perspectives of the culture studied.
Comparisons 4.2: Students demonstrate understanding of the concept of culture through comparisons of the cultures studied and their own.

Novela en video
Communication 1.2: Students understand and interpret written and spoken language on a variety of topics.
Communication 1.3: Students present information, concepts, and ideas to an audience of listeners or readers on a variety of topics.
Connections 3.2: Students acquire information and recognize the distinctive viewpoints that are only available through the foreign language and its cultures.
Comparisons 4.2: Students demonstrate understanding of the concept of culture through comparisons of the cultures studied and their own.

Leamos y escribamos
Communication 1.1: Students engage in conversations, provide and obtain information, express feelings and emotions, and exchange opinions.
Communication 1.2: Students understand and interpret written and spoken language on a variety of topics.
Communication 1.3: Students present information, concepts, and ideas to an audience of listeners or readers on a variety of topics.
Cultures 2.1: Students demonstrate an understanding of the relationship between the practices and perspectives of the culture studied.
Connections 3.2: Students acquire information and recognize the distinctive viewpoints that are only available through the foreign language and its cultures.
Comparisons 4.2: Students demonstrate understanding of the concept of culture through comparisons of the cultures studied and their own.

CORE INSTRUCTION

Warm-Up
- (5 min.) See Connections, p. 205.

Conexiones culturales
- (20 min.) See Teaching **Conexiones culturales,** #4–6, p. 204.

Novela en video
- (35 min.) See Teaching **Novela en video,** p. 206.

Leamos y escribamos
- (25 min.) Present **Leamos y escribamos,** pp. 210–211. See Teaching **Leamos,** p. 210.

Wrap-Up
- (5 min.) See Activity C, p. 211.

OPTIONAL RESOURCES
- (5 min.) Music Link, p. 205
- (5 min.) Advanced Learners, p. 205
- (5 min.) Visual Learners, p. 206
- (5 min.) Gestures, p. 206
- (5 min.) Thinking Critically, pp. 207, 208
- (5 min.) Comparing and Contrasting, p. 207
- (10 min.) Culminating Project, p. 208
- (5 min.) **Más práctica,** p. 209
- (5 min.) Slower Pace Learners, p. 209 ◆
- (10 min.) Multiple Intelligences, p. 209
- (5 min.) Applying the Strategies, p. 210
- (5 min.) Slower Pace Learners, p. 211 ◆
- (5 min.) Special Learning Needs, p. 211 ●
- (5 min.) Activity B, p. 211

▲ = Advanced Learners   ◆ = Slower Pace Learners   ● = Special Learning Needs   ■ = Heritage Speakers

Holt Spanish 1B

Lesson Planner

Teacher's Name _____ Class _____ Date _____

CAPÍTULO **9**

BLOCK 12 90-MINUTE LESSON PLAN

Practice Options
- *Cuaderno de actividades,* p. 52 ▲ ● ■
- *Cuaderno para hispanohablantes,* pp. 69–76 ■
- Reading Strategies and Skills Handbook, Chapter 9 ▲ ● ■
- *¡Lee conmigo!* Level 1 Reader ▲ ■
- *Interactive Tutor* (Disc 2) or *DVD Tutor* (Disc 2) ▲ ● ■
- Online Practice, Chapter 9 (go.hrw.com, Keyword: EXP1B CH9)

▲ = Advanced Learners   ◆ = Slower Pace Learners   ● = Special Learning Needs   ■ = Heritage Speakers

Holt Spanish 1B   Lesson Planner

Teacher's Name _____ Class _____ Date _____

¡Festejemos!

CAPÍTULO
9

BLOCK 13 90-MINUTE LESSON PLAN

STANDARDS FOR FOREIGN LANGUAGE LEARNING: BLOCK 13

Leamos y escribamos
Communication 1.1: Students engage in conversations, provide and obtain information, express feelings and emotions, and exchange opinions.
Communication 1.2: Students understand and interpret written and spoken language on a variety of topics.
Communication 1.3: Students present information, concepts, and ideas to an audience of listeners or readers on a variety of topics.
Cultures 2.1: Students demonstrate an understanding of the relationship between the practices and perspectives of the culture studied.
Connections 3.2: Students acquire information and recognize the distinctive viewpoints that are only available through the foreign language and its cultures.

Comparisons 4.2: Students demonstrate understanding of the concept of culture through comparisons of the cultures studied and their own.

Repaso
Communication 1.2: Students understand and interpret written and spoken language on a variety of topics.
Communication 1.3: Students present information, concepts, and ideas to an audience of listeners or readers on a variety of topics.
Cultures 2.1: Students demonstrate an understanding of the relationship between the practices and perspectives of the culture studied.
Cultures 2.2: Students demonstrate an understanding of the relationship between the products and perspectives of the culture studied.

CORE INSTRUCTION

Warm-Up
- (5 min.) Show students the rubric you will use to assess the writing assignment.

Leamos y escribamos
- (35 min.) Present **Taller del escritor**, p. 211. See Teaching **Escribamos**, p. 210.

Repaso
- (20 min.) Have students do Activities 1–5, pp. 212–213.
- (10 min.) Play Audio CD 9, Tr. 10 for Activity 6, p. 213.
- (5 min.) Have students do Activity 7, p. 213.
- (10 min.) Play Audio CD 9, Tr. 11–13 for **Letra y sonido**, p. 214.

Wrap-Up
- (5 min.) Go over **Repaso de gramática** 1 and 2, p. 214. Remind students of upcoming Chapter Test.

OPTIONAL RESOURCES
- (10 min.) **Process Writing**, p. 211
- (10 min.) Fold-n-Learn, p. 212
- (5 min.) Reteaching, p. 212
- (10 min.) Teacher to Teacher, p. 214
- (10 min.) Game, p. 215

▲ = Advanced Learners ◆ = Slower Pace Learners ● = Special Learning Needs ■ = Heritage Speakers

Holt Spanish 1B Lesson Planner

Teacher's Name _____ Class _____ Date _____

CAPÍTULO
9

BLOCK 13 90-MINUTE LESSON PLAN

Practice Options
- *Lab Book,* pp. 30, 59
- *Activities for Communication,* pp. 51, 71–72 ▲ ■
- **Cuaderno de actividades**, pp. 60 ▲ ● ■
- **Cuaderno para hispanohablantes,** pp. 69–765 ■
- *Teaching Transparencies:* **Situación, Capítulo 9**; Picture Stories, Chapter 9 ▲ ● ■
- *Video Guide,* pp. 83, 89 ▲ ● ■
- *TPR Storytelling Book,* pp. 50–51 ▲ ●
- Reading Strategies and Skills Handbook, Chapter 9 ▲ ● ■
- **¡Lee conmigo!** Level 1 Reader ▲ ■
- *Interactive Tutor* (Disc 2) or *DVD Tutor* (Disc 2) ▲ ● ■
- Online Practice, Chapter 9 (go.hrw.com, Keyword: EXP1B CH9)

▲ = Advanced Learners   ◆ = Slower Pace Learners   ● = Special Learning Needs   ■ = Heritage Speakers

Holt Spanish 1B   Lesson Planner

Teacher's Name _____ Class _____ Date _____

¡Festejemos!

CAPÍTULO 9

BLOCK 14 90-MINUTE LESSON PLAN

STANDARDS FOR FOREIGN LANGUAGE LEARNING: BLOCK 14

Integración

Communication 1.1: Students engage in conversations, provide and obtain information, express feelings and emotions, and exchange opinions.

Communication 1.2: Students understand and interpret written and spoken language on a variety of topics.

Communication 1.3: Students present information, concepts, and ideas to an audience of listeners or readers on a variety of topics.

Connections 3.1: Students reinforce and further their knowledge of other disciplines through the foreign language.

Connections 3.2: Students acquire information and recognize the distinctive viewpoints that are only available through the foreign language and its cultures.

CORE INSTRUCTION

Chapter Assessment

Assess
- (50 min.) Give Chapter 9 Test.

Integración
- (10 min.) See Fine Art Connection: Introduction, p. 217.
- (10 min.) Play Audio CD 9, Tr. 14 for Activity 1, p. 216.
- (15 min.) Have students do Activities 2–4, pp. 216–217.

Wrap-Up
- (5 min.) See Fine Art Connection: Analyzing, p. 217.

OPTIONAL RESOURCES
- (10 min.) Culture Project, p. 216.

▲ = Advanced Learners   ◆ = Slower Pace Learners   ● = Special Learning Needs   ■ = Heritage Speakers

Holt Spanish 1B

Lesson Planner

Teacher's Name _____ Class _____ Date _____

CAPÍTULO 9

BLOCK 14 90-MINUTE LESSON PLAN

Practice Options
- *Lab Book,* p. 30
- ***Cuaderno de actividades,*** pp. 61–62, 84–85
- *Teaching Transparencies:* Fine Art, Chapter 9 ▲●■
- *Video Guide,* pp. ▲●■
- *Interactive Tutor* (Disc 2) or *DVD Tutor* (Disc 2) ▲●■
- Online Practice, Chapter 9 (go.hrw.com, Keyword: EXP1B CH9)

Assessment Options
- *Assessment Program:* **Examen: Capítulo 9**, pp. 185–195
- *Assessment Program:* **Examen oral: Capítulo 9**, p. 196
- *Assessment Program:* Alternative Assessment Guide, pp. 244, 252, 260 ▲●■
- *Audio CD 9*, Tr. 17–18
- *Standardized Assessment Tutor,* Chapter 9
- Test Generator

▲ = Advanced Learners ◆ = Slower Pace Learners ● = Special Learning Needs ■ = Heritage Speakers

Holt Spanish 1B   Lesson Planner

Teacher's Name _____ Class _____ Date _____

¡A viajar!

CAPÍTULO 10

BLOCK 1 90-MINUTE LESSON PLAN

STANDARDS FOR FOREIGN LANGUAGE LEARNING: BLOCK 1

Chapter Opener
Communication 1.2: Students understand and interpret written and spoken language on a variety of topics.

Vocabulario en acción 1
Communication 1.2: Students understand and interpret written and spoken language on a variety of topics.
Cultures 2.1: Students demonstrate an understanding of the relationship between the practices and perspectives of the culture studied.

Cultures 2.2: Students demonstrate an understanding of the relationship between the products and perspectives of the culture studied.
Connections 3.2: Students acquire information and recognize the distinctive viewpoints that are only available through the foreign language and its cultures.

Before starting **Capítulo 10,** you may wish to teach **Geocultura: Perú,** pp. 218–221. For teaching suggestions, see pp. xv–xvi of this *Lesson Planner*.

CORE INSTRUCTION

Warm-Up
- (5 min.) See Learning Tip, p. 223.

Chapter Opener
- (5 min.) See Using the Photo and **Más vocabulario,** p. 222.
- (5 min.) See **Objetivos,** p. 222.

Vocabulario en acción 1
- (10 min.) Show **ExpresaVisión,** Ch. 10.
- (25 min.) Present **Vocabulario 1**, pp. 224–225 using Teaching **Vocabulario,** p. 224.
- (10 min.) Present **¡Exprésate!,** p. 225.
- (10 min.) Play Audio CD 10, Tr. 1 for Activity 1, p. 226.
- (5 min.) Have students do Activity 2, p. 226.
- (5 min.) Have students do Activity 3, p. 226.
- (5 min.) Present **Nota cultural,** p. 226.

Wrap-Up
- (5 min.) See **Más práctica,** p. 227.

OPTIONAL RESOURCES
- (5 min.) Common Error Alert, p. 225
- (5 min.) **También se puede decir,** p. 225
- (5 min.) Advanced Learners, p. 225 ▲
- (5 min.) Multiple Intelligences, p. 225
- (5 min.) Bell Work 10.1, p. 224
- (5 min.) Social Studies Link, p. 226
- (10 min.) Fold-N-Learn, p. 226
- (5 min.) Variation, p. 227
- (10 min.) Special Learning Needs, p. 227 ●

▲ = Advanced Learners ◆ = Slower Pace Learners ● = Special Learning Needs ■ = Heritage Speakers

Holt Spanish 1B
Copyright © by Holt, Rinehart and Winston. All rights reserved.

Lesson Planner

Teacher's Name _____ Class _____ Date _____

CAPÍTULO 10

BLOCK 1 90-MINUTE LESSON PLAN

Practice Options
- *Lab Book,* pp. 62–63
- ***Cuaderno de vocabulario y gramática,*** pp. 65–67
- *Activities for Communication,* pp. 37–38 ▲ ■
- ***Cuaderno para hispanohablantes,*** Chapter 10 ■
- *Teaching Transparencies:* Bell Work 10.1; Vocabulario 10.1, 10.2; ***Vocabulario y gramática*** Answers, pp. 65–67 ▲ ● ■
- *Video Guide,* pp. 96–97 ▲ ● ■
- *TPR Storytelling Book,* pp. 54–55 ▲ ●
- *Interactive Tutor* (Disc 2) or *DVD Tutor* (Disc 2) ▲ ● ■
- Online Practice, Chapter 10 (go.hrw.com, Keyword: EXP1B CH10)

▲ = Advanced Learners ◆ = Slower Pace Learners ● = Special Learning Needs ■ = Heritage Speakers

Holt Spanish 1B — Lesson Planner

Teacher's Name _____ Class _____ Date _____

¡A viajar!

CAPÍTULO 10

BLOCK 2 90-MINUTE LESSON PLAN

STANDARDS FOR FOREIGN LANGUAGE LEARNING: BLOCK 2

Vocabulario en acción 1

Communication 1.1: Students engage in conversations, provide and obtain information, express feelings and emotions, and exchange opinions.

Communication 1.2: Students understand and interpret written and spoken language on a variety of topics.

Communication 1.3: Students present information, concepts, and ideas to an audience of listeners or readers on a variety of topics.

CORE INSTRUCTION

Warm-Up
- (5 min.) Have students read aloud their completed sentences from Activity 1.

Vocabulario en acción 1
- (20 min.) Review **Vocabulario 1** and **¡Exprésate!**, pp. 224–225.
- (20 min.) Have students do Activities 4–6, p. 227.
- (15 min.) See Teaching **¡Exprésate!**, p. 228.
- (25 min.) Have students do Activity 7–10, pp. 228–229.

Wrap-Up
- (5 min.) See **Más práctica**, p. 228. Remind students to study for **Prueba: Vocabulario 1**.

OPTIONAL RESOURCES
- (5 min.) TPR, p. 225
- (10 min.) **Comunicación** (TE), p. 227
- (10 min.) Advanced Learners, p. 227 ▲
- (10 min.) Slower Pace Learners, p. 229 ♦
- (5 min.) Special Learning Needs, p. 227. ●

▲ = Advanced Learners   ♦ = Slower Pace Learners   ● = Special Learning Needs   ■ = Heritage Speakers

Holt Spanish 1B

Lesson Planner

Teacher's Name _____ Class _____ Date _____

CAPÍTULO 10

BLOCK 2 90-MINUTE LESSON PLAN

Practice Options
- *Lab Book,* pp. 31, 62–63
- **Cuaderno de vocabulario y gramática,** pp. 65–67
- *Activities for Communication,* pp. 37–38 ▲ ■
- **Cuaderno para hispanohablantes,** Chapter 10 ■
- *Teaching Transparencies:* **Vocabulario** 10.1, 10.2; **Vocabulario y gramática** Answers, pp. 65–67 ▲ ● ■
- *Video Guide,* pp. 96–97 ▲ ● ■
- *TPR Storytelling Book,* pp. 54–55 ▲ ●
- *Interactive Tutor* (Disc 2) or *DVD Tutor* (Disc 2) ▲ ● ■
- Online Practice, Chapter 10 (go.hrw.com, Keyword: EXP1B CH10)

▲ = Advanced Learners   ◆ = Slower Pace Learners   ● = Special Learning Needs   ■ = Heritage Speakers

Holt Spanish 1B   Lesson Planner

Teacher's Name _____ Class _____ Date _____

¡A viajar!

CAPÍTULO 10

BLOCK 3 90-MINUTE LESSON PLAN

STANDARDS FOR FOREIGN LANGUAGE LEARNING: BLOCK 3

Vocabulario en acción 1
Communication 1.1: Students engage in conversations, provide and obtain information, express feelings and emotions, and exchange opinions.
Communication 1.2: Students understand and interpret written and spoken language on a variety of topics.
Communication 1.3: Students present information, concepts, and ideas to an audience of listeners or readers on a variety of topics.
Cultures 2.1: Students demonstrate an understanding of the relationship between the practices and perspectives of the culture studied.
Cultures 2.2: Students demonstrate an understanding of the relationship between the products and perspectives of the culture studied.
Connections 3.2: Students acquire information and recognize the distinctive viewpoints that are only available through the foreign language and its cultures.

Gramática en acción 1
Communication 1.2: Students understand and interpret written and spoken language on a variety of topics.

CORE INSTRUCTION

Warm-Up
- (5 min.) Have students do Bell Work 10.2, p. 230.

Vocabulario en acción 1
- (10 min.) Have students do Activity 11, p. 229.
- (25 min.) Review **Vocabulario en acción 1,** pp. 224–229.

Assess
- (20 min.) Give **Prueba: Vocabulario 1.**

Gramática en acción 1
- (25 min.) Present **Repaso**: the preterite, p. 230 using Teaching **Gramática,** p. 230.

Wrap-Up
- (5 min.) Have students work with a partner and tell teach other three things they did this morning, using the preterite tense.

OPTIONAL RESOURCES
- (10 min.) **Comunicación** (TE), p. 229
- (10 min.) Multiple Intelligences, p. 229

▲ = Advanced Learners   ◆ = Slower Pace Learners   ● = Special Learning Needs   ■ = Heritage Speakers

Teacher's Name _____ Class _____ Date _____

CAPÍTULO 10

BLOCK 3 90-MINUTE LESSON PLAN

Practice Options
- *Lab Book*, pp. 31, 62–63
- ***Cuaderno de vocabulario y gramática,*** pp. 68–70
- ***Cuaderno de actividades,*** pp. 63–66 ▲ ● ■
- *Activities for Communication*, pp. 37–38 ▲ ■
- ***Cuaderno para hispanohablantes,*** Chapter 10 ■
- *Teaching Transparencies:* Bell Work 10.2; ***Vocabulario y gramática*** Answers, pp. 68–70 ▲ ● ■
- *Video Guide*, pp. 96–97 ▲ ● ■
- *Grammar Tutor for Students of Spanish,* Chapter 10 ● ■
- *Interactive Tutor* (Disc 2) or *DVD Tutor* (Disc 2) ▲ ● ■
- Online Practice, Chapter 10 (go.hrw.com, Keyword: EXP1B CH10)

Assessment Options
- *Assessment Program*: **Prueba: Vocabulario 1**, pp. 97–98
- *Assessment Program*: Alternative Assessment Guide, pp. 245, 253, 261 ▲ ● ■
- Test Generator

▲ = Advanced Learners ◆ = Slower Pace Learners ● = Special Learning Needs ■ = Heritage Speakers

Holt Spanish 1B — Lesson Planner

Teacher's Name _____ Class _____ Date _____

¡A viajar!

CAPÍTULO 10

BLOCK 4 90-MINUTE LESSON PLAN

STANDARDS FOR FOREIGN LANGUAGE LEARNING: BLOCK 4

Gramática en acción 1

Communication 1.1: Students engage in conversations, provide and obtain information, express feelings and emotions, and exchange opinions.
Communication 1.2: Students understand and interpret written and spoken language on a variety of topics.
Communication 1.3: Students present information, concepts, and ideas to an audience of listeners or readers on a variety of topics.

Cultures 2.2: Students demonstrate an understanding of the relationship between the products and perspectives of the culture studied.
Communities 5.2: Students show evidence of becoming life–long learners by using the language for personal enjoyment and enrichment.

CORE INSTRUCTION

Warm-Up
- (5 min.) Have students do Bell Work 10.3, p. 232.

Gramática en acción 1
- (5 min.) Show **GramaVisión 1,** Segment 1.
- (20 min.) Review the preterite, p. 230.
- (10 min.) Play Audio CD 10, Tr. 2 for Activity 12, p. 230.
- (20 min.) Have students do Activity 13–14, p. 231.
- (25 min.) Present **Gramática:** *Preterite of* **-car, -gar, -zar** *verbs* using Teaching **Gramática,** p. 232.

Wrap-Up
- (5 min.) Have students work with partners to review answers to Activity 13.

OPTIONAL RESOURCES
- (10 min.) Teacher to Teacher, p. 231
- (10 min.) **Comunicación** (TE), p. 231
- (5 min.) Special Learning Needs, p. 231 ●
- (5 min.) Advanced Learners, p. 231 ▲

▲ = Advanced Learners ◆ = Slower Pace Learners ● = Special Learning Needs ■ = Heritage Speakers

Holt Spanish 1B   Lesson Planner

Teacher's Name _____ Class _____ Date _____

CAPÍTULO 10

BLOCK 4 90-MINUTE LESSON PLAN

Practice Options
- *Lab Book,* pp. 31, 62–63
- ***Cuaderno de vocabulario y gramática,*** pp. 68–70
- ***Cuaderno de actividades,*** pp. 63–66 ▲ ● ■
- *Activities for Communication,* pp. 37–38 ▲ ■
- ***Cuaderno para hispanohablantes,*** Chapter 10 ■
- *Teaching Transparencies:* Bell Work 10.3; ***Vocabulario y gramática*** Answers, pp. 68–70 ▲ ● ■
- *Video Guide,* pp. 96–97 ▲ ● ■
- *Grammar Tutor for Students of Spanish,* Chapter 10 ● ■
- *Interactive Tutor* (Disc 2) or *DVD Tutor* (Disc 2) ▲ ● ■
- Online Practice, Chapter 10 (go.hrw.com, Keyword: EXP1B CH10)

▲ = Advanced Learners ♦ = Slower Pace Learners ● = Special Learning Needs ■ = Heritage Speakers

Holt Spanish 1B

Lesson Planner

Teacher's Name _____ Class _____ Date _____

¡A viajar!

CAPÍTULO 10

BLOCK 5 90-MINUTE LESSON PLAN

STANDARDS FOR FOREIGN LANGUAGE LEARNING: BLOCK 5

Gramática en acción 1

Communication 1.1: Students engage in conversations, provide and obtain information, express feelings and emotions, and exchange opinions.

Communication 1.2: Students understand and interpret written and spoken language on a variety of topics.

Communication 1.3: Students present information, concepts, and ideas to an audience of listeners or readers on a variety of topics.

Cultures 2.2: Students demonstrate an understanding of the relationship between the products and perspectives of the culture studied.

Communities 5.2: Students show evidence of becoming life–long learners by using the language for personal enjoyment and enrichment.

CORE INSTRUCTION

Warm-Up
- (5 min.) Have students do Bell Work 10.4, p. 234.

Gramática en acción 1
- (10 min.) Review the preterite of **-car, -gar, -zar** verbs, p. 232.
- (10 min.) Play Audio CD 10, Tr. 3 for Activity 15, p. 232.
- (20 min.) Have students do Activities 16–18, pp. 232–233.
- (25 min.) Present **Gramática:** *Preterite of* **hacer**, p. 234 using Teaching **Gramática,** p. 234.
- (5 min.) Present **Nota cultural,** p. 234.
- (10 min.) Have students do Activities 19–20, p. 234.

Wrap-Up
- (5 min.) Have students do Bell Work 10.5, p. 238. Remind students to study for **Prueba: Gramática 1**.

OPTIONAL RESOURCES
- (5 min.) Career Path, p. 233
- (10 min.) **Comunicación** (TE)**,** p. 235
- (5 min.) Multiple Intelligences, p. 235
- (5 min.) Slower Pace Learners, p. 233. ◆
- (5 min.) Special Learning Needs, p. 233. ●

▲ = Advanced Learners   ◆ = Slower Pace Learners   ● = Special Learning Needs   ■ = Heritage Speakers

Teacher's Name _____ Class _____ Date _____

CAPÍTULO 10

BLOCK 5 90-MINUTE LESSON PLAN

Practice Options
- *Lab Book,* pp. 62–63
- ***Cuaderno de vocabulario y gramática,*** pp. 68–70
- ***Cuaderno de actividades,*** pp. 63–66 ▲ ● ■
- *Activities for Communication,* pp. 37–38 ▲ ■
- ***Cuaderno para hispanohablantes,*** Chapter 10 ■
- *Teaching Transparencies:* Bell Work 10.4, 10.5; ***Vocabulario y gramática*** Answers, pp. 68–70 ▲ ● ■
- *Video Guide,* pp. 96–97 ▲ ● ■
- *Grammar Tutor for Students of Spanish,* Chapter 10 ● ■
- *Interactive Tutor* (Disc 2) or *DVD Tutor* (Disc 2) ▲ ● ■
- Online Practice, Chapter 10 (go.hrw.com, Keyword: EXP1B CH10)

▲ = Advanced Learners   ◆ = Slower Pace Learners   ● = Special Learning Needs   ■ = Heritage Speakers

Holt Spanish 1B — Lesson Planner

Teacher's Name _____ Class _____ Date _____

¡A viajar!

CAPÍTULO 10

BLOCK 6 90-MINUTE LESSON PLAN

STANDARDS FOR FOREIGN LANGUAGE LEARNING: BLOCK 6

Gramática en acción 1
Communication 1.1: Students engage in conversations, provide and obtain information, express feelings and emotions, and exchange opinions.
Communication 1.2: Students understand and interpret written and spoken language on a variety of topics.
Communication 1.3: Students present information, concepts, and ideas to an audience of listeners or readers on a variety of topics.
Cultures 2.2: Students demonstrate an understanding of the relationship between the products and perspectives of the culture studied.
Communities 5.2: Students show evidence of becoming life–long learners by using the language for personal enjoyment and enrichment.

Cultura
Communication 1.2: Students understand and interpret written and spoken language on a variety of topics.
Comparisons 4.2: Students demonstrate understanding of the concept of culture through comparisons of the cultures studied and their own.
Communities 5.1: Students use the language both within and beyond the school setting.
Communities 5.2: Students show evidence of becoming life–long learners by using the language for personal enjoyment and enrichment.

CORE INSTRUCTION

Warm-Up
- (5 min.) Review the preterite of **-car, -gar, -zar** verbs, p. 232.

Gramática en acción 1
- (5 min.) Review the preterite of **hacer**, p. 234.
- (15 min.) Have students do Activities 21–22, pp. 234–235.
- (10 min.) Review **Gramática en acción 1**, pp. 230–235.

Assess
- (20 min.) Give **Prueba: Gramática 1**.

Cultura
- (25 min.) Present **Cultura**, p. 236–237 using Teaching **Cultura**, p. 236.
- (5 min.) Present and assign **Comunidad,** p. 237.

Wrap-Up
- (5 min.) See Map Activities, p. 236.

OPTIONAL RESOURCES
- (10 min.) **Comunicación** (TE), p. 235
- (5 min.) Slower Pace Learners, p. 235 ◆
- (5 min.) Multiple Intelligences, p. 235
- (5 min.) Comparing and Contrasting, p. 237
- (5 min.) Advanced Learners, p. 237 ▲
- (5 min.) Special Learning Needs, p. 237 ●
- (5 min.) Community Link, p. 237

▲ = Advanced Learners ◆ = Slower Pace Learners ● = Special Learning Needs ■ = Heritage Speakers

Holt Spanish 1B — Lesson Planner

Teacher's Name _____ Class _____ Date _____

CAPÍTULO 10

BLOCK 6 90-MINUTE LESSON PLAN

Practice Options
- *Lab Book,* pp. 62–63
- ***Cuaderno de vocabulario y gramática,*** pp. 68–70
- ***Cuaderno de actividades,*** pp. 63–66, 67 ▲ ● ■
- *Activities for Communication,* pp. 37–38 ▲ ■
- ***Cuaderno para hispanohablantes,*** pp. 77–84 ■
- *Teaching Transparencies:* **Vocabulario y gramática** Answers, pp. 68–70 ▲ ● ■
- *Video Guide,* pp. 93, 96–97 ▲ ● ■
- *Grammar Tutor for Students of Spanish,* Chapter 10 ● ■
- *Interactive Tutor* (Disc 2) or *DVD Tutor* (Disc 2) ▲ ● ■
- Online Practice, Chapter 10 (go.hrw.com, Keyword: EXP1B CH10)

Assessment Options
- *Assessment Program*: **Prueba: Gramática 1**, pp. 99–100
- *Assessment Program*: **Prueba: Aplicación 1**, pp. 101–102
- *Assessment Program*: Alternative Assessment Guide, pp. 245, 253, 261 ▲ ● ■
- Audio CD 10, Tr. 17
- Test Generator

▲ = Advanced Learners   ◆ = Slower Pace Learners   ● = Special Learning Needs   ■ = Heritage Speakers

Teacher's Name _____ Class _____ Date _____

¡A viajar!

CAPÍTULO 10

BLOCK 7 90-MINUTE LESSON PLAN

STANDARDS FOR FOREIGN LANGUAGE LEARNING: BLOCK 7

Vocabulario en acción 2
Communication 1.2: Students understand and interpret written and spoken language on a variety of topics.
Communication 1.3: Students present information, concepts, and ideas to an audience of listeners or readers on a variety of topics.

Cultures 2.2: Students demonstrate an understanding of the relationship between the products and perspectives of the culture studied.
Comparisons 4.2: Students demonstrate understanding of the concept of culture through comparisons of the cultures studied and their own.

CORE INSTRUCTION

Warm-Up
- (5 min.) Do Bell Work 10.5, p. 238.

Vocabulario en acción 2
- (25 min.) Present **Vocabulario 2**, pp. 238–239 using Teaching **Vocabulario,** p. 238.
- (5 min.) Present **Nota cultural,** p. 240.
- (10 min.) Play Audio CD 10, Tr. 7 for Activity 23, p. 240.
- (25 min.) Have students do Activities 24–26, pp. 240–241.
- (15 min.) See Teaching **¡Exprésate!,** p. 242.

Wrap-Up
- (5 min.) Language Note, p. 239

OPTIONAL RESOURCES
- (10 min.) TPR, p. 239
- (5 min.) Slower Pace Learners, p. 241. ◆
- (5 min.) **También se puede decir,** p. 239
- (5 min.) Multiple Intelligences, p. 239
- (5 min.) Advanced Learners, p. 239 ▲
- (5 min.) Practices and Perspectives, p. 240
- (5 min.) **Más práctica,** pp. 240, 241
- (10 min.) **Comunicación** (TE)**,** p. 241
- (5 min.) Multiple Intelligences, p. 241

▲ = Advanced Learners   ◆ = Slower Pace Learners   ● = Special Learning Needs   ■ = Heritage Speakers

Holt Spanish 1B — Lesson Planner

Teacher's Name _____ Class _____ Date _____

CAPÍTULO 10

BLOCK 7 90-MINUTE LESSON PLAN

Practice Options
- *Lab Book,* pp. 64–65
- ***Cuaderno de vocabulario y gramática,*** pp. 71–73
- *Activities for Communication,* pp. 39–40 ▲ ■
- ***Cuaderno para hispanohablantes,*** Chapter 10 ■
- *Teaching Transparencies:* **Vocabulario** 10.3, 10.4; ***Vocabulario y gramática*** Answers, pp. 71–73 ▲ ● ■
- *Video Guide,* pp. 98–99 ▲ ● ■
- *TPR Storytelling Book,* pp. 56–57 ▲ ●
- *Interactive Tutor* (Disc 2) or *DVD Tutor* (Disc 2) ▲ ● ■
- Online Practice, Chapter 10 (go.hrw.com, Keyword: EXP1B CH10)

▲ = Advanced Learners   ◆ = Slower Pace Learners   ● = Special Learning Needs   ■ = Heritage Speakers

Holt Spanish 1B — Lesson Planner

Teacher's Name _____ Class _____ Date _____

CAPÍTULO **10**

¡A viajar!

BLOCK 8 90-MINUTE LESSON PLAN

STANDARDS FOR FOREIGN LANGUAGE LEARNING: BLOCK 8

Vocabulario en acción 2

Communication 1.1: Students engage in conversations, provide and obtain information, express feelings and emotions, and exchange opinions.

Communication 1.2: Students understand and interpret written and spoken language on a variety of topics.

Communication 1.3: Students present information, concepts, and ideas to an audience of listeners or readers on a variety of topics.

Cultures 2.2: Students demonstrate an understanding of the relationship between the products and perspectives of the culture studied.

Comparisons 4.2: Students demonstrate understanding of the concept of culture through comparisons of the cultures studied and their own.

Gramática en acción 2

Communication 1.2: Students understand and interpret written and spoken language on a variety of topics.

CORE INSTRUCTION

Warm-Up
- (5 min.) Have students do Bell Work 10.6, p. 244.

Vocabulario en acción 2
- (20 min.) Review **Vocabulario 2** and **¡Exprésate!**, pp. 238–239, 242.
- (35 min.) Have students do Activities 27–30, p. 242–243.

Gramática en acción 2
- (25 min.) Present **Gramática:** *Informal commands of spelling-change and irregular verbs*, p. 244 using Teaching **Gramática**, #2–5, p. 244.

Wrap-Up
- (5 min.) Give students time to make flash cards for the irregular verb forms. Remind students to study for **Prueba: Vocabulario 2**.

OPTIONAL RESOURCES
- (10 min.) Game, p. 240
- (10 min.) Teacher to Teacher, p. 242
- (10 min.) **Comunicación,** p. 243
- (10 min.) Advanced Learners, p. 243 ▲
- (10 min.) Multiple Intelligences, p. 243
- (5 min.) Special Learning Needs, p. 245. ●

▲ = Advanced Learners   ◆ = Slower Pace Learners   ● = Special Learning Needs   ■ = Heritage Speakers

Holt Spanish 1B — Lesson Planner

Teacher's Name _____ Class _____ Date _____

CAPÍTULO 10

BLOCK 8 90-MINUTE LESSON PLAN

Practice Options
- *Lab Book*, pp. 64–65
- ***Cuaderno de vocabulario y gramática,*** pp. 71–73
- ***Cuaderno de actividades,*** pp. 67–71 ▲●■
- *Activities for Communication*, pp. 39–40 ▲■
- ***Cuaderno para hispanohablantes,*** Chapter 10 ■
- *Teaching Transparencies:* **Vocabulario** 10.3, 10.4; Bell Work 10.6; ***Vocabulario y gramática*** Answers, pp. 74–76 ▲●■
- *Video Guide*, pp. 98–99 ▲●■
- *TPR Storytelling Book*, pp. 56–57 ▲●
- *Grammar Tutor for Students of Spanish*, Chapter 10 ●■
- *Interactive Tutor* (Disc 2) or *DVD Tutor* (Disc 2) ▲●■
- Online Practice, Chapter 10 (go.hrw.com, Keyword: EXP1B CH10)

▲ = Advanced Learners   ◆ = Slower Pace Learners   ● = Special Learning Needs   ■ = Heritage Speakers

Holt Spanish 1B   Lesson Planner

Teacher's Name _____ Class _____ Date _____

¡A viajar!

CAPÍTULO 10

BLOCK 9 90-MINUTE LESSON PLAN

STANDARDS FOR FOREIGN LANGUAGE LEARNING: BLOCK 9

Vocabulario en acción 2
Communication 1.1: Students engage in conversations, provide and obtain information, express feelings and emotions, and exchange opinions.
Communication 1.2: Students understand and interpret written and spoken language on a variety of topics.
Communication 1.3: Students present information, concepts, and ideas to an audience of listeners or readers on a variety of topics.
Cultures 2.2: Students demonstrate an understanding of the relationship between the products and perspectives of the culture studied.
Comparisons 4.2: Students demonstrate understanding of the concept of culture through comparisons of the cultures studied and their own.

Gramática en acción 2
Communication 1.1: Students engage in conversations, provide and obtain information, express feelings and emotions, and exchange opinions.
Communication 1.2: Students understand and interpret written and spoken language on a variety of topics.
Communication 1.3: Students present information, concepts, and ideas to an audience of listeners or readers on a variety of topics.

CORE INSTRUCTION

Warm-Up
- (5 min.) Have pairs of students use the vocabulary and expressions on pp. 238–239 to talk to each other about a trip they took.

Vocabulario en acción 2
- (10 min.) Review **Vocabulario en acción 2,** pp. 238–243.

Assess
- (20 min.) Give **Prueba: Vocabulario 2.**

Gramática en acción 2
- (10 min.) Review informal commands of spelling-change verbs, p. 244.
- (15 min.) Present **Gramática:** *Informal commands of spelling-change and irregular verbs,* p. 244 using Teaching **Gramática,** #4–5, p. 244.
- (10 min.) Play Audio CD 10, Tr. 8 for Activity 31, p. 245.
- (15 min.) Have students do Activities 32–33, p. 245.

Wrap-Up
- (5 min.) Have pairs of students do Activity 32 as an oral activity.

OPTIONAL RESOURCES
- (5 min.) Heritage Speakers, p. 245 ■
- (5 min.) Slower Pace Learners, p. 245 ◆
- (5 min.) **Comunicación,** p. 245
- (5 min.) Special Learning Needs, p. 245 ●

▲ = Advanced Learners ◆ = Slower Pace Learners ● = Special Learning Needs ■ = Heritage Speakers

Holt Spanish 1B — Lesson Planner

Teacher's Name _____ Class _____ Date _____

CAPÍTULO 10

BLOCK 9 90-MINUTE LESSON PLAN

Practice Options
- *Lab Book,* pp. 33, 64–65
- ***Cuaderno de vocabulario y gramática,*** pp. 74–76
- ***Cuaderno de actividades,*** pp. 68–71 ▲ ● ■
- *Activities for Communication,* pp. 39–40 ▲ ■
- ***Cuaderno para hispanohablantes,*** Chapter 10 ■
- *Teaching Transparencies:* Bell Work 10.7; ***Vocabulario y gramática*** Answers, pp. 74–76 ▲ ● ■
- *Video Guide,* pp. 98–99 ▲ ● ■
- *Grammar Tutor for Students of Spanish,* Chapter 10 ● ■
- *Interactive Tutor* (Disc 2) or *DVD Tutor* (Disc 2) ▲ ● ■
- Online Practice, Chapter 10 (go.hrw.com, Keyword: EXP1B CH10)

Assessment Options
- *Assessment Program*: **Prueba: Vocabulario 2,** pp. 103–104
- *Assessment Program*: Alternative Assessment Guide, pp. 245, 253, 261 ▲ ● ■
- Test Generator

▲ = Advanced Learners   ◆ = Slower Pace Learners   ● = Special Learning Needs   ■ = Heritage Speakers

Holt Spanish 1B   Lesson Planner

Teacher's Name _____ Class _____ Date _____

¡A viajar!

CAPÍTULO 10

BLOCK 10 90-MINUTE LESSON PLAN

STANDARDS FOR FOREIGN LANGUAGE LEARNING: BLOCK 10

Gramática en acción 2

Communication 1.1: Students engage in conversations, provide and obtain information, express feelings and emotions, and exchange opinions.

Communication 1.2: Students understand and interpret written and spoken language on a variety of topics.

Communication 1.3: Students present information, concepts, and ideas to an audience of listeners or readers on a variety of topics.

CORE INSTRUCTION

Warm-Up
- (5 min.) Have students do Bell Work 10.7, p. 246.

Gramática en acción 2
- (25 min.) Present **Gramática: Repaso** *direct object pronouns*, p. 246 using Teaching **Gramática**, p. 246.
- (10 min.) Play Audio CD 10, Tr. 9 for Activity 34, p. 246.
- (5 min.) Have students do Activity 35, p. 246.
- (10 min.) Have students do Activities 36–37, p. 247.
- (5 min.) Present **Nota cultural,** p. 247.
- (10 min.) Have students do Activity 38, p. 247.
- (15 min.) Present **Gramática: Repaso** *verbs followed by infinitives,* #1–2, p. 248. See Teaching **Gramática**, p. 248.

Wrap-Up
- (5 min.) Have volunteer students present the conversations they created in Activity 38.

OPTIONAL RESOURCES
- (5 min.) Multiple Intelligences, p. 247
- (10 min.) **Comunicación** (TE), p. 247
- (5 min.) Advanced Learners, p. 247 ▲

▲ = Advanced Learners ◆ = Slower Pace Learners ● = Special Learning Needs ■ = Heritage Speakers

Holt Spanish 1B

Lesson Planner

Teacher's Name _____ Class _____ Date _____

CAPÍTULO 10

BLOCK 10 90-MINUTE LESSON PLAN

Practice Options
- *Lab Book*, pp. 33, 64–65
- ***Cuaderno de vocabulario y gramática,*** pp. 74–76
- ***Cuaderno de actividades,*** pp. 68–71 ▲ ● ■
- *Activities for Communication*, pp. 39–40 ▲ ■
- ***Cuaderno para hispanohablantes,*** Chapter 10 ■
- *Teaching Transparencies:* Bell Work 10.8; ***Vocabulario y gramática*** Answers, pp. 74–76 ▲ ● ■
- *Video Guide*, pp. 98–99 ▲ ● ■
- *Grammar Tutor for Students of Spanish*, Chapter 10 ● ■
- *Interactive Tutor* (Disc 2) or *DVD Tutor* (Disc 2) ▲ ● ■
- Online Practice, Chapter 10 (go.hrw.com, Keyword: EXP1B CH10)

▲ = Advanced Learners ◆ = Slower Pace Learners ● = Special Learning Needs ■ = Heritage Speakers

Holt Spanish 1B · Lesson Planner

Teacher's Name _____ Class _____ Date _____

CAPÍTULO 10

¡A viajar!

BLOCK 11 90-MINUTE LESSON PLAN

STANDARDS FOR FOREIGN LANGUAGE LEARNING: BLOCK 11

Gramática en acción 2
Communication 1.1: Students engage in conversations, provide and obtain information, express feelings and emotions, and exchange opinions.
Communication 1.2: Students understand and interpret written and spoken language on a variety of topics.

Conexiones culturales
Connections 3.1: Students reinforce and further their knowledge of other disciplines through the foreign language.
Comparisons 4.1: Students demonstrate understanding of the nature of language through comparisons of the language studied and their own.

CORE INSTRUCTION

Warm-Up
- (5 min.) Have students do Bell Work 10.8, p. 248.

Gramática en acción 2
- (5 min.) Show **GramaVisión**, Ch. 10.
- (10 min.) Present **Gramática: Repaso** *verbs followed by infinitives,* #3–4, p. 248 using Teaching **Gramática,** p. 248.
- (25 min.) Have students do Activities 39–43, pp. 248–249. See Slower Pace Learners, p. 249. ◆

Conexiones culturales
- (40 min.) Present **Conexiones culturales,** pp. 250–251. See Teaching **Conexiones culturales,** p. 250.

Wrap-Up
- (5 min.) Review for **Prueba: Gramática 2.**

OPTIONAL RESOURCES
- (10 min.) **Comunicación** (TE), p. 249
- (5 min.) Special Learning Needs, p. 249 ●
- (5 min.) Advanced Learners, p. 251 ▲
- (5 min.) Multiple Intelligences, p. 251

▲ = Advanced Learners ◆ = Slower Pace Learners ● = Special Learning Needs ■ = Heritage Speakers

Holt Spanish 1B — Lesson Planner

Teacher's Name _____ Class _____ Date _____

CAPÍTULO 10

BLOCK 11 90-MINUTE LESSON PLAN

Practice Options
- *Lab Book,* pp. 33, 64–65
- **Cuaderno de vocabulario y gramática,** pp. 74–76
- **Cuaderno de actividades,** pp. 68–71 ▲ ● ■
- *Activities for Communication,* pp. 39–40 ▲ ■
- **Cuaderno para hispanohablantes,** Chapter 10 ■
- *Teaching Transparencies:* **Vocabulario y gramática** Answers, pp. 74–76 ▲ ● ■
- *Video Guide,* pp. 98–99 ▲ ● ■
- *Grammar Tutor for Students of Spanish,* Chapter 10 ● ■
- *Interactive Tutor* (Disc 2) or *DVD Tutor* (Disc 2) ▲ ● ■
- Online Practice, Chapter 10 (go.hrw.com, Keyword: EXP1B CH10)

▲ = Advanced Learners ◆ = Slower Pace Learners ● = Special Learning Needs ■ = Heritage Speakers

Holt Spanish 1B   Lesson Planner

Teacher's Name _____ Class _____ Date _____

¡A viajar!

CAPÍTULO 10

BLOCK 12 90-MINUTE LESSON PLAN

STANDARDS FOR FOREIGN LANGUAGE LEARNING: BLOCK 12

Gramática en acción 2
Communication 1.1: Students engage in conversations, provide and obtain information, express feelings and emotions, and exchange opinions.
Communication 1.2: Students understand and interpret written and spoken language on a variety of topics.
Communication 1.3: Students present information, concepts, and ideas to an audience of listeners or readers on a variety of topics.
Cultures 2.1: Students demonstrate an understanding of the relationship between the practices and perspectives of the culture studied.

Novela en video
Communication 1.1: Students engage in conversations, provide and obtain information, express feelings and emotions, and exchange opinions.
Communication 1.2: Students understand and interpret written and spoken language on a variety of topics.
Cultures 2.1: Students demonstrate an understanding of the relationship between the practices and perspectives of the culture studied.
Connections 3.2: Students acquire information and recognize the distinctive viewpoints that are only available through the foreign language and its cultures.

Comparisons 4.2: Students demonstrate understanding of the concept of culture through comparisons of the cultures studied and their own.
Communities 5.1: Students use the language both within and beyond the school setting.

Leamos y escribamos
Communication 1.1: Students engage in conversations, provide and obtain information, express feelings and emotions, and exchange opinions.
Communication 1.2: Students understand and interpret written and spoken language on a variety of topics.
Communication 1.3: Students present information, concepts, and ideas to an audience of listeners or readers on a variety of topics.
Cultures 2.1: Students demonstrate an understanding of the relationship between the practices and perspectives of the culture studied.
Connections 3.2: Students acquire information and recognize the distinctive viewpoints that are only available through the foreign language and its cultures.
Comparisons 4.2: Students demonstrate understanding of the concept of culture through comparisons of the cultures studied and their own.

CORE INSTRUCTION

Warm-Up
- (5 min.) Review **Gramática en acción 2**, pp. 244–249.

Gramática en acción 2
Assess
- (20 min.) Give **Prueba: Gramática 2.**

Novela en video
- (30 min.) See Teaching **Novela en video,** #1, p. 252.

Leamos y escribamos
- (25 min.) Present **Leamos**, p. 256 using Teaching **Leamos,** p. 256.

Wrap-Up
- (10 min.) Have students do Activities 1–3, p. 255.

OPTIONAL RESOURCES
- (15 min.) Advanced Learners, pp. 251, 255, 257 ▲
- (5 min.) Visual Learners, p. 252
- (5 min.) Comparing and Contrasting, p. 253
- (10 min.) **Comunicación** (TE)**,** pp. 253, 255
- (5 min.) Gestures, p. 254
- (5 min.) Community Link, p. 254
- (5 min.) Special Learning Needs, p. 255 ●
- (5 min.) Applying the Strategies, p. 256
- (10 min.) Culminating Project, p. 254

▲ = Advanced Learners   ◆ = Slower Pace Learners   ● = Special Learning Needs   ■ = Heritage Speakers

Holt Spanish 1B   Lesson Planner

Teacher's Name _____ Class _____ Date _____

CAPÍTULO 10

BLOCK 12 90-MINUTE LESSON PLAN

Practice Options
- *Lab Book*, p. 66
- *Video Guide*, pp. 94, 100 ▲●■
- ***Cuaderno de actividades***, p. 72
- Online Practice, Chapter 10 (go.hrw.com, Keyword: EXP1B CH10)

Assessment Options
- *Assessment Program*: **Prueba: Gramática 2**, pp. 105–106
- *Assessment Program*: **Prueba: Aplicación 2,** pp. 107–108
- *Assessment Program*: Alternative Assessment Guide, pp. 245, 253, 261 ▲●■
- Audio CD 10, Tr. 18
- Test Generator

▲ = Advanced Learners   ◆ = Slower Pace Learners   ● = Special Learning Needs   ■ = Heritage Speakers

Holt Spanish 1B — Lesson Planner

Teacher's Name _____ Class _____ Date _____

¡A viajar!

CAPÍTULO 10

BLOCK 13 90-MINUTE LESSON PLAN

STANDARDS FOR FOREIGN LANGUAGE LEARNING: BLOCK 13

Leamos y escribamos
Communication 1.1: Students engage in conversations, provide and obtain information, express feelings and emotions, and exchange opinions.
Communication 1.2: Students understand and interpret written and spoken language on a variety of topics.
Communication 1.3: Students present information, concepts, and ideas to an audience of listeners or readers on a variety of topics.
Cultures 2.1: Students demonstrate an understanding of the relationship between the practices and perspectives of the culture studied.
Connections 3.2: Students acquire information and recognize the distinctive viewpoints that are only available through the foreign language and its cultures.
Comparisons 4.2: Students demonstrate understanding of the concept of culture through comparisons of the cultures studied and their own.

Repaso
Communication 1.1: Students engage in conversations, provide and obtain information, express feelings and emotions, and exchange opinions.
Communication 1.2: Students understand and interpret written and spoken language on a variety of topics.
Communication 1.3: Students present information, concepts, and ideas to an audience of listeners or readers on a variety of topics.
Cultures 2.1: Students demonstrate an understanding of the relationship between the practices and perspectives of the culture studied.
Cultures 2.2: Students demonstrate an understanding of the relationship between the products and perspectives of the culture studied.

CORE INSTRUCTION

Warm-Up
- (5 min.) See Process Writing, p. 257.

Leamos y escribamos
- (35 min.) Present **Taller del escritor**, p. 257. See Teaching **Escribamos,** p. 256.

Repaso
- (20 min.) Have students do Activities 1–5, pp. 258–259.
- (10 min.) Play Audio CD 10, Tr. 12 for Activity 6, p. 259.
- (5 min.) Have students do Activity 7, p. 259.
- (10 min.) Play Audio CD 10, Tr. 13–15 for **Letra y sonido,** p. 260.

Wrap-Up
- (5 min.) Go over **Repaso de gramática** 1 and 2, p. 260. Remind students to study for the Chapter Test.

OPTIONAL RESOURCES
- (10 min.) Game Bank, pp. T60–T63
- (5 min.) Special Learning Needs, p. 257 ●
- (5 min.) Circumlocution, p. 261
- (10 min.) Fold-n-Learn, p. 258

▲ = Advanced Learners ◆ = Slower Pace Learners ● = Special Learning Needs ■ = Heritage Speakers

Holt Spanish 1B

Lesson Planner

Teacher's Name _____ Class _____ Date _____

CAPÍTULO 10

BLOCK 13 90-MINUTE LESSON PLAN

Practice Options
- *Lab Book,* pp. 34, 59
- ***Cuaderno de actividades*** , p. 72 ▲●■
- ***Cuaderno para hispanohablantes,*** Chapter 10 ■
- *Activities for Communication,* pp. 52, 73–74 ▲■
- *Teaching Transparencies:* **Situación, Capítulo 10**; Picture Stories, Chapter 10 ▲●■
- *Video Guide,* pp. 94, 99 ▲●■
- *TPR Storytelling Book,* pp. 58–59 ▲●
- *Interactive Tutor* (Disc 2) or *DVD Tutor* (Disc 2) ▲●■
- Reading Strategies and Skills Handbook, Chapter 10 ▲●■
- *¡Lee conmigo!* Level 1 Reader ▲■
- Online Practice, Chapter 10 (go.hrw.com, Keyword: EXP1B CH10)

▲ = Advanced Learners ◆ = Slower Pace Learners ● = Special Learning Needs ■ = Heritage Speakers

Holt Spanish 1B   Lesson Planner

Teacher's Name _____ Class _____ Date _____

¡A viajar!

CAPÍTULO 10

BLOCK 14 90-MINUTE LESSON PLAN

STANDARDS FOR FOREIGN LANGUAGE LEARNING: BLOCK 14

Integración

Communication 1.1: Students engage in conversations, provide and obtain information, express feelings and emotions, and exchange opinions.

Communication 1.2: Students understand and interpret written and spoken language on a variety of topics.

Communication 1.3: Students present information, concepts, and ideas to an audience of listeners or readers on a variety of topics.

Connections 3.1: Students reinforce and further their knowledge of other disciplines through the foreign language.

Connections 3.2: Students acquire information and recognize the distinctive viewpoints that are only available through the foreign language and its cultures.

CORE INSTRUCTION

Warm-Up
- (5 min.) See Find Art Connection: Introduction, p. 263.

Integración
- (10 min.) Play Audio CD 10, Tr. 16 for Activity 1, p. 262.
- (25 min.) Have students do Activities 2–4, pp. 262–263.

Chapter Assessment

Assess
- (50 min.) Give Chapter 10 Test.

OPTIONAL RESOURCES
- (5 min.) Additional Practice, p. 262
- (10 min.) Culture Project, p. 262
- (10 min.) Fine Art Connection, p. 263

▲ = Advanced Learners   ◆ = Slower Pace Learners   ● = Special Learning Needs   ■ = Heritage Speakers

Holt Spanish 1B   Lesson Planner

Teacher's Name _____ Class _____ Date _____

CAPÍTULO 10

BLOCK 14 90-MINUTE LESSON PLAN

Practice Options
- *Cuaderno de actividades*, pp. 73–74 ▲ ● ■
- *Teaching Transparencies*: Fine Art, Chapter 10 ▲ ● ■
- *Interactive Tutor* (Disc 2) or *DVD Tutor* (Disc 2) ▲ ● ■
- Online Practice, Chapter 10 (go.hrw.com, Keyword: EXP1B CH10)

Assessment Options
- *Assessment Program*: **Examen: Capítulo 10**, pp. 197–207
- *Assessment Program*: **Examen oral: Capítulo 10,** pp. 208
- *Assessment Program*: Alternative Assessment Guide, pp. 245, 253, 261 ▲ ● ■
- *Assessment Program:* **Examen final**, pp. 209–223
- Audio CD 10, Tr. 19–20, 21–23
- *Standardized Assessment Tutor,* Chapter 10
- Test Generator

▲ = Advanced Learners   ◆ = Slower Pace Learners   ● = Special Learning Needs   ■ = Heritage Speakers

Substitute Teacher Lesson Plans

These lesson plans have ben designed with the goal of making class time productive on the days when a substitute teacher conducts class. They provide instructive activities that can be administered by a substitute who does not speak Spanish. Each chapter has several days' worth of suggestions for activities.

Most activities require little preparation. Those activities that do require more preparation are signaled by a clock icon and a box containing the instructions the teacher will need to set up the activity before class starts.

These plans have been organized into three sections: suggestions for the **Geocultura,** suggestions for the Chapter, and suggestions for the **Repaso** and **Integración.** Use the suggestions for the **Geocultura** and suggestions for the Chapter at any point in the chapter. To summarize a chapter or review for a test, use the suggestions for **Repaso** and **Integración**

In the Substitute Teacher Lesson Plans, you will find suggestions for creative and fun activities for each chapter. If you prefer to have a study hall, consider having students practice the grammar and vocabuloary presented in the chapter with the following components of our series:

- ***Cuaderno de vocabulario y gramática***
- ***Cuaderno de actividades***
- *Interactive CD-ROM Tutor* or *DVD Tutor*
- the Web pages at *http://go.hrw.com. You* can find the keyword to enter throughout the pages of each chapter or **Geocultura** of the *Student Edition*.

Teacher's Name _____ Class _____ Date _____

CAPÍTULO

¡Exprésate!

SUBSTITUTE TEACHER LESSON PLANS

Capítulo puente

Research/Craft Activity

⏱ **Preparation:** You will need large index cards, felt-tip pens and/or colored pencils.

Review with the class the text on pages xii–xv of the *Student Edition*. Next, tell students to imagine that they are on vacation in a Spanish-speaking location they studied in Level 1A (Spain, Puerto Rico, Texas, Costa Rica, Chile), and would like to send a postcard home to a friend. Have students design a postcard featuring one of the regions or some aspect of that location's culture. On the other side of their postcard, have them write home telling about what they've seen and learned on their trip. Students should include in their note at least three facts they learned about the location.

Drawing Activity

⏱ **Preparation:** You will need paper, pens and colored markers or colored pencils.

Read to the class the Products and Perspectives note in the margin of page 30 of the *Teacher's Edition*. Then divide students into groups of three or four to collaborate on the design for a new Fine Arts Museum for your town. Ask each member of the group to first sketch some design ideas for the building. Then the group should look at all the ideas, choose elements from each one, and come up with a final design for the museum building. They should draw and color the final plan, name the building, and display it alongside the other designs. You may wish to have the class vote on their favorite design.

Video/Writing Activity

Have students prepare a sheet of paper in the following manner: Across the top label three columns **¿Cómo es?**, **¿Qué le gusta?** and **¿Qué no le gusta?** Down the side of the paper label the rows **Yasemín**, **el mejor amigo de Yasemín**, **Roberto**, and **yo**. Show the **VideoCultura** segments of the 1A video for chapters 2 and 3. Then have students fill in the chart with information from the video and about themselves. Students can also refer to the text of the interviews on pages 30–31 of the *Student Edition*.

Game

Have students play **Una palabra más**. See page T62 of the Game Bank in the front section of the *Teacher's Edition*. The game can be played on the board by the entire class or by teams, or by small groups at their desks using sheets of paper.

Review Activity

Have students practice the questions in **¿Quién eres?** on pages 32–33 of the *Student Edition*. They can work with a partner to ask and answer the questions, and write down the partner's responses. Students could also write their own answers to the questions for a quieter writing activity. Another option is to have students cut their answers to the questions apart and put them in a container. Have each student choose and read the answer out loud and call on another student to provide the correct question that elicits that answer.

Teacher's Name _____ Class _____ Date _____

CAPÍTULO 6

¡A comer!

SUBSTITUTE TEACHER LESSON PLANS

Geocultura—México

Culture/Drawing Activity

⊙ **Preparation:** You will need drawing paper, colored markers or pencils.

Have students look at the different pictures of folk dancers on pages 34 and 37 of the *Student Edition*. Have them describe the costumes the dancers are wearing. Then each student should draw and color their own folkloric costumes that they would like to wear if the class were to perform some folk dances. They could research other festivals in Mexico and associated costumes on the Internet if time allows.

Chapter 6

Vocabulary Activity

⊙ Have students create crossword puzzles using the vocabulary on pages 40–41. First they should write a word horizontally on their papers, then find a word that uses one of those letters and write it vertically. Have them continue in this manner until they have used a dozen words. They should next create a blank puzzle based on these words, number the boxes and create clues. They can exchange the finished puzzles with a classmate. As they work the puzzles, have them keep notes on any errors they find, and write a comment about how the puzzle worked.

Game/Grammar Activity

⊙ **Preparation:** You will need ten index cards and three die.

Have a student volunteer write one of the Spanish personal pronouns on each index card and place the cards in a stack, face down, on a desk near the board. Place the die on the desk also. Write these six infinitives across the top of the board, including the number: **1-preferir; 2-poder; 3-dormir; 4-probar; 5-tener; 6-pedir.** Divide the class into three teams. Have one member of each team go to the board, roll a die and choose a pronoun from the stack of cards. They should then go to the verb whose number they rolled and write the conjugation that goes with the pronoun chosen. The first one finished with the correct answer gets a point for his or her team. Continue until all team members have gone to the board three times.

Writing/Craft Activity

⊙ **Preparation:** You will need blank paper, colored pencils or markers.

Have students work with a partner to create a menu for their own restaurant. They can refer to page 56 in the *Student Edition* for an example. They should include five headings: **Desayuno, Almuerzo, Cena, Bebidas,** and **Postre,** then list two or three items under each category. Have them assign appropriate prices in **pesos**. The can look on the Internet for current exchange rates. They should give their restaurant a Spanish name, address and phone number and include illustrations of food items offered.

Repaso/Integración

Review Activity

⊙ **Preparation:** You will need large, blank paper and colored markers.

Read aloud the Introduction on page 79 of the *Student Edition*, under Fine Art Connection. You might also have students research Diego Rivera and Muralism on the Internet to find more examples of Rivera's work, and to understand the goals of the Mexican Muralist Movement. Then have each student choose a character from the painting on page 79 or from another Rivera painting and recreate it on a large sheet of paper. Have students combine all their pieces together on the board or bulletin board to create a mural for the classroom.

Holt Spanish 1B

Lesson Planner

Teacher's Name _____ Class _____ Date _____

Cuerpo sano, mente sana

CAPÍTULO 7

SUBSTITUTE TEACHER LESSON PLANS

Geocultura—Argentina

Culture/Craft Activity

🕐 **Preparation:** You will need large drawing paper, index cards, 8 x 11 inch blank paper, felt-tip pens and/or colored pencils, yarn or string, and tacks.

Review with the class the text on pages 80–83 of the *Student Edition*. Next, have students work in pairs to create a bulletin board display based on these pages. Ask one pair to draw and color a very large outline map of Argentina and label rivers, mountains, and major cities. Have the other pairs choose one of the cultural aspects from the pages and illustrate it on a blank piece of paper. Tell them to print the accompanying text on an index card. Put the map in the center of the bulletin board, and have students place their drawings with index cards around the map. They should use a piece of yarn to attach the cards to the appropriate location on the map.

Chapter 7

Writing Activity

After students have studied the **Vocabulario** and **¡Exprésate!** on pages 100–101 and page 104 of the *Student Edition*, have them list healthful and unhealthful habits on a sheet of paper under the headings **Sí** and **No**, respectively. Each entry should begin with a verb. For example, students need to write **comer pizza**, not just **pizza**. Tell students to be creative and exaggerate if they wish, using any of the vocabulary they have learned in previous chapters. They could decorate their papers and post them on a bulletin board under the title **Para vivir bien**.

Drawing Activity

🕐 **Preparation:** You will need blank paper and colored pencils, markers or crayons.

Have students draw imaginary creatures with more or fewer body parts than a human being. For example, creatures may have three heads, but only one arm. They should use different colors for each body part they include. When students have finished drawing their creatures, divide them into groups of four, and have them sit with their backs to each other. Each student in the group will then describe his or her creature using **Tiene...**(*It has...*). The other group members draw and color the creature according to their classmate's description. After each description, students compare their drawings to see which one is most like the original creature.

Writing/Drawing Activity

To practice the vocabulary on pages 100–101 of the *Student Edition*, have students create a cartoon animal illustrating each emotion featured. Under each cartoon, students should write how the animal feels and why. They may use any adjectives and other vocabulary they have learned in previous chapters.

Repaso/Integración

Review Activity

Have students write an essay about their own family's daily routines and what each family member does to stay healthy. They can use Activity 2 on page 120 of the *Student Edition* as a model. They should mention each family member, tell at what time they do certain things during the week, and how it is different on weekends. They should include information about what each person does (or doesn't do) to stay in shape, and what each one does to relax. Encourage them to use reflexive verbs and any other vocabulary they have learned in previous chapters.

Teacher's Name _____ Class _____ Date _____

CAPÍTULO 8

Vamos de compras

SUBSTITUTE TEACHER LESSON PLANS

Geocultura—Florida
Research/Craft Activity

⏱ **Preparation:** You will need blank paper and colored pencils or pens.

Review with the class the text on pages 126–129 of the *Student Edition*. Discuss with them the cultural information in the wrap of the *Teacher's Edition* for those pages. Next, tell students to imagine that they are working for the Florida Tourism Bureau and that they must create a brochure advertising some aspect of Florida's culture. They should illustrate the brochure and include information from your discussions. Have them include as much Spanish as possible.

Chapter 8
Video/Writing Activity

Show the **VideoNovela**, Episode 8. Then have students work in pairs to summarize in English what happens in each of the frames on pages 160–162 of the *Student Edition*. For the last frame, have them explain what the problem is and why they think the problem occurred. Then ask them to draw another frame for the **Novela** that shows what might happen when the two girls return the items to the store. They should include conversation between Celeste, Sofía and a store clerk.

Writing Activity

Have students look through the chapter and copy any six Spanish sentences or questions onto a blank sheet of paper. They should make sure they copy all spelling and punctuation correctly. Then have them work in pairs to do a dictation activity. Have one partner read a sentence to the other partner, who will write it down. Then they should switch roles, continuing until each has read all six sentences and the other has written them down. Have them check each other's papers and correct any spelling or punctuation errors.

Craft Activity

⏱ **Preparation:** You will need old magazines and catalogs, scissors, unlined paper, colored pens or pencils and tape or glue.

Have students design two outrageous outfits using cutouts from magazines, catalogs, or their own drawings. These need to be pasted and/or drawn on two separate sheets of paper. Have students label each item and give a brief description of it, including price, using the vocabulary in the chapter. Then, have them write a paragraph in which they compare the two outfits, using phrases from page 140 of the *Student Edition*. Students should favor one outfit over the other and try to sell it. Once they finish, they may deliver their sales presentation to the class.

Repaso/Integración
Review Activity

Have students look at the last pages of Chapters 1–8, **Repaso de vocabulario**, *Student Edition*, and make a list of 10 -ar infinitives that represent activities that they have done in the past several months. Next to each infinitive have them jot down notes about when they did that activity, where, and with whom. Then have them use the notes to write a narrative that describes things they have done in the past few months, using the preterite tense of the verbs. They may also write about things that other family members or friends have done.

Holt Spanish 1B

Lesson Planner

Teacher's Name _____ Class _____ Date _____

CAPÍTULO 9

¡Festejemos!

SUBSTITUTE TEACHER LESSON PLANS

Geocultura—La República Dominicana
Craft Activity

⏲ **Preparation:** You will need the *Student Edition*, index cards, and colored markers or pencils.

Hand out one index card per person and tell the students they are going to create a postcard from the Dominican Republic. On one side they should draw something found on the island. Review with students the **Geocultura** on pages 172–175 for ideas. On the other side they should write three sentences—one using the preterite tense to tell what they did yesterday, another using the present tense saying what they are doing right now, and a third sentence stating what they are going to do or planning to do tomorrow (using **pensar** + infinitive or **ir** + **a** + infinitive). As time permits, have students present their postcards to the class or else exchange with a classmate for peer-editing.

Chapter 9
Video/Speaking Activity

Show the **VideoCultura** interviews, Ch. 9. Then have students work in pairs to create their own interviews about holidays in the U.S. Tell them to use these interviews as models, and they can also refer to the *Student Edition*, pages 190–191. Each person should interview the other partner and get information about two or three holidays, dates of the holidays, how they celebrate, what they eat, and which holiday is their favorite. Have them perform the interviews for the class, and videotape them if possible.

Game

⏲ **Preparation:** You will need a timer, index cards, and pencils and paper for scoring.

Play **Categorías** as described in the Game Bank on page T60 of the *Teacher's Edition*. Have students help come up with three categories of vocabulary that they have learned so far. Follow directions for the game as described in the textbook.

Grammar Activity/Game

⏲ **Preparation:** You will need index cards and a list of **-ar** verbs.

Have students cooperate to put information on the index cards. You will need one card for each of the personal pronouns (**yo, tú, él, ella, usted, nosotros, ellos, ellas, ustedes**) and a stack of twenty or so **-ar** infinities. Students can search the glossary at the back of the textbook for verbs they have learned how to use. Place the cards in two stacks on a desk at the front of the room, pronouns in one stack and verbs in the other. Divide the class into two teams. Have a player from each team go to the board. Have another classmate draw the top card from each stack and read them aloud (then place the cards at the bottom of each stack). The players must write the correct preterite form of the verb on the board; the first one with the correct spelling gets a point for their team. Play until all teammates have been to the board three times. As a variation, have them write the present progressive form of the verb instead of or in addition to the preterite.

Repaso/Integración
Review Activity

⏲ **Preparation:** You will need plain paper, pencils or pens.

Have students review holidays and related vocabulary by using the Fold-n-Learn Activity on page 212 of the *Teacher's Edition*. They should follow the directions given in the text. They can also use the same format to practice other vocabulary. Have them write vocabulary words on the top door tabs, and the English equivalents underneath the tabs.

Holt Spanish 1B   Lesson Planner

Teacher's Name _____ Class _____ Date _____

¡A viajar!

CAPÍTULO 10

SUBSTITUTE TEACHER LESSON PLANS

Geocultura—Perú
Video/Writing Activity

Show the **GeoVisión** video for Chapter 10. Then call on students to read aloud the information on pages 218-221 of the *Student Edition*. Next, have each student write five simple questions and answers in English based on the information on these pages or in the video. Collect the papers and ask students to study quietly while you choose ten of their questions. Have students close their books and get out a clean sheet of paper. Read aloud the ten questions and have them write answers. You may have students exchange papers to grade them as you give the answers, and then collect the quizzes.

Chapter 10
Vocabulary Activity

⏱ **Preparation:** You will need index cards or small squares of construction paper.

Have students make flashcards by illustrating 15–20 of the words from **Repaso de vocabulario** on page 261 of the *Student Edition*. Students should draw a picture of each item on one side of a card, then write the Spanish word on the other side of the card. In pairs, have students test each other using their sets of flashcards.

Writing Activity

Have students open their books to page 242. Tell them to imagine that the pictures in Activity 28 are photos from several of their own family vacations. Have them write five sentences about each picture and make up details to describe where they were in each photo, when it was, who the people are, and what they were doing in each place. They can also write sentences that tell what people were wearing. Remind them to use the preterite tense when describing clothing and activities.

Video/Speaking Activity

Show the **Videocultura** video for Chapter 10. After watching the three interviews, have students turn to pages 236–237 in the *Student Edition*. Have them copy on a sheet of paper the questions from the interviews, leaving room to write answers. Then have students work in pairs to interview each other using the written questions. They should write the responses given by their partners in spaces after the questions. If time allows, have students perform the interviews for the class.

Repaso/Integración
Review Activity

⏱ **Preparation:** You will need poster boards or large sheets of drawing paper, pencils, and markers or colored pencils.

Have students review **Geocultura** at the beginning of each chapter in the *Student Edition*. Ask them to choose one of the areas and create a poster with illustrations depicting the most interesting areas and aspects shown on the text pages. Tell them to include text, in English or Spanish, that describes the illustrations. Make sure they put a title on their poster. Hang the finished posters around the classroom, and have students vote on the poster that most inspires them to want to visit that country.

Holt Spanish 1B   Lesson Planner